RETHINKING ORIENTALISM: WOMEN, TRAVEL AND THE OTTOMAN HAREM

D1471855

WDRAWN FROM
THE LIBRARY
UNIVERSITY OF
WINCHESTER

KA 0421921 X

RETHINKING ORIENTALISM

୫ ଓ

WOMEN, TRAVEL AND THE OTTOMAN HAREM

୫ ଓ

R EINA L EWIS

RUTGERS UNIVERSITY PRESS
NEW BRUNSWICK, NEW JERSEY

UNIVERSITY OF WINCHESTER

305.4095G
LEW   0421921X

First published in the United States 2004
by Rutgers University Press, New Brunswick, New Jersey

First published in the United Kingdom 2004
by I.B. Tauris & Co. Ltd.

Copyright © 2004 by Reina Lewis

All rights reserved.
No part of this book may be reproduced or utilized in any form or by any means, electronic or mechanical, or by any information storage and retrieval system, without written permission from the publisher. Please contact Rutgers University Press, 100 Joyce Kilmer Avenue, Piscataway, NJ 08854-8099. The only exception to this prohibition is "fair use" as defined by U.S. copyright law.

Library of Congress Cataloging-in-Publication Data and
British Library Cataloguing-in-Publication Data are available upon request.

ISBN 0-8135-3542-5 (cloth)
      0-8135-3543-3 (paper)

Printed and bound in Great Britain by TJ International Ltd, Padstow, Cornwall

FOR

LAURA AND HELENA,

ဆ ର

MY SISTERS,

MY FRIENDS

❧ CONTENTS ❧

List of Illustrations

ഔ Note on Language ൦

Before 1928 people in the Ottoman Empire and the early Turkish Republic wrote down the Ottoman language in the Arabic script. In 1928 this Ottoman or Osmanlı form was replaced by modern Turkish, written in the Roman alphabet and purged of many of the Arabic and Persian features that had characterised Ottoman. For people writing in English, like the authors featured here, the transliteration of Ottoman words, names and place names was not necessarily standardised and has now been replaced by the modern Turkish version of transliteration. The transition to modern Turkish also changed the use of several letters, so that, typically, b became p, d became t.

Where words appear in quotations from primary sources dating before 1928 I have retained the Ottoman form or early twentieth-century transliteration. In my commentary I have used the contemporary Turkish form of current or Ottoman terms.

Personal names appear throughout as used by their authors (e.g. Zeyneb not Zeynep, Edib not Edip). Major historical figures, such as sultans, appear in the modern spelling, except when they are referred to in quoted material from the period. The same applies to place names.

Ottoman naming conventions also changed during this period. Traditionally Ottomans did not use surnames; people of middle to upper rank were distinguished by an honorific and those of lower status were often identified by function. The respectful way to address a woman of some status was to follow her personal name with hanım (meaning lady, or woman). Men of status could be known as bey, paşa, effendi (in ascending order of importance).

Surnames were introduced in the 1930s, when Mustafa Kemal took on Atatürk as a second name (and validation of his role as father of the nation). I use Mustafa Kemal and Atatürk as interchangeable.

I have used the honorific hanım for the Ottoman women featured here (except for Halide Edib who had acquired a second name by the time she wrote her memoirs). However, I have used the modern spelling of hanım, rather than the various transliterations around at the time (variously, hanum, hanoum, khanoum and so on).

This means that Zeyneb Hanım appears in quoted material and in the bibliography as Zeyneb Hanoum (the transliteration used in her book), but in my commentary as Zeyneb Hanım. The same applies to any other Ottoman women appearing in quotations and in my commentary. The authors featured here are inconsistent in their use of the honorific, and I have tried wherever possible to follow their lead, since this gives the clearest sense of their writing and indicates the extent to which they were au fait with Ottoman conventions. So, for example, Demetra Vaka Brown refers to her intimate friends by their personal name only, but uses the honorific when she introduces characters who are senior in age or rank or to whom her relationship is more formal. The other authors make similar accommodations of naming conventions.

Wherever possible I have tried to render Ottoman terms in modern usage, using Turkish diacritics. Most letters are pronounced the same as in English, with a few exceptions:

c	j
ç	ch
ı	like the io in lotion
ş	sh, as in yaşmak, yashmak
ğ	silent, lengthens preceding vowel

✄ ACKNOWLEDGEMENTS ✄

Research can be a lonely business, but I have been lucky enough in this project to have really felt myself to be part of a community of scholars that has sustained me with kindness and taught me how to improve. Whilst it is the plague of inter-disciplinary work to be insufficiently expert in each area, I have been supported by the encouragement of researchers in all of its constituent fields, many of whom have generously shared with me their particular knowledges. At the very start of this book, I was inspired by the encouragement and advice I received from Süheyla Artemel, Nedret Kuran Burçoğlu, Saliha Paker and Zehra Toska. Over the years that followed I have cast my net widely, and although they must take no responsibility for any remaining errors, this book has benefited greatly from the expertise that was shared by Nermin Abadan-Unat, Hulya Adak, Margot Badran, Jo Bristow, Elizabeth Childs, Julie Codell, David Doughan, Edhem Eldem, Caroline Evans, Ben Fortna, Shirley Foster, Indira Ghose, Dan Goffman, Sarah Graham-Brown, Süheyla Kirca, Lois McNay, Jan Marsh, Barbara Mead-owcroft, Annelies Moor, Nicole van Os, Mary Roberts, Katrina Rolley, Anne Summers, Meyda Yeğenoğlu and Sarah Waters. Much of the material in this book has remained obscure, known to few and studied by less: but the turf wars that often mar academia have been entirely absent from those who do study these sources. I owe a debt of gratitude to Yiorgos Kalogeras for providing me with copies of primary material on Demetra Vaka Brown and for his thought-provoking responses to my work – my analysis has developed as a direct result. It has been my great joy to have come to know a group of scholars who share my fascination with this subject and my deep privilege to have worked closely with them: this book owes a tremendous debt to conversations with Nancy Mickle-wright, Teresa Heffernan, Carolyn McCue Goffman and Elizabeth Frierson. They have all at various points read (and sometimes re-read) drafts of chapters and been willing to face a thousand email enquiries. Their friendship strengthens me more than they can know.

During the many years that this book has been in development, it has been my good fortune to be invited to publish from it. In so doing I have benefited from the editorial input of many colleagues and I thank those responsible for the fol-lowing: earlier versions of Chapter Three appeared in Shoma Munshi (ed), *Images of the 'Modern Woman' in Asia* (London, Curzon, 2002); and in Phil Cohen (ed), *New Ethnicities, Old Racisms* (London, Zed Books, 1999); and in *Anglo-Saxonica: Revista do Centro de Estudos Anglisticos da Universidade de Lisboa* (3:14–15, 2001); elements of Chapter Five and Chapter Six were rehearsed in Louise During and Richard Wrigley (eds), *Gender and Architecture* (London, John Wiley, 1999); Amelia Jones and Andrew Stephenson (eds), *Per-forming the Text/Performing the Body* (London, Routledge, 1999); *ISIM*

Newsletter, International Institute for the Study of Islam in the Modern World (8, September 2001); and in Alison Donnell (ed), 'The Veil: Postcolonialism and the Politics of Dress', *Interventions* (Special Topic, 1: 4, 1999). This book has also benefited from its many outings as conference papers; those who have been my interlocutors have taught me much, and I thank especially Sara Ahmed, Julia Clancy-Smith, Vojtech Jirat-Wasiutynski, Wendy Leeks, Maria Teresa Malafaia and Álvaro Pina.

At so many points in the process of compiling this book – a period punctuated by major life changes and protracted periods of illness – I have had recourse to seek advice and support from friends. I owe a debt of gratitude to the combined wisdom (and collective patience) of Karen Adler, David Bate, Deborah Cherry, Peter Horne, Maggie Humm, Elizabeth Langland, Sara Mills, Peter Morey, Alison Oram, Susannah Radstone, Andrew Stephenson, Karen Wolny and Sally Wyatt, some of whom also acted as unofficial readers for sections of the book. The list of people who have listened to me moan, angst and generally carry on (whilst still treating me as if I was an interesting person) and who have between them offered invaluable guidance on all aspects of life and books includes Linda Adelson, Hidemi Asano, Steve Behrer, Allison Bennett, Alice Bloch, Monika Bobinska, Dawn Collins, Jo Entwistle, Marian Fixler, Caroline Freeman, Roberta Garrett, Judy Greenway, Andrea Jones, Katherine Klinger, Bridget Lawless, Sandra Levy, Caron Lipman, Helen Lowe, Sally Munt, Lyn Nead, Barbara Norton, Jeff Ostericher, Ben Page, Leylâ Pervizat, Sophie Powell, Anne Marie Rafferty, Melissa Ragona, Nell Randall, Ruth Schmidt, Simon Schmidt, Don Slater, Veronica Slater, Kate Stockwell, Kate Sturge, Deanna Sullivan, Laura Sullivan, Azucena Tejada and Lizzie Thynne. Having friends around, book or otherwise, has truly saved me several times over the past few years. I thank also Jane Harrison and Andrew Chevalier. At I.B. Tauris, my editor Philippa Brewster has been everything an editor should be and I thank her for her belief in this sometimes unwieldy project. Susan Lawson has been invaluable on numerous production dilemmas.

The research has been generously supported by a Research Fellowship from the Leverhulme Trust and a sabbatical given under the Research Leave Scheme of the Arts and Humanities Research Board of the British Academy. Staff in both organisations have been incredibly helpful and I want particularly to thank Mrs Jean Cater at the Leverhulme Trust for her kindness and understanding. Sabbatical leave from the University of East London, made possible by colleagues in the School of Cultural and Innovation Studies, has also been invaluable, as has the school's kind contribution toward production costs. Every effort has been made to trace the copyright holders of the illustrations reproduced in this book. The publishers would be glad to hear from any copyright holders they have not been able to contact and to print due acknowledgement in the next edition.

Specialist library assistance has been forthcoming from staff at the British Library, the Women's Library, London Metropolitan University, the Houghton Library, Harvard University, the Women's Library and Information Centre, Istanbul, SOAS Library and Senate House, University of London. I have also been helped by library staff at the University of East London, especially Hugh Bowman and Lorraine Williams.

On the home front, my poor family have been heroically trotting out the same phrases of encouragement repeatedly – and with feeling – for some time now: knowing they are behind me is what spurs me on. So, with much love, I thank Estelle and Hilly, Laura and Helena and Pete. Probably the worst job has fallen to Valentine Schmidt, who has risen valiantly to the challenge of accommodating my work needs whilst still managing to make sure we had a life, and who only once asked me, 'Is it finished yet?' Well, now it is: I know it, and I, haven't been easy, but I hope we have been worth it.

UNIVERSITY OF WINCHESTER
LIBRARY

ഊ INTRODUCTION ര

I track how stereotypes change, how they are and have been challenged and how in their terrible flexibility they continue to structure the terms of contemporary power and oppression. After working on this book for some years, I found myself drafting this introduction during the second Gulf War, again chasing new and old stereotypes. In class, as during previous campaigns in the region, my students and I tried to piece together how best to understand the neo-Orientalisms that informed both pro- and anti-war rhetoric, as the American-led 'coalition against terror' deployed the 'forces of civilisation' against a spectre of Islamic barbarism whose conceptualisation was horribly repetitive in its inventive reframing of Orientalist knowledges.

In these and other instances, the effects of what Gayatri Spivak (1985) terms the 'epistemic violence' of imperialism and neo-colonialism link the contemporary situation to the sources in this book. Not just because familiarity with historical attitudes to the Orient and to women from Islamic societies can help trace the forms of contemporary prejudice, but because an understanding of how racialised subjects intervened in imperial and Orientalising discourses, even as they were positioned by them in the very forms of their cultural enunciation, can illuminate the possibilities and limitations of resistance.

In this book I focus on a series of little-known or ignored English-language publications about segregated life by Ottoman women from the beginning of the twentieth century. Their travel accounts, memoirs and fictions reveal a gendered counter-discourse that challenges Occidental stereotypes. As well as engaging directly with Western Orientalist discourse, they also intervene in Ottoman debates about female and national emancipation. The group of women writers that form my study travelled between Turkey, Britain, the United States of America and the rest of Europe, as well as within the Ottoman Empire. Their writings are connected to each other by personal contact and by ideological debate. The writings of the Ottomans Halide Edib, Demetra Vaka Brown and the sisters Zeyneb Hanım and Melek Hanım are joined by the British author Grace Ellison who, in addition to travelling to Turkey and advocating the Turkish cause in the British press, was instrumental in bringing Zeyneb Hanım and Melek Hanım into print. Joined by a desire to promote the emancipation of Ottoman women and divided by politics, nationality, class and ethnicity, these women were united in their determination to alter the West's conception of the 'Oriental woman' – the term that they use throughout their writing.

For Ottoman women writers this was a project of cultural and political intervention aimed at several different audiences. For me, in trying to rethink Orientalism, their voices and those of the Western women with whom they were in dialogue illustrate how the West was never the sole arbiter and owner of

meanings about the Orient. As has been argued also by Jill Beaulieu and Mary
Roberts, Orientalism was a discourse framed by the responses, adaptations and
contestations of those whom it constructed as its objects. As the sources in this
book reveal, Orientalist knowledges were challenged at their very 'historical
moment of inception', not just from a postcolonial perspective (Beaulieu and
Roberts 2002: 2). In this light, it is important, as Julie Codell and Dianne Sachko
Macleod emphasise, to recognise the 'historical and dialectic, as well as discursive' nature of Orientalism (Codell and Macleod 1998b: 1). To focus on the
dynamism of the dialectic foregrounds the agency of Orientalised peoples and
highlights the reciprocal effect of the imperial experience on Western national
and individual identities and cultural forms (Codell and Macleod 1998b, Beaulieu and Roberts 2002, Benjamin 1997). The Orient thus appears as a site of
reception and production, not just as a source of raw material for cultural products whose consumption is assumed to occur only in the Western centres
'privileged as interpretive sites' (Beaulieu and Roberts 2002: 5). Orientalised
subjects, such as the authors featured here, entered into resistant forms of cultural
production, whose selective take-up of Orientalist styles, forms and techniques
produced a variety of alternative voices. Their politicised rewriting of Western
harem literature does, as Zeyneb Çelik argues, dissolve the 'frozen' categories of
Orientalism, disrupting assumptions of 'both the coloniser's unilateral power and
the disquieting powerlessness of the colonised' (Çelik 1996: 204). But the
contradictions between their texts also make clear the multiplicity, and sometimes mutual exclusiveness, of resistant positions.

The years covered by these women writers witnessed tumultuous changes during which the ailing Ottoman Empire, for so long the 'sick man of Europe', saw
its territories decrease and its population alter as it shifted into the modern
nation-state that is today's Turkish Republic. The lives of women, and of all
Ottoman subjects, changed dramatically as social reform accompanied political
reform, with the condition of women being hotly debated by all sides of the political spectrum. The last generation to be raised in segregated households, these
writers chronicle personal desires and dissatisfactions that were an intrinsic part
of political debate. The elite segregated households into which Halide Edib,
Melek Hanım and Zeyneb Hanım were born (the same types of households that
Demetra Vaka Brown grew up observing) were to have become a thing of the
past for the next generation. The reach of this transition is represented by Halide
Edib, the youngest writer of this group, whose second marriage to Adnan Adıvar
was the new type of affective monogamous union emblematic of the new nationalist society.

Operating almost as a litmus test, women's desires for education and the right
to choose a (monogamous) husband, and to live in their own home (not the
extended family of the segregated system), suggest the importance of Western
models to the idea of liberation. The equation of liberation with modernity had
since the Tanzimat reforms of the nineteenth century (1839–76) been one that
was always conducted in relation to the pros and cons of Western ideas.[1] Since

the time of the Western-inspired intellectuals of the Tanzimat and their opponents, the status of Ottoman women operated for women and men as a crucial
indicator of the state of the empire and of individual progress (Fleischmann
1991). Ottoman women publishing in the West could be sure that a home readership would anxiously engage with their views.

Since the publication of Edward Said's seminal volume *Orientalism* in 1978,
numerous studies have challenged Orientalist assumptions about the East's
innate inferiority. In many different geographical and historical contexts it has
been demonstrated how the Orientalist binarism between East and West contributed to a view of Western superiority that frequently supported Western colonial
and imperial rule. Further developments have stressed the heterogeneity and
instability of Orientalist discourse (Lowe 1991, Bhabha 1994), demonstrating
that its force was rarely hegemonic and uncontested (Çelik 1996). These have
been augmented by excellent analyses of how the dynamic of Orientalist discourse and its complicated pleasures also called into being the very selfhood of
the Western subject (Young 1990, Yeğenoğlu 1998, McClintock 1995). As the
field developed, scholars pointed to the varied and widespread forms of popular
Orientalism, some arguing against the presumed culpability of Western Orientalists (MacKenzie 1995, Clarke 1997). Others questioned the usefulness of
Orientalism itself as a concept, seeing it as sometimes too widely (mis)applied
and recommending its replacement by more specific categories (such as anti-
Arab, anti-Islam and Eurocentrism, Keddie 2002). Another debate focused on the
extent to which the imagined exclusivity of Orientalism's fictional binary divide
structured not only the nature of Orientalist discourse but also anti-imperial and
postcolonial resistances (al-'Azm 1984, Nader 1989, Carrier 1992, Morley and
Robins 1992). The ways in which Orientalist and imperial discourses are also
gendered has been the subject of much valuable work in postcolonial studies, as
has attention to the role of gender in anti-colonial and postcolonial politics (Burton 1992, Mills 1991, Chaudhuri and Strobel 1992, Ware 1992, Ong 1995,
Parker, Russo, Sommer and Yaeger 1992, Sharpe 1993), and to the contested
place of race in the development of feminist thinking and practice (Mohanty
1988, Mohanty, Russo and Torres 1991, Bhavnani 2001). Scholarship is now
more than ever aware of how gender identities are racialised, and of how racialised identities are themselves imbricated in gender and class discourses.[2]

This book takes an interdisciplinary approach to evidence of Ottoman
women's social and cultural agency to intervene on a number of fronts in discussions about the value and limits of Orientalism as a discourse and as a theoretical
paradigm. Its focus on sources with a female point of origin brings a new element to existing challenges to masculinist histories of Orientalism. Introducing
Ottoman sources also provides an example of 'indigenous' cultural agency that
demonstrates the other side of the classic Orientalist paradigm. That these
sources are by Ottoman women is particularly important because they speak of
practices of resistance that are charged by differences of both ethnicity *and* gender. This is not to privilege their Orientalised status as a mark of 'purity' within

imperial and gender inequalities, nor to understand gender as a homogeneous or stable category. Rather, the importance given to the different ethnic and class positions of these writers undercuts any singularity that might be accorded to the category of Oriental or Ottoman (or third world) woman, thus also interrupting some of the orthodoxies that have emerged in contemporary feminist post-colonial theory. To this is added a critical attention to the hybrid reformulations of Western cultural forms that emerge from the specific social, cultural and political historical situations from which these individuals speak. This is done in order to address the impact of these differently enunciated voices on their audiences in the West and the East, emphasising the complex overlapping addressees constructed by their writing.

But as well as their reading publics, they were also writing for each other. A central tenet of my argument is the importance of the dialogue between the Ottoman authors and Grace Ellison, through which some of their books came into being and their textual strategies can be evaluated. Presented also as emblematic of other such dialogues (see Lewis and Micklewright 2004), this serves to illustrate that the Orientalised Ottoman woman (presumed to be silenced rather than speaking) was in fact engaged in diverse forms of political and cultural activity. It also demonstrates that Ottoman women were connected textually and socially to a web of other women (and men) throughout and beyond the region, all of whom, constituting a series of segregated and unsegregated publics, recognised the importance of their writing activities. In restoring these sources to view this book characterises the segregated domains of Ottoman women as spaces of political agency and cultural production. It thereby contributes to the recasting of critical thinking about the institutional and symbolic significance of the harem – that most fertile space of the Orientalist imagination.

Despite the exponential growth of postcolonial studies and although Turkey and the Ottoman Empire feature large in representations associated with Orientalism, little attention has been paid to the case of Turkey, or to the Middle East more generally. Yet, Turkey and the late Ottoman Empire provide another paradigm for the analysis of (competing) colonial powers and the political and cultural effects of Euro-American imperial policy. This book, then, can also be understood as an intervention into postcolonial historiography and theory, using the Ottoman study as corrective to the narrowness of what postcolonial studies (often taking the South Asian experience as paradigmatic) regards as the colonial and the postcolonial. A transfer of attention to the postcolonialities of the Middle East would, as Deniz Kandiyoti urges, diversify this picture geographically and methodologically, by recognising 'not only the historical specificity of their colonial encounters but also the very different modalities and temporalities of their insertion into world capitalist markets' (Kandiyoti 2002: 282). She identifies three factors – global market relations, local social stratification and the differing roles of religion – as essential for the construction of postcolonial analyses that can take into account 'struggles over resources, legitimacy and meaning' (Kandiyoti 2002: 294–5).[3] It is in this context, at the conjunction of two fields, that this book hopes to operate, introducing to postcolonial studies the specificities of the late Ottoman situation (which only briefly after the First World War involved direct European colonial rule) and bringing to the reading of Ottoman sources the critical perspectives of postcolonial and gender theory.

This is not to present these different fields of scholarly endeavour as either securely bounded or internally unified. So, for example, if Turkey has usually been outside the scope of postcolonial studies, Ottoman women have until very recently generally been outside the scope of Turkish historical studies. Paradoxically, one area where women's history does feature large is in Turkish republican historiography which has always given a heightened role to the celebration of the Anatolian woman liberated by the revolution. But it has had little to say about the struggle of women for those rights or the history of women's activism in the late Ottoman period (with the exception of the nationalist heroine Halide Edib). Indeed it is only recently that scholarship has turned to the study of the late Ottoman period. The reasons for this as Zehra Arat (1999c) and Elizabeth Frierson (1995) both argue, were political and linguistic. The politically motivated break from the Ottoman past, seen most dramatically in the adoption of the Latin script in 1928, 'kept the following generations completely detached from their past' (Arat 1999c: 10) and helped promulgate acceptance of republican historiography. The inability of generations raised after the establishment of the republic to read Ottoman records went hand-in-hand with what Frierson characterises as a 'sense of civilisational superiority to the Ottomans' which was so entrenched that 'foreignness in the case of Ottoman history, is not entirely a matter of national boundaries' (Frierson 1995: 57). Nationalist history, in depreciating all that was linked with the immediately pre-republican past, denied the agency of Ottoman women, picturing them as helpless slaves to sultanic and religious despotism (Frierson 1995: 57) from which the nationalists were held to have liberated the entire population. This volume is, among other things, directed as a contribution to the developing analysis of how Ottoman women were active in seeking their own liberation in their own terms.

Though to varying degrees prominent and successful in their day, the authors in this volume will be largely unknown to Western readers and not too familiar to readers in Turkey and the Middle East. To remedy this, my twinned introductory Chapters One and Two provide full author biographies. These are located through a critical summary of the political and social changes attending the end of the Ottoman Empire during which these authors lived and wrote, including reference to recent historiographical debates and developments. This book aims to offer examples and critical perspectives that will build on and add to current developments in Middle Eastern women's studies, where the reclamation of women's history is still a relatively new but rapidly growing project (Badran and Cooke 1990, Meriwether and Tucker 1999, Keddie 2002, de Groot 1996) and where women's sources are frequently read evidentially rather than critically. The often felt inapplicability of contemporary cultural, literary and postcolonial theory to Middle Eastern and Ottoman sources is one of the reasons that has so far prohibited a wider take-up. Part of my project in this book is to demonstrate how selected elements of gender theory and cultural criticism can be usefully applied to the Ottoman experience. These sources need to be analysed as mediated representations, not neutral evidence, and this can be done through a mixture of historicised materialist and textual analysis that attends among other things to matters of genre, market, narrative strategy and reception.

But if cultural theory can reframe understandings of the Ottoman past, attention to the specificities of the Ottoman female experience can also unsettle some of the standardised formulations of feminist postcolonial theory. While problematising the classificatory terms which define the category 'Oriental woman', this book contributes to feminist, postcolonial and literary studies as an example of life-writing by women who are racialised but who are not part of the subaltern – the embryonic proto-class grouping whose subjugated position keeps them outside of the means of representation – that has become such an important model for postcolonial studies. Regularly extrapolated beyond the specific Gramscian definition of subalternity, and particularly in the turn to gender, the focus on subalternity has drawn attention to individuals and groups whose generally localised actions have fallen outside the scope of historical narratives of national emancipation (Young 2001). Spivak's (1988b) famous assertion that 'the subaltern cannot speak' is a reminder that the subaltern is by its very definition outside the archives. (Once the subaltern has access to representation it is no longer subaltern.) As her return to the subject (Spivak 1999) makes clear, even when the subaltern voice is apparently heard, spoken by others on her 'behalf', her enunciators can position her so as to articulate a compliant version of dominant discourse. To imagine that the colonised or the oppressed are automatically in opposition to colonial or imperial power would be to simplify the nature of colonial power and to misrecognise the power of local class and ethnic power differentiations. As Spivak, Kandiyoti and others have demonstrated, the collaboration of local elites who frequently saw their own class position strengthened by association with the colonising power should not be disregarded. To search only for evidence of 'pure' oppositional 'native' voices would also dismiss the ways in which Western discourses of modernity were embraced by colonial and postcolonial elites as the way forward for the decolonised nation.

Spivak is clear that it is important to be attentive to the particular balances of power (and power between women) in different historical and colonial circumstances. Postcolonial and literary studies retain a tendency to regard non-Western women through the lens of subalternity. The resultant heroicisation of the oppressed can obscure the web of local relations which provide the context for and often the limits of resistance. This myopia threatens to disregard the specific social status of women in the colonised and postcolonial world and runs the risk of painting women as either heroines or villains: this loses the ability to see how women's progressive or radical politics in one area may be counterbalanced by an investment in oppressive practices in another. In the complex processes by which imperial power connects to local patriarchies and class systems, the conditions for the emergence of progressive gender politics may come not only from a social background that is not of the most oppressed but may take the form of practices that create or perpetuate the continued subjugation of other women and men.

For these reasons I have been at pains in this book to draw out the place within local social relations that, among other factors, gave Ottoman women access to the means of cultural production. Emphasising the individual class position of these writers highlights the gulf between how they saw themselves and how they were seen by their readers in the West, who encountered them within imperial and Orientalist discourses that generally positioned Ottoman women as inferior. As I discuss in Chapter One it is clear that Ottoman women were aware that they could be diminished by the West in ways that were sexual (the lascivious odalisque), temporal (the Orient as a zone out of time locked in a pre-modern past), social (unable to distinguish Ottoman class difference, Oriental women were pictured as either sultanas or slaves), and cultural (the ignorant, lazy harem woman). Even though some representations were positive (notably Lady Mary Wortley Montagu's *Embassy Letters*, published in 1763), Ottoman women knew what they were up against. The writers intended specifically to challenge some of the Orientalist stereotypes through which Ottoman women were perceived. But they also had recourse to these stereotypes to sell their books and were at times personally attached to them because the positive elements of stereotypical imagery (such as the renowned charity of Ottoman women) were important to their self-image. It is this clash, generally characterised as the clash between the self-image of the colonised and their representation in colonial discourse, that has been the basis of so many explorations in postcolonial theory. Emphasising the authors' interactions with existing knowledges about the East shows how they were able to intervene in Orientalist culture with a self-conscious ability to manipulate cultural codes that is not normally attributed to the inferiorised, silenced, woman of the harem stereotype.

All the Ottoman women in this book found their personal and social positions of origin to be altered by their dialogue and experience of travel and engagement with Orientalist culture. This applied to Grace Ellison who, two centuries after Montagu, also found much to admire and envy. Revelling in the pleasures of a colonial-style upward mobility, she could not but feel the contrast between the protection afforded to Ottoman women (supported by many men in their bid for emancipation) and the unyielding market forces and vilification of feminists with which women in Britain had to contend. For Ellison, Zeyneb Hanım, Halide Edib and Demetra Vaka Brown it was impossible to be entirely unaware that their knowledges were (regarded as) situational: they all knew that their publications were sold on the basis of a point of origin whose appeals to authenticity (seen in titles like *A Turkish Woman's European Impressions* and *An Englishwoman in a Turkish Harem*) brooked no revision. As a field predicated on the authenticity of the female author who was presumed to have actually been there, harem literature placed a premium on authorial experience. But not just any sort of author would do. The status and sales of the books published by all the writers covered here depended on the creation of specific sorts of gendered identities – calibrated in relation to class, race, religion, ethnicity and nation.

It is for this reason that I return repeatedly to the often conflicting authenticating identities that their publications constructed and that were in turn contested, reinforced or reconstructed by their initial readers. In this, I am not searching for the authentic voice of the silenced native woman (Chow 1994). I am looking at how, in specific historical and cultural situations, the resistant engagement of Orientalised subjects gives voice to the enunciation of alternative transculturated identifications. These alternative modalities are brought into being by the very conjunction of local and international economics, politics and cultures that mark both the conditions of possibility for their emergence and the limits within which they have to operate. Do the dizzying and mobile identifications assumed by these authors, Ottoman and Western, demonstrate the articulation of what Chela Sandoval (1991) calls the differential form of oppositional consciousness? Though Sandoval is writing about a largely postmodern phenomenon of 'US third world feminist' political praxis, I recognise, in the inconsistent but targeted cultural interventions of Ottoman women writers, her characterisation of a radical consciousness; one that can never give total allegiance to any explanatory grand narrative (feminist or otherwise) that is unable to account for the inherently contradictory experience of the subject marginalised by racialisation.

In their forays into the already commodified representation of Oriental female lives, these women show an ability to read their 'current situation of power' and respond tactically with the self-conscious selection of the 'ideological form best suited to push against its configuration' (Sandoval 1991: 15). Looking for the insurrectionary possibilities of their accounts does not, as Sara Suleri (1992b) warns, overvalue (racialised) experience as the ultimate marker of a iconic radical subjectivity. Given the unavoidable and inflated value of the (racialised, gendered) first person that structures their attempts to intervene in Orientalism, attention to their sources can reveal both the compromised articulation of an Orientalised female voice and its impact on the dominant cultural codes that it navigates. For a citational discourse like Orientalism, which relies for its power on the repetition of recognisable elements (of Western Orientalist knowledges), these female Oriental sources from behind the veil are simultaneously a possible threat and a possible augmentation (Kondo 1997). With the veiled woman serving, as Meyda Yeğenoğlu (1998) points out, as Orientalism's iterative element par excellence the books that come from her pen will be unavoidably significant for a cultural market driven by the sexualisation of racialised difference.

Whilst concepts of authenticity were central to the production of their work and are again at the level of critique essential to my study of them, I am not presenting these books as the rediscovered native (or subalternised) voice about whose impossible enunciation Spivak writes so cogently. Although bringing their books back into circulation is one of the aims of this recuperative project, this exercise is not simply one of re-inscription. The nature of their highly mediated 'speaking' and my engagement with it can best be understood as what Spivak, in reconsidering the subaltern, terms an 'interception' – '[a]ll speaking, even seemingly the most immediate, entails a distanced decipherment by another, which is, at best, an interception' (Spivak 1999: 309). This, as Jill Didur and Teresa Heffernan point out, draws attention to the relational and transitory nature of the 'inevitable displacement that accompanies any attempt to read a definitive meaning or intent in the actions or statements of others, and how speech as interception also productively points to the binary – the two points – in which it is so often trapped' (Didur and Heffernan 2003: 4). This always situated and relational nature of the Ottoman and Western writers is what most concerns my study. It traces the movement of their speech acts as they shift restlessly and creatively between the binary poles of the Orientalist and imperial discourses that structured their encounters with each other and their readers. The cultural capital of the 'native' voice and the curiosity to see behind the veil certainly helped these authors into publication. But they could not control the reception of their work nor ensure that their attempts at self-representation were cross-culturally legible to their Occidental audiences.

Accordingly, Chapter One pays particular attention to the field of harem literature into which their books emerged and whose conventions they anticipated, detailing the role of the Anglo-American publishing industry in the creation and circulation of Western and Middle Eastern women's harem narratives. The chapter's author biographies set them in context with each other through their meetings and correspondence and trace their interventions in the publication process.

In Chapter Two, the individual life-histories of the Ottoman writers and Grace Ellison are set in an account of the events and personalities of late Ottoman and early republican social, political and economic history. In considering the debates about gender and national emancipation that framed their experiences (and to which they contributed) the chapter's problematisation of classificatory categories culminates with the question, 'who was the Oriental woman?'

Chapter Three turns to the central tropes of the Western Orientalist fantasy – the harem and polygamy – to examine how Western and Ottoman women intervened in their depiction. Aware that the stereotype of the harem lady determined Western attitudes to the empire, progressive Ottomans offered a critical evaluation of harem relations alongside a discriminating analysis of Western feminism. Their determination to develop a localised emancipatory discourse found echoes in Ellison and Vaka Brown, who were under no illusions about the rigours of Western so-called freedom, though they were often reluctant to relinquish their connections to treasured habits of old-fashioned harem living.

Chapter Four takes as its theme the representation of Orientalised female beauty. Descriptions of women, their clothes, their bodies and their beauty were a structural feature of Orientalist discourse and often operated in Western women's writing as a way to classify the Oriental domestic about which they were held to have particular knowledge. The depiction of female manners and bodies also provided an opportunity for the articulation of fantasy and the erotic in Western women's writings. This chapter examines the prominence given to female beauty in the writing of Demetra Vaka Brown, arguing that the eroticised exchange of female gazes was essential to her performance of an Orientalised femininity that the West could rarely recognise.

Chapter Five returns to the harem, this time conceptualising it in terms of spatiality. Analysing how its segregating spatial relations exerted a socialising force on subjects within and beyond the Islamic community, this chapter animates the stereotypically deadened space of the harem to consider it as a social text whose interpretation was differently available to variously racialised subjects. Detailing the hybridity of modern Ottoman spaces, the chapter contrasts Ellison's thrilling escapades in a veil with the complicated participation of Ottoman women in non-segregated spaces at the turn of the century, culminating in an analysis of women's nationalist assertion of gendered spatial rights during the Allied occupation after the First World War.

Chapter Six extends the discussion of cross-cultural dressing with an analysis of the photographs that illustrate these books. Integrating an understanding of the ethnic and racial nature of gender identities into theories of gender performativity, it recasts the binarisms often held to inhere in cross-cultural dressing in light of the varieties of Ottoman responses to European dress. With the photographs operating to validate the reality of their books, a reading of the combative relationship of Ottoman and Western women to codes of ethnographic authority is united with the cultural turn in ethnography to explore the different pleasures and possibilities of dressed and depicted bodies for subjects travelling between East and West.

The conclusion revisits the question of authenticity that haunted these books and determined the market for harem literature. It examines the difficulties Ottoman women faced in performing a modern identity in the context of the West's resolutely nostalgic commodification of Ottoman female life. The right to recognise and define the composite nature of late Ottoman modernity, of which the body of the Orientalised woman was emblematic, was fought for by all the writers in this book with an investment in nostalgia that ranged from the imperial to the nationalist to the diasporic.

HOW TO USE THIS BOOK

Because I anticipate a readership drawn from several different fields I have tried to make it possible for everyone to share in this book's particular interdisciplinarity. My way round this has been to outline historical events and theoretical protocols as I go along: where these are grindingly familiar, I am assuming you will simply flick past them. For similar reasons, you will find that some quotes from the primary sources recur in different contexts where I want to re-examine them to make different points. This is also a function of using material unfamiliar to most readers. In my efforts to share with you my fascination with these sources, I want, in a quaintly old-fashioned way, to make these writers as alive to you as possible, at the same time as treating their books as texts suitable for rigorous critical analysis. In order to maintain the cross-referentiality of my diverse fields and methods of inquiry, you will find that the structure of this book is of inter-linked rather than discrete chapters; as I trace for you the journey that I took in rethinking Orientalism.

NOTES

1 On the infiltration of Western ideas into Egypt and other Arab parts of the region see Abu-Lughod (1963).

2 See also Said (1993). In addition to the works cited above, examples of the range of responses to Said and an indication of the spread and development of work in postcolonial studies can be found in the anthologies compiled by Williams and Chrisman (1993), Ashcroft, Griffiths and Tiffin (1995) and Lewis and Mills (2003). See also Young (2001).

3 For an excellent overview see also Cole and Kandiyoti (2002) and the special issue of *International Journal of Middle East Studies* (34: 2, 2002) to which it is the introduction.

CHAPTER ONE

ജ Harem Travellers ര

SELLING THE HAREM

There is no denying it – as a topic, the harem sold books. From the eighteenth century on, whether you wrote about living in one, visiting one, or escaping from one, any book that had anything to do with the harem sold. Publishers knew it, booksellers knew it, readers knew it and authors knew it. And women the world over who had lived within the harem's segregating system knew it too. Not so entirely divorced from the conventions of Western culture as stereotypes of the isolated odalisque suggested, they cannily entitled their books with the evocative words 'harem', 'Turkish', 'Arabian' or 'princess', and pictured themselves in veils and yaşmaks on the front cover. All this even as they wrote about lives that were the opposite of what the curious West expected to find.

This book, my book, also has the word 'harem' in the title. And I, too, need it to pique the reader's interest even as I struggle from the start to control the peculiar fecundity of its associations. But I cannot avoid 'harem' because it is so central to the writings and reception of Ottoman women and to the dialogue that I want to talk about between Ottoman and Western women at the beginning of the twentieth century. In this conversation, women who were the last generation to experience the harem system of the Turko-Circassian Ottoman elite documented female lives on the cusp of immense social change. In memoirs, travel writing, autobiography and fiction, Ottoman women told the story of harem life, described the struggle for female emancipation and engaged in a cogent critique of the so-called liberation of Western women – all the while battling with the need to accommodate and challenge the Western stereotypes that created the market for their books.

Western women had for two centuries been doing their best to sate the appetite of a Western readership curious about harem life. Their ability to have actually seen the space forbidden to Western men gave their books a unique selling point and they worked it: varying from the conversational to the titillating, from the friendly to the outrageously judgemental, Western women delighted in depicting themselves as visitors and temporary inhabitants of the harem's rarefied space. But if Western women had something to sell, accounts by women who were presumed to have actually been formed by the harem's socialising regime operated at a real premium. Of course, this interest was not without its drawbacks. The Orientalist assumptions about the innate inferiority of the all-so-fascinatingly exotic East meant that Ottoman women (like other women writers from within the Islamic world) were writing, and knew they were writing, in the context of stereotypes that filled the minds of their readers before they even opened the book. Trying to illustrate how life in the harem was not quite as Europe imagined it, whilst also arguing for reform of the segregated system, brought Ottoman writers up against the prejudices of the West whose stereotypical assumptions survived with remarkable longevity despite the interventions of Western women travellers and writers.

The West's curiosity about harem life was first satisfied to any extent by the now famous letters from Constantinople of Lady Mary Wortley Montagu. Penned in 1717 during the period of her husband's ambassadorship to the Ottoman Porte, her *Embassy Letters* (published posthumously in 1763) provided the first female-penned account of the inside of the harem. Writing against the already prevalent codification of the polygamous harem as a space of sexual depravity and random cruelty, Montagu's observations took a culturally relativist stance, presenting Ottoman women as possessing freedoms not available to their European counterparts. Her willingness to evaluate the harem, seen in men's (imaginary) accounts as the ultimately 'other' space of the Orient, in relation to Western domestic gender relations, was to become typical of Western women's harem literature. For men, the harem woman trapped in a cruel polygamous sexual prison was a titillating but pitiful emblem of the aberrant sexuality and despotic power that characterised all that was wrong with the non-Christian Orient. But for women, as Billie Melman (1992) has demonstrated, the harem could be conceptualised in relation to their changing concerns with their own domestic and social arrangements. Rather than operating only as a voyeuristic sexual sphere, the harem began to appear in the manners and customs model that privileged female access and prioritised the intersubjective observation (Clifford 1986) of the gendered participant (see also Melman 1992). This is not to evacuate the sexual and the fantastical from women's writing, nor to minimise the presence of cultural and political prejudice; Western women's accounts were heterogeneous and contradictory. They offered clashing commentaries based on differing amounts of access and expertise and, though marketed on the 'truth factor' of their having actually been in a harem, must not be read as simply realistic, unmediated or unembellished. Their writings were historically contingent, so that whilst they all contributed to a shift towards a comparative social evaluation of the harem, the terms of their interest changed according to their own domestic concerns.

In the century and a half between the publication of Montagu and of Grace Ellison, Zeyneb Hanım and Melek Hanım, Halide Edib and Demetra Vaka Brown, harem literature had become a large and popular area of women's literary activity. After Montagu's corrective to men's accounts, the unreliability of anything but a female-authored source became widely accepted and, with a veritable 'eruption' in Britain of publications by women in the 1850s, harem literature was regarded by the second half of the nineteenth century as a uniquely female area of cultural production (Melman 1992). Women's insights into the harem were enthusiastically, though not uncritically, received and women were well aware that their access to the mysterious harem would make their books or articles desirable. After the flush of publications in the 1850s numbers rose steadily until they peaked in the 1890s. Though numbers of new books published after that started to decrease dramatically (to below the 1850 level), the field remained popular until, during, and after the First World War.[1] The authors covered in this book entered a field of harem literature that had become a well-established area of female publishing and inherited a general readership whose appetite to know more about the region was a continuation of the mid-Victorian enthusiasm for works on the classical and modern Middle East (Melman 1992).

The vast mid-nineteenth-century expansion in harem literature was made possible by, among other things, the increased opportunities for safer travel. This meant that more women were visiting the Middle East, still most often with male relatives but sometimes now alone. With Cook's tours operating to Egypt from 1869 the numbers of foreign women in the Middle East grew dramatically. No longer restricted only to the upper classes and aristocracy, travel became more and more part of the upper- and middle-middle-class experience (though still beyond the means of the lower-middle classes, Melman 1992). Travel and hopes of travel fuelled a market for books that could be read by a general readership as part of their preparation for the trip and by those imagining from their armchairs. Harem literature was part of a vast range of publications on the region that fed the desire for information on foreign lands and societies. As well as the general reader, publications on the Middle East also met the needs of specific communities of readers concerned with existing and new areas of investigation that ranged from Egyptology to social welfare, from biblical studies to costume. Elements of all these concerns can be found explicitly and implicitly within harem literature as women travelled with a variety of social and political agendas (missionary and secular).

The rising numbers of women travellers also led to a change in the nature and frequency of harem visits. Once a novelty of the few, trips to harems were, by the mid-nineteenth century, a staple of the tourist itinerary, bringing about changes in Ottoman and Western women's experiences of each other. Where Murray's guide book in 1847 advised women visitors to seek introductions for harem visits from consular staff, by 1871 it was advocating that Western visitors cultivate Turkish friends as a way into the harem (Melman 1992). The increased demand was such that, as Annie Jane Harvey noted in 1871, 'every year it is more difficult for passing travellers to gain admittance to the harems' (Harvey 1871: 8).

The increased numbers of Western women in the region with their insatiable demands for harem visits, and the fact that the by now formalised nature of visits to elite harems made them frustrating for visitors who wanted to 'really' see Ottoman domestic life (Harvey 1871), led to changes in both the nature of the harem visit and its depiction. Travel was no longer restricted to the European aristocracy, whose dealings had been only with the most elevated of the local elites. Foreign women began to visit and report on Muslim households from less elevated social strata, providing a view of harems of the middle classes rather than only the imperial elite. This was accompanied by what Melman identifies as the Victorian domestication and desexualisation of the harem.[2] In this the focus moved away from the aristocratic eighteenth-century interest in libertarian sexual mores that characterised Montagu's account (where Ottoman women's ability to engage in sexual intrigue was envied) to the preoccupation with bourgeois definitions of respectability that characterised Victorian writers (where the ability of Ottoman women to own property and deny their husbands access to their bedchambers were the subject of envious comparisons, see also Chapter Three). By the early twentieth century, writers such as Ellison were comparing male support for Ottoman feminism to the masculine hostility encountered by suffragists at home.

For all that harem literature was rooted in the exposure of Ottoman domesticity, it was always also a genre through which Western women were able to mount a sustained and interventionalist political discourse about international relations. Political opinion among women writers was divided and historically specific, informed by contemporary Western debates about foreign policy and divisions between the Western nations. In the late Victorian and Edwardian period especially, this strain of foreign policy commentary became more pronounced, as Western women's first-hand observations of life in the Middle East brought them up against the anti-Muslim prejudice that they felt determined Western strategy. This is seen most pronouncedly in women's discussion of the controversy surrounding the Ottoman Armenian massacres of the 1890s and the events before and during the Balkan Wars of 1912–14, when Ellison was writing. Her sense of injustice at how the West could overlook evidence of Christian Bulgarian barbarity in 1913 (see Chapter Two) continued a strain seen two decades earlier in Mrs Max Müller (Georgina Adelaide Grenfell, 1897) and by the more contemporaneous American writer Anna Bowman Dodd (1904). Both Müller and Dodd, like Ellison, contrasted the West's blind support for the Armenians with its dangerous indifference to the ways in which Ottoman state oppression affected Muslims as well as the minority populations. The lost opportunities to work with progressive Muslim opposition groups were decried by all three, who saw wider social change as a precursor to Ottoman gender and national liberation.

If the harem offered a platform for Western women's macro-political pronouncements they still had to gain entry to it. The problems of access reported by Harvey do not only reflect the increase in demand driven by the growing numbers of foreign arrivals. The trouble and awkwardness of the Western harem visit did not always please Ottoman women, who 'object[ed] to be made a show of' (Harvey 1871: 9) and were not always willing to accommodate foreign curiosity. Nor were they happy to be commodified in published accounts that transgressed Islamic codes of privacy, which forbade discussion of domestic life outside the family (Heffernan forthcoming). Western women writers admitted that Ottoman women were angered by visitors whose subsequent activities exposed their private lives and evidence suggests that elite Ottoman women used their class status to restrict the (literary and visual) cultural activities of their visitors (Roberts

2002). Ottoman women's frustration at being constructed as tourist spectacle did not diminish as the century wore on. Musbah Haidar writing of her childhood at the turn of the century was contemptuous of Mrs Bristol, wife of Admiral Bristol, the representative of the American government, to whom her mother was required to show hospitality: dissecting the Orientalist assumptions of foreign visitors and their inability to recognise local class status she pilloried the ignorance of the visiting women who, as her sister complained, '"only come to gape and stare"'. When Mrs Bristol, who admitted 'she had never been in such a cosmopolitan and elegant circle' as she found in Istanbul, was plainly amazed to find Haidar's royal family using an 'exquisite Sèvres tea service', Haidar tiraded:

> What did these people imagine they would find or see? ... Women in gauzy trousers sitting on the floor?
> In their abysmal ignorance these foreigners did not realise that many of the veiled ladies of the Harems were better born, better read, spoke several languages and dressed with a greater chic than some of their own most famous society women. (Haidar 1944: 173–4)[3]

Their encounter with this type of continued ignorant and prurient curiosity fuelled the determination of Ottoman women to publish in the West. Their decision to break with cultural norms denotes the seriousness of their determination to take on the Western prejudices with which they were so clearly familiar. This willingness to expose family life to the Western reader, and to insert a Muslim female voice into a mixed gender domain (Najmabadi 1993), needs also to be seen in relation to the development of an internal Ottoman public discourse about gender mores and modernity that was increasingly a feature of their home society by the mid-nineteenth century (see Chapter Two). It is in this context too that publications by Ottoman men appeared in the West, often written whilst in political exile, like Halil Halid's *The Diary of a Turk* (1903). Like their female counterparts men's Western publications were directed at multiple audiences: the different groups of Western readers (who were presumed to know more or less about Ottoman and Islamic society), Ottomans in the West (often in political or personal exile), Ottomans at home and in the Ottoman dominions and Muslims outside the Ottoman Empire.

The first accounts by Ottoman and Muslim women appeared in Europe in the last quarter of the nineteenth century and were, like all the Ottoman sources discussed here, from elite women. Whilst Western harem literature had widened its scope to include middle-class writers and to discuss harems outside the upper elite, for Middle Eastern women to be literate and able to intervene in European-language literary culture an elite background was a pre-requisite. Books like Melek Hanım's two-volume set *Thirty Years in the Harem: or the Autobiography of Melek-Hanum, Wife of H.H. Kibrizli-Mehemet-Pasha* (1872) and *Six Years in Europe: Sequel to Thirty Years in the Harem* (1873) and Emily Said-Ruete's *Memoirs of an Arabian Princess: Princess Salme bint Said ibn Sultan al-Bu Saidi of Oman and Zanzibar* (1888) were written in English and French and appeared also translated into other European languages. Though their stories were not always believed (Melek Hanım in particular was held to be unreliable by some reviewers), they were widely read and discussed (see also Lewis 1996, Lewis and Micklewright 2004). Melek Hanım and Said-Ruete were part of the commencement of an engagement in print with the West and were joined by the occasional article and report. But the first real cluster of English language depictions of harem life by Ottoman women came later, at the start of the twentieth century, just as the elite harems started to become a thing of the past and in the last flush of harem literature in the West. This was the period when, in Istanbul (and in Cairo), feminism emerged as a widespread political movement in the region.[4] As I discuss in Chapter Two, it was not until the later nineteenth century that changes in Ottoman society and cultural practice made possible the conditions necessary (including an increase in women's education and travel opportunities) for the emergence of Ottoman women's writings in greater numbers.

Whilst harem literature was past its period of greatest expansion, the Ottoman writers I am studying entered into a still healthy market and one that was marked by the longevity of the stereotypes about Ottoman society that their predecessors from East and West had been challenging. Though the West had known and widely reported that the Ottoman state had been engaged in a process of modernisation since the mid-nineteenth century, the presumption of its timelessness and exoticism continued especially in relation to the harem (Childs 1989). The harem woman (often equated with the odalisque, or trainee, of the imperial harem, and who was generally understood in the West as a concubine) remained the pivot of Western Orientalist fantasy. Her figure haunted all women writing from the harem who felt personally misrepresented. But the stereotype of the indolent, ignorant harem inmate was also a major concern to male writers in the late Ottoman and early Republican period who knew it determined how their whole society was seen by the West (see Chapter Two).

Ottoman women publishing in the West joined with their male compatriots in wanting to correct Western misconceptions about Ottoman society but they also wanted (as did many men) to intervene in Ottoman gender relations. Their awareness of Western prejudices made it complicated for them to express their reservations about regional gender restrictions whilst also correcting assumptions about a way of life that was, by the turn of the century, rapidly becoming defunct. Their books must always be understood in relation to this dual axis. Their work constitutes a new instalment in the field of Western harem literature, a reverse discourse that offers not just the other side of the coin but that self-consciously intervenes in the racialised discourses of gender to be found in both the East and the West. But they did not write outside Western literary conventions and the publishing industry. It is important to consider the extent to which the scope and conventions of harem literature impacted on the creation and circulation of their books. Although much of the publishing industry information that I would wish to have had is sadly unavailable, I want to bear in mind how the conventions of harem literature, as well as the wider Orientalist cultural framework, would have variously and unevenly determined the way they presented their accounts, the way that their editors advised them, the type of illustrations that were chosen and the ways in which their work was received.

Harem literature was from the very start citational, drawing its authority from the specific and general rebuttal of male Orientalist fantasy. This field of 'alternative' Orientalisms has been seen variously to undermine the stability of Western Orientalist knowledge and power (Lowe 1991, Mills 1991, Lewis 1996) and to augment it, acting as a supplement to male knowledge that maintained rather than dislodged its ultimate authority (Yeğenoğlu 1998). The importance of citation in all strands of Orientalism (and Occidentalism) developed as a characteristic of the field and from the late eighteenth century women authors cited each other in both agreement and disagreement. In this Montagu was talismanic, invoked throughout the nineteenth and early twentieth century. Reviews compared women to each other and to male sources. Male sources were connected to women's writing through quotation and footnotes and directly through personal contact (such as Sophia Poole whose *An Englishwoman in Egypt: Letters from Cairo*, 1844, was written at the request of her brother, the famous ethnographer Edward W. Lane). In my sample, Grace Ellison's book is fronted with an introduction by the esteemed Cambridge Orientalist and expert on Persian and Ottoman poetry, Edward G. Browne. The politics of citation, especially as they are linked to questions of authenticity, are a significant factor in all these sources. Ottoman writers directly and indirectly engaged in textual dialogue with each other, with Western women and with male writers from both East and West.

The connections between women's books were often personal as well as textual. In the biographies that follow I map out how the Ottoman authors, Halide Edib, Demetra Vaka Brown, Melek Hanım and Zeyneb Hanım who populate my book, linked with the English Grace Ellison to form a chorus of often dissenting voices. Together they provide a study for the final phase of harem literature – the documentation of the harem's decline.

The quantity of biographical information and publishing history available on these authors varies substantially and so the biographies in this chapter are uneven in length and content. I have endeavoured to piece together as much as possible in each case (though more will I am sure come to light after publication). The biographical information given here is designed to be read alongside the historical and cultural synopsis and commentary provided in Chapter Two, where I make clear the specific and general points at which these authors and their families intersect with and contribute to national and international events. Following my discussion of the field of harem literature at the start of this chapter, I have in the author biographies integrated material about their publishing careers. Again, this is uneven (I have far more on Vaka Brown, for example, than on others), but it is used to establish general points about the market for all their work and to analyse the ways in which Ottoman women and Ellison negotiated publishing practice in Britain and the United States.

ZEYNEB HANIM AND MELEK HANIM

These two sisters were the daughters of Sultan Abdülhamit II's Minister of Foreign Affairs, Noury Bey.[5] Their grandfather was a French nobleman, the marquis de Blosset de Chateauneuf, who had fallen in love with an Ottoman woman whilst in the service of the sultan as a military officer. Converting to Islam, he took the name Reschid Bey and made his life in Constantinople (Ternar 1994: 21). His wife came from Circassia, a region in the Caucasus mountains renowned for its fair and beautiful women who (as I discuss in Chapter Three) had for generations found prominence as concubines and wives in the harems of the Ottoman elite. Their eldest son was Noury Bey and he gave his daughters Zeyneb Hanım and Melek Hanım a liberal education on Western lines. They were tutored by English, French, Italian and German governesses and spoke five European languages as well as the 'three Oriental languages [Arabic, Persian, Ottoman] necessary for cultured people' (Melek Hanoum 1926: 130). But as they grew older their childhood liberties ceased and they were required to take the veil and adopt the role of typical elite Turkish woman. Already unhappy at these restrictions, the final straw came when their father arranged a marriage for his eldest daughter, Zeyneb Hanım. Although her husband – her father's secretary and protégé (who did go on to succeed him as Minister for Foreign Affairs) had good prospects and was a liberal, educated man – Zeyneb Hanım could not reconcile herself to an arranged marriage. It was this that acted as the catalyst for their interaction with the famous French Orientalist novelist known as Pierre Loti.

In 1906 the author Pierre Loti (the pseudonym of naval officer Louis Marie Julien Viaud, 1850–1923) published his last novel, *Les Désenchantées*. Known for his travelogues, this was his third story set in Constantinople and followed the success of his first Orientalist novel *Aziyadé*, initially published anonymously in 1879 (followed by a sequel, *Fantome d'Orient*, in 1892). In *Aziyadé* he had told the story of how the protagonist, a loosely disguised alter ego sharing the same name as his pseudonym Loti, had fallen in love with a beautiful Circassian slave woman, married to a Turk, who had killed herself in despair when the handsome English ensign was sent back to Europe. Based on his stay in Istanbul in 1876 the story transformed his association with a woman named Hakidjé, renamed as the eponymous Aziyadé, into a hugely popular romance. (Though Hakidjé had not killed herself and in fact lived until 1880, Lerner 1974). In 1906, he published another novel in which another Turkish woman also died for love of the *gaiour*. After a successful career in which his hugely popular novels were generally understood to be loosely autobiographical, this, his last novel, featured a protagonist even closer to home – the successful French novelist 'André Lhéry'. Lhéry's liaison with three Turkish women, one of whom's distracted love for him drove her to suicide rather than be forced to remarry her estranged husband, was the story of *Les Désenchantées*. And again, this woman did exist, but not quite as Loti imagined – and again she did not die.

The three Turkish women who contrived to meet the novel's hero had in fact met the French author, and had provided him with details to authenticate his tale. But they were far more instrumentalist than merely window-dressing yet another Orientalist romance: they had their own agenda and it was for this reason that they initiated the liaison that led to *Les Désenchantées*. Two of these women were the Turkish sisters Zeyneb Hanım and Melek Hanım and it is with their writings that my book is concerned.

Like many Turks, the sisters were familiar with Loti's books and 'knew them almost by heart', regarding him as 'a friend of the Turks [and of] our civilisation' (Melek Hanoum 1926: 132). Indeed, Zeyneb Hanım had already written to him in France in 1902 to thank him for *Aziyadé*. Dissatisfied with their lives, the two sisters were convinced that if only European intellectual opinion could be harnessed to what they saw as the desperate plight of the educated Turkish woman, then change might be brought about. When in 1904 they learned that Loti was again stationed in Istanbul, they determined to enlist him to their cause. Aware, as were most of his readers, that his novels were fictionalised accounts of his own experiences, they realised that they would have to feed him appropriate material: 'we knew that if he wrote our story he must make that story his own; it was for us to construct it for him' (Melek Hanoum 1926: 133). In 1904 they wrote to him 'poste restante' and made an assignation to meet. From there the story progressed, with meetings and letters fleshing out the narrative that eventually became *Les Désenchantées*.

Named after the disenchantment felt by educated Turkish Muslim women who, though cultured, had to live by the restrictive rules of Ottoman society, the novel told the story of how Lhéry was contacted by two sisters 'Melek' and 'Zeyneb' in the hope that they could persuade him to write of their plight. The famous author enjoyed a series of meetings with them and their friend 'Djénane' in boats, cafes and charmingly old-fashioned Ottoman interiors. As well as meeting clandestinely with Lhéry, the women maintained a correspondence intended to provide him with material for the projected book. All three heroines are presented as doomed from the outset and by the end of the book they are all dead or dying: Melek from brain fever brought on, it is implied by the dread of her imminent nuptials; Zeyneb from a chest infection that she refuses to treat (thus avoiding a dreaded marriage); and Djénane by suicide – though whether this was to protest at her enforced return to her adulterous husband or because of her grief over Lhéry's departure is left unclear.[6]

But the plot gets more complicated. The two sisters were not really called Zeyneb Hanım and Melek Hanım. Their real names were Hadidjé Zennour and Nouryé Neyr-el-Nissa. And they did not operate alone but had the help of a French woman, Marie Léra, who wrote as a journalist under the pseudonym Marc Hélys. Zeyneb Hanım and Melek Hanım were the names given to his fictional heroines by Loti in order to protect their identity, for fear of imperial reprisals. The third *désenchantée*, the role played by Hélys, was identified as Djénane in the novel. In their correspondence with Loti they called themselves

Zeyneb, Neyr and Leyla (Lerner 1974), the last two of which Loti changed to Melek and Djénane for publication. Melek Hanım later explained that 'not till we met [later] in Paris did Loti ever see our faces' (1926: 133) and so 'he had no idea who we were' (1926: 134). Anyway, they knew they could 'rely absolutely on the discretion of Loti', who would have understood the restrictions against Ottoman subjects talking to foreigners, and the risk to women in particular. That he gave them fictitious names and stated in the preface that 'the heroines never existed' was, they also knew, not enough to really protect them. They determined to flee Istanbul before publication and escaped to France in 1906.

When they arrived in Nice, Zeyneb Hanım's health was already poor, with the consumption that would later take her to an early grave, but they delighted in seeing the world without a veil. Whilst in Fontainebleau in 1906 they met the British feminist and journalist Grace Ellison, who – unlike many in Europe – was a great supporter of the Turks and already very interested in the situation of Turkish women. The friendship they struck up developed over the next few years, fostered by an ongoing correspondence. Ellison went on to make several long visits to Turkey herself, sometimes reporting for the *Daily Telegraph*, and publishing several of her own books about Turkey and her travels. Later, in a typically bewildering self-contradiction (in *Turkey To-day* from 1928), Ellison claimed to have initially met the two sisters when she visited them at home in Istanbul during her first visit to the city as a 'schoolgirl tourist' in 1905. But, whether she met them first in Turkey or in France, Ellison helped the Turkish sisters to publish a book each.

In 1913 Zeyneb Hanım's book, *A Turkish Woman's European Impressions* was published in London by Seeley, Service and Co. Edited by Grace Ellison it was illustrated with photographs, some of which were taken by Ellison herself. The book is made up of Zeyneb Hanım's letters to Ellison written in Europe between 1906 and 1912 (including a couple penned by Melek Hanım) and reveals not only Zeyneb Hanım's promised impressions of Europe but also details of life in Turkey. Sometimes prompted by enquiries from Ellison, the descriptions reveal the Turkish woman's awareness of what her European audience would want to know. But the book also demonstrates the dialogue between the English and Turkish woman, as they write back and forth – with Ellison occasionally making editorial interjections to distance herself from Zeyneb Hanım's criticisms of Europe or Christianity. Melek Hanım also wrote a book, the novel *Abdul Hamid's Daughter: The Tragedy of an Ottoman Princess*, based on the life of her acquaintance the Princess Aiche. This was edited by Ellison and published by Methuen in 1913 (the same year as Zeyneb Hanım's book), with an introduction by Ellison giving her impressions of the imperial palace and the Princess. Ellison's own responses to Turkey were published two years later in her book *An Englishwoman in a Turkish Harem* – and note how effectively she manages to smuggle so many keywords into her evocative title.

By the time Ellison's book came out, Zeyneb Hanım had returned to Turkey. Up until then, the sisters had travelled around Europe, visiting Switzerland (partly for Zeyneb Hanım's health), much of France, as well as Italy, London, Spain, Brussels. Their mother had died soon after they left (of shame, Melek Hanım claimed) and they lost their father in 1908 and with him the allowance that he had continued secretly to pay them (whilst having officially to disown them). This left them insecure financially, though Melek Hanım who had that year married a Polish aristocrat, was temporarily better off – until he lost the revenue of the family estates in Russia after the Russian Revolution. With no income available, Melek Hanım earned a living as seamstress (having trained in great secrecy at a dressmaker's in Constantinople when younger). Zeyneb Hanım, who never married, returned to Turkey from Marseilles in March 1912, during the Tripolitanian War between Italy and Turkey (having been in Italy when the war broke out). Here the story muddles: Yeshim Ternar claims that Zeyneb Hanım was repatriated as an enemy alien at the start of the First World War, whilst Melek Hanım – by then married to a Pole – could stay. But if Zeyneb Hanım left in 1912, this was prior to the start of the First World War, though Melek Hanım (1926: 136) does say that Zeyneb Hanım was 'sent back to Turkey' at the start of the First World War. Ellison, in Turkey just before the war in the winter of 1913/14, met Zeyneb Hanım again, but by her second trip in 1923 she recorded her as having passed away since her last visit.

Both sisters continued to use the names of their fictional alter egos when they published in English (Melek Hanım only once references herself as Neyr in Zeyneb Hanım's 1913 volume), and I shall follow this in the way I refer to them, just as Loti will be referred to by his pseudonym throughout and Hélys by hers.[7] Not only were there confusing name changes and literary alter egos, there are also conflicting accounts of how the narrative of the novel was created. As I discuss in more detail elsewhere (Lewis 2004), Zeyneb Hanım and Melek Hanım contrived to feed the ageing Loti a version of Oriental female life that would accord with his expectations in order to publicise their cause. After publication they steadfastly maintained that they were the heroines and source of the story, giving little credit to Hélys, whom they characterise merely as a 'French lady we took into our confidence [who] corrected' their letters to Loti. Djénane was, they contended, 'no one in particular … one day it was one cousin; one day another' (Melek Hanoum 1926: 133). In contrast, Hélys claimed a central role in the creation of the story and the concoction of the letters and diaries sent to Loti, writing her own account of the making of *Les Désenchantées* after Loti's death (Hélys 1923). Prior to this, Zeyneb Hanım's book declared clearly on its title page that it was written 'by Zeyneb Hanoum (heroine of Pierre Loti's novel *Les Désenchantées*)'. In her introduction Grace Ellison asserts that they are Loti's heroines, quoting his disclaimer in the novel's preface that 'they never existed' as evidence of the need to protect their identities in the face of Sultan Abdülhamit's repressive regime and making no reference to the role of a third person. Hélys' claims are given credit by Szyliowicz (1988) and Yeazell (2000) – not least on account of the copies of her letters to Loti that she lodged in the Bibliotèque Nationale. Whoever took the greatest role, it is evident from the accounts of all three of the women that between them they not only provided Loti with local details but were also largely responsible for the structure of the book:

> we wanted to see how he composed his books. We thought that he was going to live a novel, that we would only have to follow and give him a reply. Just the contrary happened. The novel would have been finished right away if we hadn't made the incidents occur. Because he furnished nothing'. (Hélys 1923, trans. in Szyliowicz 1988: 99)

The question of whether Zeyneb Hanım and Melek Hanım were really the *désenchantées* did not haunt them so much as the critique that they were not authentically Turkish, largely on account of their paternal European bloodline. Hélys paints them as half-French, half-Circassian, reporting that their father proudly claimed that his children were 'without a drop of Turkish blood' (Hélys 1923, trans. in Szyliowicz 1988: 96), though she confuses their grandfather with their father. Some reviews at the time attempted to dismiss the veracity of their complaints by denying that they were Turkish. This dizzying trail of false identities and pseudonyms creates another filter through which are played out the claims to authorship and authenticity that stalk all my sources. For to be a 'real' Oriental woman in literature aimed at the West was always to struggle with the stereotypical presumptions about that identity.

The publication of *Les Désenchantées* was an important event whose ramifications continued for the next three decades and it is in this context that the argument over Zeyneb Hanım and Melek Hanım's role needs to be understood. The characters of the novel took on a life outside its pages and came very quickly to stand for a certain type of restricted and frustrated Turkish femininity. For commentators of different political persuasions, the totemic figure of the *désenchantées* could signify either the tragedy of a wasted life or the feckless indolence of the spoilt elite. The book itself, in the years after its publication, was seen to be creating as much as reflecting discontent among Ottoman women, often linked to the already pernicious effects attributed to French fiction. In this Zeyneb Hanım and Melek Hanım were typical, already much taken with Loti's Oriental tales before their correspondence in 1904. At the same moment Vaka Brown, in Istanbul in 1901, deplored the unedifying influence of French romance fiction in the elite harems. Visiting in 1911, after *Les Désenchantées*, Hester Donaldson Jenkins again linked the two, arguing that the 'discontent of which Loti writes is common enough, for the influence of poorer French literature on its constant readers has been to give false ideas of life, to increase sentimentality, and to arouse discontent' (Jenkins 1911: 20–1). For nearly all Ottoman writers and Western observers of this period, the effect of *Les Désenchantées* remained a touchstone for arguments about the representation of the Ottoman woman and female emancipation. The reliability of Zeyneb Hanım and Melek Hanım as representatives of Ottoman womanhood was contested even as the image of the *désenchantée* became a commonplace in the lexicon of Orientalised femininity.

The problem of authenticity that challenged Zeyneb Hanım and Melek Hanım returns over and again to the material, often operating as a way of invalidating women's accounts. Its prevalence reveals not only the desire of their readership to find the 'real' thing, a 'real' harem woman whose life accorded with that which had been so long imagined, but also indicates the differences between Ottoman and European notions of regional identity. This is something that I turn to in Chapter Two, but that also haunts another of my authors, the Greek Ottoman Demetra Vaka Brown.

DEMETRA VAKA BROWN

Demetra Vaka (1877–1946) was a Greek Ottoman and a Christian whose identification as Ottoman and as a 'daughter of the Orient' (Vaka 1923: 24) was often complicated and contradictory. This was not only to do with her emigration to the United States but also with the ways in which the changes that brought about the end of the Ottoman Empire radically resituated the identities available to its erstwhile subjects. Demetra Vaka Brown is a fanciful writer who is at times opaque and contradictory in the construction of her authorial identities.

Demetra Vaka Brown[8] was born in 1877 on the island of Büyükada (Prinkipo) in the Sea of Marmora, near to Istanbul. Whilst she at various points identifies herself as Oriental in origin and refers to herself as an Ottoman and a Turkish subject, her preferred identification was that of Byzantine Greek, coming as she did from a Greek community that had lived in Istanbul for generations and that regarded itself as heir to the great Christian empire. But though her early life was relatively segregated, revolving around the local church, the Greek school, her parents' Greek friends and Greek relatives across the region, she also had a Muslim nursemaid and came to know Muslim girls and to share their world. Her closest Muslim Turkish friend was Djimlah, the granddaughter of the local paşa whom Vaka Brown met when her father took her with him on a *bairam*, or festival, visit. The friendship continued and the luxurious pleasures of the elite harem she experienced with Djimlah provided for Demetra Vaka a counterweight to her more studious home life. The death of her father when she was eleven drastically reduced the family's circumstances and Demetra Vaka now pursued her education not just for love of learning but to be able to support her impractical mother: 'my sole purpose now was to prepare myself to become a money-earner, like a man' (*Athene* 1949, 10:3, p. 30). It was partly for this reason that she emigrated to America in 1895 as the governess and companion to the children of the Turkish consul to New York, who was also a Greek. But she also left because she was frustrated with the limited opportunities available to a Greek girl in Istanbul.

> I had a thousand and one projects for my life. Above all I wanted to become a doctor in order to minister to the Turkish women, who at the time would rather die than see a man doctor. I lived in that dream of wonderful usefulness which was to be mine, and which was to save me from the martyrdom of the women of my race.

The usual fate of a Greek girl, who has to sit and wait until a marriage is arranged for her, seemed to me the worst thing that could befall me. And if the fate of the Greek girl with money was terrible, what could I think of a girl like me, who had no dowry?

It would mean a ceaseless plotting of all my female relatives to capture a suitable *parti*. And a man would be a suitable *parti* if he had money and position, irrespective of any other qualifications. (Vaka 1914: 193–4)

When the consul was recalled, Vaka Brown stayed in New York. Here she found herself a foreigner, unable to speak English and with little opportunity to make use of her French. Eventually she obtained work offering French tuition in a private girls' school and began some small-scale writing for the leading Greek-language newspaper *Atlantis* (see Kopan 1987), deriving the greatest pleasure from answering the problem-page letters sent in by poor, barely literate, Greek immigrants. Arriving before the first influx of Greeks who moved to America in response to the Graeco-Turkish war of 1897 and a decade before the major emigration of the new century, culminating in 1909, she would have found herself among a largely male immigrant population, most living in conditions of poverty (Contopoulos 1992, Saloutos 1964). Here, once again, as a single young woman working outside the home Vaka Brown would have been at odds with the socially conservative gender norms of the Greek-American community. Feeling a connection to these struggling compatriots, she wondered that Americans should donate so much money and energy to foreign missionary work simply to 'superimpose a little Christianity upon the citizens of Japan, China, India, Turkey', when they could better help the already Christian 'foreigners in their land, whose work goes to the upbuilding of the American commonwealth' (*Athene* 1951, 11:4, p. 52).[9]

Her subsequent marriage in 1904 to the American writer Kenneth Brown took her initially to his family home in Virginia and then back to New York and finally to Boston, where they based themselves when in the United States. In New York Vaka Brown started to write in English, with the help of her husband who 'smoothe[d] and iron[ed] out the rough edges' (*Athene* 1952 13:1, p. 27). She turned to the experiences of her childhood for inspiration and her 'Turkish sketches', based on her visit home in 1901 when she was reunited with Djimlah and other childhood friends, were first published in the syndicated *Sunday Magazine* in 1905. After many rejections, they eventually appeared in book form, published in the United States as *Haremlik* by Houghton Mifflin in 1909 and in Britain as *Some Pages from the Lives of Turkish Women* (London, Constable, 1909). This was to the be the first of three accounts of her interactions with Turkish women, covering a forty-year period that spanned the end of the Ottoman Empire. This vein of reminiscence accompanied by contemporary political commentary was to become her personal style and went on to provide her with material for many other publications. She worked as a correspondent and journalist over the next twenty years for magazines such as *Appleton's Magazine*, *The Smart Set*, *Metropolitan Magazine*, *Colliers*, *Atlantic Monthly*, *Asia* and

Outlook in the United States, and *Cassell's Magazine* in Britain. After *Haremlik* her second volume of memoirs was the story of her early years, published as *A Child of the Orient* in 1914 (also by Houghton Mifflin in America, by John Lane in Britain). This followed successful serialisation in *Metropolitan Magazine* and *Outlook* in the United States. The trilogy's final volume, *The Unveiled Ladies of Stamboul*, appeared with Houghton Mifflin in 1923. For this Vaka Brown had travelled to Istanbul in 1921 to observe the social changes that had followed the Young Turk Revolution of 1908.

It is with these three volumes that I am most concerned, in particular with *Haremlik*, which covers the same period as Zeyneb Hanım and Grace Ellison, and with *Unveiled*, which runs up to the Young Turk reforms in which Halide Edib was to be so involved. I am also drawing on Vaka Brown's autobiography, covering the years up to the publication of *Unveiled*, that was serialised after her death in the Greek American magazine *Athene* (1947–52). In this retrospective view of her relations with Muslim Turkish women Vaka Brown reinvented herself yet again, presenting a further account of her Ottoman identification. The inconsistencies of this with her previous writings demonstrate both the problems of being understood in the West and the disjunctions in her own localised identity that had arisen during a period in which the terms of that identity – Greek, Ottoman, Byzantine, Oriental – were being radically reconceptualised in the East and the West. The problems of framing a meaningful identity that could be recognisable to her various readerships was acute for Vaka Brown who addressed this often in her books. In all her writing, her Ottoman point of origin was essential in providing source material and as a stamp of authority on publications that spanned memoir and travel writing, journalism and fiction.

Vaka Brown specialised in political commentary about the Balkans and the Middle East. She also authored popular fiction, especially romances, often with an Oriental theme, some of which were jointly written with her husband. For someone who relied on the income generated by her writing (her husband and she had sold their share in his family farm and lived on the interest from that capital and their writing), this ability to produce in a variety of genres was valuable (though she acknowledged that some of the 'sentimental romances' were mere pot-boilers). It is clear from her memoirs that Vaka Brown saw the political commentary as central to her work, even though the balance in her writing was sometimes considered to be too romantic. In particular her commentary on politics during the First World War was in demand – 'my price went up and up, and during the first world war, Collier's paid me a thousand dollars apiece for each instalment of "In the Heart of German Intrigue"' (*Athene* 1952, 12:4, p. 41). For this she not only interviewed the main protagonists such as Lloyd George, King Constantine of Greece and Venizelos, the Greek Prime Minister in exile, but also presented herself as a player in international events, charged with carrying messages from heads of state and trying to broker a union between the Royalists, who were maintaining a pro-German neutrality and the pro-Allied Venizelists. Depicting herself as initially a Royalist, *In the Heart of German Intrigue* (brought out in book form by Houghton Mifflin in 1918) tells of her disillusionment with the duplicitous and self-serving Constantine. By the end of the book she had come out clearly on the side of Venizelos – who eventually managed to enter Greece into the final stages of the war on the side of the Allies. Similarly her travelogue *The Heart of the Balkans*, published by Houghton Mifflin the previous year, gave an account of peoples and politics in Serbia, Bulgaria, Albania, Montenegro and Greece, based on her travels there as a teenager and after. Her geo-political orientation provided a different range to the worldview of the Americans – offering area expertise on which she was considered an authority at the time (Kalogeras 1997) – that was valued by her editors and also apparently recognised by diplomatic and political figures throughout the region (Vaka 1918). From her earliest arrival in the United States she found the isolationism of the Americans alarming, having been herself formed by the obsessive political discussions she heard as a child in her parents' house.

> ... we of the subject races were continually speculating on who would become heir to her lands, if the Turkish Empire was to go ... To the average American, world politics were of no interest until after the world wars; but to us in the Near and Middle East, politics were a living concern, since they affected our daily lives. (*Athene* 1948, 8:4, p. 9)

This fascination is presented as characteristic of the consciousness of a 'subject race' and as typically Greek. Vaka Brown provides an account of the late Ottoman experience from the position of a minority population which demonstrates not only the difference of her experience from that of Muslim Turkish women such as Halide Edib, Zeyneb Hanım and Melek Hanım but that also shows the links between them. Her early friendship with Djimlah continued and the contrast between the ease of her friend's house – where sweets abounded and school lessons seemed far away – became even more marked after the death of her father:

> ... without the restraining influence of my father, work occupied all my waking hours, except when I went to Djimlah's. It was impossible to visit the house of a Turkish pasha, at that time, and remain in the world of reality. There I took off my working garb and plunged into the warm waters of luxury, where money-earning did not exist, and where one's desires were granted by magic. (*Athene* 1949, 10:3, p. 30)

For Vaka Brown, bonded profoundly with the experience of the elite Turkish harem, her writing career began with a desire to tell things to the Americans from the 'Turkish point of view'. Her affective identification with this female world continued throughout her writing. It was, however, an association that was always complicated for a member of a minority population, and the contradictions in Vaka Brown's accounts reflect the variety of shifting positions taken up by her family and friends. Whilst the autobiography in *Athene* depicts them as 'knowing nothing' of contemporary Turks, refusing to 'learn their language, or to have any social intercourse with them. We ignored them, as they ignored us. And if they despised us because they had conquered us we despised them because they were ignorant and Asiatics' (*Athene* 1947, 8:3, p. 87), elsewhere she is clear that her father spoke Turkish and her brother also was for some time friends with a Turkish boy.

The complications of the Greek Ottoman situation are most often expressed by Vaka Brown through the eyes of her childish self, caught between the injunctions of her fiercely patriotic uncle who recounted first hand the Greek Revolt of 1821 and her darling Djimlah who did not seem quite to encapsulate the evils of 'the hateful Asiatic yoke' (*Athene* 1951, 12:2, p. 22). Growing up with tales of the lost splendours of classical Greece and the Christian empire that had once ruled Istanbul, Vaka Brown learned to be proud of her 'race' and to long for the day when they would be free from their Turkish conquerors. In addition to her childhood romanticism for the classical stories, she was tutored in realpolitik by her father who allowed her to sit in on the endless adult discussions of current affairs where she soon learned that for the Greeks all '[f]oreign political events were judged from their probable effect on us' (*Athene* 1948, 8:4, p. 13). But for a child, especially one with Turkish friends, this was bewildering and Vaka Brown frequently uses humour to present the child's confusion at the often unfounded prejudices of the Greeks and the sometimes exclusive behaviour of her Turkish friends. Her mother's position remained a single constant in the shifting play of allegiances and affections – 'my mother and Sophie [her nurse] acted as if going to [Djimlah's] home was like going into a pest-house' (*Athene* 1948, 8:4, p. 14). But these bewildering contradictions were not only external, they also represent an internal conflict as the young Vaka Brown juggled her mission of intellectual advancement with her profound desire for Muslim luxury. When the strictures of school and financial hardship at home got too much she would escape to the other world available at Djimlah's:

> … the sybarite in me which craved luxury at times got the upper hand. Then I would be take myself to Djimlah for the week end. In her great konak [the large wooden multiple family mansions of the urban elite] the sordidness of a moneyless world never entered. Amid the turmoil of my mind it puzzled me that with all my ideals and aspirations I should tolerate this other self, and enjoy the life she craved. The word 'escapist' had not then been invented, but what I really did in visiting Djimlah was to escape from the realities of life. In her house we spent hours in the bath, were scrubbed and massaged by trained attendants. We ate rich food, and we slept. We reclined on hard sofas, listening to story-tellers and singers, munched sweets and drank sherbets. Then we ate and drank some more.
>
> It was a thoroughly purposeless life, and after satiating the sybarite in me till she lay dormant, I returned to my hard life of study with alacrity, and worked harder than ever – like a sinner expiating his sin. As a matter of fact I could not have endured this life of ease for more than a week. Hard work, even discontent, became pleasant by comparison. (*Athene* 1950, 11:2, p. 23)

It is this always ambivalent association, this split within herself, that I shall be returning to in my reading of Vaka Brown's work. But the frustrating restrictions placed on female life were not just a Muslim Turkish phenomenon: Vaka Brown had to fight against the constraints of what was expected of a Greek girl too. After attending the Greek school in Istanbul, she was able in 1892 to study at the Sorbonne in Paris for two years but then was forced to remain at home for financial reasons. On her return the limitations of life in Istanbul seemed more apparent and more irksome – not just the censorship and the palace spies but the gender expectations of the Greek community:

> Before going to Paris our backwardness had not troubled me as it did now. I could see no goal for myself. The only avenues open to women of my race were marrying, or teaching in the Greek schools – an underpaid and over-crowded profession. It was a meagre outlook for one who had envisaged boundless horizons. (*Athene* 1950, 11:2, p. 22)

Suddenly, the Greeks, who had always appeared to be more enlightened than the Turks, were thrown into new relief by her experiences in Europe. Though her community had always 'obtained what progress we could from near-by Europe. (We never thought of Turkey as being in Europe)', they were evidently further removed from Europe than they had thought (*Athene* 1948, 8:4, p. 12). Driven to earn a living through necessity, but also by a desire for personal fulfilment, Vaka Brown's departure for America allowed her to escape the restrictions of both her own community and the not always so terrible Turkish yoke. The Greek schools for girls, despite the attempts of the several notable women teachers who founded the Greek feminist magazines available in the last quarter of the nineteenth century, were under the control of the Greek Orthodox patriarch and were, like the mainly middle-class Greek community, conservative in their attitudes to women.[10] We shall encounter Djimlah – as she reappears in *Haremlik* – again in Chapter Four, but for now we should remember that, when Vaka Brown criticises Djimlah in print for apparently not wanting more out of life, her critique of the Muslim household is irretrievably connected to her resistance to the limited gender expectations of her own community.

Indeed, it is the realisation that she had become harem-like even in America that prompted Vaka Brown's writing career.

> Having now regained my health [after a period of living as a country lady in Virginia in 1904], divine discontent descended upon me. Oddly enough my childhood re-possessed me … and I became homesick for everything Greek …. What aspirations had filled me then! Now I was far away from all that seemed worth living for. Had I studied and worked so hard to become little better than my opulent friends in Turkey? (*Athene* 1952, 12:4, p. 14)

Though she had a life that seems desirable to others – 'it was taken for granted that being in Virginia was all anyone could desire' (*Athene* 1952, 12:4, p. 14) – her discontent was intense. Yet again the split within her own aspirations was articulated via the stereotyped figure of the indolent Turkish woman who now encapsulated the horrors of American domestic femininity, becoming everything Vaka Brown wished to avoid. Paradoxically though, having Orientalised the horrors of American domesticity, it was her desire to save Turks from the misapprehensions of American Orientalist imperialism that spurred on her writing career. When her first sketch, about her Greek relatives in Russia, was quickly accepted by *Associated Sunday Magazines* in 1905 she embarked immediately on another. Encouraged by this success, that clearly depended on her localised familiarity with an alternative worldview, she was surprised at the reception of her next sketch about two of her Turkish friends, 'married to the same man, and living happily under the same roof'. The kindly editor emerged with her manuscript in his hand:

> 'Don't you know that the Associated Sunday Magazine is published as a supplement to a large number of newspapers throughout the country? And you bring me a sketch extolling polygamy!'
>
> 'It shows the Turkish point of view. Your readers would like to learn that, wouldn't they?'
>
> He shook his head. 'Most of our readers are church-going people. They don't like Mohammedan ways. Your article would go against all their preconceived ideas of Turkey, and they would naturally resent it.'
>
> 'Then it isn't any good?'
>
> 'On the contrary, it's better than the one I accepted ...' (*Athene* 1952, 13:1, p. 26)

She was despondent at her first rejection, but her husband urged her to keep writing whilst awaiting news from *Appleton's*:

> 'y-e-s, but he said that my description of polygamy was objectionable to the ideas of the country.'
>
> No sooner had I uttered the words than a new idea popped into my head. Why shouldn't I describe the side of the Turks that was not known here? For even the Turks, who had butchered the Greek people so mercilessly, and at times had been unspeakable, had a better side. And since internationalism alone can save our civilization, each nation should learn the better qualities of the others. (*Athene* 1952, 13:1, p. 26)

At the appointed hour she returned to *Appleton's*, where the editor proceeded to check her ethnic credentials:

> Trumbull White received me more sternly than the first time, and tapping my MS with one finger remarked: 'The atmosphere seems authentic. Did you invent this story?'
>
> 'No, it's true.'
>
> 'Then you are a Turk?'
>
> 'No, I am a Byzantine Greek, born and brought up in Constantinople. Those two girls were my friends.'
>
> He relaxed. 'It's interesting, and very well told. Have you other Turkish friends you can write about?'
>
> 'Oh yes, I can.' (*Athene* 1952, 13:1, p. 26)

From the start Vaka Brown's writing depended on the demonstrable authenticity of her Oriental point of origin and was driven by her political urge to redress the prejudice against the Turks, even despite their oppression of her Greek 'race'. These mixed agenda dominate her work and account for her contradictory attitude to the Turks. Vaka Brown is both critical of the Ottoman oppression of minority populations and horrified at Western ignorance of all things Muslim and Turkish. Yet her address is different from that of Muslim Turkish women such as Zeyneb Hanım and Halide Edib, writing as she does from outside the Muslim mainstream of Ottoman society and needing to prove her Byzantine identity to incredulous Westerners. (One haughty British woman refused to believe she was the author of *Some Pages*, dismissing her accent as just some 'Continental affectation', *Athene* 1952, 13:2, p. 22). As I discuss in Chapter Two, the position of the minority populations under Ottoman rule was different to that of ethnic and religious minorities in the West, and underwent substantial changes as the Ottoman Empire lost territories and the ideal of inclusiveness broke down in the run-up to the advent of the republic. Vaka Brown's accounts of her young life illustrate the minority populations' differentiated identities that spanned the boundaries of Ottoman power, whilst her account of living as an immigrant in America reveal how important it was to her sense of self that she retain her Ottoman background. Being both of the East and yet not of it by virtue of her Christianity and subsequently her Americanisation, her attempts to intervene in the depiction of Turkish women are marked by conflicting needs for conformity with and separation from both home and host cultures. Vaka Brown as a transculturated subject was never able to embrace totally either comfortable, insular America, or the narcotic calm of the gorgeous harem, or indeed the gender restrictions of Byzantium. Split between the work ethic and the sybarite in her self, she never wanted to give up on her Eastern origins. Indeed, as Yiorgos Kalogeras argues, Vaka Brown 'constantly experimented with the ambiguities of her ethnic identity, and finally built her career on such ambiguities' (1997: 108). Unlike comparable Greek-American authors, she published little in her lifetime about the experience of emigration. But she did, as Kalogeras also suggests, often write from an American narratorial point of view. In this light it is interesting that she initially published under the ethnic-neutral authorial identity of Mrs Kenneth Brown, only later reverting to Demetra Vaka. Her often condescending tone was directed both at Americans and at the Muslim Turks, suggesting the advantages and disadvantages inherent in the contradictory ethnic and national positions she attempted to perform. With an oeuvre that was similarly split between a pro-Turkish exoticised nostalgia and a condescending Westernised critique, she found a ready market for her sketches, novels and current affairs journalism.

But the market was not always stable and Vaka Brown, who took a keen interest in sales and promotion, initially experienced some difficulty in translating the success of her articles into a book contract. When Houghton Mifflin, who were to publish all her books in America, finally brought out *Haremlik* in spring 1909 the book was:

> an immediate success, some of the newspapers giving it a full-page review, and the 'Outlook', then in its heyday, declaring 'If it is true, it is a remarkable book. If it is not true, it is more remarkable still.' For twenty-nine years the book sold, and was published in England, France, Germany, Holland, Denmark, Norway and Hungary, while extracts from it appeared in Italian and Russian reviews. (*Athene* 1952, 13:1, p. 52)

But in 1922, when Vaka Brown was working up the material for *The Unveiled Ladies of Stamboul*, Ferris Greenslet of Houghton Mifflin was concerned that the bottom was dropping out of the market. Vaka Brown entered into a keen correspondence with him, it seems initially proposing a contract for two books, one based on social sketches, the other on political journalism (some of which had already appeared in the journal *Asia*). Their prolonged exchange reveals not only Vaka Brown's persistence and hands-on approach to her career, but also the nature of the American literary market for Oriental subjects. Ferris Greenslet was unwilling to take a two-volume deal arguing that, 'the Near Eastern field has been of late not very productive of good selling books ... I think it would therefore be a great mistake to divide the attack', urging her to 'melt the two sets of material together' (6 May 1922).[11] When Vaka Brown's response was evidently to question this he repeated that 'my general idea was to reduce the political material and increase the picturesque and story side of the book, melting the two together with the political material as a sort of frame-work for the story' (1 May 1922). Evidently she pursued the question and her subsequent correspondence elicited a frank response, laying out clearly the limited interest of the American public and the constraints this placed on the type of writing that could get published. Note that he does not regard her serialisation success as a reliable indicator of book sales.

> I thought I was fairly explicit in my letter of May 12th. Here goes again:
>
> So far as I can judge, the public has very largely lost interest in foreign post-War politics and this is particularly so of so-called 'Near Eastern' politics. They may still read magazine articles that they get for nothing along with other interesting material and pictures, and they may go to hear lectures, but they do not buy books in any adequate numbers on such subjects. I think, therefore, as I tried to say in May, that if your book is to have any satisfactory success, it must depend not so much on its portrayal of the present day situation in Turkey, as upon its romantic, flavorsome Haremlik quality, though there is no reason why it should not by indirection, convey to the reader a pretty clear sense of the mood of Turkey today. (17 August 1922)

Evidently Vaka Brown knuckled under and produced the required mix, watering down her political observations and beefing up the picturesque. Two months later Greenslet wrote approvingly 'you have made a very readable book with a wise proportion of social narrative and political observation. Whatever way events turn in the Near East in the next six months, the book, if published in the spring, can hardly fail to be "timely"' (11 October 1922). This, just at the time when the Turkish nationalists under Mustafa Kemal (Atatürk) were engaged in a war against the Allied and Greek occupation, suggests that her suspicions about American isolationism were not unfounded.

In order to pique the West's interest the packaging of a book was all important. As I noted earlier, women writers often signalled the harem in the titles of their books and Vaka Brown had already come up with the evocative *Haremlik* for her first book. In Britain, where her publishers felt 'the English would not stand for *Haremlik*' (*Athene* 1952, 13:2, p. 22), this contentious title was altered to the apparently less troubling, *Some Pages from the Lives of Turkish Women*. Thirteen years later her publishers struggled to find the appropriate title for the third part of her trilogy about Turkish women. In Boston, Greenslet worried about the proposed title – *The Unveiled Ladies of Stamboul* – fearing that whilst 'it vividly and exactly describes the theme of the book ... [it] seems, however, in the minds of some, to arouse more luxurious images than the occasion demands' (11 October 1922). Clearly, the subject of Turkish women was attractive (and still worth publishing), but it was still also contentiously sexualised. Vaka Brown responded to Houghton Mifflin's concerns with suggestions to substitute 'women' for 'ladies' or to go with the even more purple prose titles of *Stamboul: Perfumed and Blood-Spattered* or *Stamboul: the Exquisite and Ghastly*, demanding of him, 'Have you any titles to suggest? Didn't the MS give *you* any?' (15 October 1922, original emphasis). Her feisty exchange, plus a reminder in her next letter for him to think again about titles, brought forth the postscript on 17 October 1922 that 'I think we will stand pat after all on "The Unveiled Ladies of Stamboul"'.

Titles and pricing and percentages were of great importance to Vaka Brown. Her letters to Houghton Mifflin show her arguing about author royalties, which were reduced in 1922 from 20 per cent and 15 per cent to 10 per cent of the list price, and chafing them to make sure they kept her work in print. Her requests were not always considered viable: in 1921 an internal communiqué suggested that staff should

> gracefully avoid sending any of Mrs. K-B's books to the Clubs in Milwaukee ... as nothing will come of it. We have tried to follow Mrs. K-B on her speaking tours and the sending of books for possible sale has always been a waste of money. The sale has been almost nothing, even when we have good bookstores to work with, and in the case of some of the Clubs, if you ever can get the matter adjusted, the books that come back to us generally have broken corners and are unfit to place in stock (12 February 1921).

Vaka Brown's persistent intervention in the financial side of her writing practice demonstrates a willingness to engage in monetary negotiations that went well beyond the ladylike. In the struggle to support herself when she arrived in the United States she learned slowly the necessity of demanding fair pay – even when it was difficult for a young woman to behave in such a way. Later in life she and her husband relied on the proceeds of their books and journalism, and her biography is full of references to good or disappointing sales. Although her husband was clearly comfortably off, they were of relatively modest means for the middle classes and lived in a series of rented houses without a retinue of staff. Indeed, she notes that England before 'the first world war was the most comfortable place for people of moderate means, who wanted to work and play. That delightful institution of "chambers" made life so simple', (*Athene* 1952, 13:2, p. 22). The 'chambers' system, in which residential rooms were hired with hourly paid domestic staff, provided the opportunity to take on additional servants for entertaining without the need to run a full establishment. This was not the opulent luxury of the grand Ottoman *konaks* inhabited by her friend Djimlah or by Zeyneb Hanım and Melek Hanım and, as we shall see, Halide Edib. Rather, Demetra Vaka Brown was placed in the middle social spectrum of life in America and Europe, gaining access to more elevated circles through her writing.

In London she had introductions to Ford Madox Hueffer, editor of the *English Review* and founder of the *TransAtlantic Review*, which published the modernist poets such as Gertrude Stein and Ezra Pound. She also met the sensational and sensationalist New Woman novelist Violet Hunt (Ford Madox Hueffer's sometime fiancée and partner). Hunt was the daughter of the artist Alfred William Hunt and a chronicler of the Pre-Raphaelites. With Ford Madox Hueffer being the grandson of Ford Madox Brown and nephew of William Michael Rossetti, this tangible connection to the British Pre-Raphaelites must have been enchanting for Vaka Brown who had already in *Haremlik* termed one of her central Turkish characters 'my Rossetti lady' (see Chapter Four).

In Boston she and her husband moved in a literary circle, centred around the salons of Ella (Forella) Greenslet, wife of her publisher at Houghton Mifflin, Mrs James Fields, wife to one of Houghton Mifflin's proprietors, and the society and literary hostess Rose Nichols. From these contacts and introductions she knew a number of women and men, journalists, writers and poets, editors of literary journals, whose politics ranged from the campaigning abolitionism and feminism of Julia Ward Howe and Thomas Wentworth Higginson to the socialism of Lincoln Steffens and the autocracy of Amy Lowell. Lowell, the 'luminary of the Imagists' in the United States was a conspicuous figure, an arch self-publicist whose lesbian adoption of masculine-style attire was but one of her notorieties. According to Vaka Brown, having read and enjoyed *Haremlik*, Lowell urged her to make more of her exotic origins beyond the page:

> 'With your foreign face, you should dress like an oriental. You should wear such clothes that when you came into a room everybody would exclaim; "My God! Who is that?" It would be the most effective way of selling your work.'
>
> 'Why shouldn't I rely on my writing to sell itself?'
>
> 'We are living in an age of advertising. As an intelligent woman you should take advantage of it, and create a sensation wherever you go by your clothes.'
>
> 'If you dress as I tell you, you will travel in your own limousine. You will be photographed constantly, and everyone will want to see you and hear you

speak. You will receive any amount of money for lecturing, and you won't know what a strap in a streetcar is for.' (*Athene* 1952, 13:2, p. 49)

Although she was always keen to promote her work, Vaka Brown drew the line at making herself into an object of curiosity and celebrity. Indeed, she presented Lowell's overwhelming craving for 'limelight' as something that possibly restricted the poet's own creativity: 'At times I even wondered whether in reality she loved her work, or chose "imagism" as a means of becoming a luminary?' (*Athene* 1952, 13:2, p. 50).[12] But Vaka Brown did not fight shy of promoting her work, arranging lecture tours and intervening in the wording of advertisements and reviews. Her keen interest in getting the titles right was also part of her awareness of books as products, that needed help to shift from the shelves.

In fact, the 'foreign face' that was apparently so legibly non-Western to Amy Lowell was not always read as such by others in America and Europe, even though Vaka Brown would often have wished it was. Most often her foreignness is depicted as registered through her voice – her accent and use of English. Vaka Brown's own body appeared in her publications only after she had established herself with *Haremlik*, which appeared without illustrations. In 1914 in the second part of her trilogy, *A Child of the Orient*, she did use a photograph of herself as the frontispiece (Ilustration 17, p. 260 below). Here, the vaguely 'Greek' costume and winsome pose suggest that, having by now established her reputation as a respected author, she did take Lowell's advice. By the 1920s Vaka Brown's picture was regularly used in publicity and profiles; Ferris Greenslet noted in January 1921 that he had 'had the pleasure of gazing at a most seductive picture of you in some popular illustrated magazine or paper ...' (11 January 1921). And in 1923 she appeared in Western and old-fashioned Ottoman dress, alongside photographs of contemporary Turkish women, in *The Unveiled Ladies of Stamboul* (Ilustration 18, p. 261 below). But, as I discuss in Chapter Four, it is the female body of other 'Oriental' women that is most often depicted in her writing, as a way of registering racialised difference.

For all that Vaka Brown knew that her Oriental experiences were a valuable commodity, her personal investment was nonetheless conflicted. Presenting herself in a variety of guises she tracked the problems faced by an ardent internationalist who was at times overcome by a Greek 'love of race' but yet who could not bear to be mistaken for a foreigner on her return to Istanbul in 1921. In all her writings, her geo-political point of origin serves to authenticate her account – she is indeed from the Orient. But her Byzantine rather than Turkish Muslim identity works to offer a novel version of international events. Her personalised journalism inextricably connected her own experiences to international events, mapping world news and history in relation to family members spread throughout the region. She was quite clear that as a Greek the Turks were her oppressors, but also that Turkey would always remain part of her:

> '[M]y pleasure in revisiting Turkey was enhanced by the knowledge that I did not have to stay there ... yet [Turkey] remained the beloved of my childhood.

Turkey might be misgoverned, might be on the brink of revolution, but it had formerly been the Byzantine Empire, and some intangible part of me would forever be linked to this soil colonized by my forebears. If anyone could have shown me a way to be of use to her, I should have been ready to return to her. (*Athene* 1951, 12:3, p. 22)

Her way of being useful was to challenge negative American attitudes to the Turks. But it is very clear from this passage and throughout her writing that this desire to change American misconceptions about Turkey was also a way to preserve for herself the most personally meaningful version of an Ottoman identity in America. This favoured identity would among other things differentiate the internationally minded Vaka Brown from ill-informed Westerners who took no interest in Middle Eastern affairs. Presenting herself as split between the Western and the Turkish, between the need for productive work and the desire for the sybaritic existence of elite Turkish ease, her nostalgia tries to salvage from American misapprehensions a preferred version of Ottoman life. That this rests for her on the by now outmoded habitat of the elite harem – something that, like her childhood, has passed into history – explains her lack of affinity with the emancipated, unveiled women that she observed in the modern Turkey of 1921. Indeed, writing in *Unveiled* she acknowledged that 'I have been accused of describing in *Haremlik* a life as unreal as moonshine', but now, the

old system was broken to bits – gone never to return; and I, who have been accused of being its troubadour, had come back to the new system, with electricity instead of candlelight, and the mysterious figures of Stamboul replaced by unveiled daughters of the true faith; to women who sat behind desks, took down dictation on the typewriter from men they called infidels, and sold goods behind counters ... (Vaka 1923: 26–30)

Her association with the long-past Byzantine Empire staked a claim to the land and rooted her identification through her ancestors into an even more ancient ownership and power. It is not surprising that modernity in Turkey was an alienating experience for Vaka Brown. Whilst she embraced American contemporaneity and the opportunities it offered her for professional and personal fulfilment, her nostalgic identification was based on the Ottoman society of her childhood, now radically disappearing, like the Byzantine Empire before it, in the transition towards the republic.

HALIDE EDIB

An antidote to Vaka Brown's nostalgia for the old ways of the elite Ottoman order is provided by the determined modernity of Halide Edib (1884–1964), one of the leaders of campaigns for women's emancipation in Turkey. A prominent nationalist who served with the nationalist forces during the War of Independence (1919–23), Edib is the most well known of my sources. A prolific writer, she produced novels, plays and journalism throughout her long literary career. Widely regarded as one of the leading nationalist novelists, her fiction – though of 'uneven' literary merit (Paker 1991b: 283) and often criticised for its inelegant style – is widely held to represent the experiences of the generation of women who were born into the end of the empire and struggled towards the changes of the new republic (Donzel, Lewis and Pellat 1978, Adak 2003, Kandiyoti 1989a, Durakbaşa, 1993). Though most of her writing was in Ottoman and then modern Turkish, her two volumes of autobiography were written in English during her period of (probably self-imposed) exile from Turkey. It is these two volumes, *Memoirs of Halidé Edib* (1926) and *The Turkish Ordeal* (1928) that are of greatest interest to this study. Covering her childhood and the Young Turk years up to and including the fight for national liberation after the First World War, Edib's memoirs reveal the personal challenges and benefits of the transition from the old Ottoman order to the new republic narrated by one who was intimately involved in the formation of new political policy.

Halide Edib, like Zeyneb Hanım and Melek Hanım, was born into a wealthy family of the Ottoman upper class but her path to individual emancipation was to be party political. Her visibility on the national stage marked a change in the practices usually associated with Ottoman Muslim women, seen inevitably after 1906 as tragically, helplessly, Lotiesque:

> In the many books on Turkish life that have been published [the Turkish woman] has almost invariably appeared as discontented, to be sure, with her lot in life, but as showing this discontent only by making a helpless, futile attempt to evade the custom and the law to which centuries have made her subject, with intrigue and cunning as the only weapons at her command. (Ellis and Palmer 1914: 57)

Though the authors of this complaint about the over-application of the *Désenchantées* model were teachers at the American College where Edib had been a pupil, they do not name her directly – but her assertive literary and feminist campaigning was a matter of great pride to the college authorities. Edib came to symbolise the transition from the discontented harem lady to emancipated nationalist comrade.

Edib's father was First Secretary of the Sultan's Purse and hence part of the palace upper bureaucracy. Her mother died when she was a young child but her father soon remarried and Edib was raised by her stepmother (whom she called Abla, a respectful honorific meaning older sister) and her grandmother, moving between the two houses. As I discuss in Chapter Three, young Halide Edib's life changed when her father took another wife, a family dependent, Teïzé (similarly an honorific, meaning aunt), to whom Halide was intensely attached, and the household became polygamous. This change was a sharp contrast to her progressive father's Westernised ideals and brought about the eventual dissolution of the family home into two households. He did subsequently try to shelter his 'incompatible family' under one roof, in a large establishment in Scutari where each wife could have her own house and garden. But 'the curse of polygamy followed

[them] there also' and the miserable Teïzé eventually took a divorce (Edib 1926: 172–7). Prior to this, the young Edib lived for periods with her grandmother and Teïzé and sometimes with Abla, visiting between the two. But wherever she was housed her movements between the two women and their court of relatives and servants often made her the focus of their rivalries, causing her great distress and confirming her hatred of polygamy. It was not only Halide who found the split loyalties of the polygamous situation impossible – the whole situation caused considerable discomfort to her father, a man associated with progressive intellectual circles amongst whom polygamy was increasingly frowned upon (see Chapter Three).

Whilst the women who had raised her were traditional, and provided her with a stock of folklore that was to prove invaluable in her story-telling career, Edib's father gave her an education that was Westernised and determinedly modern. As well as instruction from an imam, she had an English governess and tutors drawn from among the most prominent Ottoman thinkers (including Riza Tewfik, one of the early promoters of Turkish folk culture who wrote some of the first poems using simplified Turkish language and traditional form, Edib 1926). At the age of fifteen she became the first Muslim Turkish girl to board at the American College for Girls from where she graduated in 1901. That same year she married her mathematics tutor, the famous Salih Zaki Bey, a friend of her father's and the same age as her father. Salih Zaki Bey was a renowned mathematician and philosopher, director of the Istanbul meteorological observatory and professor at the highest schools in Istanbul, then busy compiling the first mathematical dictionary in Turkish, including work on Comte whom he most admired. They had two sons and Edib helped him with his dictionary, living 'the life of the old-fashioned Turkish woman', 'confined within the walls of my apartment' (Edib 1926: 207).

When the Young Turk Revolution occurred in 1908 Halide Edib became immediately involved. With both her husband and her father – a member of the revolutionary Committee of Union and Progress (CUP) – connected to the intellectuals of the Young Turk movement, she started writing for the Young Turk daily paper, *Tanin*. Her first novel *Raik'in Annes* (*Raik's Mother*) appeared in 1909 to be followed in 1910 by the eponymous *Seviyye Talib*. This initial success was repeated two years later by the wildly successful *Handan* (1912), which established her reputation and found her a wide readership. *Yeni Turan* (*The New Turan*, 1913) explored new patterns of relations between men and women (Paker 1991b) in an explicitly nationalist context and was part of a pattern of writing that continued alongside her political work, focusing particularly on education and the condition of women. At this time her husband took a second wife and Edib left her marriage (see Chapter Three). Despite the emotional hardship of this decision which was still socially radical, and the effects it had on her physical health, Edib maintained a high level of activity in Young Turk cultural politics, associating herself particularly with the cultural activities of Ziya Gökalp and the Turkish Hearth movement (see Chapter Two). She was integral, with Nakiye Hanım, in establishing women's nursing activities during the Balkan

Wars and in starting programmes for women's education. She taught at the Women's Teacher Training College in Istanbul and acted as an inspector of schools in Istanbul – which took her to parts of the city that a woman of her class would not normally have visited. In 1916 she and Nakiye Hanım undertook a survey of schools in Syria for Cemal Paşa, then one of the leaders of the Young Turk CUP government, and she returned in 1916 and 1917 to oversee the schools development programme as well as reorganising the orphanage at Aintoura. In 1917 she married again, to Dr Adnan Adıvar who was also a prominent member of the CUP.

Throughout the period of the Allied occupation after 1918 Halide Edib continued her work for the nationalists in Istanbul and then, after 1920, in Ankara with Mustafa Kemal's nationalist government. During the War of Independence Edib was the first Turkish woman to have a rank in the nationalist military (though many women had contributed clandestinely to the military effort) where she served variously as translator, writer, editor and organiser of nursing, relief work and women's education. As well as writing for the nationalist press, this was when she wrote the novels about women in the resistance, *Atesteri Gömleck* (*The Shirt of Flame*, 1923) and *Vuran Kahpeye* (*Strike the Whore*, 1923), that went on to establish her as a leading 'nationalist writer' in the modern Turkish literary canon (Paker 1991b).

When the nationalists triumphed and government was established in Ankara, she and her husband continued to serve the nationalist cause. But they had political differences with the Kemalists and fled to London in June 1926 when their faction, the Progressive Republican Party, was suppressed by Mustafa Kemal. They stayed away for fourteen years until Mustafa Kemal's death in 1938, returning in the spring of 1939. The first four years of their exile they spent in London, which Edib had previously visited in 1909 when her life was in danger from the leaders of the counter-revolution. In London once more, she wrote her two-volume autobiography. Thereafter most of her time was spent in Paris, where her husband lectured in Turkish at the École des langues orientales vivantes, while Edib continued to write. She visited the United States on a university lecture tour in 1929 and was visiting professor at Columbia in 1931–2. Her travels and teaching also took her to India in 1935 where she met Gandhi and other leading nationalists, producing her account *Inside India* in 1937. On returning to Istanbul, Edib headed the university's English department and served for four years as an independent member of parliament for Izmir.

While she was living away from Turkey, Halide Edib wrote two further volumes of political history and commentary in English, whose publication history indicates her international reputation: *Turkey Faces West* was based on her lectures in the United States and was published there in 1930, whilst *Conflict of East and West in Turkey*, which covered the contents of her Indian lecture tour, was published in 1935 in Lahore (where some of her Turkish novels were also translated into English).[13] The political affiliations forged between the new Turkish Republic and other Asian countries still struggling for independence point to a significant English-language readership for Edib's work outside Britain, whilst her works reached an extended readership elsewhere through translations into languages such as Russian, Ukrainian and German. The links between Indian anti-colonialists and Turkey, apart from those of religion, were based also on the status of Turkey as a perceived leader of female emancipation in Asia. For Edib, in *Inside India* (which was published in London in 1937 and translated for serialisation in Turkey in 1940–1) the Hindu women of India and their Muslim sisters were like the Ottoman women of her mother's generation, awaiting the type of liberation made possible by emancipatory nationalism.

Edib's decision to write in English was directly political: after an altercation with Kemal in Ankara in the summer of 1920, when she was alarmed at his ambitious desire for absolute personal power – 'I want everyone to do as I wish and command' – she realised what she needed to do:

> I would try to recreate that period of Turkish history by preserving a faithful record of my experiences during that great ordeal … that the world might some day read it – not as a historical record nor as a political treatise, but as a human document about men and women alive during my own lifetime; and I would write it in a language far better fitted to reach the world than my own. It was that very night, as I lay in bed after the scene with Mustafa Kemal Pasha, that I determined to write my Memoirs and to write them in English. (Edib 1928: 190)

The material for the first volume of her memoirs was nearly all compiled during that summer, the year before she started writing her Turkish-language novel, the nationalist fable *The Shirt of Flame*.[14] Her memoirs did not appear in Turkish until the 1960s after she herself undertook their translation upon her return to Turkey. The decision to write in English was a calculated intervention into what Edib anticipated would become a contested, or controlled, rendition of the nationalist struggle. Penned against the backdrop of the Treaty of Sèvres when the Turkish cause looked at its most desperate, the memoirs were not published until after the nationalist triumph and the realisation of her fears about Kemal's absolutist tendencies. Her memoirs had a dual audience. They were consciously directed at an international readership whose sympathy for the Turkish ordeal she was determined to arouse, particularly in relation to Lloyd George's support for the Greek invasion after Turkey's defeat in the First World War and the accompanying atrocities suffered by the Turkish civilian population, who were demonised by the foreign press as uncivilised. But she also aimed to use the recently imported Western genre of autobiography to set down her side of the story for a Turkish readership, able to access the English account and then later the Turkish. But as Hulya Adak (2003) discusses, Edib's memoirs were not widely circulated in Turkey in the 1920s and 1930s and were only later rehabilitated into a revised republican historiography. For many years the defining narrative of the independence struggle was Mustafa Kemal's *Nutuk* (*The Speech*), the published version of his epic six-day speech from 1927 that set the seal on the Kemalist version of national liberation. Edib's two-volume foray into autobiography frames *Nutuk*; her *Memoirs*, the account of the early years, preceded it by one year and *The Turkish Ordeal* came one year later, deliberately telling her version of the War of Independence.

The Memoirs of Halide Edib sets out the story of a private individual who becomes a public figure, often using the third person to distinguish her different selves. It provides a psychoanalytically inflected history of her different incarnations, from the young girl who could not understand her mother's final absence to the young woman sick in bed after the painful divorce to the fearless 'Halide of Sultanahmet' who, overtaken by nationalist fervour, gave an inspiring speech at the vast rally against the Allied occupation in 1919. *The Turkish Ordeal* focused on the struggle for national liberation after the First World War and can be seen as directly corrective to *Nutuk*. Kemal's self aggrandising account, the 'sacred text' of the republic (Adak 2003), pictured Kemal as the lone instigator and hero of the Turkish liberation – pitting him and the Turkish nationalists equally against the Ottoman sultan (past and present) and against Kemal's political opponents within the nationalist camp, such as Edib and her husband. Edib is vilified as a traitor in *Nutuk* for advocating an American mandate for Turkey after the First World War (which she thought would protect Turkey from the Christian minority populations being 'empowered' by the Allies, Adak 2003). In her riposte, Edib not only laid out her own position, but also factored in the other nationalist leaders who had been largely excised from Kemal's account. Edib's was not the only response in print but, like other memoirs, letters and articles, her autobiography was not to be easily accessible in Turkey while *Nutuk* held sway. Her eventual 'translation' of the autobiographies into Turkish made several alterations to the original.[15] These, as Durakbaşa discusses, de-emphasised the self-analytic elements present in the English version but also, most importantly, removed and altered her criticisms of Kemal 'at a time when she wanted to protect herself from political criticism' (Durakbaşa 1993: 141). This, as Adak elaborates, transformed *The Turkish Ordeal* from refutation of *Nutuk* into praise of it. Edib's memoirs were always intended to have multiple readerships and, in contrast to their original suppression in Turkey, were received as authoritative in Britain where the *Times Literary Supplement* recognised Edib's work as, 'history written by the novelist who helped to make it happen' (29 November 1928, p. 921). But in their final Turkish version in the mid-twentieth century they became deeply compromised texts whose initial 'potential resistance' gave way in translation (Adak 2003). The changing nature of the published autobiography is a reminder of the changing and paradoxical status of Edib in Turkey. Whilst always revered as a leading nationalist novelist, she had very little political credibility for periods in the 1920s and 1930s – due largely to the historiographical hegemony of Kemal's *Nutuk*. Now Edib is given a more sympathetic reading, valued as one the few sources testifying to women's involvement in political activism, in keeping with the later twentieth century revision of republican historiography.[16]

UNIVERSITY OF WINCHESTER
LIBRARY

In 1920s Britain, writing in the language of the colonial powers – which was also the language of her education and affiliation to the United States – provided the exilic subject Edib with opportunities to explore forms of identification that were not in keeping with the anti-individualism of the republican climate. At the same time, her writing was clearly constrained by the need to deflect Orientalist projections. She had to be able to shift between both sides of the Orientalist divide: presenting the modern alternative to the harem stereotype in the West but, when home again in Turkey, needing to re-insert herself as not so anti-Kemalist and not so Westernised as to be inauthentic in the terms of the new nationalist identifications.

Halide Edib remained a public figure throughout her life. Her many publications continued to find a popular readership, with several of her novels being made into films. The literary critical attention to her work, which initially read her as a nationalist writer, has been augmented by feminist analyses of her life and work (Paker 1991b) and has recently come to be re-animated by new examination of the late Ottoman period and critiques of Kemalist historiography (Durakbaşa 1993, Adak 2003). It is impossible to discuss this period of change in women's lives in Turkey without talking about Edib, so powerful is her stamp on the era. As someone who was directly involved in bringing about the political changes that effected social change in women's lives she is invaluable to my project. But, I am restricting my study of selected moments in her oeuvre to an exploration of her memoirs, looking particularly at the early years, which correspond to the timing of the rest of my material. Much of the rest of her oeuvre, written in Turkish, falls outside the English-language scope of this project. Her prominence in Turkish history and literature means that of all the writers discussed here she is the only one to have received sustained attention and the only one about whom substantial information is available in secondary sources, so therefore less excavatory work is required.

GRACE ELLISON

A common link between these women and their English-language publications is Grace Ellison (d. 1935) who knew all the Ottoman women in this study except for Demetra Vaka Brown, who had left for America before Ellison 'first fell in love' with Istanbul in 1905 (Ellison 1928: 108). Ellison occupies a unique position as the English woman in most direct dialogue with the Ottoman authors I am discussing and as a very public proponent of Turkish interests during the troubled period from the Young Turk Revolution of 1908, through the First World War to the establishment of the Turkish Republic in 1923. She was prominent for her sympathetic writings about Turkey and is also important to this study because of her editorial work in bringing Turkish women's writing to the English-reading public.

In 1913, the year when Zeyneb Hanım's *A Turkish Woman's European Impressions* came out, Grace Ellison was making her third and longest visit to Turkey, working on her own investigation into the lives of Turkish women. The correspondence that made up Zeyneb Hanım's book tracked the two women around Europe and between Europe and Turkey, following the émigré's restless wandering and the journalist's determined excursions. When Zeyneb Hanım wrote to Ellison from London in November 1908, Ellison noted in a footnote that she had 'received this letter in Constantinople, where I was staying in a Turkish harem, having travelled there in order to be present at the first debate in the newly-opened Turkish Parliament' (Zeyneb Hanoum 1913: 181). Keenly Turkophile and of sufficient journalistic status to be given entry to the new parliament, Ellison was determined to improve the reputation of the Turks, 'to correct the errors, prejudice and hatred which have become almost part of the British national "attitude" to Turkey' (Ellison 1915: i). Her third visit in the autumn of 1913 lasted into early 1914 and produced a series of articles written between November and January that were published within a few weeks in the *Daily Telegraph*. Appearing in the final months before the start of the First World War, Ellison reported on 'Life in the Harem' almost daily in the *Daily Telegraph* between January and February 1914.

On this trip she stayed with her friend Makboulé Hanım whose acquaintance she had made in 1908 when she had met her father Kâmil Paşa, then Grand Vizier to Abdülhamit.[17] By the time Ellison returned at the end of the Balkan War, Kâmil Paşa had been ousted and exiled to Cyprus (see Chapter Two) and Makboulé Hanım was married to Nagdi Bey, a man whose loyalties were to the new government of Enver Paşa that had replaced the cabinet of her father. Ellison stayed with Makboulé Hanım for several months during which time Kâmil Paşa died and was buried in Cyprus. When Ellison first arrived Makboulé Hanım was living alone in her father's Istanbul *konak* whilst her husband was absent on duties, though he returned during Ellison's visit and she was able to observe the young couple and the constraints they faced in shifting a whole household towards their more modern domestic habits. Her account of this visit appeared not only in the *Daily Telegraph* but subsequently in 1915 in book form from Methuen as *An Englishwoman in a Turkish Harem*, illustrated with many of her own photographs. Before this volume came out she had also written an introduction to Melek Hanım's *Abdul Hamid's Daughter*, for its publication (also with Methuen) in September/October 1913. Her introductory chapter to Melek Hanım's imperial romance offers her experience of the imperial harem and a description of her meeting with the book's heroine, Princess Aiche, to whom she was introduced under the good offices of Makboulé Hanım. Ellison must have been working on Melek Hanım's manuscript in the early weeks of her stay with Makboulé Hanım, just as she had been corresponding with her sister Zeyneb Hanım when she was last in Istanbul in 1908.

An enthusiastic supporter of Turkish nationalism, Ellison returned again in the winter of 1922 to report on the fight for Turkish independence, gaining access beyond the nationalist lines during the War of Independence. This was itself a testament to her reputation and connections in Turkey since the nationalists, fighting the Allied occupation, held particular enmity for the British, whom they blamed for the Greek invasion. She interviewed Mustafa Kemal in Anatolia (possibly for the *Daily Telegraph*) and then published a fuller account in book form as *An Englishwoman in Angora* (1923). Her fifth trip in 1927 saw her reporting on the changes visible in the new Turkish Republic and its new capital in Ankara. Her boundless admiration for Mustafa Kemal as the man 'who has given freedom to women' (Ellison 1928: 7) dominates her apologist rendition of his increasingly totalitarian government. This trip appeared as an illustrated volume entitled *Turkey To-day* in 1928, a strange hotch-potch of recycled anecdotes about her earlier trips accompanied by long extracts from the writings of Zeyneb Hanım and Melek Hanım, Halide Edib and other Turkish writers. Ellison was awarded the Order of the *Shefkat nishani* (Tenderness Order), first class in diamonds (no date). Her receipt of this order, designed to honour the contribution of women, was presumably in recognition of her services to the Turkish state.[18] In her *Daily Telegraph* reports in 1914, Ellison noted the *Shefkat nishani* as an Order of Mercy awarded to ladies of high rank, worn by most of the court officials she met in the imperial harem. On that occasion, the only non-palace lady to be wearing it was her hostess Fatima, though Ellison also commented accurately – and as it turned out, presciently – that the order was awarded to 'distinguished lady visitors'. Certainly, Ellison was to become a favoured visitor, claiming that she was the first English woman to visit Angora during the War of Independence, having been given clearance by the nationalists in Ankara.

In both these later volumes Ellison reflected on her earlier trips, recycling material in a typical journalistic manner and often, confusingly, changing details and chronologies. For example, in 1928 she wrote that she first met Zeyneb Hanım and Melek Hanım in Istanbul in 1905 rather than in France as indicated in the introduction to *A Turkish Woman's European Impressions*. Claiming that theirs was the 'first Turkish house [she] visited', Ellison's later writings placed her as participant in their 'renowned' salons that were attended by 'the wives of the diplomats and all the leading personalities who passed through Constantinople', much to the pride of their father Noury Bey (Ellison 1928: 112–13).

This contradictoriness is very frustrating and hard to explain. It may be simply that over the years details became blurred, or that the need to fill pages led Ellison to revamp previous copy. But it may also be because of the exigencies of the Ottoman political situation. Certainly in the Hamidian years it would not have been safe to reveal the identities of her Turkish friends and respondents. In both *An Englishwoman in a Turkish Harem* and *Abdul Hamid's Daughter*, Ellison disguised Makboulé Hanım's identity under the alias 'Fatima' or 'Fathma' revealing her identity and that of her father only once it was deemed safe in the 1920s, by which time Makboulé Hanım's husband had been elevated to the status of paşa. I shall follow suit and refer to Makboulé Hanım as Fatima in my discussion of these two books, reverting to 'Makboulé Hanım' when that is how she is distinguished by Ellison, or when I wish to refer to the historical personage rather than the figure in Ellison's writing.

Ellison was not just an enthusiastic traveller and journalist: she was also a feminist and a campaigner. She was born in Scotland and educated in England, at Rochester girls' grammar school, and France, attending the University of Halle. For six years she was the continental correspondent of the *Bystander* and also reported for the *Daily Graphic* on the Second Hague Conference in 1907. The conference's concerns with international armament control were presumably close to the heart of a woman who, seeing herself as a cosmopolitan, also involved herself in nursing and providing for those injured by war. Ellison was the founder and Directrice Générale of the French Female Nursing Corps and raised money during a nine-month tour of the United States to establish the Florence Nightingale Hospital in Bordeaux. In 1918 she took the role of assistant to the head of the children's welfare bureau of the American Red Cross. For these works she was rewarded by the French state with the medaille d'or d'honneur, the silver medal of the French foreign office and service and wounded medals.

Her travels in the Middle East took her throughout Turkey and the Balkans, as well as into Syria and Palestine. Never marrying, Ellison travelled alone as a working journalist. On each trip she was most concerned to explore the status of women and to challenge Western misapprehensions. Unlike many Western women travel writers at this time, Ellison was unapologetically feminist and saw the dialogue between Western and Middle Eastern women as one that should specifically promote understanding and change:

> I asked Halide-Hanoum, perhaps the most active and best known of modern Turkish women, in the name of one of our prominent suffrage societies, how we English women could help the Turkish women in their advancement. 'Ask them', she said, 'to delete for ever that misunderstood word "harem", and speak of us in our Turkish "homes"'. (Ellison 1915: 17)

Frustratingly, Ellison does not specify by which suffrage organisation she was mandated. But her willingness to be publicly associated with a campaign that was in 1913/14 still vilified in many quarters in Britain (her own newspaper, the *Daily Telegraph*, ran a regular column on 'Suffragist Outrages' throughout 1913) speaks to her serious commitment. As we shall see, Ellison's desire to 'help' Turkish women is expressed through a mixture of attitudes that veer between radical and patronising, modernist and nostalgic, admiring and impatient. This bewildering concoction is not unlike her contrary attitude to Western feminism. In her 1922 tract *The Disadvantages of Being a Woman*, published as part of A. M. Philpot's 'Blue Booklets' series, she railed against the overly ambitious aims of British feminists, chastising them for presuming that ordinary women could go to the extremes of the 'exceptional minority'. Her critique centred on the point that, in basing their campaign on 'the unconsidered outcry for absolute equality', feminist leaders had 'largely killed men's protector instinct' (Ellison 1922: 10–11). Her overriding conviction was that equality was pointless for the majority of women unless they had secure wages, pension and insurance provision. But her realistic assessment of women's material needs was also part of an ideological rejection of the equality argument in keeping with others about to develop strands of modernist feminism (Heffernan forthcoming).

For a woman who often adopted a patronising tone to her Turkish colleagues, Ellison was under no illusions about the constraints of female life in the West. Indeed, she was sometimes frustrated with Turkish women, who did not seem to appreciate how lucky they were to have so much male support and did not appreciate how much social and economic security was afforded them by the obligations of the harem system. Like Vaka Brown, Ellison was torn between the desire to be financially and intellectually independent and the attractions offered to women by the sybaritic sanctuary of the Turkish harem. The challenges for middle-class women of making a living in Britain were acutely clear to Ellison as they were in America to Vaka Brown. Unlike the elite family backgrounds of Halide Edib and Zeyneb Hanım and Melek Hanım, Ellison seems to have come from a financially comfortable but not exceptionally wealthy family. Her father, Captain Ellison, was a military man and her middle-class education extended to advanced training. It is quite likely that she had some private income, though it is also likely that her earnings as a journalist were not a matter of indifference to her.

In *The Disadvantages of Being a Woman* Ellison is scathing about ladies who dabble in jobs, working for 'pin-money' between school and marriage. Such 'pin-money women', she argued, constituted 'women's greatest obstacle in work' after health concerns, effectively undercutting the living wage and making 'it more and more impossible for those who must work to earn their living' (Ellison 1922: 73). Ellison does not count herself among the 'pin-money women' or among the 'Society women' who, 'since the war, have pushed their way into literature, art, films, and the business world' in 'bewildering' numbers, leaving poor girls with no alternative but to ghost write 'Countess's' articles for a 'mere pittance' (Ellison 1922: 73–4). Ellison's opinions indicate that she regarded herself as a serious journalist – not some dabbler who needed ghost writers – and that she was still among those women to whom wages mattered. In staking an ideological distance from the dilettante upper-class lady, Ellison created an identification with women who need to earn a living. This subjective self-positioning relates both to her pecuniary needs and to a political affiliation with those less well-off than herself whose material circumstances should, she thought, be the yardstick on which are based feminist demands. But though she talks in general terms about the needs of the majority of unexceptional women, her concern is not primarily with the working classes and the poor. She is speaking about middle-class women who desire to earn a respectable living and who need to be financially secure should their menfolk fail them. In all this, her sense of urgency about women's ability to support themselves, is based on a clear agenda about preserving gender difference. Only in exceptional circumstances should married women's wages replace rather than supplement a man's family income, for 'an energetic wage-earning wife always demoralises a man' (Ellison 1922: 75). The status of the single woman was more uncertain. Reliance on the goodwill of fathers and brothers was too unpredictable, further rendering imperative the need for secure wages and a national insurance scheme that did not require women to sacrifice their femininity. The women who dispense with their femininity – discarding 'their useless hair', wearing 'substantial masculine boots with low, flat heels' and dressing 'themselves as nearly as they dare in the comfortable, ugly fashions of men' – become 'neutrals'. These hardworking creatures may benefit from being treated 'just like a man' in the world of work, but being 'no longer feminine, unable to be quite masculine' the neutral, according to Ellison, would find that her 'real friends, male and female, are few and far between' (Ellison 1922: 67).

Ellison's contrariness is part and parcel of the difficulties faced by women in the West who were trying to carve out a professional career in a period when such things were still potentially unsexing and also de-classing. It is no coincidence that her two forays in the world of work were into writing and nursing – the main areas of activity open to middle-class women.[19] Similarly, Vaka Brown, who early on realised that she did not welcome the socially anomalous position of being a governess in an American home, concentrated on teaching (the other genteel occupation open to middle-class women) before she was able to earn money exclusively from her writing. That Ellison coupled her social services role in the support and provision of nursing and nursing training with writing about Turkey was more unusual for a Western woman. Though she claimed that it was her father's tales of the East told to her as a child that inspired her travels, I want also to consider how Turkey met Ellison's personal needs as a woman struggling to achieve professional recognition in the West. Her political support for the reformist Young Turks and the nationalists is self-evident. But alongside this ran an Orientalist nostalgia for the now almost obsolete harem system of the old Ottoman elite that is at first surprising coming from a woman whose enthusiasm for the new government (and willingness to overlook Atatürk's autocratic tendencies) was criticised by reviewers in the *Times Literary Supplement* (21 June 1923, p. 413; 11 October 1928, p. 719). Her reports on the luxury of the elite harems that she visited act as indicators of her apparent self-assessment of her place in the class spectrum, and her adoption of the pleasures permitted by slave labour, indicate the limits and relational nature of her affiliation to European working women (see also Chapters Three and Five). It is the potential of the harem system to provide (particularly for single women) the protection so sorely lacking in the modern West that, I shall be arguing, influences her liking for a social institution whose reputation is found to be so damaging by her Turkish respondents. But whilst the social welfare benefits of the harem system shielded Muslim women from having to 'exercise the most hideous of professions' – as seen at home in the 'terrible degradation of our poor Whitechapel women' – it also restricted women's opportunity for economic independence by limiting them to training in the accomplishment arts rather than saleable skills (Ellison

1915: 199). This was to be a source of great hardship to women and their families in the aftermath of the Balkan Wars (see Chapter Two).

Ellison's discussion with Halide Edib reiterates how women writing about the
Middle East could not get away from the pre-eminence of the notion of the
harem – whatever their attitude to it. Ellison, the avowed feminist, herself used
the word harem in the title of her first book, knowing full well that it would help
sales. And note also how, in 1913, she was keen to point out that she received
Zeyneb Hanım's letter in a 'Turkish harem'. The possible problems of the term's
runaway signification were outweighed by its importance in highlighting the
experiential nature of her Turkish reports and thus endorsing her expertise and
authority as writer and editor: just as was the case with Vaka Brown's carefully
crafted book titles. As I discuss in Chapter Five, Ellison's political commitment
led her to stress the contemporaneity of Ottoman women even though this ran in
opposition to her personal attachment to the old ways of the harem system. In her
willingness to dilute this 'imperialist nostalgia' (Rosaldo 1993) with the realities
of modern harem life, Ellison's accounts differ from those of several other European women writers discussed by Mervat Hatem (1992). As she points out, even
women such as the Hungarian Djavidan Hanım (née Mary Torok) and the French
Eugenie Le Brun, who married men of the Egyptian elite and resided in Egypt,
tended to depict harem women as uneducated and uninvolved in politics. Writing
in this way, at precisely the time when Egyptian activists such as Huda Sha'rawi
were campaigning for women's rights, emphasised the social superiority of Europeans and would have gone some way towards deflecting criticism from women
such as these who had made 'mixed' marriages. Ellison's desire to challenge
Western stereotypes about Turkish women (while invariably replicating some of
them) was shared by Hester Donaldson Jenkins, another English writer, whose
1911 volume *Behind Turkish Lattices, the Story of a Turkish Woman's Life* sum-
marised similar ground in more general terms. Both women were intent on
honouring the same circle of prominent progressive Ottoman women campaign-
ers and writers that included at its head Halide Edib and her colleague Nakiye
Hanım as well as the older writer and feminist Fatma Aliye Hanım (see Chapters
Two and Three). In contrast, Vaka Brown presents her nostalgic pleasure in a
harem life as something which had always ultimately to be rejected in favour of a
non-'Asiatic' modernity (for a comparison of these different nostalgias, see the
Conclusion).

Early indicators of Ellison's status in Turkey and perceived status in Britain
were evident in the *Daily Telegraph*'s reports of the decision to allow Turkish
women into the university for special classes, that was announced a few days
after Ellison's articles ended. Their Istanbul correspondent cited Ellison as an
influential figure in this decision, noting that her articles had been printed in the
CUP organ *Tanin* (for which Halide Edib also wrote). The appearance of her
'deeply psychological articles' in the Turkish press were held by the correspondent to have been 'read everywhere with intense pleasure' and to 'have done not a
little towards raising the status of the Turkish woman' (*Daily Telegraph*, 7 Febru-

ary 1914, p. 11). In the next issue, the paper's editor, in a leader article, reiterated that they had 'been read very widely in Turkey' and confirmed that her work had 'we believe, given no inconsiderable stimulus to the cause of enlightenment and social freedom' (*Daily Telegraph*, 9 February 1914, p. 11). Although it is evident from the first published accounts of her 1913–14 visit that Ellison was well-connected enough to enter the palace and also to meet leading Turkish feminists and politicians, this is made more apparent in her last two Turkish books where she is more forthcoming about her political contacts with men such as Talat Paşa and Cemal Paşa who, she claimed, 'so often asked for advice about how they could give women more freedom' (Ellison 1928: 136). The tendency of the British press to overvalue the impact of British interventions means that their evaluation of Ellison's status in Istanbul must be regarded with some reservation, as indeed must Ellison's own depiction of her influence. But it is clear that she moved in elevated political and social circles and was taken seriously in Istanbul at the end of the Ottoman Empire. This continued when the nationalists come to power under her hero Mustafa Kemal (to whom she may also have had preferential access from Makboulé Hanım's husband who had been one of Kemal's military instructors). The success of *An Englishwoman in a Turkish Harem* was followed swiftly by *An Englishwoman in the French Firing Line* (publisher unknown, 1915), and *An Englishwoman in Occupied Germany* (publisher unknown, 1920), the series culminating in *An Englishwoman in Angora*. Apart from these recognisably branded products, Ellison also produced three biographies, assisting on Prince Nicholas of Greece's memoirs in 1926, writing a biography of Kemal in 1930, and producing the *Authorised Life Story of Princess Marina* in 1934 on the occasion of the princess' marriage.

Whilst her work's mix of travelogue and political commentary is not uncommon for travel writing, the fugitive nature of Ellison's personal revelations (less so in her later work) is more peculiar, given the unremittingly gendered point of origin integral to her books' production and circulation. Ellison was a woman who was obviously successful in garnering prestigious foreign assignments as a journalist and one who wanted to be taken seriously for her writing. Hers was not to be mere feminine 'puff' but work of consequence and substance. But though she aspired to the serious tone of ethnographic research (see Chapter Six), she could never get away from the selling point of her gender, often betraying an anxiety about authority and gender common to all these sources. In a context in which most female Orientalist work evolved outside institutional and formal networks of power (the Royal Geographic Society, for example, did not admit women until 1913 and Ellison was never a member, Melman 1992, Birkett 1989), Browne's attestation that 'Miss Ellison enjoyed an opportunity of seeing an aspect of Turkish life which few English women and no English men have been privileged to study at first hand' (Browne in Ellison 1915: xviii) served to pull her into the field of respected Orientalist scholarship that was otherwise largely inaccessible to women travellers and writers. Ellison herself in her subsequent publications did her best to assert her status as an authority. Reflecting on and recycling accounts of previous events allowed her to provide additional detail about her trips, thus locating her more firmly within an elevated social and political sphere. Wherever possible she took the opportunity to note the success of her earlier books, pointing out for example in 1923 that *An Englishwoman in a Turkish Harem* had been 'widely circulated in the East' (Ellison 1923: 24).

This assertion of her status also included responding to reviews and criticisms of her work and associated projects. Thus in *Turkey To-day* she elaborated again the story of *Les Désenchantées*, reprinting elements of the sisters' books and supporting Zeyneb Hanım and Melek Hanım's version over unspecified 'false statements about the[ir] motives' (Ellison 1928: 118); this I take to be an implicit refutation of Hélys' version of events. Significantly, Ellison never actually mentions Hélys, though as someone fluent in French and often resident in France she must have known of Hélys' claims and publications. Similarly, she makes little reference to other Western travel writers, male or female. In light of the citational nature of Orientalist discourse, she begins her writings (in the *Daily Telegraph*) by challenging previous misapprehensions, inflating the uniqueness of her accounts. By standing alone, she can emphasise the exclusivity of her access to the harem, her connections to prominent politicians and the value-added nature of her particular account. Though Ellison's revisiting of the Zeyneb Hanım and Melek Hanım story is partly to ward off counterclaims, I shall be considering later the importance of how the personal reappears in her work. Where once the feminine and the personal were unwelcome but unavoidable incursions into her attempts to produce an ethnographic and journalistic authority, by the latter period she is more able to play up her femininity, having now established her reputation. Further, this occurs in the context of her visits to the nationalist elite in Ankara. Here, as Durakbaşa (1993) rightly contends, the nationalist modernising project, based on a 'paternalistic protection' that encouraged women's emancipation alongside the preservation of traditional gender behaviours, was for Ellison an exceedingly attractive contrast to the unsexing and brutalising market conditions faced by 'modern' women in Britain. Seen in this light, the predilection for the antiquated harem system on the part of an avowed feminist who also supported the nationalist modernising cause seems less of a contradiction. Both the luxury of the elite harem and the chivalric comradeship of the nationalists offered Ellison the chance of a protected femininity that was almost impossible in the West (see Chapter Five).

After two centuries of Western women's harem literature, there was still a thirst in the West for more and more up-to-date information about Middle Eastern women's lives. Western stereotypes demonstrated tenacious longevity and Western women travellers still aimed to correct them – only now Ottoman women were joining directly in the dialogue. The subject of Ottoman womanhood was of tremendous concern in the Ottoman Empire where the figure of the Ottoman woman was known to be an important factor in the assumptions behind Western foreign policy. The status of women in Turkey and the difficulty of representing this accurately to a critical outside world concerned men and women on all sides of the political divide during this period of political upheaval. The dying decades of the Ottoman Empire and the early years of the republic were marked by a furious debate about Westernisation and modernisation in which the status of women operated as the signifier sine qua non. It is to this moment and to these debates, in particular to how they shaped and were shaped by the authors in this book, that I turn in Chapter Two, concluding with an evaluative response to the question, 'who is the Oriental woman?'

NOTES

1   I have drawn for this data on Melman's (1992) excellent research. Her figures cover British publications on the Middle East and the harem in Britain and survey the period 1718–1914, ending just as my sample gets underway. Her information does not cover the United States of America where Demetra Vaka Brown began publishing, and where my other authors were also published. However, the context is sufficiently similar to be valuable for both Western markets. Further analysis of the differences between the British and American publishing context and readership are integrated into this chapter's author biographies and the discussion of the individual books.

2   Melman presents the shift to a Victorian domestication of the harem and interest in the non-elite household as coincident to rather than caused by the increase in middle-class travel, whilst Ruth Bernard Yeazell (2000) suggests a more causal relationship.

3   Musbah Haidar grew up between the two atmospheres of her British mother and Arab royal father, Amir Ali Haidar, a Sherif of Mecca. Herself an Arab princess, Haidar came from a family so certain of their elite royal status that when her aunt, the head of the family from Mecca, arrived to visit them in Istanbul the offer of hospitality at the imperial palace was declined as beneath them (the sometime rivals for the caliphate) in social status, as were offers of marriage to the Ottoman royal daughters. The ignorance of foreign women whose own social status was even further below that of her family was therefore especially irritating to Haidar.

4   On Egyptian feminism see Badran (1996) and Baron (1994).

5   Though he was undeniably a prominent figure, no record of his holding this post has been found.

6   On the *fin de siècle* cult of the dead woman and women's participation in it, see also Chapter Four.

7   On the function of 'Loti' as protagonist and pseudonym, and of the created Oriental female character as sign, see Barthes (1971).

8   I am using her composite married name throughout for ease of reference though, as I discuss later this chapter, her variable authorial signature included Mrs Kenneth Brown and Demetra Vaka, both of which she sometimes used concurrently.

9   At the end of the nineteenth century the Ottoman Empire was the greatest focus for American missionary activity (Başci 1999).

10   'Feminist Discourse and the Greek Women Writers in Constantinople at the Turn of the Century', Vassiliki Lalagianni, paper presented at '100 Years of Ottoman Women', Bogazici University, 2000.

11 This, and all other correspondence referenced in this chapter, is from the Houghton Mifflin manuscripts at Houghton Library, Harvard University. See Bibliography for references.

12 Her qualms about Amy Lowell's affectations did not stop Vaka Brown from asking Lowell to read the draft of a manuscript that was giving her trouble in December 1921. Lowell's formal decline (she was busy with her life of Keats) suggests not only the poet's sense of self-importance but also indicates that Vaka Brown's place in the Boston literary set might not have been as secure as indicated in her own account.

13 *Atechden gömlek* appeared as the *Daughter of Smyrna* in 1938 some years after its initial publication.

14 Edib wrote only one novel in English, *The Clown and His Daughter*, published in London in 1935; it was serialised in an Istanbul daily the same year to great acclaim and published as a single volume there the following year.

15 I am grateful to Saliha Paker for discussing the 'translations' with me.

16 See also, Elif Ekin Aksit, 'Kadınların Hatıralarında Karsıt Söylem/ Counter-Discourse in Women's Memoirs', GETA Asistan Sunusları, Siyasal Biligiler Fakültesi, Ankara, 24 October 2002.

17 Kâmil Paşa, Kibrisli Mehmed (1832–1913) was four times Grand Vizier (1885–91, 1895 briefly, 1908–9, 1912–13) and held at times different ministries including Minister of Education (1880). I am grateful to Benjamin Fortna for discussing Kâmil Paşa. See also Shaw and Shaw (1978).

18 *Who Was Who* (1941).

19 I am grateful to Anne Summers for emphasising this point.

CHAPTER TWO

ഩ EMPIRE, NATION AND ര CULTURE

THE 'DECLINE' OF THE OTTOMAN EMPIRE

To understand the gender implications of the political climate in which the women authors featured in this book lived and wrote, one has to return to the Tanzimat reforms of the nineteenth century (1839–76). Just as the problems that spawned these reforms were to adumbrate the crises that brought about the end of the Ottoman Empire, so too did the intellectual agenda of the reformers set the territory for progressive discourse for generations to come – and inform the nature of opposition. The Tanzimat reforms included measures in education, the military and the bureaucracy that would change the balance of power in society and developed the secular influenced elite on which Zeyneb Hanım, Melek Hanım, Halide Edib, Demetra Vaka Brown and Grace Ellison reported and for whom they wrote.[1]

The Tanzimat reforms were different to previous Ottoman attempts at reform in that, with the persuasion of Western powers, they did not seek to preserve the old institutions but intended to change and modernise them through an indigenising adaptation of Western models. Begun under Sultan Mahmud II, the reforms really took off during the reigns of his sons Abdülmecit I (1839–61) and Abdülaziz (1861–76), directed by politicians such as Mustafa Resit Paşa, Ali Paşa (1815–71) and Fuat Paşa (1815–69). Their shifting alliance kept the power of the sultans in check as they developed the administration of the Porte, or government. The new measures increased centralised control through the use of a restructured army and the development of a large central bureaucracy. The state began to take an interest in many areas of its subjects' lives (schools, welfare, courts) previously left to the millets. These semi-autonomous religio-ethnic units of legislation accommodated (in a somewhat permeable manner) not only the empire's minority populations but also organised through the Muslim millet to manage administrative affairs within the empire. The concept of the millet changed with differing circumstances. The minority millets recognised not only a distinction from the Muslim majority (as in the Jewish millet) but came also to accommodate differences within faith communities (as seen in the distinctions between the Gregorian Armenian and the Greek Orthodox millets). Millets could also traverse ethnic differences: in the Muslim millet between, for example, Arabs, Turks or Kurds, whilst the minority millets also grouped faiths across ethnic divides, such as the Greek Orthodox millet which had itself managed to incorporate previously separate Balkan Orthodox patriarchates (Quataert 2000). The minority millets were in receipt of differential taxation – in return for being barred/exempt from military service – and had within this system enjoyed for centuries (in theory if not always in practice) greater rights and protections than were available to minorities in Europe.

Prior to the Tanzimat reforms the ruling class had consisted of those involved in the various functions of the sultan's imperial household (clerical/judicial, military, financial), whose power was derived from 'the delegation of the sultan's authority' (Göçek 1996: 31). Inspired by European revolutionary philosophy, the Tanzimat leaders wanted to curb the palace's absolute rule and to raise a modern, educated population. This aim was shared by the palace though for different reasons: in face of the increasing independent power of the ruling class, the palace wanted to develop a new cohort of state functionaries loyal only to the sultan as caliph and leader of the empire (Kandiyoti 1991b, Quataert 1994). Although the Tanzimat reforms are often regarded as paving the way for the development of Turkish nationalism, this was not necessarily the intention of the reformers themselves. Their aim was to reform the Ottoman state in order to preserve the multi-ethnic enterprise that was the Ottoman Empire. As I discuss later in this chapter, the decisive development of Turkish nationalism in the early twentieth century was able to emerge only after international events and domestic changes brought about a seismic shift in the ways in which Ottomans (Muslim and non-Muslim) formed regional, religious and ethnic identifications. In the mid-nineteenth century reformers were attempting to revitalise, so as to preserve it, a multi-ethnic model of Ottomanism that was already facing disintegration as local nationalisms, based on the European romantic nationalist ideal, began to take hold and subject populations tried to break from Ottoman rule frequently supported by the European powers.

The Ottomans' complex and often unequal relations with the European powers were determined by a number of shifting political, territorial and economic factors, including intra-European feuds and alliances and, latterly, the international concerns of the United States. The loss of Greece in 1830 was a major factor in the reconceptualisation of regional identities. Supported by Britain, the Greek bid for independence (beginning in 1821) was based on the articulation of a Greek national identity that was to set the patterning of other national identities in the Ottoman's Balkan and the Arab dominions, also to be (selectively) encouraged by the foreign powers. There is much debate about the nature of and reasons for the inconsistent attitude of the Western nations, sometimes supporting the breakaway Ottoman dominions, at others assisting the Ottoman state to retain territories or minimise losses. But it seems retrospectively that it was in the Western powers' overall political and economic interests to keep the Ottoman Empire intact, if weakened, until the end of the First World War. For commentators at the turn of the twentieth century the fate of the Ottoman Empire was still unclear though, to pro-Turk sympathisers like Anna Bowman Dodd, the cynical self-interest of the Western powers made it apparent that the Ottoman state would be allowed to remain 'a nation just so long as Europe sees in her the balancing weight in the Eastern question – and no longer' (Dodd 1904: 487).

One factor in this political strategising was the importance of commerce to, with and from the Ottoman Empire. Donald Quataert argues that despite the opportunities provided by Western military superiority it was in the West's economic interest to keep the Ottoman Empire intact, hence their only periodic interventions to support internal revolt. Operating trade through 'privileges and concessions' guaranteed by a central power (despite some Ottoman attempts at protectionism) was for the Western powers preferable to dealing with the series of competing local power bases sure to emerge were the empire to be dismembered (Quataert 1994: 761). Britain in particular was concerned to retain influence in the region in order to protect the overland trade route to India and to prevent the increase of Russian power. Although historians dispute the extent to which Tanzimat reforms were undertaken at the behest of the Western powers, Quataert convincingly characterises the continuation of the Ottoman Empire even in its weakened state as 'thanks to a mutual accommodation between European political and economic interests and the needs and concerns of the Ottoman bureaucracy' (Quataert 1994: 761). Certainly, as related by Vaka Brown, the Greeks of Istanbul were anxiously monitoring the Western press as the great powers manoeuvred for control. The Greeks were under no illusions that even though one power might be better for them than another – her father favouring the British as followers of classical Greek civilisation, other friends favouring the Russians as co-religionists in the Orthodox Church – they were all operating according to imperial interests. Their ambassadors in Istanbul were seen as contemptible, 'bent on squeezing what advantage they could, by pretending to espouse the cause of the subject races' (*Athene* 1948, 8:4, p. 13).

For Britain in particular (Heffernan forthcoming), the need for a centralisation of the Ottoman state was a major element of foreign policy. The impossibility of using a centralised state model (reliant on the concept of a modern nation-state) to preserve the multi-ethnic supra-national Ottoman imperial entity held within it the unforeseen but inevitable break-up of the Ottoman Empire and the development of the Turkish nationalism that was to emerge victorious after the First World War. The more centralised and effective bureaucracy developed during the Tanzimat years, that served Ottoman interests in salvaging the governance of the empire and responding to calls for reforms, was also of economic and ideological service to the West in its periodic propping up of the 'sick man' of Europe.

To produce the personnel necessary for implementing the reformers' plans and running the vast government bureaucracy, new training establishments at elementary and advanced levels were set up to offer vocational, military and civilian training. This moderated the educational control of the Muslim clergy in the state system (see later in this chapter). As Fatma Müge Göçek explains, the sultans (who had been instigating Western-style training in part since the eighteenth century) hoped that these developments would breed a new cohort of state functionaries loyal only to the sultan in order to counter the growing independent power of the ruling class who had been setting up their own 'office-households' as rival powerbases to the imperial household. At the same time equal rights were extended to the male minority populations. But the individualist ideology and concept of loyalty to the state, rather than a dynastic loyalty to the sultan/ caliph, imbibed with the Tanzimat's Western-style education, made the new training establishments of the nineteenth century into hotbeds for the revolutionary secret societies that were to challenge the sultan's rule.

Women's education was also at the forefront of the reformers' minds by the second half of the nineteenth century. Schools for girls first opened in 1858 and were extended in 1869 when elementary education was made compulsory for children up to the age of twelve (Sönmez 1969, Shaw and Shaw 1978). Sultan Abdülaziz opened middle-level schools for girls and a women's teacher training college in 1863 though, as with most women's education in this period (see later in this chapter), this was intended to create better-educated Muslim wives and mothers able to share in the Westernised concerns and social habits of their husbands' careers, rather than to produce independent women. For men, the combination of training and the security of jobs that were integral to the bureaucracy rather than gifts of the palace, that could be withdrawn at will, helped to create a class of independent-minded bureaucrats. Among these were later to be numbered Halide Edib's father, although by then the increased power of the palace machine under Abdülhamit made such positions more precarious. At the same time, the development of the economy following Western industrial models helped to foster a nascent business middle class. This consisted largely of members of the minority populations (notably Greeks, Jews and Armenians), as Muslims preferred a place in the civil service or the military to work in business or other professions. Though never as established as in the far more industrialised West, the Ottoman middle class and the bureaucrats formed a new power block that was replacing the older ruling class as the hegemonic class. The emergence of an independent bourgeoisie, consisting of bureaucrats, merchants and intellectuals (able for the first time to live independently on income as writers, journalists and teachers at the growing number of Western-run schools) fostered an independent lifestyle alongside the individualistic ideology imported from the West. Later, the Westernised intellectuals and bureaucrats were to be the driving force behind the development of the Young Ottomans who formed the late Tanzimat opposition and again in the next wave of reform under the Young Turks in the early twentieth century. But at the same time, the modernisation of Ottoman society and economy reduced the power of Muslim groups who did not benefit from roles in the new bureaucracy and resented the rights given to minority populations. It was this largely lower-middle-class and artisanal population of craftspeople, lower-ranked clerics and civil servants that were to form another opposition based often on Islam (Kandiyoti 1991b).

The Ottomans' ability to manoeuvre international events to their advantage was rapidly decreasing by the end of the nineteenth century. The break with traditional Ottoman isolationism, which had developed after the sixteenth century, accelerated during the eighteenth and nineteenth centuries and saw the empire, which had once governed vast territories and relied largely on internal trade, become increasingly dependent on European finance and locked into disadvantageous trade relations (Inalcik and Quataert 1994). As the loss of territories impacted unfavourably on the internal market, the Ottoman economy from the 1830s also began to devote more of its activity to producing raw materials for export rather than materials and manufactured goods for the internal and external markets. Much of this was driven by the preferential trade terms enjoyed by European commerce arranged under the capitulations. These concessions, granted variously to Western powers from the fifteenth century, protected foreign trade interests and gave European populations and traders in the Ottoman Empire autonomy under the power of their national consulate. The capitulations were also seen to favour Ottoman minority populations who were more likely to have links with foreign companies and to be taken on as agents, thus acquiring the protection of foreign consulates (Berkes 1964). During the course of the nineteenth century, merchants from the Ottoman minorities increasingly took over from the European companies who had once sponsored them (though the foreign merchants increased their share once the foreign-built infrastructure programmes started up from the 1870s). Whilst it had generally been held that trade was by the nineteenth century dominated by the minority populations, Quataert points out that, though Muslim merchants did indeed fail to gain a proportionate share of the market, they were not as insignificant in (internal and foreign) commerce as was until recently presumed (Quataert 1994). Muslims did remain the majority players in domestic trade, which continued until 1922 to make up the bulk of commerce (Quataert 2000), but the perception that minority populations dominated foreign trade was an important political issue for the Ottomans themselves who at various times tried to increase the share of Muslims in the merchant classes. As the Westernising sensibilities of the Tanzimat stimulated the demand for foreign goods, however, the increase in foreign trade further enhanced the power of a merchant class that was significantly non-Muslim. This picture continued into the twentieth century. Istanbul in particular showed a predominance of minority population traders: by 1911 nearly 90 per cent of merchants in the city were Ottoman Christians, mainly Armenian and Greek (Quataert 1994: 840). It was this under-representation of Muslims in the middle class that the Young Turks after 1908 aimed specifically to redress.

By the last quarter of the nineteenth century, capitulary limitations on the Ottoman's ability to restrict foreign imports meant that the Ottoman dominions functioned for the West as a good source of raw materials to whom could be sold back manufactured goods (continuing into the early twentieth century) whilst simultaneously hindering Ottoman attempts to develop their own industrial base (Quataert 1994). The influence of European politics and finance was such that in the last years of the Tanzimat the Ottoman state was hugely reliant on European loans whose interest payments took up more than half of its total revenues. The Ottoman Public Debt Administration was set up in 1881 to oversee repayment of the empire's vast foreign loans and was largely staffed by foreign and minority (generally Christian) population personnel which, like the similar employment practices of the other foreign corporations surviving from the mid century, further increased their influence in the Ottoman economy (Göçek 1996, Quataert 1994). But here again historiographical traditions are being challenged. The picture is not necessarily that of the remorseless decline of Ottoman manufacture that is usually presented: Quataert (1994) points out that after the initial decline of the Tanzimat years, Ottoman manufacture was responsive and adaptive, continuing in forms that were largely non-factory based (like the developments in the thriving handcraft-based Anatolian cotton and carpet industries) and hence invisible to observers looking for signs of Western-style industrial modernity.

The political and education reforms of the Tanzimat helped to produce a new sort of intellectual and a new opposition. By the 1860s a younger generation of men, trained in the Tanzimat's more secular system, readers of French literature and philosophy – some, like Ibrahim Şinasi, (1826–71), studying in France – emerged as part of a new intelligentsia that looked to Western and secular cultural models for form and content where once the religious orders had held sway. Replacing religious and Eastern (often Persian inspired) cultural forms with adaptations of Western models, the development of a specifically Turkish literature began, featuring the work of Ziya Paşa (1825–80) and Namık Kemal (1840–88) in the newly expanded press and the new theatres. This generation were the heirs to the initial Tanzimat reforms and from their ranks emerged the Tanzimat opposition known as the Young Ottomans. Concerned at the abuse of power possible within the vast Tanzimat machine, they were anxious to protect the pan-national, multi-ethnic entity that had been the Ottoman Empire. Although Islam continued to be the basis of all debate about reform, the Young Ottomans were distinctive in that they sought to harness the progressive potential of Islam to Western ideas of parliamentarianism and constitutionalism and to include minority populations in their Ottomanist vision of representative government.

The drive for a constitution was eventually successful, but short-lived. When Sultan Abdülaziz continued to refuse a constitution he was overthrown in favour of his brother Murat V. But Murat's mental health was of such concern that approaches were made to Abdülhamit to take the throne. Making a pact with Midhat Paşa that he would be given the throne, and not just a regency (Shaw and Shaw 1978), on the understanding that he would approve a constitution and act with the advice of ministers, Abdülhamit came to power in August 1876. The advent of the Tanzimat constitution owed much to Young Ottoman agitation and also gave Abdülhamit a chance to demonstrate progress in the sorts of visible reforms being demanded by the European powers then in Istanbul to try to resolve the crisis between Turkey and Russia over Bulgaria and Bosnia-Herzegovina. But the constitution and the representative parliament were short-lived. Abdülhamit disbanded both in February 1878, ostensibly because of the demands of the war with Russia. All power accrued again to the palace and opposition was stifled as he used the Tanzimat machinery to consolidate a net-work of spies loyal to the palace.

It is Abdülhamit's larger than life figure that stalks this book's material, for it was under his autocratic rule (1876–1909) that all these Ottoman women started their lives. Intellectuals and progressives lived in fear of his legendary spies and were hidebound by the difficulty of overcoming his consuming censorship – which applied not only to publications but also to the freedom to speak to for-eigners and engage in public political debate. Vaka Brown on returning from Paris, where she had been fired up by the quality of fervent political debate, found the Hamidian climate increasingly onerous:

> The repression of the spy system had not been so noticeable to me before. Now it seemed as if people had become even more reticent in their talk. My few acquaintances who had lived abroad never dared discuss any public affairs even remotely connected with Turkey. (*Athene* 1950, 11:2, p. 22)

Zeyneb Hanım and Melek Hanım, whose family life was connected to the palace, dreaded discovery by his spies and both tell the story of a neighbour, a writer, who disappeared in the mysterious way that perceived enemies of the sultan were wont to do. Halide Edib, when at the American College for Girls, found herself chased by a boatload of palace police after spies had laid information that her teacher had taken her to have tea on board an American's yacht moored in the Bosphorous. Eluding the police, who had been sent to 'prevent a Turkish girl from going abroad a foreign ship', she was only able to free from prison the boat-man who assisted her after some 'good friends of father's explained to his Majesty that I was hardly sixteen and had no intention whatever of attempting to run away from Turkey' (Edib 1926: 198–200). Later, her older sister Mahmoure Abla became the 'first victim of the old [Hamidian] regime in our family', when her husband was arrested after his family fell foul of a powerful palace clique. Once released from house arrest, Mahmoure Abla went into exile with her hus-band to Jerusalem, returning only in 1908 'with all the other exiles' (Edib 1926: 223–7). Halil Halid (1903) similarly represents the reign of Abdülhamit as one characterised by cronyism and informers, recounting his struggle to achieve a government position and the attempt to recruit him as a spy. In twice fleeing to Europe, Young Turk Halil Halid was typical of men in the opposition who shifted back and forth to Europe depending on the safety of Istanbul or the Turkish dominions. Though, with Ottoman subjects unable to gain their passport without Palace permission to travel, movement outside (and sometimes inside) the empire was very difficult. It was for just these reasons that Zeyneb Hanım and Melek Hanım's flight was carried out under conditions of secrecy. Unable to obtain their own passports, they disguised themselves and travelled under the false identities of their Polish music mistress and her daughter.

But though he is often presented as ogre, increasingly isolated in the park-estate of the Yildiz Kiosk palace, Abdülhamit in fact brought to fruition many of the reforms and modernisations of the Tanzimat plan. Overseeing continued economic development, he continued with the modernisation of the armed forces, vastly extended the Tanzimat school system and encouraged cultural activity as national literacy increased. Whilst the Tanzimat reformers were more uncritically pro-Western, Abdülhamit's extensive education programme was, as Fortna (2002) argues, based on adaption not adoption of Western education. Aiming to unite Western science with Islamic values, Ottoman officials (including the father of Grace Ellison's friend Makboulé Hanım, Kâmil Paşa, who wrote on this as minister of education in 1880)[2] were convinced that the economic power of Western nations was linked to their superior scientific abilities. Determined to access this power for the Ottoman state, they focused on the parlous education available to the Muslim population. Seeing themselves, as Fortna explains, in an adversarial relationship with the well-funded foreign and missionary schools (who taught science along with Christianity) and in competition with the better organised schools run by the minority populations, the education reformers under Abdülhamit created a new Ottoman education model. This indigenised Western science and integrated religious teaching via the clergy to produce 'an environment of patriotism and observance while educating their charges in those subjects deemed necessary to help the Ottoman Empire catch up with the West' (Fortna 2002: 244).

With the increase of education and the undoubted influence of the secular ideology that accompanied Western knowledge, the population began to read as never before. Despite Abdülhamit's intensive censorship rules, a range of opinion avoided censorship and reached the public just as it had during the Tanzimat. Vaka Brown, like many, relied on the foreign press brought in under the foreign post offices whose autonomy was guaranteed by the capitulations. Such was the demand for these crucial papers – '[they] had a value no newspapers in a free country possess' – that she often stayed up all night 'to read them quickly, so that they might be lent to others' (*Athene* 1950, 11:2, p. 23).

Abdülhamit further developed the empire's infrastructure (in conjunction with foreign companies), including railroads and communications. In Istanbul, where all these writers grew up, changes were marked, with the advent of street lighting, paved streets and public transport. On a daily basis life for the upper echelons of Ottoman society was increasingly punctuated by the objects and habits of Western culture: furniture changed as chairs and tables replaced, or often co-existed alongside, traditional divans. Halide Edib experienced one such startling transformation when her stepmother took over what had previously been her grandmother's house, using decoration to signal a change in power; 'Granny's room no longer had that pleasant white-covered divan; it was Abla's room and had European furniture … I had the feeling of being a stranger' (Edib 1926: 155). For many, as I discuss in Chapters Three and Six, the consumption of Western goods was fast becoming an accepted facet of life; the issue was how to use and adapt such goods and technologies without being swamped by Western ideas and morals.

In all this, the status of women was never far from the centre of debate. The rule of Abdülhamit is widely characterised as a period in which imperial policy tried to adopt elements of Western modernity that it could consider 'material', such as electricity and locomotives, without being tainted by what it considered 'moral', or rather immoral. Concerns about the influence of Western immorality inevitably centred on perceived threats to the Islamic regulation of female sexuality, such as prostitution and divorce (Berkes 1964). In the late nineteenth century the initially pro-Western thrust of Tanzimat modernising reforms shifted into an anti-Westernism that offered alternative routes to power and social stability. This included an Islamist reaction against the equality granted to non-Muslim subjects who were seen by many to have benefited disproportionately from the reforms. Pan-Islamism, supported by Abdülhamit, aimed to revive the role of the sultan caliph as head of all Muslims (not just those in his realm) who would have had an overarching loyalty to the sultan as caliph and head of the universal *umma*, the world congregation of the faithful. This plan to unite all Muslims not only aimed to offer leadership to the many Muslim nations conquered by Western imperialism but also, by extending the sultan/caliph's authority, to give him more leverage with the Western powers. But it excluded the non-Muslim minority populations. The other supranational ideology developing at this time that was to play a key role in the eventual development of Turkish nationalism (see later) was pan-Turanism, or pan-Turkism, which aimed to unite ethnic Turks inside and outside the Ottoman Empire, stressing the linguistic and ethnic affiliations of Turkic speakers from across the region, including Russia, the Caucasus, China and Central Asia.

All sides played out their debates across the figure of the Ottoman woman. Pan-Turanism countered the Islamist defence of 'traditional' practices such as polygamy (pictured as a moral alternative to immorality and to 'Parisian vices', Berkes, 1964: 285) with the construction of an imagined past that figured female emancipation as an indigenous pre-Islamic Turkic tradition. This was a strand of thinking that was to have great significance within nationalist ideology in the twentieth century (Kandiyoti 1991b). In the meantime women were swift themselves to challenge defences of polygamy: in 1891 Fatma Aliye Hanım (1862–1936, daughter of the Tanzimat cleric and reformer Cevdet Paşa), herself a translator, novelist and contributor to the women's press, criticised clerics who argued that polygamy was a natural law that Islam merely recognised rather than created (Berkes 1964: 285):

> If we believe that Islam had universally valid principles, we ought to declare that the monogamous marriage is the one enjoined by Islam and that the verse of the Kur'an enjoining man to remain with one wife is in accordance with civilisation. It is only then that we can justify our position.[3]

Arguing against the cleric Mahmud Es'ad, she maintained that biological arguments were irrelevant, framing her response in moderate Islamic terms. Her fusion of Islam with selected Western innovations was in keeping with liberal ideas of the time, notably with those of her father and the prominent reformer and constitutionalist Ahmet Midhat Paşa (1822–84) – one of the initiators of the Turkish-language novel – who promoted her writing. Opposed to slavish Westernisation for its own sake Midhat Paşa argued that the Turkish character should be embellished, not replaced, by Western civilisation. As Fatma Aliye Hanım demonstrates, the proto-feminist critique of polygamy was carried out on a discursive stage which inevitably framed debates about gender in relation to the competing ideologies and associated moral values of Westernism, anti-Westernism and Ottoman reformism.

The economic developments of the Hamidian regime were accompanied by an increased restriction of personal freedoms which grew to be so far reaching that they touched the lives of vast sectors of the population. It was this that led to the advent of another liberal opposition known as the Young Turks, a loose grouping of opposition factions, some in Istanbul, some elsewhere in the Ottoman Empire, but many in Europe where they were freer to operate. These secret societies, often with military men as key members, consisted of Muslims and representatives of minority populations. The extent to which Turkish nationalism was implicit or explicit in Young Turk politics is a matter of debate, but it would appear that the agenda of the early Young Turks was not focused on Turkish nationalism. Instead, the Young Turk congresses in 1901 and 1907 that fomented plans for the 1908 revolt were still enmeshed in Ottomanism and consisted of representatives of the different minority populations of the Ottoman Empire who all wanted an end to Abdülhamit's control. From the start the sometimes tenuous Young Turk alliances were racked by intense differences of opinion and local ambitions. The group that were to prove the most powerful were the Committee of Union and Progress.

Hated as Abdülhamit was, even the Young Turk revolutionaries of 1908 were not intent on deposing him. They aimed to reform his government and limit his power through the reactivation of the Tanzimat constitution. The Young Turk Revolution of 1908, which brought Halide Edib into public political life, ushered in the second constitutional period that lasted until Turkey's defeat in the First World War in 1918. When the sultan agreed to bring back the constitution, the CUP engineered a change of grand vizier to keep the balance of power between government and palace. The compromise candidate was Kâmil Paşa. Not a CUP supporter, Kâmil Paşa sided instead with the Ottoman Liberal Union Party, which had emerged as the main faction within the Young Turks to oppose the CUP. The Ottoman Liberal party was under the leadership of Prince Sabaheddin, now back from Paris. His decentralist position aimed to retain the Ottomanism of the early Young Turks by giving minority populations equal rights and autonomy *within* the empire. It was to Sabaheddin that Vaka Brown was to dedicate her 1923 book *The Unveiled Ladies of Stamboul*, seeing in his inclusive politics a chance to retain the multi-ethnic society that she so valued. But the Young Turk government, even as the sultan attended the grand opening of the new parliament (witnessed by young reporter Grace Ellison), had to face continual strife in the

Balkans and in Crete as subject populations agitated for independence and neigh-bours tried to gain Ottoman territory. Vaka Brown retrospectively represents the view of the minority populations, initially inspired by the Young Turks she met in Paris in 1892–4:

> As our international group enlarged, other Greeks came into it. Two of these were adherents of the Young Turks movement ... These Greeks took me to other meetings where the principal speakers were Turks whose slogan was that in their country there should be no Christians or Musselmen, no Greeks, Arme-nians, Kurds, or Arabs. All should be citizens of Turkey, working for the good of Turkey.
>
> It sounded very fine and I became an adherent of the movement ... [but] on closer acquaintance with the leaders, a distinctive mistrust was born in me. ... [one of the leaders] revealed more than he probably intended to. What they meant by saying that all the citizens of Turkey should be equal, was that Greeks, Armenians, Arabs, Kurds – Christians and Mohammedans – were all to become Turks. 'We are the people to whom Turkey belongs. The others should become like us. Only when they all become Turks can the country progress.'
>
> It would have been useless to point out to him that other races – the Greeks, for example, with an intellectual heritage of thousands of years – could not become backward Asiatics, like the Turks. (*Athene* 1950, 11:1, p. 19)

Although her vitriol has the benefit of hindsight, unofficial channels brought her news of communitarian violence very soon in the months after the 1908 revolution:

> [W]e heard of the revolution in Turkey, and it made me happy to think that the people might at last have a chance. Even my mistrust of those 'Young Turks' I had known in Paris, did not keep me from hoping that the government would inaugurate a regime under which Mussulmans and Christians could live and work happily together, – until letters from friends in Turkey, but mailed in Greece, brought the information that the non-Turkish element throughout the country was being secretly persecuted. Yet English writers following their nation's policy of bolstering up Turkey, wrote glowing accounts of Enver, Talaat, and Djemal, the triumvirate which had risen to the surface, like other scum. (*Athene* 1952, 13:1, p. 27)

Vaka Brown with her minority population background was not surprised to learn of the breakdown of the Ottomanist dream and, of course, supported the Cretan revolt. To her Grace Ellison's support for the Young Turks, whom Ellison saw as insufficiently favoured by the British, would have seemed typical of Britain's biased policy. The advances in women's conditions for which Ellison applauded the Young Turks would not have saved their reputation for Vaka Brown, for whom the gender agenda could not take priority over concerns of ethnicity and nation.

In Turkey the losses sustained under the first year of Young Turk rule did not recommend the new order. Kâmil Paşa became a rallying point for conservatives and disgruntled Muslims, anxious that minority populations were being unfairly advantaged. But though he was not opposed for some time by the CUP, they did eventually move a vote of no confidence in him in early 1909. This show of power by the CUP, who had just appointed the first CUP grand vizier in his place, was one of the factors that prompted the conservative and Islamist opposition to mount the counter-revolution that briefly restored Abdülhamit to absolute power. But the Macedonian army was loyal to the CUP and, under the leadership of Mustafa Kemal and other officers, marched on Istanbul. There, they defeated the Istanbul army which was loyal to the sultan and deposed Abdülhamit in favour of his brother Mehmet Resat V who reigned, in a much reduced capacity, until 1918. It was these changes at the palace that paved the way for Zeyneb Hanım's safe return to Istanbul.

The rest of the Young Turk period saw the culmination of the Tanzimat reforms, including the most dramatic legislative changes in women's rights prior to the republic, in the context of almost continual warfare that cost many lives and brought the empire to its knees. Though often considered a period of CUP rule, the 1909–18 era was, as Shaw and Shaw point out, a time punctuated by continued factionalism among the Young Turks, with (often short-lived) splinter groups jockeying for position and the power of the army always to be taken into consideration. It was in one of these reshuffles, in this case in the wake of the Italian victories in Tripoli in November 1911, that Makboulé Hanım's father Kâmil Paşa was brought back into government as a member of what was intended to be the more impartial cabinet of Gazi Ahmet Muhtar Paşa (1839–1918).

THE BALKAN WARS, THE FIRST WORLD WAR AND THE CRISIS OF OCCUPATION

Whilst the Ottomans were focused on Tripoli, the Balkan nations banded together to push for independence, starting the first of two Balkan wars in October 1912. Turkey quickly lost most of her European territories, while the Bulgarians advanced on Istanbul. The Muhtar cabinet resigned and Kâmil Paşa was brought back as grand vizier by the other Young Turk groups in an attempt to keep the CUP from controlling the cabinet. As a man well connected with Britain, it was hoped that he would be able to persuade the European powers to intervene in the Balkans.[4] To this end Kâmil Paşa directed the London negotiations in December 1912 during the initial cessation of warfare in the Balkans. Fearing that Kâmil Paşa was about to give away the besieged city of Edirne (Adrianople), the CUP led by Enver Paşa staged a dramatic coup d'etat on 23 January 1913, replacing Kâmil Paşa at gunpoint. Still trying to keep the London Conference going the new cabinet offered compromise terms. But these were rejected by the Bulgarians and war resumed. Kâmil Paşa continued to agitate against the CUP, trying to organise a counter-coup, with British backing, to bring back the Liberal Union. He was discovered and arrested in the final days of the Balkan War. The war was brought to a bitter end for the Ottomans with the Treaty of London on 30 May 1913, by which time Turkey had lost Crete and nearly all her European territories. But the plans against the CUP went on, resulting in the eventual assassination of a CUP minister. At this, the CUP cracked down on the opposition, exiling Kâmil Paşa and those others who escaped the death penalty; thus establishing the CUP as the dominant party.

Under the triumvirate led by Enver Paşa, the more nationalist CUP government took up military action once more when the Second Balkan War started after Greece and Serbia had formed an alliance against Bulgaria. An attack by Bulgaria led to the declaration of war on 8 July 1913, with the Ottoman Empire joining Montenegro and Romania against Bulgaria in the following fortnight. Vaka Brown, who had spent considerable time in the Balkans (written up as *The Heart of the Balkans* 1913), wrote later that she

> would have felt less sympathy for the Bulgarians had I been able to foresee …
> that in 1913 they would destroy the Balkan Confederation – which might have
> saved the peace of the world – and seek to subjugate their allies, Serbia and
> Greece. And I should have hated them could I have imagined the bestialities
> perpetrated by them as partners of Germany in the two world wars. (*Athene*
> 1950, 10:4, p. 36)

Finally, at the end of July, Bulgaria gave in and an agreement was brokered in Bucharest on 10 August 1913. For Vaka Brown, anxiously following the international news, the American lack of interest was perpetually frustrating: '[t]o Marion [an ex-pupil travelling with them] and my husband [the Balkan War] was just another European squabble. To me it was the continuation of the Greek War of Independence, which began in 1821 (*Athene* 1952, 13:3, p. 16). Although Turkey had triumphantly regained Edirne, by the end of the Second Balkan War the Ottoman Empire had lost most of what remained of its European territories and associated revenues. Since the more densely settled European territories had in 1850 accounted for nearly half of the entire Ottoman population, this marked a remarkable loss of population. It also produced a demographic shift towards what was to become a Muslim majority in Ottoman lands, once the other Christian dominions were eventually lost, especially as many Balkan Muslims migrated south after independence (Quataert 2000).

The change in the balance of power in the Balkan region (especially Austro-Hungary's anxiety about the development of a powerful Serbia), that was eventually to lead to the First World War, meant that things were still volatile when Grace Ellison visited Istanbul in the aftermath of the Balkan Wars in October 1913. Turks were not reassured that peace was to be lasting and the city was still reeling from wartime hardship and personal losses. On the political front, negotiations were still ongoing about the status of the Aegean islands that had been referred to an international commission under the terms of the Treaty of London.

At the point when Ellison was writing her missives from an Istanbul harem, Turkey was being urged by the European powers to give up the islands of Chios and Mitylene that it considered essential to the protection of the Western coast of its empire in Asia Minor. Unlike Vaka Brown, who considered the British to be always biased in favour of the Turks, Ellison found British foreign policy appalling. To her, given the continued faith that Turkey continued to place in the British, it amounted to nothing less than a betrayal:

> Turkey trusted herself to the arbitration of Great Britain particularly amongst the Powers. Now, here am I, the guest of this people, submitted to the humiliation of hearing it is the Foreign Minister of my country who has ordered Mitylene to be handed over to the Greeks. Has Sir Edward Grey ever stopped for a minute to think what that means? An Island five kilometres from the Turkish coast to be given to the Greeks! It is as if some foreign Power had ordered us to hand over the Isle of Wight to the Germans! Was that decision made without even looking at the map? ... (Ellison, *Daily Telegraph*, 6 February 1914, p. 7)

Part of Ellison's mission was to emphasise the high regard in which the British were held by the Turkish population as she endeavoured to foster British support for the Young Turk government and to convince her British readers that Britain must maintain its influence in the region. Prior to her outrage about British action on the Aegean islands, Ellison explained that right 'in the heart of Asia the word "England" stands for something almost superhuman', as exemplified by the heir to the Turkish throne who confided to Ellison his gratitude that England 'shed her blood for us [in the Crimean War]' (Ellison, *Daily Telegraph*, 6 February 1914, p. 7). Britain's support for the Turks in Crimea was not of course without self-interest, serving as it did to protect the overland route to India in the face of Russian incursions. Tellingly, Ellison contextualises her commentary on international political negotiations through an explanation of how European imperial rivalries were built into the very structure of the Ottoman household. This is demonstrated by the ascendancy of the English governess in elite households:

> In the families where there are two governesses, an Englishwoman and Frenchwoman, it is the Englishwoman who is given the position of trust, the Englishwoman who sleeps in the children's room, the Englishwoman who buys their clothes; in short, whatever the mother cannot do herself she prefers the Englishwoman to do for her. 'The Englishwoman told me so therefore it must be true,' is a phrase which I myself have heard ... (Ellison, *Daily Telegraph*, 6 February 1914, p. 7)

To throw this advantage away seemed ludicrous to Ellison who 'cannot but despise this Liberal Government, which is doing its best to destroy that wonderful prestige'. The *Daily Telegraph* itself took a leader line in favour of the Turkish position, arguing that if the Turkish Empire were to be reduced to its territories in Asia Minor, it should be allowed to retain the islands in order to secure its Western shoreline. For Ellison, the British government's 'interfering' jeopardised the Ottoman's complex juggling of regional demands at which they were as practised as the mistress of the not untypical household made up of 'a Greek cook, an Armenian bonne à tout faire, and Albanian cavass [guard] and a Turkish gardener' whose violent quarrels she must arbitrate. Recognising that the Turks have made mistakes, she still urged against the 'humiliation' of further 'bungling' European intervention. The link between domestic diplomacy (by women in the household) and the international stage is made even clearer:

> I am asked by a correspondent, 'What do I think of the future for Turkish women?' How can I speak optimistically of the future of a country on the brink of war? For war with Greece means, no doubt, that Bulgaria also takes part, and then the whole ghastly business of the year 1913 must be gone through again. But if there is a war, I, for one, will stay with the Turks and nurse the sick. I shall work with the Red Crescent Society, but I shall wear round my neck a cross, and on that cross the Saviour of the world, his arms stretched out in pity towards the whole world. (Ellison, *Daily Telegraph*, 6 February 1914, p. 7)

Ellison's ardent identification with the Turks is inflected with a Christianity that is often found to be wanting in her eyes when judged against the benefits of Islam. The following paragraph contrasts her imagined multi-faith nursing protest with the recent misuse of the Christian cross by the Bulgarians in their massacre of Turkish civilians during the Balkan War: 'that they should carry the Cross and wage [their 'savage'] war in the name of the Cross, what Christian can ever forgive it?' A few years earlier in 1895 Mrs Max Müller (Georgina Adelaide Grenfell) similarly criticised England's partisan support for Abdülhamit's Christian subjects, whilst condemning the Armenian massacres she regretted that the opportunity had been lost to encourage the also oppressed Muslim population to be a force for progressive change in the empire as a whole.

Despite the hyperbole of Ellison's political treatise in this her last article in the *Daily Telegraph* series, her association of war and nationalism with women's emancipation was well advised. The Balkan Wars and their aftermath became a mobilising moment for Turkish women, whose labour in all manner of fields was found to be necessary in the absence and death of so many men. As well as the social services undertaken by the Red Crescent, Muslim women started to work in nursing – a remarkable incursion into public work, especially for the previously sheltered middle classes.[5] Feminism and nationalism became inseparable in the Turkish context as the importance of female emancipation and the promulgation of the monogamous Western style rather than Islamic polygamous family became a central plank in the Turkist ideology of Ziya Gökalp, who became CUP's main ideologue when it came to power in 1913. Initially an Ottomanist, like many of the Young Turks, Gökalp was at first a pan-Turanist who moved towards a nationalist position in the face of the evident breakdown of the pan-national imperial ideal. But by 1913 it was clear that this Ottomanist ideal was unmanageable and Turkish nationalism was beginning to gain a hold. Women's emancipation was to become central to Turkish nationalism with the recognition of the importance of women's work in the war effort during the Balkans, the First World War and the War of Independence going on to form a core strand of Mustafa Kemal's struggle for independence and the social changes of the early republic. It was in these struggles that Halide Edib achieved prominence, being instrumental in setting up the first women's nursing projects during the Balkan Wars (see Chapter Three). Makboulé Hanım also worked in the Red Crescent hospitals but by this time, when Ellison was back in Europe writing up her *Daily Telegraph* articles for her book, the First World War had started and Turkey had entered on the side of the Germans. The two women united in their nursing endeavours – one nursing the Allied wounded in the Red Cross hospital in Bordeaux and the other running Red Crescent facilities in Istanbul – were separated by international hostilities, unable to meet or receive news of each other (Ellison 1928).

Turkey's alliance with Germany was driven by Enver Paşa, who, in contrast to Kâmil Paşa's connections to the British, had longstanding contacts in Berlin. Although popular opinion in Turkey and much of the government still favoured Britain and France, fear of Russia's expansionist desires put problems in the way of a partnership with the Triple Entente. Hastened by a secret deal with Germany, Enver Paşa eventually persuaded the other members of the triumvirate, Talat Paşa and Kemal Paşa, to forge an alliance with the Central Powers on the promise of help to regain lost Ottoman territories. But the defeat of Germany in 1918 and the terms of the armistice marked the deathknell of what was left of the Ottoman Empire. Turkey's surrender cost it all its remaining Balkan and Arab provinces and – worse still – the Allied forces under the leadership of Britain were able to partition Anatolia and occupy Istanbul. It was at this point that the Ottomanism of the first generation of Young Turks finally gave way to the development of a Turkish nationalism that had been incubating in the younger generation of Young Turks and was to be fostered by the resistance to the foreign occupation. Thus came about the Turkish War of Independence (1918–23) and the rise to leadership of Mustafa Kemal, military hero of Gallipoli.

With the collapse of the Ottoman Empire, the Hamidians' imaginary division between the material and the moral was discarded as Mustafa Kemal forged ahead with a policy of nation building and modernisation that specifically emulated a secular Western model, within the context of emerging Turkish nationalism (Berkes 1964). While the extent to which an exclusive Turkish nationalism was a foundational part of the Young Ottoman and Young Turk reformist agenda has been much debated, Quataert (2000) suggests it can partly be explained by historiographical needs of the Ottoman successor states – of which Turkey is just one. For emergent Arab or Balkan states the spectre of evil Ottoman oppression was important in the development of new narratives of national identity. Similarly, the nationalists in Turkey after 1922 also needed to distance themselves from the sultanic regime and emphasised the longevity of a legitimising Turkish national consciousness.

The presence of foreign troops in Istanbul was a shock of great magnitude to the population and revealed in a new way the different allegiances of the Muslim and minority populations. Selma Ekrem, then a schoolgirl at the American College for Girls, described how she and the other Muslim girls could scarcely stand to talk to the girls from minority populations who were excited by the arrival of the Allied troops.

> They who had shared the hardships and sufferings of war with us could not share our sorrow now that the Allies had come to Stamboul ... At college mournful groups of Turkish girls pored over the newspapers ... We could not bear to look at the other girls, those who were not Turks, and who lived their happiest days in our blackest ones. The rustle of non-Turkish newspapers drove us out of rooms, the sight of enemy flags made us shut our eyes ... Let them flaunt their joy in our faces, ... The Turks were ready to give their lives to drive that [Greek] army away – and then we had Moustapha Kemal. (Ekrem 1931: 236–42)

Ekrem's teenage rush into nationalist indignation was emblematic of the massive shift in consciousness that the end of the empire brought about for the Muslim Turkish population.

WHO IS THE ORIENTAL WOMAN?
SHIFTING NOTIONS OF OTTOMAN SUBJECTHOOD

In the late Ottoman era and until the First World War most people in the empire would have considered themselves to be Ottoman subjects and to see their future as part of an Ottoman Empire. For some populations, like the Greeks – as Vaka Brown testifies – the sense of national or ethnic identity and desire for autonomy was longer established. For others, revolt was often about gaining greater powers within the Ottoman system, not dismantling it. For many individuals the Ottoman entity was not questioned. In the Anatolian provinces Turkish national consciousness was in many ways one of the last national consciousnesses to assert itself in the region. Previously individuals, if they thought about it at all, would have considered themselves as subjects of the sultan, mediated by their affiliation to a millet, or, if Muslim, by their loyalty to the sultan as caliph.

The Ottomans traditionally called themselves Ottomans (Osmanlı), a dynastic affiliation that did not equate to a national identity. Prior to the mid-nineteenth century, 'Turk' was not a word applied to themselves by the Ottomans and even then only rarely and with much debate. As the *Times Literary Supplement* review of Edib's second volume of memoirs in 1928 commented, '[w]hen the author was born it was almost impossible for an Osmanli to imagine that there could be such a thing as "Turkey" apart from the dominions of the Ottoman Padishah – the word was purely foreign and he never thought of himself as a Turk' (29 November 1928, p. 921). But Turk was how the Western powers had long referred to all members of the Ottoman Empire, collapsing Ottoman onto Turk and Turk onto Muslim in a way that ignored the heterogeneity of the Ottoman state and the specificity of Turkish ethnicity. By the eighteenth century, in the West, 'going Turk' meant converting to Islam and 'Turk' could refer to Muslims inside or outside the Ottoman dominions, though its previous comprehensive associations lived on in Western usage until the final years before 1908 (Dodd 1904). Evidently, there was a huge gap between how the Ottomans saw themselves and how the West named and regarded them.

Divisions within the Ottoman Empire were between those of faith, as in the millets, not nationality or race. Muslim Ottomans had submerged their identity (more thoroughly than most populations in the region according to David Kushner, 1977) within the supranational community of the Islamic *umma*. Moreover, within the multi-ethnic Ottoman Empire, birth was not necessarily the determinant of social status – historically until the eighteenth century the practice of conscripting non-Muslim slaves into the military and the imperial household service meant that these converts to Islam could rise to positions of great power and would have seen themselves as Ottomans. Similarly, in the nineteenth century Zeyneb Hanım and Melek Hanım's grandfather, a French Christian, converted to Islam in the service of the sultan. Conversion itself was not always necessary: non-Muslims could also hold prominent offices of state, such as the Greek Ottoman consul whom Vaka Brown accompanied to New York. For non-Muslim women, excluded from positions in the military or the bureaucracy, alliances through marriage or concubinage with imperial or elite families gave access to social status within the Ottoman elite. Women slaves could also progress to powerful careers as functionaries in imperial and elite harems. It would therefore have been common in elite households to have non-converted women from different religions and ethnicities whose allegiance and affective identification would have been to the social category of Ottoman.

The Ottoman tradition of supra-national loyalty which had begun to weaken by the end of the eighteenth century (Berkes 1964) was challenged in the nineteenth by local nationalisms fostered by the self-interest of European powers: with the Greeks as discussed earlier, and also, most devastatingly for the Ottomans, with the Arab Revolts that were strategically fostered by Britain during the First World War. Thus the Ottomans were challenged by non-Muslim minority populations and by non-Turkish Muslims, all of whom felt disadvantaged by the Ottoman system. By the end of the First World War the pan-Ottomanism of the Tanzimat era had been irrevocably shattered as different nationalist campaigns took advantage of the increasingly weak Ottoman Empire's inability to control its dominions. The wider social and ethnic base that had supported the reforms of the Tanzimat and shown potential as the Young Turks first came to power disintegrated in the face of competing national aspirations. Opinion is divided about whether nationalisms in the region predated the movement for breakaway states or were created to forge a national identity for the resultant states (see Quataert 2000). But it is clear that after 1908 the Tanzimat Ottomanist vision of heterogeneity was on the wane. This heterogeneity in the Ottoman population was often remarked upon by Western visitors. As Heffernan (forthcoming) points out, the terms in which the West evaluated this social mix changed as Western nationalist discourses further developed. By the end of the nineteenth century what had once been regarded as religious variety in the Ottoman population was being increasingly translated into one of ethnic and racial mixing. Within this confusion of ethnicities, Istanbul was sometimes presented as an almost miscegenated city whose lack of homogeneity was read as a sign of the 'sick man's' weakness by Western commentators accustomed to the mythic homogeneity of the 'imagined' communities (Anderson 1983) that made up the narratives of the modern Western nation-states. This leads Heffernan to suggest that Western sponsorship of the Turkish reforms had within its sight a project of social re-engineering, aiming to effect a Western-style homogeneity through the transformation of religious millets into ethnic/national categories on the model of Western national identity.

Göçek (1996) however, argues that the dissolution in the *fin de siècle* of the earlier pan-Ottomanist model was not as inevitable as is often presented. The end of the Ottoman model was not simply due to the inexorable rise of local nationalisms, but was directly contributed to by the inability of the Muslim political leadership to recognise the continued and structural discrimination faced by minority populations. It was these grievances, alongside the often Islamic complexion of Ottoman reform ideologies, that, Göçek contends, led the minorities to place their faith in regional independence and that, with the Turkification of the new nation-state, cost Turkey its commercial ability. But, as Edib makes clear in the first volume of her memoirs, the development and definition of Turkish national identity was never a seamless process. In the streets and among the intellectual elite of the Young Turks in the years before 1918, different formulations of nationalism were in constantly debated circulation, generally in the context of a resolute Ottomanism.

All the terms of identification circulating in these debates were unstable and context dependent. In general, if Ottomans before the end of the nineteenth century had used the term Turk at all it might have referred to 'the ignorant nomad or peasant of Anatolia, often with derogatory connotations' (Kushner 1977: 2), certainly not to the proud Ottoman leaders of an empire. The contentious reframing of the term Turk in the 1860s, with the development of a 'Turkish' newspaper, generated much discussion as the Ottoman population struggled to formulate a new language of identity. The Tanzimat reforms extended the definition of Ottoman to include the newly equal rights of the minority populations, but Abdülhamit moved to claw this back via pan-Islamism. It was this that partly drove the determined pan-Ottomanism of the early Young Turk generation in exile in Europe at the start of the twentieth century, whose factions included Turks and members of the minority populations all equally disenchanted with Abdülhamit's denial of Tanzimat ideals. But in the years after 1908, pan-Turkism and Ottomanism were to be replaced as Turkism – influenced by the longstanding intellectual exchange with Europe – emerged as the dominant ideology.

European Orientalists had, since the development of Turkology in the eighteenth century, started to throw light on the role of pre-Islamic Turks in Asia and Europe. By the mid-nineteenth century, their linguistic studies of Turkic languages and the construction of an honourable history for Turkic speakers in the development of civilisation were becoming known to Ottomans.[6] Ideas spread to Turkey via Turks studying abroad, Westerners visiting Istanbul and, in the mid-nineteenth century, the arrival in Ottoman dominions of European revolutionaries fleeing the failed revolts of 1848 (who combined with Turkology the romantic nationalism of Central Europe). Ottomans studying abroad or in exile, and those at home, began to engage in debates about language, history and identity in the context of nascent discourses of nationalism. Within this there were overlapping and competing areas of interest. The Russian Turks who arrived in vast numbers in the late nineteenth century brought with them new knowledges about the Tartars and other non-Muslim Turks of Central Asia, which – for some – nurtured dreams of a pan-Turanic polity spanning Ottoman and Russian dominions that lasted into the First World War.

The demise of regional alternatives that stressed Ottoman, ethnic or religious affiliations in favour of a Westernised model of the nation-state did not mean that opposition to Westernism disappeared, although it did develop in new forms. This was no doubt influenced initially by the strong anti-Western sentiment held by many Turks after the Western-supported losses of Ottoman lands in the Balkan campaigns. This was exacerbated by what they saw as Turkey's poor treatment by the great powers during the First World War and then driven to boiling point by the ultimate insult of the foreign occupation of Istanbul.

When the Allies occupied Istanbul in 1918 many of the nationalists moved to Ankara, where Mustafa Kemal was co-ordinating national resistance. Halide Edib and her husband stayed in Istanbul until 1920, so she was there when the Greeks invaded Izmir in 1919. This event was calamitous for the beleaguered Turks and compounded the Allied occupation of former Ottoman territories. The invasion was the culmination of Greece's long-held dream of uniting the Greek populations on both sides of the Aegean. Having joined the Allies towards the end of the war, the Greek Prime Minister Venizelos gained Allied support for the occupation of Izmir, and the Greek fleet was greeted with joy by the city's Greek residents. A campaign of murder and terror ensued, often assisted by the local minority population. Events at Izmir, and the subsequent appropriation of further territory by the triumphant Greeks, galvanised support for the nationalist forces and opposition was vocal. In Istanbul Halide Edib made her now famous passionate speech at a public rally in Sultanahmet Square (23 May 1919). This venture into public politics by a woman was remarkable – for although Edib was well known as a writer, her presence in public was still a radical departure.

The period in which the Allies occupied Istanbul and partitioned Anatolia was presided over by Mehmet Resat V's successor Mehmet VI (Vahideddin), whose co-operation was secured by the British. When the recently elected nationalist-sympathising parliament was dissolved under British pressure, in March 1920, Kemal made Ankara the official base of the nationalist government in opposition and was joined by supporters fleeing Istanbul, now entirely under British control. In Ankara the Grand National Assembly was established on 19 March 1920 with Kemal as its president. Halide Edib and her second husband Adnan Adıvar arrived in Ankara on 1 April 1920 having fled into hiding to avoid arrest after the closure of parliament. Once there, Edib served closely with Kemal and the nationalist leadership and with them was condemned to death in May 1920 by the Istanbul government, then collaborating with the Allied powers. She was in Ankara in time for the first meeting of the Assembly that was opened on 23 April 1920, with her husband serving as minister for health and later as vice president of the Assembly. Halide Edib, meanwhile, worked with colleagues to set up a press bureau, translating foreign reports and issuing communiqués from the Ankara government to counter Istanbul/Allied briefings against them. The constitution was passed on 20 January 1921.

When the Istanbul government accepted the terms of the Treaty of Sèvres (10 August 1920) under which Turkey lost all her European and Arab territories the nationalists declared them to be traitors. The war continued with the campaigns against the Greeks acting as the deciding factors. Halide Edib volunteered and was made a sergeant, rising to the rank of sergeant major. Finally, in September 1922, the nationalists won the war and the lengthy negotiations commenced that were to lead to the Treaty of Lausanne on 24 July 1923. The Turkish Republic was declared on 29 October 1923, with Kemal as its first president. During that period the sultanate was ended, and the caliphate was temporarily restructured as a civil appointment, but this too was dissolved upon independence in 1924 (despite heavy opposition from within the Grand National Assembly as well as without).

The debate about secularisation was one of several subjects that divided nationalist factions in Ankara. The Islamists were opposed for obvious reasons and wanted a more strongly Islamic state. Others, known as the Westernists, among whom were included Edib and her husband, supported a Westernising policy but were loyal to the ideal of the Tanzimat constitution, which conceptualised the state as Islamic and therefore to be headed by the sultan/caliph. They were vocal in their opposition to the abolition of the caliphate, arguing instead that the modernity of the West was to be embraced along with free market economics but within the context of a strongly reformed Islam, cured of superstition and the obscurantism fostered by a conservative clergy eager to hold onto power. In contrast, the Easternists saw an Eastern social and political model as an alternative (Edib 1928, Berkes 1964). Encouraged by the Bolshevik Revolution that had ended the Russian Empire, the Easternists (not all of whom were Communists) saw the end of the Ottoman Empire as a chance to promote affiliations between peoples on a new level and looked to foster alliances with other Muslim nations in the struggle against Western imperialism. Their radical secularist programme (including women's suffrage) may have accorded with many of Kemalism's aims but not with his free market economics. The debates of the war years continued after independence but Kemal moved increasingly towards autocracy, constructing a programme of top-down reform to be implemented by strong and uncontested leadership. As he moved towards a one-party system, Westernist opposition figures and groups, including Halide Edib and her husband, reformed as the Progressive Republican Party (PRP) in November 1924. But by June 1925 the PRP, along with the Turkish Communists, had been suppressed, Halide Edib and Adnan Adıvar went into exile in Britain. The terms of their exile remain unclear, and though Adıvar was cleared *in absentia* of any part in the June 1926 plot against Kemal's life, they remained away until after the president's death.

It was the exclusionary potential of Turkism that was to provide Kemal with an ideology to unify and encourage the war-torn nation into the aggressive modernisation of state and society that he felt was necessary for Turkey's economic independence (Berkes 1964). Gökalp, who died in 1924, was never as anti-clerical as Atatürk was to become, though his Turkist ideology proved a far more effective challenge to Islam than Westernism (Berkes 1964). Moving away from his earlier more pan-Turanist position, Gökalp developed the ideas of his mentor Durkheim to emphasise the role of nation rather than society, and turned to the pre-Islamic Turkish past for the roots of a popular social structure. Turkism provided an affective link to the heroic Turkic peoples of ancient Central Asia without hankering after the now lost Ottoman territories essential to the geographically more extensive pan-Turkism or pan-Turanism of the Young Ottomans. The ideological shift required to get Turks to think of themselves as Turks was enormous.

The discussion about the development of the Turkish language (away from the influence of Persian and Arabic forms) that was to be so influential in the development of Turkish literature and Kemalist language reform, took on new life in the context of the international exchanges of the turn of the century. As Kushner points out, the widely accessed newspapers of Abdülhamit's time were censored, but discussion about politics could be transferred into other territories: the fervent debate about language and literary form was also a coded debate about politics and identity. In this endlessly shifting controversy, all the terms by which were designated the populations of the empire became unfixed, with millet being reconceptualised in some quarters outside its usual signification of a faith community. The Turkish identity that was being formed was also in its early stages often pan-Turkist, in keeping with other European romantic nationalisms like those of the Germans and Poles that were also not linked to securely bounded states (Lewis 1968). Whilst the Young Turks in exile and in 1908 were initially committed to Ottomanism, by the time regional nationalisms and the First World War had decimated Ottoman territories the smaller geography imagined by Gökalp's Turkism came into its own. This simultaneously shifted the terrain away from the pan-Islamic complexion of much pre-war rhetoric: although the loss of Christian territories – and the forced migrations of population exchanges with Greece after the First World War – had in fact rendered what was left as a largely Muslim entity, Turkism was significant in helping to untie the link to Islam by stressing the valour of the pre-Islamic Turks. Previously, this had been an era of little interest to the Ottomans whose historiography had been dynastic in concern and restricted therefore to the post-Islamic period (Lewis 1968).

The labels that are attached to Ottoman women authors have to be considered in relation to these changing ideas about national, regional and religious identity. As I noted in the introduction, they all knew the value of a regional identification for the sales of their books, though it is hard in the absence of archival evidence to tease out the relationship between the publication process (commissioning, editing, reviews) and their shifting forms of personal identity. Whilst they variously use the terms Turkish and Ottoman, they are united in all calling themselves Oriental – a term not in common usage today and one that is sometimes considered to have derogatory overtones, as well as being remarkably imprecise. But yet this is the term that is used by and about them, so I do at times refer to them as Oriental women. But who or what is the 'Oriental woman'? It is best to imagine that I am using the term 'Oriental' with inverted commas to signify that it is to be understood as a constructed, relative term, not simply as one of neutral, geographic description. One could also put inverted commas around 'woman', but I am taking it as read that gender and femininity are understood to be constructed terms of identification, not natural givens. 'European' is, of course, similarly non-natural. The easiest way to think about how I am using 'Oriental' is to consider it as a classification for one who has been *Orientalised*; that is racialised in the specific terms of an Orientalist discourse, which is also gendered and classed.

The elements that made up the identification Oriental changed over time and were, in the case of Orientalised subjects writing for the West, repositioned by changes in both local and international discourses of racialised difference and concepts of empire and nation. Bowman Dodd in 1904 gives a sense of how surprising this shift in terminology could be to the outside observer. She wryly speculates on the political implications for the internal coherence of the Ottoman state of altered Western conceptions of the Ottoman population. Having marvelled at the Western habit of defining Turks as anyone 'living south of Austria and Hungary' she notes how

> [m]issionaries still further complicate the confusion in the popular mind, by their free use of the word 'heathen.'... With the comparatively recent revolt of the Greek Christian in the north several exceptions to this universal classification have been made. The greatly exaggerated 'Bulgarian atrocities' made known the hitherto unsuspected fact that Bulgaria called itself Christian. When Servia [sic] and Montenegro joined the Bulgarians in their revolt against the Turkish yoke two more 'Christian' nations were born out of the vague and misty Eastern fog of 'heathendom.'
>
> The Armenian made his entrance upon the political stage in similar dramatic fashion ... [and] still another 'Christian' nation was differentiated from the 'heathendom' of Turkey. (Dodd 1904: 426–7)

The shift from the multi-ethnic identification of Ottoman to the exclusive republican identification of Turkish occurred during the collective life span of the authors covered here, and was experienced and judged by them in different ways. The non-fixity of the designation 'Oriental woman' is also important in relation to internal, local differentiations between Oriental women. Halide Edib, who identified herself as Oriental, was a Turkish Muslim who started her life as an Ottoman subject and became a Turkish citizen with the establishment of the republic in 1923. Demetra Vaka Brown also called herself Ottoman and identified herself as of the Orient, yet she, though born and raised in Turkey, was of Greek Christian descent. Although Vaka Brown professed great affinity with segregated life, she was not Muslim and knew segregated society only as a visitor to Muslim houses. In both their work a range of other Oriental and Occidental gendered categories are deployed, such as Armenian, Albanian, Perote (the non-Muslim Ottomans living in the Pera region of Constantinople, also the European/foreign quarter, see Chapters Three and Five), Levantine, Syrian, Negro and Circassian, all of which are portrayed as having different meanings for Ottoman or Occidental readers and which often had different meanings in different places. Many of these terms went on to change dramatically with the breakdown of pan-Ottomanism and the advent of local nationalisms.

For Vaka Brown this posed particular problems. Her identification was rooted in the complexities of an Ottoman subjecthood that she often characterised in relation to her Byzantine heritage. Her allusions to the great Christian empire place her as Christian and Greek, but not as Athenian – emphasising her roots in Istanbul. This Byzantine identification was a popular if mythic allegiance among diaspora Greeks at the turn of the century, linked to longstanding hopes for a return to the 'Great Idea' of the Hellenic Empire. It also offered Vaka Brown a way to distance herself from the Athenians whose support for Constantine she deplored and whose invasion of Anatolia (even under her much-admired Venizelos) she did not support. Instead, she played up the connection of Byzantium to contemporary Istanbul and presented herself as an Ottoman, still struggling in the final months of the empire to salvage an Ottoman identification that she knew was beyond repair. In 1922 she dedicated *Unveiled* with these words to the failed Ottomanist leader Prince Sabaheddine:

> We met when the army of your race and that of mine were clashing on the battle-field; yet there was no prejudice, no antagonism, no hatred between us. You knew me to be a Greek by blood, and born in Turkey; yet you accepted me as Ottomans should accept each other – as children of the same empire ... we came together, not as a Turk and a Greek, but as two Ottomans, loving the Ottoman Empire, our birthland, with the same kind of love, wishing for it progress and civilization. (Vaka 1923: v)

That her plan for reconciliation – the Turks ceding Istanbul to the Greeks in order to retain their Anatolian provinces – would have placed Turkey firmly outside Europe and as part of Asia, puts a different spin on the inventedness of Europe. But this passage shows the intensity of Vaka Brown's investment in Ottomanism, despite the repeated challenges she faced in the context of the war against the Greeks. Ottoman was important as a form of identification that, like Byzantine, allowed her to retain the nuance of a regional identity that transcended anything as limiting as a nation-state. In this context, her presentation of herself as American, particularly in *In the Heart of German Intrigue*, reflects a chosen identification with the country that she associated with personal and political freedom; 'a land where there was liberty of thought and liberty of action' (Vaka 1918: 1). For Vaka Brown, identity oscillated between alliance with and difference from the Turks and the Greeks and the Oriental. But though she embraced the label of Ottoman, she was more reticent to name herself as Oriental, often using the term to refer to the differences between herself and her Muslim friends: 'I the Greek, with the instinct of the merchant, ... she, the Oriental fatalist ...' (Vaka 1909: 50). When she does identify herself as Oriental it is either used at one remove – 'daughter of the Orient' – or as a label given approvingly from outside – 'I knew you belonged to us Oriental women' – both of them affirming her claim to belong.

Even though these women were writing in a period when issues of collective identification were a matter of heated public and personal debate, they could not predict how the political situation would develop. So for Zeyneb Hanım, who fled Istanbul in 1906 and whose first letters date from two years before the 1908 revolution, Turk was possibly still a difficult term; potentially negative amongst the Ottomans themselves and often experienced as derogatory when projected onto the Ottomans by the West. It had not yet reached widespread usage as a form of self-identification in the Ottoman Empire. Yet Zeyneb Hanım's title, *A Turkish Woman's European Impressions*, sets up a geographical divide that, at the time she started writing in 1906, might well have had different connotations for her than for her readers. This would have altered again by the time it was published in 1913, when she was returning to a war-torn Turkey that was beginning to see the necessity for Turkish nationalism. By the time Edib was drafting her memoirs in 1920 and completing them for publication in England in 1926, the reclamation of the term Turk had become a central part of nationalist ideology and the basis of the new republic. For the nationalists, Ottoman now stood for all that was wrong with the sultanic abuses of the old order: backward, superstitious, non-modern. In their determination to carve a new modern nation-state, the language, alphabet and habits of the Ottoman past were to be spurned in favour of a new Turkic culture and identity. But none of this has a clear-cut historical trajectory: despite the momentous shifts in concepts of identity, the meanings of particular terms and their associations were sometimes consistent. For example, in the two decades that separate the memoirs of Edib and Zeyneb Hanım, they both understand Turk to refer to Muslims when they are writing about their experiences at the turn of the century. It is also in this sense that Vaka Brown uses Turk. But for her the identification as Ottoman was particularly important because she was not Muslim; Ottoman and Oriental allowed her to claim a regional identification that would be disallowed by the more specific Turk, just as Greeks would be excluded from the new Turkish Republic.

When these authors use the term Oriental, they know it is powerful and often out of their control. It is therefore to be regarded as an imaginary category that has attached to it a series of contested and shifting meanings. Whilst it is a commonplace of current critical practice to see all identifications as constructed and contingent, these writers faced the same struggle over terminology and identity a century ago. In their determined mission to write their stories for a Western readership they made strategic use of a term common in the Orientalist discourses that framed their interaction with the West.

Though the influence of their Western editors and publishers is, unfortunately, impossible to track, questions of terminology would have factored in different ways in the production and distribution of their books. Writing in a second (or third or fifth) language for a target audience framed by Western Orientalist discourses, they all struggled to find ways of naming themselves that could make sense for their Western readers – in the context of the different imperial policies and Orientalist discourses of the Western nations they encountered. Their writings are framed by local debates about identity, loyalty and class and are positioned in particular ways through their travels and publication activities in East and West.

CHANGES IN WOMEN'S SOCIAL CONDITIONS

Gökalp's combination of Western ideas in an emphatically Eastern and Turkist social context tried to avoid the appearances of slavish Westernisation (Fleming 1999). It provided a powerful model of society and gender that was not based on religion and helped shift the terms of the debate away from Islam which, since the Tanzimat period, had constituted the only viable terrain for debates about gender (Kandiyoti 1991b). The Turkic turn in gender debates could thus also appeal to nascent Turkish nationalist sentiment. As Kandiyoti puts it, 'with respect to women what might have been rather unpalatable in the form of Western influence was recuperated by nationalist discourse' (Kandiyoti 1991b: 36). Halide Edib was also clear in her American lectures that the apparent 'return to our origins ... [is a belief] consciously propagated by a considerable number of intellectuals, partly for the sake of making these changes acceptable to the masses' (Edib 1930: 213). With the loss of the empire, Turks were now to think of themselves as a nation, with national aspirations and an ability to fill all national roles, including those that had previously been left to minority populations. The Turkists wished to see developed a Turkish middle class and had since the early years of the Second Constitutional Period been using organisations such as Turkish Hearth to encourage Turks to develop roles in industry and trade to support the national economy and help rid Turkey of its dependence on foreign capital (Kandiyoti 1991b). In this, women played a crucial role: as emblems of the new national modernity; as workers contributing to the welfare of the state; and as mothers raising a new generation that was not hidebound to the old ways.

From the start, measures for female emancipation were a key part of Kemalism's modernising policy. Although legislation encouraging female education and employment had been in the foreground from the Young Turk period, polygamy and women's married rights were now the subject of intense debate and activity. As the nationalists sought to modernise the vestiges of empire into a nation-state, it became increasingly important that women (be seen to) contribute to the cultural and economic development of the new republic.

The Young Turks had changed marriage legislation to improve women's rights in 1917 when the Family Code brought marriage under state regulation, rendering a religious ceremony alone insufficient for legal recognition. It also made limited provision for women to initiate divorce, notably in relation to polygamy, which a woman was now able to stipulate against and over which she was entitled to a divorce if her husband married again against her will. The religious leaders who had vociferously opposed the reforms of the Young Turks' Family Code in 1917 continued to oppose the newer reforms of the National Assembly and the adoption of the Swiss Civil Code in 1926. The Civil Code made marriage a purely civil matter, gave equal divorce rights to men and women and specifically prohibited polygamy, something which had only been discouraged in the 1917 Family Code. This effectively ended religious control of civic life. The Code did not give women full equality: the custody of children, though now shared, reverted to the husband in case of dispute; the right to decide the place of domicile remained with the husband; and women's right to work depended on the explicit or implicit permission of their husband (Z. Arat 1994). But it was regarded at the time as the most advanced form of female emancipation available in the Middle East.

After the 1908 revolution the population, especially in the larger urban centres, began to move more freely in public spaces. For women in particular this marked the beginning of serious change. The different regulations about the veil and about women's use of public spaces are discussed in more detail in Chapters Three and Five, but the overall picture was one of increased, if uneven, liberalisation in dress codes and social etiquette. Veiling had always been a habit of the urban rather than the rural population and, as a marker of status, was part of a system of seclusion that, like the harem, was a feature of life for urban upper-class and royal women more than any others. In cosmopolitan Istanbul, where these writers lived or congregated, social habits and the incorporation of Western goods had long been far in advance of rural communities and most other Ottoman cities. But whilst, as I argued earlier, the harem system of segregation was of immense interest to Western onlookers, seclusion and the accompanying habit of polygamy were of disproportionate importance to Ottomans themselves (Duben and Behar 1991). The women writers under discussion here span the generation that saw the decline of the veil as a mechanism of seclusion; from Zeyneb Hanım and Melek Hanım who lived under Abdülhamit's increasingly severe dress regulations, to Halide Edib who famously 'unveiled' at a rally in the American College in 1912. Although there was much mis-reporting of her symbolic action – which involved only the removal of the *peçe*, or face veil, rather than the complete uncovering of her head and hair – the significance of her intervention points to the enormous political and cultural capital that women's outerwear had for Turks and Westerners alike. The second constitutional period saw an increase in women's occupation of spaces outside the home, but public and political anxiety that their dress and demeanour should remain properly modest continued (see Chapter Three). Women's access to mixed gender space was made possible and regulated by continued segregation on public transport (see Chapter Five), whilst attendance at theatres or restaurants in the company of men, rather than of women, was forbidden (Shaw and Shaw 1978).

One of the main factors in changing women's roles was increased provision for women's education. State secondary schools increased under Abdülhamit, often run along French educational lines and teacher training facilities for women were extended from 1870. In addition to the state schools the different millets also ran their own schools which were brought under state regulation after 1869. Advanced education and professional training remained largely seg-regated until the late nineteenth century, with few non-Muslims attending the state training establishments (further deepening the split between the Muslim bureaucracy and the non-Muslim commercial bourgeoisie, Göçek 1996). But the millet schools remained a popular parental choice as many feared the secular influence of the state schools and Muslims worried about the Christian flavour of the (often foreign) staff and the French influenced curriculum (Shaw and Shaw 1978). Vaka Brown, for example, never attended a state school. Her primary school was Greek and when she started at college in Istanbul in the 1890s it was inevitable that she would attend the Greek Zappeion college where instruction was in Greek. After returning from the Sorbonne, she transferred to a private French school to continue her education in French. In the second constitutional period higher education opportunities increased for women with limited access to women-only classes at the university in Istanbul made available in 1914 (for which reports in the *Daily Telegraph* gave Ellison some credit) plus the establish-ment of training for women in fine art and music in 1917. Access to mixed classes in science and literature followed in 1921, whilst the law college admit-ted women in 1921–2, followed by the medical college in 1922–3 (women's midwifery training had commenced in 1842). In most of these mixed classes women were still sectioned off from men (Taşkiran 1973, Shaw and Shaw 1978).

Up to and including the second constitutional period most elite Muslim women were generally educated by European governesses who, though very mixed in ability and learning, introduced Western literature, ideas and habits into the harems. The inadequate and supercilious Western governess was deplored by Zeyneb Hanım, with Edib assessing that the extent of their damage left unharmed only 'the fortunate few who were not morally maimed by some of the foolish and unworthy creatures who call themselves governesses'.[7]

Zeyneb Hanım and Melek Hanım, as was typical, received a Western-style education at home, and religious instruction from an imam. Halide Edib's educa-tion was more unusual: though she also had governesses (English and French) and religious instruction at home, her progressive father also sent her out to school. He had determined that she was to be given a Western upbringing and dressed her in European clothes: 'short, dark blue frocks in winter, all English-made, and white linen in summer. Her arms and legs were bare after the manner of English children, which shocked her granny and made her anxious lest she should catch cold' (Edib 1926: 23). But the young Edib was less worried about the temperature than that 'she looked different from other children of her age and class [and] attracted attention', plus she envied the 'gorgeous-colored silk gowns, frills and ribbons, even jewels' of the other little girls (Edib 1926: 23). These Western clothes marked her as different even at a time when, as I discuss in Chapter Six, elite women were regularly wearing and adapting Western fashions.

Further distinguishing her from her peers in the Turkish (Muslim) elite, was her father's decision to send her to a Greek-run kindergarten. Unusually for Muslims of their class, they were not living in the Muslim quarter of the city but resided near Yildiz (where her father worked) in an area populated by Greeks and Armenians. Her experience of being the only Muslim Turkish girl in primary school continued when she became one of the first Turkish girls to attend the American College for Girls in Scutari, on the Asian coast of Istanbul. Established as a high school in 1879, the American College for Girls (or Constantinople College as it was colloquially known) obtained degree awarding powers in 1899. Initially run by the American Women's Board of Missions, the college often played down its missionary activities (which had anyway been largely directed at non-Protestant Ottoman Christian minority communities) and in 1905 became formally independent from the Mission Board.[8]

In 1893–4 Edib attended the American College for Girls as a day student, being too young to board, but was forced to leave after a year when Abdülhamit issued an *irade*, or imperial decree, forbidding her attendance. As she noted in a footnote, *irade*s, usually matters of general policy, could also be applied to a single individual as was the case with her unorthodox schooling. This anxiety about Turkish men and women coming into contact with foreigners, and about the potential proselytising of the missionary college, was typical of the Abdülhamit regime. The *irade* attests to the prominence of Edib's family and indicates the public nature of individual female incursions into previously unsanctioned spheres. Edib returned to the American College for Girls in 1899, and went on to become their first Muslim student to graduate at degree level.

Given the importance of education to reformists in the Ottoman Empire and the new republic, it is not surprising that Edib, in the years before her exile, focused her attention on school provision. She was invited by the CUP government, most of whom were known to her personally through family and class connections, to inspect secular schools in Istanbul and also undertook with Nakiye Hanım to reform the independent *evkaff* or religious school system, adding for the first time teaching in modern science to their tradition of religious instruction. In much of her education reform she worked closely with the British educationalist Isabel Fry, who had first written to Edib in response to Edib's letter to the *Nation* in 1909. In this Edib had extolled the values of Anglo-Saxon education which, based on their 'sacred ideas of womanhood and home', accounted for Anglo-Saxon civilisational superiority.[9] Responding to Edib's plea for British educators to 'come and help dispel the dark clouds of ignorance',[10] Fry, from a prominent British Quaker family, made several visits to Turkey, sometimes at the invitation of the CUP government. She offered Edib refuge in London when she first fled Turkey in 1909, and again on a second visit made in 1911.

The nationalists continued the reforms of the Tanzimat and second constitutional era. Education was, as Zehra Arat explains, considered by the Kemalists to be essential to their project of economic, social and political transformation: 'the most effective way of transforming the Ottoman subjects into "nationalist" citizens with modern and secular minds' (Arat 1999b: 158). The nationalists opened new teacher training colleges and encouraged teachers to take posts in the country. Here teachers, men and women, were expected to teach progressive social habits by example (wearing 'modern' clothes, making monogamous marriages) to the whole rural community, not just by rote to children in the classroom (Woodsmall 1936). Women now able to enter university were aware that their status as flag-bearers for the new order opened them to particular scrutiny. A woman medical student, talking to Frances Woodsmall, was quite clear that she and her cohort were 'considered not merely as individuals, good, bad, or indifferent, like men, but as representing women as a whole. We cannot afford to fail; it would be considered that higher education for women is a failure. If we succeed it means that we have advanced the whole idea of women's ability' (Woodsmall 1936: 229).

Alongside these new opportunities came new looks as changes in women's appearance were debated and engineered alongside their entry into education. But the new style did not mean a loosening of control over women's appearance. As Zehra Arat's interviews with women educated in the early years of the republic demonstrate, dress and demeanour continued to be strictly policed. Short hair, which generally meant a bob, was the most encouraged, 'because it fit well into the officially promoted hygienic image of the "modern woman"' (Arat 1999b: 168–9). The association of beauty with health rather than indolence can be traced back to another important facet of educational reform from 1908 – the emphasis on physical education, especially for girls. Gymnastics become a formal part of the school curriculum and were much vaunted (Edib features photographs of girls doing gymnastics in her first volume of memoirs) as an antidote to the stereotype of the indolent, supine harem woman of the Ottoman order. The link is made explicit by Woodsmall, who was much taken with the new physical regime.

> This emphasis on physical exercise for Eastern girls is naturally producing a new ideal of feminine beauty. The Turkish beauty contest would not award the prize to the languorous girl of the Ottoman Empire Period, who was suited to sit on a soft Turkish divan in a palace on the Bosphorous with lustrous eyes shadowed by kohl, a decorative figure from Pierre Loti's *Désenchantées*. The

new standard would make quite different requirements for beauty of figure and bearing characteristic of the modern athletic Turkish girl of the New Republic. (Woodsmall 1936: 81–2)

In the period from the *désenchantée* Zeyneb Hanım to the nationalist Edib the definition of female beauty had changed from the Ottoman ideals of Zeyneb Hanım, who – as I discuss in Chapter Three – could not understand why European women spent so much time on 'unladylike' sporting activities, to the revolutionary callisthenics of Halide Edib's school systems. With it changed the body shape, deportment and habit of a generation of Turkish women. The languid odalisque that Western readers expected to find in accounts of the harem had always been a fantasy, but by the time Zeyneb Hanım and Edib were writing she was even more a fiction. Yet she remained present in their writings as part of the Orientalist discourse about female beauty and racialised identity that I discuss in Chapter Four.

Halide Edib was also instrumental in establishing the first formal association for women's rights, Teali-i Nisvan Cemiyati (The Society for the Elevation of Women) in 1908. This was joined by other associations for promoting women's welfare, education and work. The urgent national need of the Balkan Wars and the First World War proved to be a mobilising moment for many women: women's organisations sponsored women in nursing and provided vocational training so that they could support themselves and their families and contribute to the national economy. Though poor women had always earned money, the war years saw poor and middle-rank women enter nursing in modest numbers (working mainly as auxiliary carers) and an increase in the charity work undertaken by elite women.[11] With rich women boycotting imported textiles and clothes in favour of domestic products, the women's branch of the Red Crescent Society sold embroideries sewn by genteel women and offered training in seamstressing. Some women even opened their own shops and ateliers (Durakbaşa 1993). The contrast to Melek Hanım's clandestine sewing lessons a decade earlier could not have been more extreme.

The nationalists, and subsequently the Kemalists, certainly saw the liberation of women as crucial to the building of the new nation. But, as I discuss in Chapter Three, recent feminist studies have argued against the traditional image of Kemalist munificence, suggesting that his vision of female liberation was limited to women's potential service to the state. As Ayşe Durakbaşa (1993) argues, the image of the hardworking Turkish woman contributing to the new republican society was essential to the nationalist modernising project. Instead of the 'degenerate' and 'parasitic' Ottoman harem lady that to their frustration still symbolised the country in the minds of the West, the Turks would be represented by the stoic Turkish man and his modern female wife/companion. Her emergence into public service, often in nursing and teaching that could (as was the case in the West) be coded as an extension of her role as wife and mother (to the nation), was not about individual fulfilment but about contribution to society, very much the tone of Edib's memoirs. In this light, it is argued, can be read Kemal's discouragement of an independent women's movement (Jayawardena 1986, Kandiyoti 1991b, Tekeli 1986, Z. Arat 1994, Frierson 1995 and see Chapter Three). The Kemalists' functionalist conceptualisation of women's emancipation as a benefit for the nation rather than something undertaken and/or led by women themselves followed a long tradition of Ottoman reform in which liberal men's desire to 'modernise themselves [was achieved] through focusing their attention on women' (Fleischmann 1999: 100). By writing out signs of existing female agency (at all levels of society) and presenting women as helpless victims of sultanic abuse awaiting nationalist liberation, the Kemalist account re-inscribed the Western presumption of Ottoman women's total subjugation (Frierson 1995).

The increased visibility of Turkish women in the public world and at work (see Chapter Three) did not end Western curiosity. The Orientalist obsession with the hidden Oriental harem woman that had fuelled the market for women's accounts now transferred to an intense curiosity with her newly visible counterpart. It was not just the West that fed this latest incarnation of Orientalist curiosity: the nationalists and Kemalists were well aware of the propaganda potential of the liberated nationalist woman and pictured her widely in the international arena (Abadan-Unat 1981b, Durakbaşa, 1993, Fleischmann 1999). But there was a clear class differentiation in the new roles for women: for the nationalist elite there was the ideal of the educated professional women, whilst for the majority of the female population the inspirational model was the stoic Anatolian peasant wife and mother, heroine of the war effort. Not only was the educated professional woman not intended as a role for all women (Durakbaşa 1993), but her potency as an image of the new Turkey derived in no small part from her elite class origin. In Egypt, too, it was the public participation of the previously secluded elite harem woman which most captivated the West and which therefore offered particular benefits for nationalist self-fashioning on the international stage (Hatem 1992). Thus despite his warning about the drop in the market for Near East publications, Ferris Greenslet was perfectly confident in the value of what Vaka Brown would produce from her research trip home in 1921. Writing to her in advance of what was eventually to be published as *The Unveiled Ladies of Stamboul*, he glowed that her trip would be a 'wonderful opportunity to present to American readers a full and vivid view of contemporary Turkish life, and the aims of the Turkish people' (1 February 1921).[12] For Grace Ellison, whose writing also spanned this period, and for Halide Edib, who published in English post-Independence, the ability of images of the Orientalised woman to sell books had changed but not diminished in the transition from Ottoman to republican society.

LITERATURE, LANGUAGE AND IDENTITY

The literary context in which the Ottoman writers were producing had also undergone radical changes, integral to the development of Tanzimat, Young Turk and nationalist ideologies. Literature and literary styles became one of the key arenas for debating the benefits of Westernisation for a programme of modernisation. In 1833 the Translation Chamber was established in Istanbul to train Muslims in European languages so that diplomatic papers could be prepared for use by the government. As Saliha Paker (1991a) points out, this soon came to act as a school for aspiring Ottoman writers and politicians, many of whom started their careers in the translation service. Further training establishments were inaugurated in the 1850s and 1860s to select and translate teaching materials that would introduce Western science and humanities into the Ottoman education system. The need to find Turkish equivalents for the style and concepts of European literature, decisions about which (highbrow or populist) sources should be translated, and different opinions about the need to be true to the style rather than just the content of the original, all formed important stimuli to the ongoing disputes about altering Ottoman literary language and forms that had a political and social significance beyond matters of aesthetics alone (Paker 1991a).

As the consciousness of a Turkic heritage developed through the nineteenth century, the lack of a purely Ottoman language became a matter of intense significance. Written in the Arabic script with many allegiances to Persian and Arabic linguistic and literary structures, the language of literature and of the Ottoman court was felt by many to be overly elaborate and ideologically bound to a non-progressive past. In the Tanzimat era the state of the language indicated the state of the empire and Young Ottoman intellectuals were keen to use language reform as a vehicle for political reform. Successive generations continued to simplify and Turkify the Ottoman language, culminating in the abolition of the Ottoman Arabic script by Kemal in 1928.

From the start the move towards language reform was inseparable from the desire to introduce and integrate the progressive ideology of revolutionary Europe. This was seen in the new language and styles used in translations and most notably in the new style of Turkish literature that emerged in the late 1850s. The man credited with leading the development of the new writing, and with bringing French literature and revolutionary philosophy to the Ottoman court, was the poet, dramatist and editor/journalist Ibrahim Şinasi. While training in the scribal department of the military school he was introduced to Western ideas and literature by foreign officers seconded to the arsenal – one of whom was the conte de Chateauneuf, Zeyneb Hanım and Melek Hanım's grandfather. According to Melek Hanım (1926), it was her grandfather who was responsible for Şinasi's interest in all things French and to whose influence, therefore, 'can be traced indirectly the whole modern Turkish movement' (Melek Hanoum 1926: 130). This personal, if overstated, connection emphasises the sisters' place in the genealogy of progressive modernising literature and explains why they were so willing to place their trust in the mobilising effects of literature: they really thought that an intervention from Pierre Loti would swing the international mood in favour of change for Ottoman women. In the context of Istanbul they were not entirely wrong – Ottoman readers of Ottoman and foreign literature had long used literature as a way to engage in overt and covert political debate and, as I discuss in more detail in Chapter Three, literature had and was understood to have a central role in the dialogue about women's emancipation. Just as in Europe (Flint 1993), much concern was expressed about the effects of women's reading habits. Members of the elite, like Zeyneb Hanım and Halide Edib, would have been literate in at least one European language (as well as Persian, Arabic and Ottoman) and so would have read French literature in the original. Ellison was dismayed that many English books were only available in poor French translation and urged British publishers to do more to counteract the primacy of French literature – anticipating the political influence this would afford. Similarly, Demetra Vaka Brown waxed sarcastically (see Chapter Three) about the insalubrious effects of too much French fiction.

Translated literature reached vast sections of the public. Literacy rates (albeit based on unreliable census returns) had improved in the wake of Tanzimat educational developments and Abdülhamit's policy of school building. Literacy rose from 2 per cent in 1868 to about 15 per cent in 1900, dropping after the First World War to 10.6 per cent in 1927 (Yapp 1991). Habits of reading aloud meant that books and newspapers had an audience far beyond the literate. During the Tanzimat much translated literature was quite high brow and would have been accessed by a relatively small number of readers, but under Abdülhamit (who was a great fan of detective fiction) more popular literature was translated and reached a much wider audience. When the Sherlock Holmes series printed in English became newly available in Istanbul, Halide Edib, to the 'childish delight' of such intellectuals as her father and her husband Salih Zeki Bey, 'read [them] out in Turkish', acting as on-the-spot translator. In this she paralleled the activities at the palace where, as

> Father used to tell us … the interpreters in Yildiz were translating them as fast as they could, for Abdul Hamit had an extraordinary liking for criminal and police stories, especially for those of Conan Doyle; the chief of the royal wardrobe, Ismet Bey, read them all night behind a screen. (Edib 1926: 207)

Literacy, which had once been the province of the clergy, became during the last quarter of the nineteenth century an increasingly popular habit as the population learned to read for pleasure, now that romances, science fiction and crime writing were available in weekly instalments. As Berkes points out, whilst such 'froth' was preferred by Abdülhamit's censors who restricted overtly political ideas or international news, literary conventions (such as the crime novel's rational rather than divine explanation for events) and the regular coverage of foreign trivia (curiosities in science and geography) in the ever increasing numbers of newspapers and magazines meant that 'features that were unconventional and even believed to be incompatible with Muslim beliefs surreptitiously crept into the mental make-up of the people through publications' (Berkes 1964: 278). In addition, the censorship was never absolute: Vaka Brown for example was able to import foreign books on political subjects under the kind offices of an 'influential man' who would meet her at the custom house and inform the officials that all her books were of an Islamic nature (*Athene* 1950, 11:2, p. 23). Print culture offered a route to new knowledge and ideas that did not rely on access to power networks, thus extending Western concepts of the individual to large sections of the population (Göçek 1996).

With the development of the first Ottoman printing press in 1835 and the first non-government newspaper in Istanbul in 1840, a programme of publishing outside religious and government organisations grew and continued (within the context of censorship and closure) throughout the period. Newspapers and magazines were in general even more important to the genesis of progressive thinking than novels and poetry, and a press for women also developed. Starting during the Tanzimat as supplements and magazines (in Turkey and the Ottoman dominions (see Frierson 1995, 2000b, Baron 1994), by the 1880s and 1890s, women were served by a vast range of (often short-lived) stand-alone publications. The magazines, on a range of general and specialist themes, often aimed to assist women in the adaptation of selected elements of Westernising modernity (Frierson 2000b). At the turn of the century, the women's press in Istanbul continued to be a vibrant forum for debating social change, expanding again in the second constitutional period (Şeni 1995, Nicole van Os, in conversation), and offered important publishing opportunities for women (see Chapter Three). Ellison noted in 1914 that some 'women writers' were in fact the female pseudonyms of men who undertook to write feminist articles while 'the number of women writers here is still very limited' (Ellison, *Daily Telegraph*, 29 January 1914, p. 8). But despite this possibility, women were, as Frierson points out, writing in large and increasing numbers for the women's press and sending in correspondence. The longest running women's journal was *Hanımlara Mahsus Gazete* (*Ladies' Own Gazette*, 1895–1909) that, as she notes, was supported by Abdülhamit. Whilst apparently extending his control over the press this royal mandate, Frierson argues, gave women a chance to present themselves as agents of the sultan's authority. The journal's typical recourse to an Islamic framework, seen in the writing of Fatma Aliye Hanım a regular contributor to *Hanımlara Mahsus Gazete*, further legitimised their claims that women needed education and opportunities in order to raise better Muslim children by presenting them as loyal subjects serving the needs of the caliph's Islamic empire (Frierson 1995). Education was one of the most important topics in this and other women's journals though, as Frierson points out, the terms of women's demands became increasingly less apologetic as the *fin de siècle* wore on.

Women readers encountered the West and the lives of Western women in nearly every issue. Running from the trivial and curious to statistical reports of Western women's inroads into the professions, the women's press offered a snapshot of Western female life that was celebratory and critical by turn, often giving contradictory commentary within a single issue (Frierson 2000b). The magazines did not advocate slavish imitation of Western life but sought to direct their readers on how to 'accept as well as reject various Western influences, and adapt the acceptable influences into Ottoman and Muslim norms' (Frierson 2000b: 178). This, in combination with the developing discourse of scientific (i.e. educated) housewifery, was an important facet of the Ottoman attempt to develop a indigenous modernity. Like the society of which they were part, this domestic modernity – 'intrinsically Muslim [and] non-Western' – was by the run up to 1908 being conceptualised in increasingly Turkish and Muslim rather than Ottoman terms, with the minority populations being more and more associated with all that was wrong with Western modern immorality (Frierson 2000b). This mix of familiarity, misconception, envy and critique in Ottoman women's attitudes to Western women greeted Grace Ellison and the returning Demetra Vaka Brown when they went to Istanbul. When they saw the West for themselves it also structured the travel experiences of Vaka Brown, Zeyneb Hanım, Melek Hanım and Halide Edib. For women, as for men, knowledge of the West was mediated through print culture and literature, with many Western women writers being translated and serialised in the women's as well as the general press.

Whilst Western novels in the original and in translation were achieving an ever greater public, the novel in Turkish began to emerge in the 1870s (Finn 1984). Most notable here were the novels of Ahmed Midhat Paşa and Namık Kemal who frequently fictionalised discussion of the situation of Turkish women as a means to advocate social and political reform (Sönmez 1969). Fatma Aliye Hanım, the first woman 'to be acknowledged as a novelist' (Paker 1991b: 279), also took a moderate line, arguing in her novels from the 1890s for the rejuvenation of early Islam's egalitarian practices. By the time Halide Edib was writing her first novels in the 1910s, the form was already established as a vehicle for social investigation and the early success of *Handan* (1912) was one of the factors that propelled her into a ceaseless round of public speaking against the Allied occupation.

Şinasi's protégé, Namık Kemal (1840–88) pushed the development of drama in Turkish (Paker 1991a) with his patriotic play *Vatan Yahut Silistre* (*Fatherland*) of 1873. Namık Kemal, like most of the Ottoman patriots in the 1870s, aimed to unite all members of the empire in loyalty to place or country (*vatan*) under the Ottoman caliph. But the implicit link of the *vatan* to the community of believers in the *umma* made it insufficiently attractive to minority populations. As the remnants of the Ottoman Empire fell away in the twentieth century, *vatan* made the transition to the Turkist ideal of the nationalists. Namık Kemal's play was a cause célèbre and he, like other Young Ottomans, experienced periods of exile under both Abdülaziz and Abdülhamit. One associate who avoided exile was Zeyneb Hanım's father Noury Bey. Just as her grandfather had been an associate of Şinasi, so too in the next generation was her father a close friend of Namık Kemal. Edib, who met Noury Bey through her own father when she was a child, records that Noury Bey and Namık Kemal 'had passed their early life together, mostly in Paris', though, 'for some reason or another Abdul Hamit, after crushing Namık Kemal, had overlooked Noury Bey and some other less prominent leaders of the movement' (Edib 1926: 175).

During Abdülhamit's reign the development of journalism as a full-time non-government profession and the vast increase in press publications swelled the ranks of independent writers and pushed the call for a simplified language that would expand their public audience (Rofé 1969). Ottoman Turks needed to have a language that could 'create and propagate science' to close the perceived gap between Turkey and the West (Edib 1926: 314). Others sought to avoid Hamidian censorship by developing a high literary language, like that of the short lived but influential *Servet-i Fünum* journal (*Treasure of the Sciences*), established in 1896. The leading light of the art for art's sake 'New Literature' movement associated with the journal was Tevfiik Fikret (1867–1915) who went on to be a dominant force at *Tanin* in 1908.

This new CUP paper, with which Halide started her writing career, 'appeared as an event in the country'. 'No other paper had such a brilliant position, such an enormous sale and popularity' (Edib 1926), yet it soon became the focus of the opposition. Edib's husband Salih Zeki Bey was their science correspondent and other literary luminaries from the New Literature group contributed. For the young Edib, 'it was flattering to collaborate with the famous writers of the day [while she] was entirely unknown and was just at the beginning of [her] career' (Edib 1926: 262). For someone still living a largely segregated life this writing activity, with its assumption of a public voice, was a change of tremendous proportions. It made her a conduit through which women could express their grievances, and this in turn contributed to her political mobilisation (see Chapter Three). In the pages of *Tanin* and the many other papers that were springing up to represent views of all persuasion, religion and women were the ideological battle between revolutionaries and conservatives (Edib 1926). In her desire to reform religious institutions Edib was far less anti-clerical than Tevfik Fikret whose profound humanist secularism went hand in hand with his Ottomanist convictions that the 'tyranny' of religion was one of the negative forces of division that threatened the inclusiveness of the Ottomanist ideal (Edib 1926: 264).

Perhaps the most important cultural organisation for the development of nationalist views of a new society was the CUP-backed Turkish Hearth (Turc Ocaği or Ojak). This was formed in 1912 and was at first pan-Turanistic and not linked to any party (Edib 1926) but soon took Gökalp's Turkic turn as the nationalist tendency developed. The emphasis was on educational rather than directly political activities, though its celebration of Turkish folk culture and lessons in Turkish history were a central tenant in the CUP and nationalist's programme of encouraging a sense of national Turkish identity as an antidote to the now outmoded and politically useless (to them) ethos of Ottomanism and Islamism. Turkish Hearth was the first organisation to arrange events for a mixed audience; Edib was elected as their only woman member in 1912. Voted onto the council in 1918, she helped bring in regulations permitting wider membership for women. Edib herself used simplified language in her writing and drew on folklore for her fiction, remembering one occasion when Gökalp (her friend until they fell out over educational reform and political differences in 1915) chastised her for making *Handan* too much influenced by Europe and insufficiently distinct in her Turkishness (Edib 1926).

FAMILY NETWORKS, CLASS AND SPATIAL LOCATION

It was not just Gökalp that Halide Edib knew personally: she had contact with many of the Young Turk leaders and their literary and cultural ambassadors through connections of her father's and her first husband (himself a friend of her father), as well as family links to prominent members of the revolutionary community. Although she went on to make her own way in the nationalist elite, again marrying a prominent man, her imbrication in a social context of elite politicians and intellectuals was not untypical in providing the conditions of emergence for a woman writer and activist in this period (see also Frierson 1995, Paker 1991b). The Young Turks may have been revolutionaries, but, as Berkes points out, like the Young Ottoman generation before them, they came from a class accustomed to governing in the military and the civil administration. Their revolutionary and reformist activities were spurred on by a belief that the nature of that governance needed to be different. This class background and tradition of leadership continued with the nationalists and Kemal, whose top down reforms were in the tradition of social engineering that started with the Tanzimat. Edib came from these same circles. Her patriotism was also that of the obligation of the elite, inseparable from her intrinsic class consciousness: her two volumes of memoir are marked by a romanticisation of the heroic Macedonian fighter and the loyal Anatolian peasant whose deferential support for Edib on her travels and in Ankara spurred her on. It was her class position that first led her into public service where her earliest activities in nursing and education were, like those of women in Britain, commissioned by and undertaken through a network of social connections that were rooted in her family and underpinned by her elite status. What was distinctive about this, not in itself uncommon, instance of women gaining access by proxy to circles of power, was that in the late Ottoman context power was not necessarily determined by financial capital: for the bureaucratic bourgeoisie it was cultural capital that gave it 'its own social resources and its own vision of the future of Ottoman society' (Göçek and Balaghi 1994b: 80). The individualistic ideology acquired during their Western-style training led to a vision of society based on ties to colleagues and to state rather than one based on dynastic loyalty to sultanic and divine absolutism. As primary sources from the period demonstrate (Göçek 1996), the student experience politicised men who, often operating within the secret political societies of the nineteenth and early twentieth centuries, regarded each other as brothers to whom was owed extreme loyalty. This was the paternal and marital network that helped advance Halide Edib.

In this light, her father takes on a very significant role as the force behind her progressive and Western-style education. It was he who took the lead in decisions about her schooling and in presenting her to the radical intellectuals of the day. It was the same in Zeyneb Hanım and Melek Hanım's household, though their mother was still alive. Edib remembers being introduced to their father, Noury Bey, by her father when she was a mere seven-year-old and recalls being permitted to attend Noury Bey's 'intellectual and musical salon'. Here, 'the talk was on a high intellectual plane; but politics was carefully excluded. It would not have been safe to do otherwise; Abdul Hamid's spies were everywhere' (Edib 1926: 175). She makes no mention of his daughters who would have been her near contemporaries and maybe she – young enough to be present unveiled amongst the men – did not see them. But they were there. For it was they – 'hidden behind screens – who played and sang for his guests' (Melek Hanoum 1926: 130). Like Edib's family, it was their father who drove their Western education, 'first of all for his own enjoyment'. In this he was like many men of his generation who wanted educated daughters and cultured wives, but who expected them to marry and become 'Eastern in the full sense of all it meant' for a woman. The gap between the generations of women who experienced the rapid changes of the beginning of the twentieth century can be summed up in Zeyneb Hanım and Melek Hanım's characterisation of their mother who 'spoke only Turkish, and cared not at all for Europe and its ways, though she never once raised her voice to question the master's (our father's) will in any way. She was a Turk of the old school, and between her and us was a gulf that could not be bridged' (Melek Hanoum 1926: 130). It is these personal dilemmas of modernisation, this gap between generations of women and between men and women's expectations, that is raised over and again by Demetra Vaka Brown's respondents in Chapter Three and by Halide Edib's account of her two marriages.

It was not just Vaka Brown's Turkish friends who felt alienated from their mothers. In a pattern wholly similar to that of Zeyneb Hanım and Edib, Vaka Brown owed her education to her father – the man who encouraged her love of learning, helped her to talk politics and who left provision in his will for her education. All her affinity was to him and to her mother she seemed alien, a situation made worse after his death when her mother resented the money put aside for Demetra's schooling. Vaka Brown was aware of 'the lack of sympathy between my mother and myself ... in my desire to acquire knowledge, I neglected what my mother considered the graces of youth, and this created a chasm between us. Years later I was able to appreciate her point of view, and to wish I had been able to feel it then' (*Athene* 1950, 11:1, p. 19).

The importance of liberal fathers for this generation of Ottoman women cannot be underestimated.[13] In signifying their own progressive modernity through an investment in their daughters' education, whilst also (especially for Zeyneb Hanım and Melek Hanım) ensuring that they lived by a conventional code of female morality, these fathers at the end of the nineteenth century anticipated what Durakbaşa identies as the Kemalist male psyche's 'obsession with bringing up exemplary "daughters of the Republic"' who would ensure the family's social esteem through both 'appropriate sexual behaviour and ... achievements in accord with "modernity"' (Durakbaşa 1993: 16). Education for women in the 1920s and 1930s was most often at their father's instigation and bore a direct relationship to their father's own educational attainments (Z. Arat 1994). In contrast, many of the mothers of educated girls had no education themselves and were sometimes even opposed to it. The gulf between Zeyneb Hanım and Melek Hanım and their mother at the turn of the century was experienced on a wider scale after the birth of the republic, as women's participation in education dramatically expanded.

Neither should one underestimate the importance of an elite background, for it was this family status that gave women like these authors access to the progressive milieu that nurtured their intellectual development. As Durakbaşa (1993) illustrates, this was particularly important for women: whereas the legacy of the Tanzimat education system had meant that men from relatively humble backgrounds could rise to prominence through the military and civil schools and then government appointments, women did not have access to these individual routes to advancement. Having to rely on family connections meant that only women 'from the semi-aristocratic konaks of Istanbul could count as "modernist women"' (Durakbaşa 1993: 103). Kandiyoti (1991b) points to a similar situation in the provinces, demonstrating how the recently emerged Turkish/Muslim middle class (assiduously fostered by the Turkists in the second constitutional period) came to provide a nesting ground for women's public political expression. For metropolitan women, such as Halide Edib and Grace Ellison's friend Makboulé, it was family and class connections that enabled them to take a lead in the newly developing roles available to women. In the context of seismic national events like the Balkan Wars it was their social connections that included them among the great and the good running the new Red Crescent hospitals and overseeing school developments. For Vaka Brown, who was neither Muslim, Turkish nor elite, the route to personal development was fostered by her father and to some extent by personal contacts (her friend Djimlah providing an initial entrée to Turkish female society). Her tangential social position followed her to America where she was initially quite impoverished. Not only was she part of a minority population in Turkey and an immigrant in America, but her status in the American-Greek community was also apparently subject to challenge – on the basis of her tenuous class position at home and because she published in English rather than Greek.[14] Her rendition of a modern Ottoman identification, whilst it shared many foundational aspects with the other writers, was also quite distinct.

In these ways personal circumstance formed part of the individual conditions of emergence for the writing of female agency with which this book is concerned. Although the authors discussed here took very different political views, they were all involved in a project to reframe for themselves and for their Western readers the definition of Oriental womanhood, able now to represent themselves in local and international cultural discourse as never before for Ottoman women. Yet the social locations that were integral to their political and cultural mobilisation in Istanbul, were drastically misidentified by the generalising force of Orientalist discourse. To redress this, Halide Edib and Zeyneb Hanım tried to emphasise distinctions of race and class. But, because the signs of Ottoman social status did not automatically translate for the West, this worked with only varying degrees of success (see Chapter Three). Regarded as inferior by the West in racialising terms, they were not the 'natives' of India or Africa. Although they were from an empire they experienced the policies and expansionism of Euro-American imperialism. 'Imperialised' rather than colonised subjects, these authors were positioned as both essentially Oriental and potentially Westernised. This oscillating otherness preoccupied the Ottomans almost as much as it did the West, but for different reasons and to different effect. The impact of the loss of the Ottoman dominions and the new forms of individual and collective identification it required were felt by Halide Edib in 1920:

> It was about the end of May. I had just read a certain British statesman's speech on the 'Big Stick Policy' for the East and had translated it. I was surprised at the storm of rebellious feeling it gave rise to in me. I realised then to the full that we were no longer a nation of empire-builders who were unconscious of their own superiority complex, as we had been not long ago – ten years before this speech would have left us calm and cold; instead we had now become of the peoples who suffer from the superiority complexes of other great empire builders.

The speech, which 'clearly defined those two standards for East and West which the whole East so resents', similarly enraged Mustafa Kemal. '[M]oved by it as perhaps never before [h]is low voice become loud and hoarse as he spoke out his indignation':

> 'They shall know that we are as good as they are! They shall treat us as their equal! Never will we bow our heads to them! To our last man we will stand against them till we break their civilisation on their heads!' Rhetorical as this may sound to-day, the 'we' and the 'us' had some meaning then, though he may have been unconscious of it. It was as if the whole East were crying out in his voice.
>
> I felt at that time that even the massacres by the Greek army, and the Allies' high-handed occupation of Istamboul were insignificant compared with the insufferable assumption of superiority by the West. (Edib 1928: 148–9)

Edib's outrage at the 'superiority complex' of the West was directly connected to her recognition that the Turks had now lost their own version of the comparable imperial superiority that would once have diminished the charge of Western imperial discourse. Now that the empire was gone and they were themselves occupied, the emotional and material effects of Western imperialism would impact on their sense of self as never before. The alliance with the rest of the East was reconfigured from a longstanding regional and religious affiliation (of leadership, alliance and contestation) into a union of anti-colonial politics. Yet, for the nationalists, urgently debating the values of Western-style modernisation, the retaliative gesture could never be one of simple repudiation. Kemal would

UNIVERSITY OF WINCHESTER
LIBRARY

'break their civilisation' in its superiority but not reject completely its forms: the Turks would remake themselves to prove incontrovertibly their equality with the West.

As Edib illustrates, none of these colonial and postcolonial relations were straightforwardly matters of domination and resistance but were always a complex and changing set of interconnected checks and balances, producing varied subject positions within each socio-political territory. As these authors and their contemporaries endeavoured to work out how to position themselves in relation to the West, the image of the Orientalised Ottoman woman remained a central battleground in the struggle for self-definition at home and abroad. The representation of the harem was the space in which it was fought.

NOTES

1 In this and other chapters I have drawn extensively on the secondary sources available to which I would also direct readers in search of further detail and commentary (Shaw and Shaw 1978, Berkes 1964, Inalcik and Quataert 1994, Kandiyoti 1991b, Quataert 2000).

2 See Fortna (2002).

3 Fatma Aliye *Nisvan-i Islam* [*The Women of Islam*] (Istanbul 1891), in Berkes (1964: 287). She also published another work, *Taaddüd-i* [*Polygamy*] in 1899. See also Chapter Five.

4 Kâmil Paşa was more than simply well-connected in Britain; the rise and fall of his career periodically influenced Britain's treatment of the Young Turks. Writing a retrospective of his career in the *Daily Telegraph* in January 1913, Count Leon Ostrorog, describes how on the occasion of Kâmil Paşa's removal in 1909 the Young Turks, anxious to alleviate British fears that this symbolised an anti-British turn in government policy, mounted an immediate public relations campaign, telegraphing the London press and sending a deputation to the British embassy in Istanbul. But the embassy gave them short shrift, and the English newspaper in Istanbul, the *Levant Herald*, began 'a campaign of the utmost violence against the Young Turks' (*Daily Telegraph*, 24 January 1913, p. 13). In a climate where attitudes to the disposition of European power and influence in the region were an inevitable factor of Turkish politics, the perception of Kâmil Paşa's loyalty to Britain coloured judgement about him in Turkey, making him a rallying point for the pro-British factions and a figure of opposition for those against. This was reflected in Britain where coverage of his eventual downfall in 1913 reflected imperial concern about the loss of Britain's favoured politician in the Porte (see also Shaw and Shaw 1978).

5 Though as Fleischmann (1999) points out, nursing – like other welfare organisation work – was potentially less challenging if understood as an extension of the Islamic charity work conventionally undertaken by the elite. With a long history of Muslim women endowing schools, hospitals or water fountains (Meriwether and Tucker 1999), this new hands-on charity work extended the philanthropy that had previously brought women by proxy into public attention.

6 The first grammar of Turkish was published in English in 1832, giving a positive account of Turkish history, see Kushner (1977).

7   Edib, letter to the *Nation*, 1909, in Jenkins (1911: 25).
8   I am grateful to Carolyn Goffman for answering enquiries about the college. See also Goffman (2002).
9   Edib, letter to the *Nation*, 1909, in Jenkins (1911: 25).
10 Edib, letter to the *Nation*, 1909, in Jenkins (1911: 26).
11 Actual numbers remain unclear, as does the balance between voluntary nurses and those in receipt of payment. I am grateful to Nicole van Os for her discussion of these points.
12 Correspondence from the Houghton Mifflin manuscripts at Houghton Library, Harvard University. See bibliography for references.
13 I am grateful to Gayatri Spivak for her discussion of this point.
14 Kalogeras and Frierson, private correspondence.

CHAPTER THREE

๛ HAREM: THE LIMITS OF ๛ EMANCIPATION

REWRITING THE HAREM

By the time that Halide Edib, Zeyneb Hanım, Demetra Vaka Brown and Grace Ellison were writing in the early twentieth century, the West's image of the secluded, polygamous Oriental woman had accrued the layers of myth, rumour and stereotype of a longstanding fascination. The vision of the harem as a sexualised realm of deviancy, cruelty and excess has animated some of the West's best known examples of dominant Orientalism from fine art, to operas, to novels and popular literature. For political thinkers, the (inevitably sexualised) tyrannies of Oriental despotism provided a foil to Europe's own image of just governance, be it monarchy or republic. In a variety of discourses the veiled, secluded Oriental woman became the perfect image of the non-citizen. In Britain the 'plight' of the Oriental woman and of enslaved concubines occupied missionaries and early feminists alike in the nineteenth century, especially after the abolition of the slave trade in 1807 and the emancipation of slaves in British territories in 1833. As the other European powers moved towards abolition in the decades leading up to the middle of the century, world attention turned to the Ottoman and Arab slave (Toledano 1982). In alternative and proto-feminist strands of Orientalism, the plight of the harem inmate could be invoked as a metaphor for women's oppression in Britain or as a spectre of what was to be avoided in even the most apparently egalitarian of marriages (Zonana 1993). But the veiled, secluded Oriental woman was not always represented as a hapless victim.

Some Western sources, women travellers in particular, were concerned to debunk such stereotypes: from Lady Mary Wortley Montagu in 1763 onwards, there was a strain of women's writing that explained the relative freedoms available to women within a segregated world, freedoms (like the ability to own property) that sometimes outweighed the rights of their European contemporaries. As Melman has illustrated, European writers evaluated the Oriental segregation of the sexes in relation to changing European concerns: this could be the enviable ability of Muslim women to own property and connive in sexual affairs in the eighteenth century, or their power to refuse their husband entry to their chambers in the nineteenth. Whilst the real or imagined status of Oriental women came to operate as an index of female liberation for Western discussions of emancipation, women from the 'Orient' were themselves actively concerned with their own status and liberation. This chapter analyses how Ottoman women presented their struggle for emancipation to these Western onlookers. Despite the overwhelming importance of Western ideas and practices for the signification of modernity and progress, many Ottoman women conceptualised a specifically Eastern vision of emancipation and engaged in a clear-sighted evaluation of the relative merits of Occidental liberation. Rather than see these women's accounts as simple or unmediated descriptions of the true experience of Ottoman women, I want to look at how the struggle to create a narrative voice that can speak as an Ottoman and as a woman without being subsumed under the various stereotypes in operation, is itself part of the political fight for emancipation at home and understanding abroad.

The condition of Ottoman women was inevitably discussed in both East and West in relation to the harem and polygamy. The system of segregated living, irrespective of whether it was accompanied by polygamy, was for a long time common to many different ethnic communities in the Middle East and the Mediterranean, where codes of honour and shame encouraged the seclusion of women. This was often allied with restrictions concerning modesty that veiled or otherwise protected women from the public gaze. The separation of domestic space into the public quarters of the *selamlik* and the private family space of the harem does not have an overtly sexual connotation in the popular sense of sexual activity, although it is do with concepts of male and female sexuality in the broadest sense. The harem (meaning sacred or forbidden) is that part of the house forbidden to men who are not close relations. It is thus the family rather than public space of a domestic dwelling and as such would be where women and children lived and where any indoor work of the family took place (Keddie 1991). For most families those living in the harem would include the wife of the eldest man (the head of the family) and any daughters, daughters-in-law and their children. Children of both sexes had access to the *selamlik*, girls only being secluded when they took the veil at the onset of puberty. Most people lived in some simple form of this multiple – that is, cross-generational or extended – family.

Contrary to Western expectations, few harems housed more than one wife of any single man and those that were polygamous were usually restricted to two of the total of four wives permitted by religious law. Polygamy was for long periods and certainly by the nineteenth century an expensive practice that was mainly the preserve of the elite. Polygamy was clearly in decline by the late nineteenth century as observed by Lucy Garnett (1891) who found only one polygamous household (with two wives) among the many she visited. But though rare, it did continue and Fanny Davis maintained that for the elite polygamy was still a relatively common practice. She noted that Halide Edib identified it as being 'rare in the families who had no slaves' (Edib 1926: 41), surmising that for families affluent enough to own slaves polygamy was more commonplace. Certainly, for the elite women in my sample polygamy was within their immediate or family experience: nineteenth-century sources like Melek Hanım (1872) and Emily Said-Ruette (1888) depicted polygamous households in the circle of royal

families and their upper-level officials; at the turn of the century several of Demetra Vaka Brown's respondents were involved in polygamous unions; whilst Edib
described her own experience of polygamous households as a child and as a
wife. Yet by 1915 Grace Ellison's hosts in Istanbul were hard-pressed to find a
polygamous set-up for her to visit. As Ellison's expressed desire to meet polyga-
mously married women illustrates, polygamy had accrued a symbolic importance
out of all proportion to its actual practice. As a marker in the debate between tradition and modernisation it was dwelt on obsessively by both Westerners and, as
we shall see, the Ottomans themselves. Nonetheless, to find the ultimate model
of the complex polygamous harem complete with multiple wives, concubines
and eunuchs that fascinated the West, one would have had to look to the imperial
harem of the sultan (see Penzer 1936 and Peirce 1993). Whilst for the most elite
households of the royal court this provided an aspirational model, it was as far
removed from most people's lived experience as royal residences are today.

Although polygamy, however infrequently practised, remained a largely Muslim practice, mechanisms of segregation and seclusion were at various times
prevalent in different capacities throughout most Middle Eastern populations.
But their impact was always contingent. As Nikkie R. Keddie demonstrates,
class was often a major determinant. Since seclusion was a signifier of status,
restrictions on women generally impacted more on elite and urban women than
on poor and rural female populations (Keddie 1991, Hume-Griffith 1909). Like
all cultural practices seclusion methods varied in intensity and popularity over
time and over region, but it is clear that increased foreign presence was often a
precursor to increased seclusion. Without realising that veiling and seclusion
were regularly utilised by diverse Middle Eastern populations as a form of resistance to foreign colonial intervention, Occidental visitors would have come away
with the impression that what they witnessed was typical and timeless, rather
than seeing it as a development in response to their own presence. These Western
assumptions and misapprehensions formed the backdrop to Ottoman women's
writing. By the last decades of the Ottoman Empire both seclusion and polygamy
had come to be associated almost entirely with Islam in the minds of the West,
and the harem, as a mechanism of seclusion, was understood as essentially and
unavoidably polygamous. This persisted despite efforts to challenge it: Lucy
Garnett in 1891, writing two decades before Ellison, was already challenging
specific images in the British press (this time in the *Academy*) of harem 'pris-
ons'. She did this by citing not only her own experiences but the accounts of
previous women travellers such as Lady Craven (1789) that emphasised the 'liberty' of Ottoman women (Garnett 1891: 439–40).

Segregated and, by implication, polygamous life was thus central to both the
dominant Western Orientalist fantasy and the challenges to it provided by Ottoman women. The reasons for this can be divided into four. First, the mythic
sexualised polygamous harem was the pivot of a well-established Western fantasy of Oriental depravity, which was both proof of the Oriental's inferiority and
source of much pleasurable and envious contemplation.

Secondly, the prevalence of the harem trope was well known to Oriental women, whether or not they identified themselves as feminist, who in their various ways set out to debunk this myth and present the harem as a home not a brothel. Since the nineteenth century, Oriental women had been puncturing myths about the relative evils of Occidental and Oriental marriage. In 1888 Emily Said-Ruete compared polygamy favourably with the hypocrisy of Christian marriage, 'Is it not bitter irony and delusion to talk of only "one" wife?' (Said-Ruete 1888) and argued that the benefits of Muslim family life outweighed the evils of polygamy. She revealed the frequency with which she encountered assumptions based on the stereotypical harem.

> How many times have I been asked: 'Do please tell me how can people in your country manage to live, with nothing to do?' I had the pleasure of answering this question six or eight times over at a large party ... [where people are] firmly convinced, moreover, that women in the East do nothing all day but dream away their time in a shut up harem, or, for a change play with some luxurious toy. (Said-Ruete 1888: 48–50)

As Said-Ruete and other Occidental and Oriental women pointed out in the 1860s, 1870s and 1880s, polygamy was already restricted to elite and traditional families. For most men it was too expensive, for most women it was unacceptable. But, as twentieth-century sources make clear, its symbolic importance continued unabated.

The primacy of the harem myth is illustrated by Grace Ellison's determination to challenge the Orientalist rarefication of the term. Arguing that the 'Turkish woman is not what Europe generally imagines her to be' (Ellison 1915: 16), she cited the philanthropic and educational activities of Turkish women as they moved towards their own version of modernity. She wrote specifically about how 'harem' operates as a sign within Orientalist discourse, giving this account of her first discussion with Edib, by then an acknowledged leader of the emerging Turkish feminist movement:

> I asked Halide-Hanoum, perhaps the most active and best known of modern Turkish women, in the name of one of our prominent suffrage societies, how we English women could help the Turkish women in their advancement. 'Ask them', she said, 'to delete for ever that misunderstood word "harem", and speak of us in our Turkish "homes". Ask them to try and dispel the nasty atmosphere which a wrong meaning of that word has cast over our lives. Tell them what our existence really is.' (Ellison 1915: 17)

Like Said-Ruete in the previous century, Edib also criticised the supposed superiority of Christian marriage. But she was no apologist for polygamy. In her 1913 introduction to Zeyneb Hanım and Melek Hanım's letters Ellison wrote that she was explicitly warned not to use harem in the title of her lectures, as evidence of the prurient connotations of the word:

> I have sometimes spoken on Turkish life, and been asked those very naïve questions which wounded the pride of Zeyneb Hanoum. When I said I had

actually stayed in an harem, I could see the male portion of my audience, as it were, passing round the wink. 'You must not put the word "harem" in the title of your lecture,' said the secretary of a certain society. 'Many who might come to hear you would stay away for fear of hearing improper revelations, and others would come hoping to hear those revelations and go away disappointed.' (Ellison, in Zeyneb Hanoum 1913: xvi)

Clearly, the 'improper revelations' concerned polygamy and concubinage, concepts inseparable from the term harem in the minds of the West. Again in 1915, in the first chapter of her defiantly entitled volume *An Englishwoman in a Turkish Harem,* Ellison elaborated the sexual overtones elicited in response to her announcement that she desired to return to the 'calm and peace of an Eastern harem'.

> To the Western ear, to be staying in a Turkish harem sounds alarming, and not a little – yes, let us confess it – improper. When, before I left my own country, I had the imprudence to tell a newspaper correspondent that I was longing to get back to the quiet harem existence, I was accused of 'advocating polygamy,' for to the uninitiated the word 'harem' means a collection of wives legitimate or otherwise, and even the initiated prefers to pretend he knows no other meaning. (Ellison 1915: 2)

Neither warning about the sexual connotations of the term harem stopped Ellison from using it in the title of her book which, with its potent combination of signifiers of gender, space and nation, was either designed to challenge directly such prurient assumptions or to capture precisely such a market. In the end, I suspect, Ellison's title aimed to do both:

> A chapter, at least, on harem life will always add to the value of the book; for the word 'harem' stirs the imagination, conjures up for the reader vision of houris veiled in the mystery of ages, of Grand Viziers clad in many-coloured robes and wearing turbans the size and shape of pumpkins, and last, but not least, is supplied for the reader's imagination a polygamous master of the harem, and they have made him the subject of their coarsest smoking-room jokes. Poor Turks! How we have humiliated them! The Turk loves his home and he loves his wife. He is an indulgent husband and a kind father. And yet we judge him from the books which are written, not to extend the truth about a people, but only to sell; the West expects to hear unwholesome stories when it reads of the Eastern homes, and all these falsehoods are put into circulation by expelled governesses and Perote ladies, who have given an ugly form and soul to all that passes behind the door through which they are rarely privileged to enter. (Ellison 1915: 15)

As one who did intend to 'extend the truth', Ellison was still captivated by the exoticism of Turkey and did not wish to diminish the differences between East and West into a bland homogeneity. She recognised the specificity of women's oppression in the East but also agreed that the solution must be localised. To this end she engaged in a strategy of information-sharing which aimed to disabuse the West of its misapprehensions about the harem. This was done in order to promote sympathy and understanding for Turkey and prepare the ground for the recognition of the idea that the West might not necessarily have the answers, but that there might be an Ottoman resolution to Ottoman women's concerns. Having previously demonstrated her clear understanding of the stereotypes that Turkey was up against, Ellison was still at pains in 1915 to point out that polygamy was virtually extinct, even in the imperial household. She extended her discussion of polygamy substantially between filing her reports for the *Daily Telegraph* and refashioning them into a book. But she still noted that Western observers assumed that every woman in a given household was a 'wife'. So again, like the particularisation of the harem, the mythic status of polygamy is quantified and qualified. It is this combination of ethnographic/scientific curiosity and wilful sexual titillation (even those who knew 'prefer to pretend') which was activated by all writings on the harem and with which Ottoman authors knew they had to contend.

Thirdly, it is clear that whilst the phantasmagorical harem plagued Ottoman women in their dealings with the West, the harem as an experiential domestic system of segregated living was the very real terrain on which Ottoman women fought for liberation. So when Ottoman women wrote about their domestic lives in English they were simultaneously trying to encode themselves as 'Oriental' women in a way that wrested their image back from the 'misrepresentations' of dominant Orientalism *and* to argue their case against the forces of conservatism at home. In the struggle for self-definition and autonomy these Ottoman woman writers contested their subordinated position in relation to both Western imperialist knowledges and local Ottoman gender relations.

Fourthly, as discussed in Chapters One and Two, the harem system in particular and the status of women in general had, since the Tanzimat reforms of the nineteenth century (1839–76), become a central issue in the fight against the sultanate and subsequent national liberation struggle. As in many national and development struggles all sides tried to make the status of women their particular property. Attitudes to female emancipation shifted regularly in the intense factionalism of Turkish politics between the Tanzimat, the second constitutional period instigated by the Young Turk Revolution in 1908 and the formation of the republic in 1923. Over a prolonged period intellectuals and politicians sought to reform the Ottoman Empire of what was increasingly seen as an outdated autocratic regime, and bring it into the modern world. For many intellectuals and politicians of quite diverse political persuasions, modernity – of which female emancipation was considered an element – was equated in part or in whole with the West. In most of these discussions the West was a central model, to be variously emulated, adapted or rejected (Berkes 1964). It is within this matrix of competing definitions of what was truly Oriental, Ottoman and Turkish and how to ameliorate women's conditions that nineteenth- and twentieth-century Ottoman women writers represented the old and new woman of what came to be called Turkey.

THE PROBLEMS OF THE MODERN WOMAN

The conservative Demetra Vaka Brown and the revolutionary Halide Edib had quite different politics, but they both stressed the need for a specifically Ottoman or Turkish route to female emancipation. Simply copying the West would not do. This view was shared by Zeyneb Hanım and Melek Hanım. None of them disputed that the three decades in which they were writing were a period of change for Turkish women, but their attitudes both upheld and contradicted the changing political trends towards the West and female emancipation coterminous with their books. This is in part because they were writing for a international as well as local audience and were therefore engaged in a dialogue with the West whose misinformed attitudes about Ottoman women they anticipated and challenged. But it was also because they had in various ways an investment in the lived experience of being 'Oriental women'. The publicly political Edib, who saw military service as a writer and translator in the war of independence and spoke at public rallies, experienced the personal challenges of trying to enact social change: in 1908, even as she was writing for the constitutionalist CUP newspaper *Tanin*, she was still 'not emancipated enough to go to the newspaper office' and knew only those men who were the 'most intimate friends' of her husband and father (Edib 1926: 265). The others, such as the poet Tevfik Fikret, she knew only through their published work.

Whatever their political differences, all the writers I have looked at begin by challenging the stereotype of the Oriental woman as docile, ignorant, inactive and uneducated. Writing from elite backgrounds they are all at pains to stress the noble characteristics of Ottoman womanhood: they may be unlike their European or North American sisters in many ways, but the difference may often be to the Ottomans' advantage. Without denying the disadvantages of the Ottoman attitude of fatalism, these writers emphasise Ottoman women's active role in philanthropy (Edib), their legendary hospitality (Vaka Brown and Ellison), and great 'natural' nobility. Vaka Brown in particular, writing at the turn of the century, poses the natural grandeur and justice of the Ottoman woman against the false sophistication and misguided passions of the over-educated European new woman. Her cruel characterisation of the Occidental feminist grows as the book develops:

> There was so much of the sublime in them [Turkish women], which is so lacking in our European civilization. I felt petty and trivial every time I found myself facing one the those conditions which they understood so well. It is true that in Europe and America there are, and have been, women who sacrifice their lives for big causes. But as a rule it is a cause to which glory is attached, or else some tremendous thing that they half understand, and to which they give themselves blindly because of its appeal to that sentimentality which is so colossal in European women. And through their self-abnegation they [Turkish women] were reaching heights unknown to us of the Western world. (Vaka 1909: 128)

The image of the Western 'New Woman' recurs often in all these sources. For Vaka Brown, the Occidental 'New Woman' is often depicted as intemperate, over-educated and misguided, with all the advantages accruing to her more natural Ottoman sister. The pitfalls of blindly mimicking the American way are indicated in the account of her meeting with Houlmé, her friend Djimlah's half-sister, who has been given an 'enlightened' Western-style education, only to find that she cannot settle for a segregated life. Raised by her grandfather, 'a Turk of the new school, which believes women ought to be educated to be the companions of men' (Vaka 1909: 137), Houlmé was betrothed to her cousin Murak with whom she had played and been educated until she took the veil at fourteen. Promised to him as his only wife, she nonetheless begs her grandfather to send him away to Europe for three years so that she may really be sure that, having seen the world, he chooses only her. Now, of course, she is missing him desperately and feels all the evils of her transitional situation, caught between Western ideas and Eastern life: 'Since they let us share your studies they ought to let us lead your lives and if this cannot be done, then they ought not to let us study and know other ways but our own' (Vaka 1909: 147). Houlmé's problem is that she now thinks that a man 'must be to his wife what she is to him, all in all. Is this not what Occidental love is? I did not use to think this way till I read your books. I wish I had never, never known' (Vaka 1909: 148).

The impact of Western books, notably novels and romantic fiction, is illustrated by the contrast provided by Houlmé's sister Djimlah who, though also raised with a Western education, seems unaffected by them. To this point Houlmé responds, 'True ... my sister is educated as far as speaking European languages goes but she has never been touched by European thought [she still believes that] her husband is her lord, the giver of her children'. Knowledge of Western languages is less the problem than familiarity with Western literature. Vaka Brown repeatedly limits the impact on Ottoman women of Western ideas to a concern with men and romance. Whilst this also fits in with her support for the refusal to export American feminism wholesale in favour of an indigenous development over time, it also allows her to trivialise Turkish women's aspirations. By keeping discussion of liberation firmly within the bounds of the domesticated realm of romance, Vaka Brown is able to appear marvellously contemporary and journalistic (a selling point) whilst simultaneously weaving in a popular narrative of love stories. She thus captures the market both for popular romance and the exotica of harem travelogues.

Although Vaka Brown presents this obsession with romantic love as a childish distraction from the real issues of female emancipation and social change, opposition to arranged marriages was something that did greatly concern progressive Ottoman men and women in the period leading up to the restitution of the constitution under the Young Turks in 1908. The complex signification of love as an ideological idea even if not matched by actual practice shifted, as Alan Duben and Cem Behar have shown, in the years between the Tanzimat and the formation of the republic. The individualism spawned by the liberal ideas of the

Tanzimat led to a valorisation of love among the political elite in the 1860s and 1870s. During the years of Abdülhamit's rule when political free expression was severely censored, many opponents of the Hamidian regime turned to the expression of personal liberty as a stand-in for the political self expression they were denied, often focusing on the issue of freely chosen, as opposed to arranged, marriages. The role of Western, mainly French, literature in the development of this political discourse cannot be ignored.

> Love, or *amour*, as it was often referred to by privileged Ottomans [after the French literary and political writings that inspired them], came to stand for so much more than just an intense personal relationship. It came to be associated with a political passion at the same time. The state was equated with the father, and autocratic, backward political arrangements with patriarchalism and restrictive marriages. *Amour* and *liberté*, then, went hand in hand in a wave of intellectual liberalism that swept Istanbul intellectual society in the politically oppressive decades before the turn of the century. Such passions were domesticated, repressed and channelled in socially acceptable ways during the pre-First World War years. (Duben and Behar 1991: 88)

Despite Vaka Brown's critical overlay, the pull of romantic love evidenced by the Ottoman women in her account marks the legacy of this earlier period, especially as her visit took place in 1901, before the revolution of 1908. The women that Vaka Brown interviewed are depicted as her contemporaries in age and would have been, therefore, young enough to have spent their pre-marital years in the Hamidian era when love, a prominent theme of the early Ottoman novel (Sönmez 1969), 'was often a euphemism, perhaps one might say a displacement, for liberty' (Duben and Behar, 1991: 92). They would have experienced the heightened trauma of the conflict between modernising expectations and traditional practices. Houlmé, who turns out to be relatively conservative in her attitude to changing gender roles, does not believe that the Westernising experiment leads to personal happiness. When Vaka Brown asks her how she would raise any daughters she were to have, Houlmé's response calls for moderation – attempting to make the change in one generation is too fast.

> 'I do not think Turkish parents have any right to experiment with their children. I should not like to give my daughters this burden of unrest. I should like to bring them up as true Osmanli women.' 'Then you disapprove of the modern system, of education that is creeping into the harems? Were you to be free to see men and choose your husbands would you still disapprove?' 'Yes. It took you many generations to come to where you are. Back of you there are hundreds of grandmothers who led your life and worked for what you have today. With us it is different: we shall be the first grandmothers of the new thought and we ought to have it come to us slowly and through our own efforts. Mussulman women, with the help of Mahomet, ought to work out their own salvation, and borrow nothing from the West. We are a race apart, with different traditions and associations.' (Vaka 1909: 148–50)

In contrast to Houlmé's conservatism, her other friends are ardent feminists and want 'immediate freedom'. They '"look upon [me] with mistrust as if I were a traitor"' (Vaka 1909: 150). Their urgency is demonstrated by their choice of the French anarchist Louise Michel (1830–1905) after whom they name their group (Vaka 1909: 151–2).

Houlmé takes Vaka Brown to a meeting of the 'suffragettes of the harem' and Vaka Brown is quite scathing. The women's plans in her opinion are ill-thought out and immature. With dripping sarcasm she notes that the required uniform of grey *çarşaf*s – to symbolise the new dawn – is abandoned in favour of corsets and contemporary French fashions the minute the meeting ends. With no men present the veils make an ideological point for the all women meeting, but to Vaka Brown the specially purchased *çarşaf*s are simply there to create a gratifying sense of mystery and conspiracy. After giving the whispered password 'Twilight' Vaka Brown and Houlmé are ushered into the meeting room:

> In a large hall stood the rest of the gray symbols of dawn all so closely veiled as to be unrecognizable … It was all very mysterious and conspirator-like. The nine windows of the room were tightly shuttered, that no unromantic sunlight should fall upon the forerunners of the new epoch.

Vaka Brown continues in this trivialising tone and is most unimpressed when the leader proposes that six of their number should kill themselves to draw attention to their campaign.

> … I was utterly disgusted at the whole meeting. I might just as well have been in one of those silly clubs in New York where women congregate to read their immature compositions. These were totally lacking the sincerity, the spontaneity, and the frankness which usually characterise Turkish women. (Vaka 1909: 163–6)

Over lunch, at which point most of the women reappear in Paris fashions, Vaka Brown is relieved to see that the women, 'drawn from the flower of Turkish aristocracy', return to type: 'over the meal the great cause was forgotten, and they were again spontaneous Turkish women'. Later, however, the discussion resumes and Vaka Brown is asked for her views. Again, much of the discussion centres on the relations between the sexes. On the subject of the non-polygamous man, she challenges their vision of the romantic Western hero who meets every female need.

> 'Few men are women's companions intellectually.' I said, having listened to as much as I could without replying. 'The only men who are the companions of intellectual women are half-baked poets, sophomores, and degenerates. Normal men, nice men, intelligent men, never talk the tomfoolery women want to talk about. They are too busy with things worth while to sit down and ponder over the gyrations of their souls. In fact, they don't have to worry over their souls at all. They are strong and healthy, and live useful lives without taking time to store their heads with all the nonsense women do.'

Those forty women breathed heavily. To them I represented freedom and intellectual advancement and here I was smashing their ideals unmercifully. I pretended not to notice the effect of my words and continued:–

'If you expect real men of any nationality to sit down and talk to you about your souls, you will find them disappointing. As for American women, they are as different from you as a dog from a bird. Whatever they do cannot affect you. They are a different stock altogether.' (Vaka 1909: 169)

Vaka Brown repeatedly emphasises that the differences between Occidental and Ottoman women mean that their liberation must follow a separate path.[1] After Houlmé's lament that her unrealistic expectations and subsequent suffering were prompted by the uncritical consumption of Western fiction, Vaka Brown stresses that Occidental liberation is not always as easy as it appears to be in French novels. Her suspicion that literature is the fount from which the suffragettes have derived many of their immature ideas is confirmed when one eighteen-year-old 'girl' demands the freedom to travel the world. Vaka Brown is ruthless in her response:

'My dear child,' I said, 'you could not go alone for half a day without having all sorts of things happening to you.'

'But that is just what I want,' she retorted. 'I am tired of my humdrum life, when such delicious things as one reads of in books might be happening to me.'

This girl in her youth and simplicity was really revealing the cause of their malady. They were all fed on French novels. (Vaka 1909: 170)

This diagnosis of the evils of novels and romance is ironic coming from Vaka Brown who herself earned money from publishing 'sentimental romances' (*Athene* 1952, 13:2, p. 49). Writing with her husband Kenneth Brown she produced 'melodramatic' romances,[2] generally set in the Orient which, like *In the Shadow of Islam* (1911), pre-empted the exoticised eroticism of the desert romance that was to be so scandalously popularised by E. M. Hull's *The Sheik* in 1919. Though they sold well, the romances were considered to be beneath Vaka Brown's true talents by literary figures such as Amy Lowell. However, for all that she trashes French literature (which had a long established risqué reputation), Vaka Brown, as Kathlene Postma points out, used middlebrow romantic fiction to explore alternative roles for women.[3] She also, as argued by Kalogeras, emplotted her own autobiographical account, *Child of the Orient*, as a series of episodic 'miniature' romances. Placing herself in this way as part of a constructed heroic Greek history allowed her to 'further her interests in the romance of emancipation she composes' (Kalogeras 1991: 40). In her own writing, romance as form and as genre was able to perform a variety of often subversive and personally meaningful roles, even if it sometimes sat oddly in her mixed oeuvre.

But in *Haremlik* Vaka Brown's response to Turkish women's romance-induced fantasies is stinging, though she struggles to challenge their misapprehensions about 'the seamy side' of American civilisation:

'I do not deny that there are American women who have parted with decency, and whom one divorce more or less does not affect; but the really nice American women have as much horror of divorce as any well-bred European woman.'

Zeybah Hanım retaliates that she had read in newspapers that women can divorce and remarry on grounds even of 'incompatibility of temper':

'I believe' – here the learned lady threw back her head, and turned to the rest of her audience – 'that a nation that has such laws has them not for those who have parted with decency, but for the nice women, in order to help them rid themselves of undesirable husbands. I hear that courts proclaim that a woman may not only get rid of her husband, but that the husband shall continue to support her. Can you tell me after that America does not uphold divorce?'

I was rather staggered by her argument, although I knew that fundamentally she was mistaken.

'What you say is true, in a way,' I admitted; 'but the fact remains that nice American women do not believe in indiscriminate divorcing.'

'Oh, well, there are always backward women in every country. I was told by an American lady, once, that not to be divorced nowadays was the exception. And wait till the women have the power to vote. That is the one thing the American men are afraid to grant to women, because they know that then women will make laws to suit themselves.'

I did not ask Zeybah Hanoum how much farther women could go, with the ballot, than she thought they already had gone, in the home of the free. (Vaka 1909: 170–3)

Vaka Brown's sarcasm is not her last resort; she is given the opportunity to be openly directive. As an antidote to their literature- and misinformation-induced 'malady' Vaka Brown recommends the Turkish women to take advantage of the benefits offered to women by Islam. They should campaign for change in a more moderate and 'sensible way', and

take into consideration the others who are involved in it. For example, I should think that you ought to tear down that banner of 'Down with the Old Ideas!' and put up another reading: 'Respect for the Old Ideas. Freedom to the New!'. Then, instead of closeting yourselves together behaving like imitation French anarchists, you ought to have your meetings in the open. Since you all wear your veils, you can invite the men who are sympathetic to your movement, to take an interest in it. Little by little, more men will come, and also more women. Really your troubles are not so serious as those of European women because under the laws of the Koran women have many privileges unheard of in other countries. The Mussulman system is very socialistic. What you want is to be free to mingle with men. Since you want it, you had better have it, though you are overrating the privilege. There is a great deal of poetry and a great deal of charm in your system; but if you don't like it, you don't like it. (Vaka 1909: 175–6)

Vaka Brown's admiration for the traditional harem system, which, 'seems to me admirable on the whole', may seem surprising for a woman who now lived in

America, was not yet married, and worked as a teacher and a journalist. By the time she was writing these episodes that went on to be published as *Haremlik*, Vaka Brown was married and developing a career in political and social journalism about the Middle East and the Balkans. Although she is quick to note that she could not stay in the Orient – 'he who tastes of American bustle can never again live for long without it' (Vaka 1909: 221) – she cannot condemn it out of hand. Her fondness for *konak* life means that she cannot recognise the predilection for romance as a burgeoning discourse of individual rights. Duben and Behar (1991) note how both in novels and their interviews with elderly Istanbularis the phrase 'the end of *konak* life' comes to signify the end of an era, typified by gracious living and multiple family dwellings. The emergence of a 'modern' nuclear family on a Western model based on companionate love-marriage was not just about individual choice, it also drastically re-ordered the previously patriarchal and cross-generational structure of family and civic society. In contrast to the pro-Westernism of many progressives, Vaka Brown's need to commodify the East as a recognisable Orient for her Western readers in conjunction with her own mainly conservative politics works against a recognition of the value of social and political change. Although Westernisation was contested by many who also opposed Hamidian autocracy, there is something very peculiar about Vaka Brown's need to defend a system which her American modernism might well render unappealing. This resistance is driven by her investment in elements of Orientalism (see Chapter Four). Whilst part of her selling power is her ability to reveal the inside of harem life to an Occidental audience, and although as a self-identified Oriental woman she has an investment in challenging some negative Orientalist stereotypes, Vaka Brown does not really want to see changes in harem life. Her critique of the Turkish feminists' idealisation of romantic love, whilst also an accurate indication of the idealisation of the West typical of many strands of Turkish Westernism over the late Ottoman period, allows her to patronise her Turkish hosts (despite herself selling romances) and assert a Western superiority to which she as a hybrid subject can subscribe. Ottoman women were also critical of the limits of Western 'liberation', but Vaka Brown's rendition of the feminist meeting allows no such sophistication to those who wish to end their *konak* lifestyle.

THE POWER OF POLYGAMY

Vaka Brown's nostalgia for the charm and luxury of the elite harem is directly disputed by Halide Edib. Whilst to the West the idea of polygamy might invoke 'the sugared life of harems pictured in the *Haremlik* of Mrs Kenneth Vaka Brown, it was not so in the least' (Edib 1926: 144). As part of her mission to represent the reality of Ottoman lives she uses a footnote to discredit the Western etymology of Vaka Brown's title.

> The word haremlik does not exist in Turkish. It is an invented form, no doubt due to a mistaken idea that 'selamlik' (literally, the place for salutations or greeting, ie., the reception-room, and therefore, among Moslems, the men's apartments) could have a corresponding feminine form, which would be 'haremlik.' The word is, however, a verbal monstrosity. 'Harem' is an Arabic word with the original sense of a shrine, a secluded place … Hence it came to be identified with the seclusion of women, either by means of the veil or by confinement in separate apartments; and hence again it came to be used for those apartments themselves. (Edib 1926: 144)

Again and again women recognise the power of words as they engage in struggle over the meaning of the terms that defined their lives. Unlike Vaka Brown, Edib, who was directly involved in Young Turk and nationalist reforms, presents the harem as a stifling environment and polygamy as an institution which must be resisted. She left her first husband when he took a second wife and challenges all romanticisation of polygamy.

> I have heard polygamy discussed as a future possibility in Europe in recent years by sincere and intellectual people of both sexes. 'As there is informal polygamy and man is polygamous by nature, why not have the sanction of the law?' they say. (Edib 1926: 144)

Edib rejects this idea though, like Said-Ruete, she is unstinting in her criticism of the supposed superiority of Western Christian marriage. Whilst she also wants to assert the benefits of a specifically Ottoman emancipatory politics, and has no objection to exporting to the West valuable Ottoman qualities or habits (selfless-ness, patriotism, lack of elitism), polygamy is not an example she would have the world follow. Notably, she removes polygamy from the privatised realm of indi-viduated romance and locates it within the social unit of the household (which includes children, servants and relations) where the hurt is even worse than the injury done to a wife who shares her husband with a 'temporary mistress'.

> Whatever theories people may hold as to what should or should not be the ideal tendencies as regards the family constitution, there remains one irrefutable fact about the human heart, to whichever sex it may belong. It is almost organic in us to suffer when we have to share the object of our love, whether that love be sexual or otherwise. I believe indeed that there are as many degrees and forms of jealousy as there are degrees and forms of human affection. But even sup-posing that time and education are able to tone down this very elemental feeling, the family problem will still not be solved; for the family is the primary unit of human society, and it is the integrity of this smallest division which is, as a matter of fact, in question. The nature and consequences of the suffering of a wife, who in the same house shares a husband lawfully with a second and equal partner, differs both in kind and in degree from that of the woman who shares him with a temporary mistress. In the former case, it must also be borne in mind, the suffering extends to two very often considerable groups of people – children, servants, and relations – two whole groups whose interests are from the very nature of the case more or less antagonistic, and who are living in a destructive atmosphere of mutual distrust and a struggle for supremacy.

On my own childhood, polygamy and its results produced a very ugly and distressing impression. The constant tension in our home made every simple family ceremony seem like a physical pain, and the consciousness of it hardly ever left me.

The rooms of the wives were opposite each other, and my father visited them by turns. When it was Teïzé's turn every one in the house showed a tender sympathy to Abla [previously the only wife, Halide's mother having earlier died], while when it was her turn no one heeded the obvious grief of Teïzé ...

And my father too was suffering in more than one way. As a man of liberal and modern ideas, his marriage was very unfavorably regarded by his friends, especially by Hakky Bey,[4] to whose opinion he attached the greatest importance ... Among the household too he felt that he had fallen in general esteem, and he cast about for some justification of his conduct which would reinstate him. 'It was for Halide that I married her,' he used to say ...

The wives never quarreled, and they were always extremely polite, but one felt a deep and mutual hatred accumulating in their hearts, to which they gave vent only when each was alone with father. He wore the look of a man who was getting more than his just punishment now ... (Edib 1926: 144–7)

Halide Edib abhorred polygamy. Her description of the trauma it caused for the whole household refuses to see it as an individual matter. Although Fanny Davis cites cases of harmonious polygamous households, she also records that even in cases where wives were scrupulous in their observation of etiquette and rank, their children and servants could not always be relied upon to behave and often acted out the rivalries and tensions between the wives and their camps (Davis 1986: 92). For Edib, Vaka Brown is dealing with fantasy, not reality. To Edib, represented as the voice of the 'New Woman' of the Turkish Republic and writing some years after Vaka Brown's first publication, the harem produced a state of mind that was not healthy. The end of the old ways that Vaka Brown sees as a sad Ottoman decline, Halide Edib celebrates as a new, modernising order. But she is torn: she also wants to represent all that is best about Muslim women of the old order (their contribution to the war effort, for example). For her the harem figures as both a confining and restricting space and a place from which good things can develop, as she simultaneously tries to demonstrate the deadening effect of the harem system and celebrate the agency of Ottoman/Turkish women.

One might have thought that it was only the West which assumed polygamy would be so disproportionately significant in the lives of Muslim women. Yet its presence in these sources and the evidence about Istanbul lives of this period gathered by Duben and Behar suggest that for Ottoman social commentators, too, polygamy assumed a centrality in discussions of Ottoman society and morality that was out of all proportion to its actual occurrence. As Duben and Behar have demonstrated, statistical analysis of Ottoman archives reveals that polygamy was rarer even than Ottoman reformists themselves imagined. Led by faulty data, the discussion of *amour* and marriage emerged in the last two decades of the nineteenth century as part of an obsession with what was mistakenly assumed to be a decline in Istanbul's Muslim population and an impression of wider participation in polygamy than was actually the case.

Using the 1885 and 1907 census, Duben and Behar deduce that in the entire period only 2.29 per cent of married men in Istanbul were polygamous, which means that only 5 per cent of women were at any one time in a polygamous marriage – a figure relatively low when compared to Arab countries at the time (Duben and Behar 1991: 148–9). Most polygamous unions involved only two wives, with very few involving three, and none in their sample including the maximum religious allowance of four wives. Their sample, like the sources in this book, was based in Istanbul, which was throughout this period a more rapidly Westernising and modernising place than the rest of Anatolia. For most men and women involved in a polygamous union, the polygamous element would account for only a part of their lived experience: typically a first wife might live the first 80 per cent of her married life monogamously, leading Duben and Behar to reposition polygamy as a *process*, one stage in a series of marriage events that could be conceptualised as a sequence of 'successive though overlapping monogamies' (Duben and Behar 1991: 155). For the years of this study polygamy remained exceptional in practice, restricted mainly to the rural population or in Istanbul to men of a religious background or high ranking government officials – such as Edib's father and her first husband. But even among the elite the possibility of a second wife for 'a man married to a gentleman's daughter', who might also have a powerful family behind her, would be 'no light matter' and, as Halil Halid opines, were such men 'so injudicious as to take another wife, they would very likely render their lives the reverse of peaceful' (Halid 1903: 48).

Polygamy continued to be symbolically important to all sides during the modernising moments leading up to and including the formative years of the establishment of the republic. The furore against polygamy in the late nineteenth and early twentieth century

> was part of the larger ideological battle for egalitarian gender relations and a modern Western way of life; it probably had little effect on what were rather low polygyny rates even at the beginning of the period. But polygyny had great symbolic value for Ottomans and for many foreign observers of the Ottomans. (Duben and Behar 1991: 158)

Feelings ran high and Duben and Behar suggest that both Western and Ottoman sources be treated with caution since Western sources are too likely to reproduce the Orientalist excess beloved of their readers and Ottoman sources are far more likely to feel able to articulate an anti- rather than pro-polygamy position. Attitudes to and experiences of modernisation were often conflicting. As the Westernising political elite in the late nineteenth century sought to move away from the anti-modernising associations of polygamy, the royal council pledged to restrict themselves to only one wife – a 'diplomatic' wife – who could be involved in visits with the wives of foreign ambassadors in Pera. Driven as this was by a desire to present as modernised to the Western observers, it should

hardly be surprising that at least one politician was found to have a secret polygamous family of other wives and children whose existence had not previously
been known (Davis 1986: 93). Even Ahmed Midhat Paşa – who supported Fatma
Aliye's campaign against polygamy – remarried, and without the prior consent of
his first wife (Davis 1986: 90). Edib's own experience contains a similar set of
contradictions. She was raised by a Westernising, progressive father who took a
close interest in her education and socialisation (see Chapters One and Two), yet
the household she knew best was the *konak*-style multiple family arrangement
typical of the Istanbul Muslim elite, with her grandmother and other relatives living with her for prolonged periods. The biggest contradiction in her Westernised
young life was the transition to polygamy when her father remarried. The evident
distress this caused him, as well as Edib and the rest of the household, speaks to
the personal difficulties inherent in such epochal shifts in social structure. The
sort of quandary raised by Vaka Brown's respondents, the classic 'caught
between two cultures' so beloved of twenty-first-century social commentators,
again indicates how the move to Western family models was generally patchy,
uneven and fraught with contradiction. As I discuss in Chapter Six, the adoption
of Western goods, clothes and habits signified all manner of vague social pro-
gressiveness but was also experienced as a process of transition in which both
old and new were fused in an often uneasy coexistence.

   Whilst many progressives had been arguing for increasingly equal marriages
since the Tanzimat, attitudes to the nature of Ottoman family life and the role of
women kept shifting and were inevitably contradictory, as demonstrated in the
Ottoman women's magazines sampled by Duben and Behar. In 1895 one of the
first Ottoman women's magazines, the *Hanımlara Mahsus Gazete* (*Ladies' Own
Gazette*) was preaching egalitarian and companionate relationships for men and
women: 'the family should be characterised by a most sincere, most affectionate
atmosphere. Just as it is desirable that husband and wife be close to each other in
age, they should also have an intellectual and emotional relationship.'[5] Yet in
1913 *Kadınlar Dünyası* (*Woman's World*), organ of the Ottoman Society for the
Protection of Women's Rights (Durakbaşa 1993) and the main feminist journal
of the Young Turk period, published articles claiming both that such needs were
still unmet, 'in the first instance, we have no family life'[6] and that things were
fine, 'other than with a few exceptions our family life is very satisfactory'.[7] As
individuals struggled to come to terms with the personal implications of changes
in married life, even the internalised unspoken traditions of household etiquette
became a sparring ground. Women had traditionally referred to their husbands
using the 'siz' (vous) form of address with the honorific title 'bey' (Mr) or
'efendi' (sir), whereas men had typically addressed their wives with the familiar
'sen' (tu) form and used either her personal name or the generic title 'hanım'
(wife), but now this was under attack. One contributor to *Kadınlar Dünyası* supported this traditional demarcation of status, maintaining that 'it is improper to
repeat one's husband's name and so one refers to him as "our man" or "father of
such-and-such child",'[8] whilst another raged that 'our women address their hus-

bands as "efendi". Whereas that is a term of address used by a slave towards a master. That means that we are just so many slaves'.[9] Similarly the ideal marriage age for men and women was also under debate, with an increasing emphasis on raising the age for girls so that they could be more educated. For men, the necessity that they be mature and financially solvent was widely recognised. Immature marriage was felt to be financially ill-advised and responsible for a high divorce rate, thus incompatible with the move towards egalitarian unions. *Kadınlar Dünyası* augmented this again in 1913. 'Neither should the male be the ruler, nor the female the ruled. A man is a woman's life-long companion'.[10] By the war years the emphasis on women shifted increasingly to their role as mothers, as other popular women's magazines elaborated the necessity of a female education that would produce good companions and better mothers. This re-evaluation of conventional gender and marital roles formed the climate in which Ottoman women wrote and were read.

Women's journals such as these certainly reached an upper- and middle-class readership and would have been the reading matter of all the women writers I am discussing and of Vaka Brown's respondents. However, such ruminations on social change were not only of interest to the elite: the magazine's recommendations also served as aspirational for their wider class readership. If at first the contributors and readers of the women's press were upper-class (wives and daughters of high level bureaucrats), it is evident from price, advertisements and content that by the 1890s both readers and writers were coming from outside the elite (Frierson 1995, 2000b). This challenges conventional understandings of the pre-1908 women's press as a purely elite phenomenon. Beth Baron similarly finds in Egypt evidence of readers from outside the middle classes. In addition to the increased numbers of literate women, habits of reading aloud meant that the illiterate had access to the press too. Men could hear newspapers read aloud in coffee houses in Istanbul or in streets in villages. Women would not be participants in these public spaces but, as Baron demonstrates, women did have parallel routes of access. If one female member of a household was literate she would read to the others. As female participation in education increased, the ideas promulgated in the new women's press, which were often available in schools, would find their way into more and more homes. Magazines were passed on to other households and kept for later re-reading. In these ways the new women's journals of the late nineteenth and early twentieth centuries reached an audience wider than their actual subscription numbers (Baron 1994: 80–93) and were, as Frierson (2000b) demonstrates, essential in assisting women to work out the modelling of an alternative non-Western modernity. With gender politics acting as guarantor of Muslim and Ottoman morality, in Turkey, as elsewhere, the debate on women's changing role in society was public and widespread. Edib notes that it was the subject which caused the most controversy in *Tanin*'s coverage of issues in the early years of the second constitution.

> Among the progressive thoughts which 'Tanine' advocated and which aroused the bitterest opposition was that of the emancipation of woman. The very

mention of giving her an equal chance in education and of elevating her social status enraged the conservatives. They did not realize that 'Tanine' was not yet a party organ and that its ideas about the emancipation of women and the complete westernization of all the Turkish institution were put forth on its own responsibility …

I received a great many letters on widely varied subjects. Sometimes my correspondents asked social questions, sometimes political ones, but each took care to send me a long exposition of his own views. Some of the letters were about family problems and secrets; no Catholic priest could have received fuller and more candid confession than did I during those months … Besides these letters I received visits from a great many women belonging to different classes who came to me with their personal troubles and asked advice. It was through these visits that I first became aware of some of the tragic problems of the old social order. I am indeed grateful to those humble women who brought to me their difficulties in their relations to their families and societies. I got much valuable life material from their stories. The surface of the political revolution was of passing interest, but the undercurrents of life, which started in the social depths of Turkey, drew me irresistibly into its whirlpool. (Edib 1926: 267–70)

Although Edib was avowedly and publicly progressive on women's issues, not least as one of the founder members of one of the first women's associations in Istanbul, her presentation of Turkish feminism is very different from Vaka Brown's. For Edib, this momentous event in the annals of female emancipation is subsumed under the wider national crisis of the Balkan Wars. Female emancipation is located almost entirely within the fight for a wider social and, crucially, national emancipation as Turkey fought to hold onto its European territories. In the winter of 1912 Istanbul was flooded with refugees and wounded troops, as the Bulgarian army advanced South. Many families in her circle left the city, but Edib remained, having sent her servants and children to safety elsewhere. This is how she introduces the foundation of Teali-Nisvan Cemiyeti (The Society for the Elevation of Women):

I stayed in Fatih [Istanbul] at Nakie Hanum's house and worked with the women of the Taali-Nisvan Club for relief and nursing. We, with some teachers and some educated Turkish women, had formed that first women's club. Its ultimate object was the cultivation of its members. It had a small center where the members took lessons in French and English. It also opened classes for a limited number of Turkish women to study Turkish, domestic science, and the bringing up of children … There was a feministic tendency in the club, but as a whole it kept within the bounds of usefulness and philanthropy, and we tried to maintain a quiet tone, avoiding propaganda, which becomes so ugly and loud and offers such an easy way to fame for any one who can make sufficient noise.

The club organized and opened a small hospital with thirty beds in Istamboul. A young surgeon and a chemist, both husbands of club members, volunteered to help; … We took only privates. As the Balkan war saw Turkish women nursing men for the first time, any little human incident became a tremendous scandal. (Edib 1926: 334–5)

Edib's disapproval of attention-seeking feminists is of a quite different register to Vaka Brown's. For Edib, personal emancipation is presented as part of
national emancipation, and publicity-seeking might distract from that. Also, by
the 1920s when Edib was writing, an individualist emphasis on love had been
recomplexioned as reactionary in favour of a view that registered the modern
Western family as the foundational unit of the new republican society. Tracing
the political travails of love, shows how attitudes to the nuclear family and individualism had shifted. For late nineteenth-century Ottomans, the quest for
personal romantic fulfilment represented a progressive-minded attack on the old
order and its associated repressive patriarchal family and state structures. By the
time of the Young Turks in the early twentieth century, individualism had, as
Duben and Behar demonstrate, come to 'be associated with anti-nationalism,
moral corruption and even treason' (Duben and Behar 1991: 94). By the end of
the First World War the discursive terrain had shifted again as the companionate
nuclear family was reactivated by Kemalism as a national model, although the
previously associated liberal individualist ethos was not encouraged. Gökalp saw
the late nineteenth-century Westernists of the *Servet-i Fünum* (*Treasure of the
Sciences*) journal, associated with the New Literary Movement, as decadent and
un-Turkish and now emphasised the nuclear family as a Turkist structure. The
way that he subordinated individual passions to the greater need of the nation and
society indicates, as Kandiyoti suggests, the extent to which 'defining responsible social adulthood in terms of monogamous heterosexuality' was part of a
wider regulation of sexuality that, as well as reforming women's roles, sought to
bring under control the 'unruly' sexualities permitted by the (cross-class and
cross-ethnic) homosocialities of female and male segregated society (Kandiyoti
1998: 280). It is in this context that Duben and Behar note that most autobiographies or journals left by educated Ottomans from this period tend to be political
rather than personal in their tone and content. Reading Edib's treatment of her
life, loves and politics in this light requires a consideration of the extent to which
her account was partly determined by the changing status of feminism in Kemalist politics.

TRANSITIONAL FEMININITIES:
MAKING A SPACE FOR WOMEN IN THE NEW REPUBLIC

Women's emancipation was taken up as a standard in the fight for the republic,
and was central to Kemal's anti-religious social reforms. Policies advocating
female emancipation were of huge symbolic importance for the new regime as a
way of signalling their distance from an antiquated and morally impoverished
empire. They also allowed the Turkish Republic to present itself as modernising
on a local and international stage. Kemal was vocal in his praise of women, registering their contribution to the War of Independence and linking this to their
crucial role in society. Few elite women, like Edib, actually served at the front

(Fleischmann 1999). The majority of combat and front-line supply duties were undertaken by the peasant women who were specifically honoured as a symbol of the new nation by Mustafa Kemal:

> The Anatolian woman has her part in these sublime acts of self-sacrifice and must be remembered with gratitude. Nowhere in the world has there been a more intensive effort than the one made by the Anatolian peasant women.
>
> Woman was the source of a vital dynamism: who ploughed the fields? She did. Who sowed the grain? She. Who turned into a woodcutter and wielded the axe? She. Who kept the fires of home burning? She. Who, notwithstanding rain or wind, heat or cold, carried the ammunition to the front? She did, again and again. The Anatolian woman is divine in her devotion.
>
> Let us therefore honour this courageous and self-sacrificing woman. It is for us to pledge ourselves to accept woman as our partners in all our social work, to live with her, to make her our companion in the scientific, moral, social and economic realm. (Kemal, 1923, in Kandiyoti 1991a: 35)

He repeatedly returned to the need to change women's role in society, often citing in public speeches the errors of the old ways which wasted women's potential.

> A civilisation where one sex is supreme can be condemned, there and then, as crippled. A people which has decided to go forward and progress must realise this as quickly as possible. The failures in our past are due to the fact that we remained passive to the fate of women. (Kemal, 1923, in Jayawardena 1986: 36)

In 1928 Grace Ellison, writing in *Turkey To-day* of her meetings with Kemal, was overwhelmed by his progress in social reform: 'he has given freedom to women, a stupendous reform that has had its repercussions through the East. Already in Syria, Palestine, India and China, his name is mentioned with reverence and awe' (Ellison 1928: 7). In contrast to Ellison's unbounded admiration for Kemal, feminist critics now are re-evaluating his commitment to women's liberation. Some recent commentators have argued that Kemalism wanted to control the boundaries of feminism, too much of which would be seen as a distraction (Jayawardena 1986) and that consequently the early republic preferred a centralist 'state-sponsored' feminism to the development of an autonomous women's movement (Kandiyoti 1991a: 42, Tekeli 1986). Zehra Arat (1994) argues that a feminist development of women's individual consciousness of themselves as women was never Kemalism's aim. Maintaining that Kemal's policies on women cannot be called state feminism because they did not have a 'feminist' intent to demolish patriarchy, she argues that Kemalism only ever aimed to elevate Turkish women to the still subordinate status of women in the West and that gender- and class-specific interests were to be subsumed to the goals of 'corporate nationalism'.

Most historians agree that Turkish feminism began with elite and governmental initiatives and not as a grassroots movement. Correspondingly, its impact was uneven and class-biased. In a pattern that lasted from the early republic to the late twentieth century, the ability to benefit from reforms concerning women (from education to dress) was available more to urban and elite women than to the majority of the female population, who lived in rural communities that remained traditional in their gender organisation (Abadan-Unat 1991). The top-down nature of republican reforms meant that women's rights far exceeded their actual participation in social, economic or political life. Unlike Europe and North America where legislation dragged behind social change, in Turkey government policy moved in advance of women's changing consciousness and experience. When the conservative forces in the National Assembly tried in 1924 to reverse some of the 1917 changes to marital law the press chided women for their inactivity:

> The proposal … has passed through the Sharia and Justice commissions with-out a murmur from women. Almost all newspapers have cried out against this law. However, our women who engage in demonstrations without justification and at every possible occasion, did not act. We have witnessed this silence with surprise as well as some despair. Where were our young ladies filling sections of university classes, where those founding political parties in the pursuit of chimera? The Turkish Republic is insulting you with its own laws, why are you not crying out? (Necmettin Sadak, 21 January 1924, in Kandiyoti 1989b: 139)[11]

There was a disjunction between government-led feminist policies and the expe-rience and social consciousness of women themselves. Although there was a small group of elite women who were vocal (and this must be to whom Sadak refers), even they were circumspect in their public actions. In many ways the elite modernising men who had promoted female emancipation since the Tanzi-mat aimed their politics at education and marriage in keeping with an implicit and at times explicit intent to educate women into better – i.e. modern – mothers and companionate wives for the modernised Turkish man. This did not necessar-ily involve public political participation for women. Despite his public praise of women's role, Kemal was conspicuously reluctant to intervene in debates in the National Assembly, where the traditionalists still held considerable sway and opposed advances in female emancipation.[12] He was at times more pro-active the other way and controlled the development of an autonomous women's move-ment. He declined to authorise the Women's People's Party founded in June 1923 and advised them instead to form an association. This, the Turkish Women's Fed-eration (1924) was dissolved in 1935 after the Twelfth International Federation of Women took place in Istanbul, due to direct pressure from Kemal (Kandiyoti 1991a). Toprak suggests this was because the Congress had passed pacifist motions, inspired by speakers from Britain, the USA and France, that were at odds with Turkish defence policy.[13]

Nermin Abadan-Unat (1981b) and Sirin Tekeli (1986) suggest that republican decisions to make feminism central to their early policies were largely opportun-istic. Locally, support for feminism could be used as an attack on the caliphate (regarded as a prime enemy since the sultan and the clergy had made an accommodation with the occupying powers in Istanbul and issued a fatwah against Kemal and the nationalists in Ankara). Internationally, it showed that the East could lead the West, granting women the vote (municipal suffrage in 1931, full suffrage, for women over 21, in 1934) in advance of European countries such as France and Italy. And, importantly, it was hoped that female emancipation and apparent democratisation would differentiate Kemal's new one-party state from Hitler's, whose regime was conservative in relation to women's roles in society. This explains why female suffrage was encouraged, even though it was far in advance of women's proportionate participation in party politics.

Well aware of the political currency of the 'liberated' Turkish woman on the international stage, Kemalism's modernising ideology prioritised educating women so that they could make a public contribution to republican society. But, as Durakbaşa demonstrates, this was combined with 'an extremely conservative, puritan sexual morality', ensuring that women's new roles did not transgress (modified) conventions of female propriety (Durakbaşa 1993: 16). Kandiyoti, who emphasises that the woman question had been central to discussions of Ottoman political and social reform since the Tanzimat in the nineteenth century, sees the particular complexion of early republican gender reforms as a direct historical consequence of the perceived crisis in the Ottoman social fabric and the rise of Turkist sentiment. Thus by the early 1930s, revisionist republican historiographies were painting the Turkish national identity (now conceived of as based on a 5,000-year-old, and therefore pre-Islamic, Turkic presence in Central Asia) as one that 'was deemed to have a practically built-in sexual egalitarianist component' (Kandiyoti 1989b: 143).

One illustration of the repositioning of women's demands as part of a national, rather than only a gender, issue is Edib's endorsement in the 1920s of women's contribution to the world of work. This is in contrast to writers published in the early years of the century like Vaka Brown and, as I shall discuss shortly, Zeyneb Hanım. Women had already taken on a limited involvement in work outside the home before Kemal emerged as a leader at the end of the First World War. He inherited previous measures permitting women's public labour from the Young Turk era when imperial *irade*s (decrees) permitted women to work during the war years in factories (munitions, textiles, food) and nursing, though their dress and demeanour were still strictly policed (Kandiyoti 1991b, Quataert 1991). Apart from the economically vital nature of women's productive labour, the cultural capital of women's new and, crucially, public working lives was also immense for the Kemalists. But then so was the primacy of women's reproductive labour as mothers of the nation and hence guardians of the new ways, the latter being a goal of female fulfilment whose promotion was never neglected (Z. Arat 1994).

> The most important duty of woman is motherhood. The importance of this duty is better understood, if one considers that the earliest education takes place on one's mother's lap. Our nation had decided to be a strong nation. Circumstances today require the advancement of our women in all respects. Therefore,

our women, too, will be enlightened and learned and, like men, will go through all educational stages. Then women and men, walking side by side, will be each other's help and support in social life. (Kemal, *Nutuk*, 2, 1989, pp. 89–90, in Z. Arat 1994)

In light of these changes in public perceptions of women's role can be seen the tensions in Edib's work between an overarching nationalist rationale, that provided an alibi for feminism, and a very personal account of her own response to the limitations of the old order and the sometimes frightening challenges of the new. Edib's journey towards emancipation – which she, like Vaka Brown, stressed must be developed in specifically Turkish terms – chronicles her changing consciousness. Edib, who is more radical in her gender politics, rarely depicts herself as a feminist. Steeped in nationalist modernising ideology, she disapproved of British suffragists and their 'noisy' tactics, regarding the campaign for equality with men for its own sake as tantamount to 'the revolt of one sex against the other's domination' (Edib 1928: 197). In this her sentiments were in keeping with those of many Turkish feminists whose assertion of women's rights to emancipation was accompanied by a moderate line on gender relations. Edib played a major role in 'creating images of the new Turkish woman'. Her fiction, Kandiyoti argues, casts the 'nationalist heroine ... as a self-sacrificing "comrade-woman" who shares in the struggles of her male peers'. Kandiyoti links this to Gökalp's emphasis on the innate equality of Turkish social relations in which the key characteristic of the Turkish woman was presented as 'her *iffet*, ie. chastity and honour' (Kandiyoti 1989b: 143). Edib's heroines, she claims, are often represented as an asexual 'sister-in-arms' whose chastity and virtue are never in doubt, an illustration of how the nation's need for emancipated but moral citizens determined the self-representation of women of the Kemalist generation like Edib. In contrast, Saliha Paker (1991b) insists that Edib's fiction contains many more varied explorations of female sexuality, desire, frustration and choice. Seen en masse her fiction, Paker maintains, represents a much fuller galaxy of contemporaneous attitudes to women and marriage, not all of them popular.

Edib's autobiographical writing is marked by the conflicts inherent in those discourses of gender, sexuality, nation and morality that frame the terms of her personal experience. Her two-volume memoir covers the shift from the affluent life of her father's Istanbul *konak* to the spartan existence of the nationalist elite in Ankara and reveals Halide Edib's own shifting identification with different models of Turkish womanhood. Whilst she does, as I mentioned earlier, want to counter the Western stereotype of the useless, sexualised sequestered woman with a defence of the many wonderful qualities of the upper-class lady, her identification with this mode of femininity is itself overtaken by the newly emergent no-frills femininity of the nationalist ideal. This is seen in her embrace of the challenging conditions of life in Ankara with the nationalists. When Izzet Paşa and his party from the Istanbul government met with the Nation Assembly in Ankara he visited Edib in her 'rickety' apartment that 'must have seemed to him to be a mere mud hut'. When 'both the pashas involuntarily exclaimed, "Poor Hanum Effendi! Oh, poor Hanum Effendi!"',

> The tone of pity in their voices actually hurt me and made me feel rebellious almost to the point of wanting to be rude. Pity was a shock to my state of mind in Anatolia at that time. The continual hardships we were all suffering and the ever-present dangers amidst which we lived made us believe in what we were trying to do as being an almost superhuman task, and we were exalted enough to pity those who were so impressed by obvious externals that they missed the inner meaning of our efforts and were blind to the presence of a national spirit which was invincible in the face of the worst possible daily discomfort. But they did look so fine as they came in and brought back my old world to me in my little hut with such genuine affection, that I only said in a laughing tone, 'Please don't pity me; it is my choice.'
> And I was really happy to receive them, after all, in my tiny room, as they each offered me some token from Istamboul – biscuits, eau-de-cologne, chocolate – gifts for a civilised but childish woman who had gone into the wilderness. (Edib 1928: 235–6)

In the making of the new nationalist Turkish identity, the replacement of the atrophied Ottoman order is symbolised by the rejection of the effete and politically immature woman she once was. Halide Edib, who replaced one form of elite status with another (now a member of the nationalist elite cadre), will now channel the energy that once went on fripperies into making a productive contribution to the welfare of the nation – militarily, socially, politically and culturally. In her affective (but always limited) identification with the stoic Anatolian woman, Edib in her memoirs lays out the anti-individualist nationalist ideal. Sirin Tekeli (1986) argues that this first generation of women who were 'ascribed' an identity by the state were so passionately involved in their sense of modernisation that they did not see that they had been fed a 'schizophrenic illusion'. The chance to represent the new modern woman was available to elite women who, in between being publicly visible as perfect modern wives and mothers, were given the opportunity to train as professionals, not realising that such goals – which Tekeli argues were not self-selected but ascribed – bore no relation to the experience and opportunities available to the majority of the nation's women whom they were supposed to represent.

As Durakbaşa (1993) elaborates, the entry of women into the world of work was accompanied by an 'extra attention' to domestic duties that brought the new sociological ideas, beloved of Gökalp, into the home. It is no coincidence therefore that alongside their nursing duties the Teali-i Nisvan club also organised classes in domestic science and child development, at the same time as encouraging women to extend their 'natural' nurturing roles into public nursing.[14] As the family emerged as central to the modernising project, social education also aimed to facilitate changes in the relations between the sexes, and the companionate marriage and professional wife became the ideal for the nationalist elite. For Halide Edib writing of how her life was in 1912, this (in the form of her second marriage to Adnan Adıvar) was still to come. At this point she was still being dutiful wife to her much older first husband.

The conditions of her first marriage to Salih Zeki Bey are glossed over in her memoirs with a mere announcement, after having described her admiration for this older man, a friend of her father's and sometimes her tutor.

> I graduated in June, 1901, and I married him at the end of the same year. We had a delightful apartment with a lovely view in Sultan Tepé. We furnished and prepared it together. No little Circassian slave bought from the slave-market at the lowest price could have entered upon our common life in such an obedient spirit as I did. (Edib 1926: 206)

Although in the passage below she calls this a love match, Duben and Behar describe it as an arranged marriage (Duben and Behar 1991: 95). Her reticence about her feelings for him, his position as friend of her father and the reference to her subodinate, pseudo-enslaved, status do indicate that even if not strictly arranged this was not a marriage of equals. However, Edib loved motherhood and lived what she presents as a happy traditional married life – though it was interrupted by periods of anxiety and depression.

> [After a serious operation, Edib felt depressed] Something was hurting me in an unutterable way. I seemed a foolish child playing with words and as though I had missed the essence of life. What had I missed? I had made a love marriage. I had two babies who made me realize the full ecstasy of motherhood. I could not complain much of the details of my daily life, for they were more or less the same as the daily life of the great majority of other Turkish women. I did not envy the bustle and the empty pleasures of the few more or less described by Pierre Loti. I never had 'hat and ball' longings. What I had missed and what wanted, I did not know. (Edib 1926: 229)

The only named woman's complaint about marriage is projected away from Edib's own experience and signalled by the 'hat and ball' cravings typified by Vaka Brown's contacts and exemplified for many by Zeyneb Hanım and Melek Hanım. A footnote explains these cravings as the desire 'to go out unveiled in a hat like Christian women and to dance'. Edib's rejection of the hat and ball life-style occurs in a context of public concern about the corrupting effects of Westernisation on young women. In the pre-republican years when Edib contracted her first marriage, the Turkish press regularly worried about this: '[t]here are many women who think doing housework is disgraceful. They enjoy making themselves up and just sitting round or flitting about town. The influence of novels is great in this respect.'[15] Such hat and ball behaviours would only have been available to women of bureaucratic and commercial classes, a small part of the population, and left most families unchanged. The few public cases were enough to produce a moral panic about the effects of such Westernisation on the Muslim population as a whole. The Western way of life was a predominant theme in early Turkish fiction and Edib's heroines were often Westernised and European dressed (depicted as a precursor to liberation). In contrast, in her memoirs the section on married life presents her as living a quiet and secluded life. She only hears of the revolution in 1908 when her husband reads of it in the newspapers brought to them at their country retreat on Burgaz (Antigone), a quiet island in the Marmora (Edib 1926: 252). Yet even her subsequent involvement in revolutionary politics cannot insulate her from the persistence of the old ways.

> In 1910 I was having serious domestic trouble. I felt that I was obliged to make a great change in my life, a change which I could not easily force myself to face. Salih Zeki Bey's relation with and attachment to a teacher looked serious enough to make it seem conceivable that he contemplated marriage. A believer in monogamy, in the inviolability of name and home, I felt it to be my duty to retire from what I had believed would be my home to the end of my life. But knowing Salih Zeki Bey's passing caprices of heart and temperament I wanted to be absolutely sure, before breaking up my home, of the stability of his latest attachment. I therefore took the little boys with me and went to Yanina near my father with the intention of waiting there for a few months.
>
> At my return Salih Zeki Bey told me that he had married the lady, but to my great surprise he added that polygamy was necessary in some cases, and he asked me to continue as his first wife. There was a long and painful struggle between us, but at last he consented to a divorce, and I left what for nine years had been my home.
>
> It was a cold April night when I [left] with the boys ... What now seems an almost ordinary incident in a woman's life was then of supreme importance and the cause of great suffering to me. My foolish heart nearly broke. I think the women of Turkey must be more used to divorce nowadays, for one hears little of broken hearts in the many divorce cases that now take place there.

Edib, who had spent much of the previous year feeling unwell, was shortly after this diagnosed with a 'serious chest weakness'.

> Salih Zeki Bey's second marriage had aroused such personal curiosity that every eye probed me hard to see how I bore my own trouble after having written so much about other people's. I remember one fat woman in particular among my acquaintances who used to come with stories about the love-making of the new couple and watch my face with obvious curiosity. I neither questioned nor commented; I had a strange feeling of wonder at her apparent desire to see me suffer. I passed the test of vivisection rather successfully I believe, for my calmness and apparent lack of interest made her after a time drop the subject. Still it was a great pity that every one spoke of me as having consumption at this moment of my life, for consumption is ridiculously associated in the public mind with disappointed love.
>
> I allowed myself no sentimental self-analysis or morbid philosophizing at this time, such as I had occasionally indulged in during the other serious illnesses I had gone through. I meant to conquer all physical ills, and I meant to make a home for my sons equal to the one they had had to leave, and to surround them with a happy and normal home atmosphere. I was determined to live, and not to leave them to the sort of life which children have when their mother is dead or crushed in spirit.

> As I write these lines I feel as if I were writing of the life of a young woman who has passed away. I see her lying on a simple bed of high pillows; I see her struggling to write her daily articles or short stories; and I hear her cough continually. Then in the evening lights blaze over the waters, the little boys come back, and she makes painful efforts to conquer her wild desire to kiss and hug them. They chatter about the American school they attend, and finally they go down to dine with granny, while she is left alone in the twilight room, ... In the autumn of 1910 I was once more going on with my lectures and lessons, and the cough and fever had gone. Beside my lessons and writings I had become a busy public speaker. (Edib 1926: 307–10)

Note that, since this occured before the 1917 Family Law, Edib had no right to a divorce but had to prevail upon her husband to grant one. It was precisely this situation – of a first wife confronted with an unwanted second union – that the right of veto in the 1917 legislation was designed to ameliorate. Edib's circumspect restraint and brief references to her husband's 'passing caprices' suggest that other affairs had been weathered; what made this one different was his intention to marry the woman and introduce her into family life. But Edib, by now a published novelist writing regularly on literature and women's issues, expresses no anger at Salih Zeki Bey. She presents a dignified front as she attempts to overcome the unwanted notoriety of the divorce. Fast-living and modern – or, as many saw it, low – morals are not for her. Edib's self-presentation is as a wronged woman suffering for her principles. It is very important at this stage in her narrative, which comes after her first indictment of polygamy in the account of her father's experiences, that Edib differentiates her desire for a modern, Western-style nuclear family from the excesses and immoralities associated in the press with scandalously Westernised young women. At the time of Edib's divorce and through the years of the Balkan and First World Wars, the Turkish press continued to worry that, for some women, the allure of a Westernised lifestyle was based on a desire for decadence in which freedom was equated with a lack of any moral code or restraint. A quote from 1926 gives a sense of this prevailing panic:

> these days women have become alienated from many of their responsibilities. They want neither to look after their children, nor do anything else! These women are the daughters of men who raised them in dance halls ... A misunderstood modernity has made women lazy ... perhaps this situation results from their rather sudden emergence from seclusion into a free style of life.'[16]

It was this concern about decadence and low moral tone that Gökalp set out to transform with his concept of an essentially moral and Turkish experience of modernity. The attendant sacrifice of self and emphasis on women's and men's involvement in child-rearing as part of their contribution to the new nation can be found in Edib's autobiography where she presents herself devoted to motherhood and immersed in a busy domestic life. This is in contrast to her earlier fiction where, as Paker (1991b) points out, female liberation is sometimes clearly linked to sexual liberation. This can be seen in *Seviye Talib*, published in the same year as her divorce, unlike the later novels which produced what came to be seen as the typical Edib protagonist: the heroine who subordinates all personal desire to the national cause.

In her memoirs Edib's version of Western-influenced modernity and egalitarian gender relations includes a strong moral code. In this Edib distances herself from media representations of free-living Turkish women and from her own sexually 'deviant' female characters, as well as from the radical advocates of free-love among European utopians and feminists. Instead, she aligns herself with a feminist tradition that sought to reform marriage with a moral agenda. As Lucy Bland (1995) makes clear, in relation to British feminism in the years prior to the First World War, from the late 1880s onwards most feminists, whilst bitterly opposed to the inequities of marriage law and custom, were determined to reform rather than abolish the institution and saw their campaign in distinctly moral terms. Men would be encouraged to overcome the 'beastly' sides of their natures whilst women would, through legal change and sexual education, learn to assert their own rights over their bodies. The stigma of unrespectability was considered intolerable and ill-advised by the largely middle-class feminist grouping. Interestingly, Bland notes that, while advocates of free-love or free-union saw relationships as ideally monogamous and long-term, many critics – feminist and otherwise – worried that men would use free-love as a way to access more than one woman. European feminism was haunted by the spectre of polygamy and concubinage as a potential of male sexuality the world over.

Edib's memoir illustrates the conflict for women between living out their politically ascribed role as modern and educated and the tenacity of traditional attitudes to female sexuality. As Durakbaşa deduces from memoirs and interviews with professional women alive in the early years of the republic, women were required to adopt a public demeanour in keeping with traditional concepts of 'modesty' whilst also manifesting 'modernity'. Their professional status was designed to make them equal to men without shaking off the 'patronage' of their 'fathers and Kemal Atatürk, the symbolic father of all the nation and especially of women.'[17] In fiction from the 1930s, active participation in left politics was often the preferred route out of female frustration, rather than the depiction of an all too dangerous active female sexuality as was sometimes presented in Edib's early fiction. The moral tone of Edib's memoir distances her from both the disreputable Modern Misses of Istanbul balls and the free-love ideology of those European feminists who sought to dismantle the model of the nuclear family just as Turkey was trying to transfer it. Edib's links with British feminists tended to be with more respectable organisations and individuals such as Isabel Fry (though she also met the more scandalous birth control campaigner Margaret Sanger).[18]

It is where female emancipation merges into the republican project that the differences between the conservative Vaka Brown and the radical Edib become most clear. Vaka Brown writing in 1923 was troubled by the reforms of Mustafa

Kemal. She could not like the new woman of the republic, regarding the unveiled female street-sweepers with concerned horror:

> Turkish women, with uncovered faces, and clad in gray trousers, were sweep-
> ing the streets … Many of them were young and had pretty faces … The sight
> of these feminine street-sweepers never lost its poignancy. It was not so much
> that I resented women doing this work; for work is the noblest thing in life, and
> useful work through which a whole city becomes cleaner and healthier is dou-
> bly worth doing. What pained me in the sight of these silent, gray figures,
> forever cleaning, forever dodging the heedless traffic, was the thought that
> these were the women who in the days of Osmanli pride had been bought and
> cared for and kept secluded. They had then been the joy-givers of a conquering
> race. Now those conquerers, beaten and humbled, were letting their women
> clean the streets over which for more than five centuries they had forbidden
> them to walk unveiled. (Vaka 1923: 10)

For Vaka Brown, who depicts several women happily ensconsed in polygamous households, the unveiled Ottoman woman is a sad sign of Ottoman decline.
In her narrative of nostalgia it is the privilege of class as much as different gender
relations that she craves and her alleged admiration for plucky, modern, unveiled
Istanbul shop-girls is conspicuously muted. But, despite her nostalgia for a Muslim past that was never hers, her predominant mode of self-presentation is as a
go-getting Greek who makes things happen, in contrast to the Turkish women's
resignation in the face of divine will (Vaka Brown's 'resigned happiness' was
only ever temporary). But she is also scornful of Western feminism. Her own less
than elite background and her tenuous class situation in the USA also prompts
her pseudo-gentrifying allegiance to the disappearing lifestyle of the Muslim
Ottoman elite. Class is always an important corollary to gender identifications; it
facilitates Ottoman women's involvement in nascent feminist and republican
politics and provides the luxury integral to the exoticism that pleases Occidental
women.

THE PRICE OF FREEDOM:
CLASS, SLAVERY AND CONCUBINAGE

The engagement with the West that characterised many women's consideration
of female emancipation often reveals a shifting relationship between the constituent discursive terms of nation, class, race, ethnicity and gender. In Zeyneb
Hanım and Melek Hanım's account of their travels to Europe in the early 1900s
the West figures as often as a disappointment as a positive model. Zeyneb Hanım
gives a clear exposition of how Turkish women perceived the constraints of
Western liberation. Like the feminists who spoke to Vaka Brown (1909), she and
her sister started out with an elevated idea of European female life. But these
illusions were soon challenged:

It seems to me that we Orientals are children to whom fairy tales have been told for too long – fairy tales which have every appearance of truth. You hear so much of the mirage of the East, but what is that compared to the mirage of the West, to which all Orientals are attracted?

They tell you fairy tales, too, you women of the West – fairy tales which, like ours, have all the appearances of truth. I wonder, when the Englishwomen have really won their vote and the right to exercise all the tiring professions of men, what they will have gained? Their faces will be a little sadder, a little more weary, and they will have become wholly disillusioned.

… When in Turkey we met together, and spoke of the Women of England, we imagined that they had nothing more to wish for in this world. But we had no idea of what the struggle for life meant to them, nor how terrible was this eternal search after happiness. Which is the harder struggle of the two? The latter is the only struggle we know in Turkey, and the same futile struggle goes on all the world over. (Zeyneb Hanoum 1913: 186–8)

The emphasis on the tiring pursuit of dubious pleasures is constant in Zeyneb Hanım's letters. The two sisters missed the quiet ease and companionship of Turkish social life and were bemused by the ceaseless, and to them pointless and graceless, activities of the European upper and middle classes (sports, skating, soirées). The negative depiction of female entry into the professions fits in with their experience of a privileged elite lifestyle that, formed without a northern Protestant work ethic, did not see wage labour as an ennobling event. As Vaka Brown reported from the Istanbul feminist meetings, Turkish women craved emancipation in terms of education, freedom of movement and sexual politics, rather than a right to work. Similarly Ellison noted that progressive Ottoman men did not 'even want [their wives] to work' only to accompany them to social events like Western women (Ellison 1915: 30). The ways in which Melek Hanım and Zeyneb Hanım's gendered identifications were class- and race-specific are highlighted by Zeyneb Hanım's next lines. In order to argue that concepts of happiness vary across cultures, she brings in another and subordinate subject, in the naked body of her African slave.

Happiness – what a mirage! At best is it not a mere negation of pain, for each one's idea of happiness is so different? When I was fifteen years old they made me present of a little native from Central Africa. For her there was no greater torture than to wear garments of any kind, and her idea of happiness was to get back to the home on the borders of Lake Chad and the possibility of eating another roasted European. (Zeyneb Hanoum 1913: 186–8)

Having previously discussed the myths or mirages that the East and the West hold about each other, Zeyneb Hanım now deploys a stereotype about the 'South' that transcends the East/West divide. The stereotype of the cannibalistic African primitive was a staple of Western popular imperialism and Orientalism by the late nineteenth and early twentieth centuries (Hulme 1986). In Ottoman sources, which make clear distinctions between Ottomans, Europeans and non-Arab Africans, references to cannibalism also occur, though less frequently, often associated with tales of childhood fear.

Zeyneb Hanım uses the cannibal image as a tongue-in-cheek joke for her European audience, but it is also part of her own Ottoman lexicon of racialised division, something that she and her Occidental readers can share. Tellingly, neither she nor her English editor Ellison saw any need to remove or explain it (and Ellison did use footnotes elsewhere to explain what she saw as Zeyneb Hanım's misapprehensions about European life). The figure of the naked African cannibal does what she is meant to do: she simultaneously exemplifies the non-universality of human happiness, thus naturalising the different aspirations of Turkish (Muslim) and English women, whilst also uniting the Turks with the Europeans thus separating them from the Africans. This supports Zeyneb Hanım's (and Ellison's) argument for a separate Ottoman route to female emancipation without positioning Turkish women as too different. But, because the African slave represents the worst of human depravity, the differences between Occident and Orient are minimised: Turkish women, although different from European women, are far more like them than they are like the uncivilised savage. Although it is not clear whether for the purposes of the cooking pot a Turk would count as European, the story certainly serves to separate Turkey from the more primitive-coded others of imperial Europe without merging her as one with Europe. The humorous tone with which the slave's cannibalism is invoked deflates the threat that such alleged practices provide for Europeans and reinforces the African's subordinate position. Enslaved, young and uncivilised, without the power to enact her revenge, the African's inferiority elevates and unites the Occidental readers and Ottoman Muslim writer.

As seen, Edib used slavery as an apparently benign metaphor for her feelings at the outset of her first marriage. She also, like Zeyneb Hanım, refers to cannibalism in joking reference to being told such tales as a child, again in the context of a young enslaved African. When the new slave girl arrived she was put to bed in Edib's room. Her younger sister Neilüfer was petrified:

'I am afraid to be left alone with her, Halidé Abla,' she answered. 'Art thou sure she is not a cannibal?'

We were told a great many stories of cannibals, and their characteristics according to our information were two canine teeth sharper than other people's and a tail. I did not believe in these stories, but all the same I … looked at her. Under the colored night-light she laughed nervously at my face. It was a strange grimace rather than a smile, and her white teeth shone brilliantly. She looked more like a black kitten showing its teeth when it is frightened and at bay than a child. Politeness forbade my making further examination, but I told Neilüfer that I had examined her teeth and she was not a cannibal …

[Later] when Reshé learned enough Turkish to talk, it was most amusing to hear her impression of the first night in my room. They were identical with Neilüfer's. Some one had told her in Yemen that white people, especially those of Constantinople, were in the habit of eating Abyssinians. She was accordingly waiting to be killed and eaten any moment. (Edib 1926: 167–8)

Whereas Edib can construct an identificatory metaphor with a 'white' Circassion slave, the figure of the cannibal is strictly associated with a 'black' child and kept more distant. In this Edib was not alone. Hester Donaldson Jenkins in 1911 reported the same tale told by Saliha Hanım (daughter of Tewfik Effendi) of how as a girl she and her new Abyssianian slave (also called 'Resha') spent a sleepless first night for fear of becoming each other's dinner. The cannibal myth that was common to Ottoman children and those who served them takes on a new significance when it appears as reported material to the Western observer or reader. The childhood story becomes an important component in the Ottomans' bid to be placed at the 'white' end of Western racial hierarchies. The attempt to be recognised as having the same powers and responsibilities as other colonial powers and imperial autocracies had long been an established part of Hamidian statecraft (Deringil 1999), and those in opposition felt the same. Halid Halil writing in 1903 was shocked by the 'revelation' that an article in the *Spectator* on the challenges of civilising the 'dark races' included Turks amongst the primitives (1903: 137), though his dismay might have been tempered by his general sense that 'in no other country in Western Europe is Turkey more misunderstood than in Britain' (1903: 1).

In Edib reference to blackness as a differentiating identity also occurs in relation to the black servants in her father's house, most notably her Nubian wet-nurse Nevres Badgi. On making the traditional Ramadan visit to her 'milk-mother's' house the young Halide was disgusted by the 'incurable smell of colored people, so hard to a sensitive white nose to bear, however that nose may love the owner of the smell' (Edib 1926: 63). When sleeping in Nevres Badgi's room Edib describes how the space in the dark 'seemed to thicken so as to solidify Nevres Badgi into a hard black mass, so hard that one could bite it, as Mark Twain says, but never be able to chew it without breaking one's teeth' (Edib 1926: 63). The allusion to Twain's writing about African Americans ties her description into a regime of representation that would have been recognisable for a Western reader. It also further aligns the Turkish Muslim Edib with the 'whites' of the Occident. This racial polarisation is endorsed by the 'chocolate-colored American negress' on the boat to Egypt who recognises Edib as looking like her daughter '[who] is white'. Marking out a racialised identification was difficult for Ottomans, especially for the Muslim Turks who hovered uncertainly on the edge of whiteness in the minds of the Occident, being at one moment the 'sick man of Europe' and at another irredeemably Asiatic. Jenkins, displaying a common interest in the pigmentation of the Turks, notes that after 'so much intermarriage with Circassians … the race had become light in colouring', unlike the Armenians or Persians who remain darker (Jenkins 1911: 167). 'Cannibalistic' slave girls may have been an unremarkable feature of Edib's and Zeyneb Hanım's childhood mythologies but when recounted to the West, in the context of the harem, the combination of slavery and race brought in a different associative chain of meaning to do with gender, sexuality and oppression.

Apart from the generic Orientalist spectacle of harems full of odalisques (implicitly understood as enslaved concubines) references to the ethnic and racial heterogeneity of the Ottoman population were easily assimilable to a well-established feminist tradition in which slavery in general, and the sexual slavery associated with the harem in particular, operated as a metaphor for Western women's oppression in marriage. For centuries after the demise of serfdom and slavery in medieval Europe, the African slave and the harem slave had stood as potent symbols of oppression in debates about liberty. This was especially so in relation to Occidental women's emancipation. When European feminism is linked to slavery in the Oriental harem the sexualised aspects of female bondage become paramount, as slavery and seclusion mingle in a fantastical display of projection, sympathy and titillation. In campaigns against the international slave trade feminists and abolitionists highlighted the moral and sexual evils of slavery whether in British territories or North America. But it was in conjunction with the Eastern harem that feminists found their most productive territory for comparison. The harem offered not only the worst example of the patriarchal husband's power over his wife but also the spectre of concubinage and the ultimate sexual subordination of women, whether legally free or enslaved. As Joyce Zonana (1993) points out, when Jane Eyre rankles under Rochester's benign despotism Charlotte Brontë could be sure that her character's *cri de cœur* – 'I'll not stand you an inch in the stead of a seraglio ... [I'll] preach liberty to they that are enslaved – your harem inmates amongst the rest ... and I'll stir up a mutiny' (Brontë 1847: 297–8) – would be instantly comprehensible to her readers. This image of the harem inmate as a symbol for the imprisonment of (Western) women in marriage had not faded by the time of the 'New Woman' in the late nineteenth century. In her 'New Woman' novel *A Superfluous Woman* (1894) Emma Brooke wrote of 'lovely girls ... bought and sold in the London marriage market very much as Circassian slaves are sold to a Turkish harem' (in Bland 1995: 132). Melek Hanım self-consciously uses the same trope but links it directly to the issue of race: 'the cloistered, pampered existence we were forced to lead in our father's harem did not satisfy us. The European blood in us seemed to revolt against this "slavery," and we were in consequence far more unhappy than we ought to have been' (Melek Hanoum 1926: 130). Making a bid for maximum Western sympathy the émigrée Ottoman emphasises that, however much Eastern women agitated against seclusion, the pain inflicted on one with 'European blood' was more of an affront.

Brooke was not alone in displaying a knowledge of the specificities of the Ottoman slave system (in her reference to Circassians) at the same time as perpetuating the Orientalist assumption that all Oriental harems were inevitably spaces of domination and cruelty. To think about Western attitudes to and interactions with Ottoman slavery requires an understanding of the characteristics of the Ottoman slave system and its place in the harem. Not least because the Ottomans themselves were incensed when Westerners associated their slave system with American plantation slavery and regularly insisted on the distinctions between the two (see also Toledano 1982, Lewis 1990, Davis 1986).

Unlike the North American system, the Ottoman slave trade was governed by the laws and conventions of Islam. Under these regulations slaves had certain rights which were generally, although not universally, observed. No free-born Muslim could be enslaved, so slaves were generally obtained from outside the empire or from non-Muslim populations. Islam encouraged but did not require manumission although it was a common Ottoman tradition to free slaves after seven years (after which many stayed in their master's service as free servants). Additionally, owners often freed slaves in their wills. Many sources maintain that Ottoman slaves were regarded as part of the household and treated as one of the family (Davis 1986: 100, Tugay 1963). This is emphasised by Vaka Brown who proclaims that 'slavery in Turkey is not what the word implies in Christendom. A slave in Turkey is like an adopted child, to whom is given every advantage according to her talents … slaves are always better off than if they stayed at home' (Vaka 1909: 119). Though Ellison agrees that slaves are never harshly treated and regard their owner's house as their own, sometimes refusing to leave once they have been freed, she likens them to well-behaved servants rather than relations (Ellison 1915: 26). Although some women slaves were purchased explicitly as concubines rather than as domestic labour, all women slaves were liable to be sexually subject to their masters.

Concubinage did not have the legal status of a marriage, but the relationship implied some rights; any children from the union were considered free-born, regarded without stigma and entitled to an equal share of the inheritance when their father died. Upon bearing children, their mother could no longer be sold to another owner and would become free on her master's death, if he had not already married her as was often the case on the birth of a child (Bouhdiba 1975, Davis 1986, Lewis 1990). Unlike slave-owners in the West, Ottomans relied on import rather than 'breeding' to replenish slave numbers. To Ottomans, different forms of slavery were seen as quite distinct, with their own pricing and practices and patterns of decline. According to Toledano's figures (1982), agricultural slavery, for example, was in decline by the nineteenth century (except for a few increases in demand) and was openly discouraged whilst by the late eighteenth and nineteenth centuries the most significant slave trade by far was in African women[19] for domestic labour and Circassian, Georgian and Abyssinian (Ethiopian) women for concubines and wives in elite households. With slaves' value reflecting a racialised hierarchy of beauty, Caucasian women were held in the highest esteem, followed by Abyssinians who were considered to be the lightest skinned Africans (Lewis 1990). This outnumbered the trade in male slaves for any purpose. The harem slave trade, regarded as largely consensual, was seen as a recognisable route to advancement. Since the conventions of polygamy required other wives and concubines (whose numbers were not limited) to be subservient to the first wife, it was common by the nineteenth and early twentieth centuries for the second wife to be a freed slave or concubine. Such a woman would, Davis notes, already be in the habit of subordination to the mistress of the household and therefore constituted less of a threat to the primacy of the first wife. Thus men, whose first wife was usually a free-born Muslim Ottoman woman, found it easier to manage polygamy if other differentials of rank were mapped onto the hierarchy of wives. Although Islamic law required a husband to treat all wives equally (often interpreted as a rotation of sexual intimacy) many Muslim parents did not want to marry their daughters into a secondary situation, which further extended the practice of taking concubines as subsequent wives (Davis 1986: 88–9). Bouhdiba (1975) in contrast, speaking on a meta-historical level about an Arab-Muslim culture, suggests that wives often saw concubines as more of a threat than other wives since, as slaves, they were not subject to the same conventions of seclusion and modesty and were able to go about in the street and be seen unveiled by visitors. He characterises the concubine in the elite harem as 'the intruder par excellence', sometimes better educated than the wife or wives and bringing with her an erotic exoticism of far-off places and customs. Concubines were in any case seen less and less since by the 1890s the harem slave trade was also in decline, due in part to the worsening economic fortunes of the elite.

In the first half of the nineteenth century, as the European powers themselves eventually moved towards abolition, attention increasingly turned to the Ottoman trade. The British in particular were keen to suppress and abolish the Ottoman trade, and the Ottomans did between 1840 and 1880 undertake several measures to restrict the trade. Eventually in 1880 they signed an Anglo-Ottoman convention for the suppression of the African trade and in 1908 the Young Turks revived the clauses in the 1876 constitution abolishing slavery. Although many of the attendants in the *konaks* at the turn of the century would have been legally free (Davis 1986: 114), it is evident that some slavery continued into the twentieth century. Certainly, Edib's experience of an elite household with African slaves cannot be explained as only representing slaves who were purchased before the 1880 regulations. The young Reshé must have been sold to her family some time in the 1890s. As Toledano (1982) points out, Ottoman policy on slavery, though clearly influenced by relations with European powers, generally followed its own agenda and did not comply with what had for Britain initially been a desire for total abolition. Significantly, he argues, Ottoman concepts of the social place of slavery and of personal status were fundamentally unchanged and uninfluenced by the concepts of human rights that informed Western interventions. The various attitudes of Ottoman sultans and politicians depended on how the empire's need for different types of slave labour could be balanced against the urgency of good relations with Europe, rather than an ideological commitment to abolitionism. British ambassadors reported many frustrations in trying to progress with abolition and with reform.

The Caucasian trade in 'white' slaves is a case in point here. Slaves, mainly women, from the Caucasus regions of Georgia and Circassia were very important to the harem slave trade, but also gained the attention of the West for whom the prospect of 'white' slavery was particularly troubling. Circassian women occupied a special position in domestic slavery, being legendary for their pale beauty and much sought after for elite harems and the palace. Though nominally Muslim and therefore not legally enslaveable, Circassians had their own traditions of slavery in which parents often sold their children into slavery or young girls volunteered, since to many the prospect of life in an elite Istanbul harem was preferable to a hard life in the Caucasus. Although numbers of slaves from the Caucasus were in decline from the early nineteenth century after Russia annexed the region (creating opportunities for black slaves to rise to positions of greater privilege previously reserved for whites, Lewis 1990), Britain's main chance to intervene in the Caucasian trade came with the Crimean War when Britain and France supported the Ottomans against Russia. After intense lobbying for the abolition of the whole Caucasian trade, the porte agreed to stop the Georgian slave trade but managed to hold onto the more valuable trade from Circassia. The commitment to the Circassian slave trade can be seen in instances where the Ottoman government was moved to intervene directly, such as when traditional conventions of kinship support and non-coercion were disrupted. After the Crimean War in the 1860s, when the Russians were keen to depopulate the Caucasus of their troublesome Muslim population, they encouraged, at times enforced, migration. The hardship of the immigrant families and kidnapping by unscrupulous dealers meant that many children were enslaved and separated from their families, where previously slave families had been kept together. Attempts to rectify this were made by the Ottoman government through the Immigration Commission, even buying their freedom to reunite families in cases of unlawful enslavement. The tradition of non-coercive Circassian slavery continued, particularly the purchase of Circassian women for elite harems (see Garnettt 1891, Davis 1986, Toledano 1982). In 1870 Sir Henry Elliot, the British ambassador to Istanbul, realised how indelicate it might be to raise the subject of Circassian slavery since the grand vizier's Circassian wife had been a slave and so had been or were the wives of many other important officials (Toledano 1982: 170, see also Said-Ruete 1888).

An important sign to the West that they were gaining ground was the closure of the slave market in Istanbul in 1847. Toledano depicts this as a totally Ottoman initiative in the context of the Tanzimat reforms (prompted by reports that slaves were being badly treated in contravention of Islamic law) although open slave trading might also have been seen as inappropriate to the desired image of Istanbul as a modernising capital city. Certainly, Westerners were regular visitors to the slave market, which had become a feature of the tourist itinerary as well as a staple of high and popular representation. The slave trade did not cease, nor was it intended to, with this measure. It simply became clandestine, often to the cost of the slaves who – having now to endure a journey made harsher and more treacherous by the need for subterfuge – died in greater numbers before reaching their destination (Garnett 1891). At the upper end of the trade the tradition continued whereby upper-class women (often apparently unaware of the horrors of the journey) bought Circassian girls and educated them into cultivated and elegant women to go as concubines and wives to elite harems, or trained them as dancers and entertainers (occupations not respectable for Muslim women). Vaka Brown among others reports on this. Although there was serious money to be made in such ventures it was not only finances that prompted women to undertake such transactions: to be seen attended by cultivated Circassians was a sign of status and women could align themselves with powerful households through the placement of their trainees. If the slave managed to marry her master, the alliance could prove to be even more useful. Often, enslaved Circassians were considered as suitable wives from the outset, entering their new homes as free women. Women who did not specifically purchase and train slaves would still often consider it part of their duty to educate the slaves who came to them as young girls and arrange good marriages for them. Whilst Circassians might be intended for the highest of social alliances, many less exceptionally valued women slaves would be assisted to marry, often being given their freedom along with their dowry.

The religious and cultural conventions that followed from such diversification in the Ottoman slave trade were often blurred for Western observers and critics, as was the ensuing social and ethnic delineation of the slave population. That the term Circassian was known in the West as a racialised signifier of enslaved beauty does not necessarily mean that the West would have a corresponding awareness of the specifically Ottoman social experience of slavery. To the British, by and large, in their opposition to the trade, a slave was a slave was a slave. On the other hand, Ottoman slavery continued to be a source of interest to the Occident in ways that were not entirely condemnatory. Even as their husbands met with officials to negotiate the end of the trade, the wives of European ambassadors and diplomats were engaged in a round of harem visits in which slave girls were part of the exotic spectacle in which they delighted (Blunt 1881, Poole 1844, Lott 1866). Vaka Brown's digressions on elite harem slavery are there as entertainment not horror stories.

Zeyneb Hanım and Melek Hanım moved from race to other markers of social stratification. Zeyneb Hanım's need to be separated from race 'primitives' occurs infrequently in her writing but another separation – between herself and the European working class – is frequently constructed. It was clearly imperative for Zeyneb Hanım to be recognised as a lady and seen as distinct from a primitivised working class. She regularly remarked on Western activities that seem to her unladylike (sporting exercise that leaves women with red cheeks and disordered clothes for example) and was traumatised by the possibility of not being 'taken for a lady'. This potential loss of class status colours her response to English feminists. In this account of a feminist meeting, differences of class rather than nationality are paramount.

> Since I came here I have seen nothing but 'Votes for Women' chalked all over the pavements and walls of the town. These methods of propaganda are all so new to me. I went to a suffrage street corner meeting the other night, and I can

assure you I never want to go again. The speaker carried her little stool herself, another carried a flag, and yet a third woman a bundle of leaflets and papers to distribute to the crowd. After walking for a little while they placed the stool outside a dirty-looking public-house, and the lady who carried the flag boldly got on to the stool and began to shout, not waiting till the people came to hear her, so anxious was she to begin. Although she did not look nervous in the least she possibly was, for her speech came abruptly to an end, and my heart began to beat in sympathy with her. When the other lady began to speak quite a big crown of men and women assembled: degraded-looking ruffians they were, most of them, and a class of man I had not yet seen. All the time they interrupted her, but she went bravely on, returning their rudeness with sarcasm. What an insult to womanhood it seemed to me, to have to bandy words with this vulgar mob. One man told her that 'she was ugly'. Another asked 'if she had done her washing,' but the most of the hateful remarks I could not understand, so different was their English from the English I had learned in Turkey.

Yet how I admired the courage of that woman! No physical pain could be more awful to me than not to be taken for a lady, and this speaker of such remarkable eloquence and culture was not taken for a lady by the crowd, seeing she was supposed 'to do her own washing' like any woman of the people.

The most pitiful part of it all to me is the blind faith these women have in their cause, and the confidence they have that in explaining their policy to the street ruffians, who cannot even understand that they are ladies, they will further their cause by half an inch. I was glad when the meeting was over, but sorry that such rhetoric should have been wasted on the half-intoxicated loungers who deigned to come out of the public-house and listen. If this is what the women of your country have to bear in their fight for freedom, all honour to them, but I would rather groan in bondage. (Zeyneb Hanoum 1913: 189–91)

Gender appears as an identification calibrated by class as well as race or ethnicity. Changes in women's status achieved at the cost of losing the class-specific privileges of their position as ladies may not be worthwhile. It was not only the Ottoman women who found street meetings potentially demeaning. British suffragists themselves found street activities an endurance before they learned to manage their role as public spectacle (Tickner 1987, see also Chapter Six). Zeyneb Hanım remained unconvinced, concluding:

I do not pretend to understand the suffragettes or their 'window-smashing' policy, but I must say, I am even more surprised at the attitude of your Government. However much these ill-advised women have over-stepped the boundaries of their sex privileges, however wrong they may be, surely the British Government could have found some other means of dealing with them, given their cause the attention they demanded, or used some diplomatic way of keeping them quiet. I cannot tell you the horrible impression it produces on the mind of a Turkish woman to learn that England not only imprisons but tortures women: to me it is the cataclysm of all my most cherished faiths. Ever since I can remember, England had been to me a kind of Paradise on earth, the land which welcomed to its big hospitable bosom all Europe's political refugees. It was the land of all lands I longed to visit, and now I hear a Liberal Government is torturing women. Somehow my mind will not accept this statement. (Zeyneb Hanoum 1913: 236)

LOOKING EAST AND LOOKING WEST

Compared to Europe, Turkey might not be so bad. Ottoman women writers evaluated female status in the West in relation to their own home conditions, just as European women had long looked East for a comparison or a contrast. By the twentieth century, whilst clearly still concerned with the practice and representation of polygamy, Ottoman women were widening the discussion to cover the conditions for the emergence of social and political emancipation in both East and West. And the West did not always come out on top. In contrast to the negative treatment of suffragists in England, ranging from rudeness to brutality, Ottoman women had the advantage of substantial and active male support, something which Ellison after her British experience found 'still almost incomprehensible' (Ellison 1915: 65). For Vaka Brown, the men, whose support for female emancipation she so admired, were part of a wider national liberation project with which she could not entirely agree. The influx of Westernisation threatened all that she held dear. At the end of the her 1909 volume she gave her conclusions about the 'Turkish suffragettes':

> The most noticeable thing about them was that they were attracted only by the worst features of our Western civilization. It was my opinion at that time – although recent political events do not seem to have borne me out – that Turkey would be better off without any influx of European thought.
>
> … The most discouraging thing about Turkey is that, while the old-fashioned Turk is a man on whose integrity you may depend, as soon as the Turk becomes Europeanized he loses his own good qualities, without obtaining those of the West – exactly as the American Indian does. He is so vitally different from us, and his mind is so naif and unspoiled, that the result of contact with our sophisticated thought is very harmful. I agree with Houlmé that Turkey ought to work out her own salvation. (Vaka 1909: 189)

The concepts of national, racial and ethnic difference that inform this conclusion were integral to the way that her books were read in Turkey. In 1923 Vaka Brown recounted discussions about the reception of her first two books with older Ottoman women who had experienced the transition from empire to republic and the attendant shifts in their personal and social life. They make clear the international and local dimensions that colour responses to her work.

> Dilara Hanoum was not one of my old-time friends. I had met her only recently at another Turkish lady's house, and she had taken an interest in me because I was to write about Turkey. She was also good enough to say of my book 'Haremlik': 'You are the best singer I know of what was good in our old system.' Her opinion was in odd contrast to that of the younger generation, who

wanted to tear the book to pieces as glorifying a system which it was the pride
of the Young Turks to have extirpated. (Vaka 1923: 57)

Dilara Hanım asks Vaka Brown what sort of book she will write now about
Turkey.

'I think I shall write "Haremlik, Twenty Years After".'
'And I suppose you will say what dreadful people we have grown to be, now
that we are trying to become emancipated and progressive, and have lost the
charming life you depicted.'
'Of course, aesthetically I cannot help being disappointed at the loss of
much that was attractive and dramatic in the old life. But I am thrilled at the
way you – the Turkish women – have accepted the change. You may become
the pioneers of progress for the women of the whole of Asia.'
… [Dilara responds] 'We may never meet again, but since you are going to
write some more about Turkey, I should like to tell you certain things that may
help us all. I hate Europe only because she is the enemy of Asia. You are not
just a journalist: you write so that you may help – I have felt that in your books
– and you genuinely like us. There are only two people who love the Turks, you
and Pierre Loti; but, whereas he wants to keep us as we are, to please his aesthetic sense, you wish us to progress. Well, the difference between Europe and
Asia is the way the word "progress" is understood. To Europe progress means
only material prosperity – wealth. She wants us to progress solely in order that
she may make more money out of us …' (Vaka 1923: 67–70)

Vaka Brown is torn between the need to advocate progress and a nostalgia for the
elegance of the old ways (see also the Conclusion) that is indicative of the shifts
in her ethnic self-presentation between 1909 and 1926 (and again in the posthumous autobiography of 1947). If her first attempt at memoir marked her as
predominantly Oriental, this identification had changed by her second volume, *A
Child of the Orient*, in 1914 to include an emphasis on her Greekness and the
labelling of the Turks as Asiatic, a term scarcely used in 1909 but that peppered
the memoir of 1947. The status of Ottoman women had become for Vaka Brown
in 1923 a smaller fixture in a composite political picture concerned with the
European mandate, foreign aid and pan-Asian resistance to Western imperialism.
The elite harem life of her youth became a symbol of the best qualities of Turkish
national life which need to be modified in relation to modernity, but which
should not be rejected out of hand for what she sees as a bitter and untrustingly
nationalist callous modernisation.

The iniquities suffered by women in the liberated West were keenly felt by her
and by Ellison who, for all her romantic affections for Turkish life and people,
was careful in the final analysis to depict herself as intrinsically not part of the
harem world: '… that I should have to depend for male society exclusively on
my blood relatives – Heaven forbid!' (Ellison 1915: 196). Whatever the pleasures of masquerade *à la turque* (see Chapter Five) Ellison had to establish
beyond any doubt that she was not really Oriental. When a Turkish woman asked
what it was like to mix with non-familial men, Ellison represented it as a physio-

logical instinct and need: 'To ask me what it means to mix freely with men is almost like asking what it means to have lungs. I never stopped to think, but I know I should die without them' (Ellison 1915: 196). For the avowed feminist Ellison, the contrast with Turkey makes the limits of Western freedom all the more keenly felt:

> I came here with perhaps just a little of the 'downtrodden woman of the East' fallacy left, but that has now completely vanished. To me, as an Englishwoman, there are sides of this life which would irritate me into open rebellion ... But then, after all, is not everything relative? ... If we in the West possess what is known as the 'joy of liberty', have not so many of us been deprived of the blessing of protection? If the Moslem women are 'possessions' they are 'cherished possessions' and treated as such. (Ellison 1915: 195–8)

> ... The Turkish woman is proud and insists that her dignity be respected, and personally, I know few who would put up with the 'polygamy' which women of the Latin races are obliged to accept ... (Ellison 1915: 58–9)

The relative merits of protection and free-market liberty put Ellison in what she knows is a difficult and contradictory position:

> 'Is it absolutely necessary for them to come to us for assistance?'
>   This is the question I have asked so many Turkish women. They must think I argue almost like a reactionary. Yet I have not defended the harem system. There is, however, so much in the Turkish home life which is beautiful that I would prefer to see them progressing on the lines of their own civilisation, rather than becoming a poor imitation of us. Let them come to us and learn to organise their studies; the rest they can, if they will, manage for themselves. (Ellison 1915: 197–8)

Impressed by the luxury of elite Ottoman homes and seduced by the charm of Oriental hospitality (see Chapter Five), the tensions for women between Oriental 'slavery' and Occidental freedom are not lost on Ellison. She is not surprised that Zeyneb Hanım seeks succour in Turkey after the rigours of Western 'liberation':

> I had not seen her since she so resolutely and for ever closed the book on her European experiences and our first meeting was just a little painful. Zeyneb ... had gone forth with a flourish of trumpets to try the great, wonderful liberty of the West, – a woman who cast aside her own civilization to throw herself before the altar of ours. She was not prepared for our civilization, she was not armed for the fray, the hurricane of progress took her off her feet, and now ... she is back in the little Yali [summerhouse] again. (Ellison 1915: 187)

Whilst the reviewer of Zeyneb Hanım's book in the *Times Literary Supplement* found that Turkish women generally prefered life in the harem to female existence in Europe, he, or perhaps she, dismissed as 'negligible exceptions' the *désenchantées*' well-aired complaints about segregation and seclusion. In what was to prove a string of accusations of inauthenticity, the writer rehearses Zeyneb Hanım's European bloodline to dismiss her as an atypical and therefore unsuitable respondent.[20] For information on harem life he recommends instead the stories of the British writer Marmaduke Pickthall where 'there is no questioning the authenticity of the picture'. Pickthall, who was later in 1920 to convert to Islam (and the cause of Indian nationalism) had already been resident for some years in Lebanon, India and Egypt and is here found to be acculturated in ways that yield valuable 'insight',[21] whereas Zeyneb Hanım is pictured as a doomed hybrid full of contradictions. Her 'inherited disposition' leads her to revolt: 'she is apparently one of those women who belong by temperament to the rebels [but] [s]he detests the suffragists; yet but for her high breeding and traditional fastidiousness she has the making of one.' Although she benefited from the 'clear vision' typical of the harem woman, her cultural mix meant that 'steeped in French decadent literature [she] would be unhappy in any society.' This 'morbidity' coupled with her amusing – and sometimes to the point – observations about English life was not enough to overcome for the reviewer the fact that 'a nation is not so easily atomized by a foreigner'. That Pickhall is apparently perfectly able to 'atomize' Egyptian life, and segregated harem life at that, does not appear to be a problem. This classically Orientalist preference for Occidental sources as authorities about the East (Said 1978) illustrates the significance to gender of concepts of authenticity. Zeyneb Hanım's Ottoman identification is understood by a Westerner as impossible to resolve, even though in local terms it makes perfect sense. But, as with Edib's rejection of Vaka Brown's version of the harem, when it comes to speaking for the segregated Ottoman woman, the issue of who has the right to represent her is paramount. Whilst the *Times Literary Supplement* reviewer and Edib have different agendas their two examples hint at what was at stake in the contest over the authenticity of sources.

By the time Ellison published her unashamedly Turkophile *Turkey To-day*, she had largely relinquished her nostalgia for the elegant living that was already, when she made her first visit, only a vestige of past glories and was full of the more rugged splendours of Mustafa Kemal's revolutionary society. Turkey is hailed as a beacon of female emancipation in the Middle East and Kemal as its architect. She recalls how the women she met on her first visit seemed doomed: when she left her friend on that occasion 'we astonished our entourage by bursting into tears. The whole question of women's freedom seemed to me so hopeless and pathetic. The women were too cultured to be happy and too unorganised to revolt – isolated rebellion as in the case of Zeyneb was useless – and one felt there was so little one dared to do, or could do ...' (Ellison 1928: 151).

But with the advent of Mustafa Kemal all that had changed. As far as Ellison was concerned he has 'given freedom to women, it is he who decides her destiny' (Ellison 1928: 230). Though the *Times Literary Supplement* was to criticise *Turkey To-day* for not identifying Kemal as a dictator and for showing no sympathy for the many Turks who were unhappy at the enforced repudiation of some of their 'most cherished customs and ideals' her admiration for his modernisation project is wholehearted.[22]

[Kemal had] made up his mind that Turks should take their place in the Councils of Europe on equal terms ... and this could never be done until women

were the partners of men. Besides, no right-thinking Turk cared for the harem.
He was as ashamed of the words harem and polygamy as he was of his fez. The
coarse smoking-room jokes about his home life and polygamy, as well as the
conspicuous place his fez gave him in European assemblies, he deeply
resented. He knew he was being classed as 'a native,' he asserted almost too
emphatically his belief in Western home life and avoided using the word
'harem,' whilst the women, to escape pity, pretended they had never been in
bondage. (Ellison 1928: 82)

In racialised hierarchies of civilisation and power, the old Turkey of harems and
hanıms could too easily be relegated to the status of inferior and infantilised subject nation. For the new republic, the public presentation of women was of
tremendous symbolic importance in determining how Turkey could interact with
the Western powers and the rest of Asia.

It was also important to Western feminists interested in the international struggle for women's rights and alive to the propaganda potential of foreign
comparisons. The British suffrage paper *Votes for Women* reporting on the 1908
revolution noted that 'the British Ambassador at Constantinople lost no time in
congratulating the sultan on having granted to his subjects those rights of representative government, which the British government deny to women of their own
country' (3 September 1908, p. 426). *Votes for Women*, for which Ellison wrote
in 1912, showed particular interest in the active, at times life-endangering, role
played by women in the intrigues leading up to the 1908 revolution.

> Readers of Pierre Loti will not need to be reminded that among Moslem
> women of to-day there is a standard of culture and a knowledge of the world's
> political events equalling anything among women of the West, and they will
> not be surprised that the aspirations towards freedom, so sadly unrealised by
> the French author's women friends, have at last found partial expression. Turk-
> ish women, it appears, have been in the employ of the Young Turk party in
> work which, if not impossible for men would, at least, have been very difficult
> of safe accomplishment, and it is significant of the change which seems to be
> colouring Eastern views about women, that when in Salonika a lady of distinc-
> tion, the wife of a young Turk officer, appeared in the streets unveiled and
> carrying a banner on the day that the Constitution was proclaimed, far from
> meeting with criticism, she was applauded, and her husband's comrades pub-
> licly kissed her hands.[23]

Allusions to Loti's *Les Désenchantées* are ubiquitous in these reports, as are references to class. Identified specifically as ladies, the report applauds these
unveiled women who 'wore European dress, and had all the charm of high-bred,
cultured women'. Whilst Zeyneb Hanım was horrified at the de-gentrification
faced by British suffragists, the reporter here notes that, 'in order to parry spies in
their dwellings, several ladies in Monastir had of late years dispensed with servants, performing menial duties themselves', sacrificing for the national good the
marks of status in the privacy of their home.

Ottoman writers, though not all rushing head-long into an intense Westernisation, certainly review their own position through an Occidentalist filter (Nader

1989). When the sometimes too rosy tint of this lens is found to be false – Zeyneb Hanım's fairytales – Ottoman women are confirmed in their sense that their emancipation must be specifically Oriental, a selective amalgamation of Eastern and Western ideas.

In the context of a debate about seclusion, where to discuss or gaze on women was traditionally an affront, the style and beauty of Oriental women come into play as crucial markers of racial, sexual and political modes of identification. The immensity of this shift is revealed by the decision in 1930 to enter Turkish women in European beauty contests. When the championing of unveiled Eastern beauty was vindicated by a win in 1932 the beauty queen was celebrated with 'a civic ovation comparable to the triumphs accorded to great national heroes' (Woodsmall 1936: 55). The langorous Loti heroine had been replaced by women trained in gymnastics – undertaking in public exercises that in 1908 Zeyneb Hanım had found shocking and unappealing in Europe. The visibility, appearance and body of the Turkish woman underwent material changes as the signification of the category 'Oriental woman' shifted for both Orient and Occident. But though her image was modified, the symbolic importance of the Oriental woman never lost its primacy as a currency with which to represent the Orient in both East and West. It is to this that I turn in the next chapter.

NOTES

1 As Nader illustrates, the differences between Eastern and Occidental men are also important: in her case study of mid-twentieth-century Libya, she finds that women who had built their hopes on a companionate marriage based on their (often shared) reading of Western mass market romance found that even when the family adopted a modern, Western nuclear format, 'although the form was Western the content was Eastern'. Even though the couple had more privacy, they still 'tended to lack the shared interests and emotional bonds characteristic of the Western *ideal* couple, and could not change' (Nader 1989: 337–9 original emphasis).

2 Overton (1928: 316) described her novels as 'somewhat on the order of F. Marion Crawford romance – perhaps rather more melodramatic'.

3 In *In the Shadow of Islam*, what at first seems to be a typical exotic romance, with its emancipated American heroine overwhelmed by the sexual attractiveness of the Oriental hero, is transformed into a story of female political dedication as Millicent Grey, in Istanbul in the weeks before the 1908 Young Turk Revolution, turns her back on sexual union and determines instead on a life of political purpose. As Postma points out, the hero, a Young Turk leader and cousin of the sultan, is rendered unappealing in political terms (his initially Ottomanist vision of inclusive democracy is replaced by a despotic Turkish nationalism as he turns his back on his mother's Albanian Christian heritage) in order to allow the heroine to reject marriage and explore her political agency. I note that whereas in Hull's *The Sheik* the 'boyish' heroine is guided towards a conventional marital plot resolution when the 'sheik' who aroused her womanly passions turns out not to be so Arab after all (miraculously it emerges that he is of European and aristocratic parentage), in *Shadow*, the emancipated Milli-

cent is saved from the lower sexual passions that are aroused by the Oxford-educated, European-like Orhkan when he becomes overtaken by his Oriental, i.e. Turkish, heritage. The racialisation of sexual desire serves paradoxically to usher one emancipated woman towards (an albeit exciting version of) reproductive femininity and to take another out of its orbit and into celibacy. Kathlene Postma, 'American Women Readers Encounter Turkey in the Shadow of Popular Romance', conference paper at 'A Century of Ottoman Women', Boğaziçi University, Istanbul, 2000.

4 Ibrahim Hakki Paşa was grand vizier from 12 January 1910 to 29 September 1911.

5 Mehmed Hilmi, 'Hayat-ı aile', *Hanimlara Mahsus Gazete*, 1895, pp. 2–3, in Duben and Behar (1991: 217–20).

6 'Çocuklarımız' (Our Children), *Kadınlar Dünyası*, 29, 15 May 1913, p. 1, in Duben and Behar (1991: 197).

7 'Bizde hayat-ı aile' (Our Family Life), *Kadınlar Dünyası*, 27, 15 May 1913, p. 2, in Duben and Behar (1991: 197).

8 Sacide, 'Kızlarımızın çehizi ne olmalı?' (What should our daughters' trousseaux/ dowries be? More intellectual training), *Kadınlar Dünyası*, 97, 22 July 1913, p. 3, in Duben and Behar (1991: 225).

9 Nesrin Salih, 'Türk Kızları' (Turkish Girls), *Kadınlar Dünyası*, 47, 2 June 1913, pp. 2–3, in Duben and Behar (1991: 225).

10 'Müsavat-ı hukuk' (Equality of Rights), *Kadınlar Dünyası* 30, 16 May 1913, p. 1, in Duben and Behar (1991: 220).

11 The conservative proposal, which was eventually defeated, aimed to lower the legal age of marriage to nine years for girls and to remove the first wife's right to veto subsequent polygamous marriages, one of the gains of the 1917 Family Law.

12 Apologists would argue that he preferred to use public speeches to build up a groundswell of opinion supporting reform, rather than force things through at a legislative level, see Z. Arat (1994).

13 Z. Toprak, '1935 Istanbul Uluslararasi "Feminizm Kongresi" re Baris', *Dusun*, March 1986, cited in Kandiyoti (1991: 41–2).

14 For other examples of modernising discourse in the creation of 'new' women as wives, mothers and citizens in the Middle East see Abu-Lughod (1998).

15 Aziz Haydar, 'İçtimaî dertlerimizden: izdivaç kanınlık' (Some of our social troubles, marriage, femininity), *Kadınlar Dünyası*, 82, 7 July 1913, pp. 1–2, in Duben and Behar (1991: 198).

16 Feridun Necdet in *Sevimli Ay*, 1926, in Duben and Behar (1991: 197).

17 A. Durakbaşa (1987), 'The formation of "Kemalist female identity": A historical-cultural perspective', unpublished MA thesis, University of Boğaziçi, in Paker 1991.

18 I thank Judy Greenway for this information.

19 The Lake Chad region from where Zeyneb Hanım's slave girl originated was at the core of the major slave route through North Africa to the Mediterranean and then across to Istanbul.

20 'Veiled Women', *Times Literary Supplement*, 13 March 1913, p. 107.

21 Pickthall's 1913 novel tells the story of an English governess who marries the son of her employer and acclimatises to Turkish ways.

22 'Turkey To-day', *Times Literary Supplement*, 11 October 1928, p. 719.

23 'The Woman Movement in Turkey', *Votes for Women*, 20 August 1908, p. 395.

CHAPTER FOUR

ᔥ EROTICISED BODIES: ᔦ REPRESENTING OTHER WOMEN

ORIENTALISM AND ORIENTALISATION

Whilst the evocative and detailed description of Orientalised women was an expected trope of material about the Orient, the emphatic use of the female body as a marker of racialised difference in the writings of Ottoman women was more than mere allegiance to cultural convention. This chapter focuses on the codification of Oriental women's bodies as beautiful in a consideration of how the gaze is racialised and sexualised at the point of both production and of reception. Different types of 'Oriental' women are displayed for the reader in a highly visual style of literary description characterised by references to the 'sister arts' of painting and poetry. These 'word portraits' institute a regime of representation – the presentation of 'Oriental' women by 'Oriental' women – that can be analysed in relation to the dominant modes of Orientalist spectacle with which their readers would have been more familiar. The images also set up a series of racialised ethnic and national differences that splinter the dominant Orientalist version of a generic Orient or Oriental. Localised differences have a function in the construction of alternative Ottoman femininities important to the textual self-inscription of their authors. Beauty signifies in and through a series of looks that, in a number of different ways, gender and racialise both the objects of the gaze and the owners of the look. This is seen particularly in the books of Demetra Vaka Brown whose repeated commentary on the beauty of Ottoman women is too pronounced to ignore, particularly in her first book *Haremlik* where she returns to the intimate friends of her youth, now become grand hanims.

Ottoman writers use descriptions of female appearance and beauty to present a series of racial and ethnic Ottoman identities that they evidently expect to be only partially comprehensible to their Occidental readership. Their efforts to explain regional Ottoman differentiations of race and ethnicity – that are unremittingly gendered and classed – to a readership of presumed outsiders is suggestive for an analysis of how the reiterative qualities that Judith Butler (1990) sees as essential to performative gender identities can be applied to identities based on race and ethnicity. Operating as mechanisms to incorporate subjects into social order, performative phrases or actions literally do, or enact, what they say as they are said: thus the doctor who says of the new-born baby 'it's a boy' literally attributes a gender to the infant as s/he says it, just as a marriage comes into legal being as the official pronounces the words that name it. Butler uses theories of performativity to emphasise how gender is constructed and non-natural, seeing it as an identification that is secured through the repeated performance of socially accepted signs of masculinity or femininity. Much of the interest generated by theories of performativity has centred on questions of gender identity and of theatrical spectacle, whether it be formal or informal drag performances, theatre, film or performance art (see Jones and Stephenson 1999 and Chinn 1997). I am going to use the emphasis on the instability of identity foregrounded by theories of performativity to think about the construction of racialised and ethnic identities in literary texts. In this and the following chapter I explore if and how performative statements are able to operate across cultures, where the consensus necessary for the recognition of performative actions may not be shared.

When the main claim to fame of Ottoman women's books was that they could sell themselves as the 'accurate' revelation of a still largely hidden world authenticated by the 'real' Oriental status of their female authors, I want to ask how much manoeuvrability their authors had in relation to the types of identifications with which they aligned themselves? When they explicitly and implicitly invoke European visual art in their depiction of Oriental women, is it useful to consider their emerging representations in relation to discussions of the embodiment of performative spectacle? Do the authors' fluctuating processes of identification with and separation from the variously racialised female subjects of their books show something new about the functioning of those contradictory and shifting processes of identification that have emerged as central to discussions about performativity (see also Brah 1996)? This chapter analyses the identificatory positions for authors and readers that are produced in and by these sources in relation to an Orientalist gaze that is conceptualised as plural rather than singular, and as polysemic in its potential to produce diverse positions of spectator pleasure and identification.

I want to return for a moment to consider the Orientalist discursive conditions in which these texts emerged. As discussed in Chapter One, the sexualised display of the Oriental female body was a central strand of Western Orientalism, fully developed and well known by the second half of the nineteenth century. But I would not want to characterise this as a display whose only audience was male. I agree with many other scholars in the field who argue that that the dominant codes of Orientalist art prioritise a male visual pleasure and that this is bound up in the construction of imperial identities and the subjective investment in imperial power relations (Nochlin 1983, Richon 1985, Tawadros 1988). None of that is contested: pictures by male artists such as Jean-Léon Gérôme, Eugène Delacroix, John Frederick Lewis and Ludwig Deutsch were prevalent in the Salons and Academies of Europe. But women were also consumers, attending exhibitions, viewing Orientalist visual culture through the print and periodical reproduction that reached beyond the middle classes, and collecting colonial postcards (MacKenzie 1995, DeRoo 1998). Women as well as men looked at

Orientalised female bodies and were well schooled in the logic of the Orientalist fantasy harem.

Western women did not only consume Orientalist imagery, they also produced it. As I argued in *Gendering Orientalism* (Lewis 1996), there was a painterly female Orientalist gaze in operation in the nineteenth century, the products of which circulated in the same venues as paintings by Decamps, Ingres or Gérôme. More is now known about the variety of nineteenth-century women's visual Orientalism (Roberts 2002, Cherry 2000). Whether they liked them or not, critics nearly always read a painting's female point of origin as essential to its meaning. The terms of this gendering might be variable, but gender remained central to the reception of women's art or literature. At the turn of the twentieth century, this was still the gender-specific context in which Ottoman women's writings were received. Only now, merchandised in relation to their experience of the harem, their geographical/ethnic point of origin differently racialised the text. But if, as Melman has demonstrated, the European woman was inevitably positioned at one remove from the nascent superiority of the ethnographer's gaze, then the woman coded as Oriental was situated even further from any space of cultural authority (Melman 1992). As Ottoman women inserted themselves into a Western representation system, one must consider the role played by their depiction of female beauty in this process of transculturation.

As discussed in previous chapters, the classification 'Oriental woman' was not straightforward and could encompass differences of religion, region and ethnicity in keeping with the heterogeneity of the Ottoman population. Yet the terms of this heterogeneity were not fixed in either their value or their meaning, operating as variable categories that were deployed, contested and remade in Ottoman sources. As Ottoman writers tried to reframe their gendered Ottoman identities for themselves in the context of books directed at a primarily Occidental audience, they struggled with the slipperiness of language and the liabilities of a mode of writing dependant on concepts of authenticity. In a transculturating movement their terms of identification shifted from a local to an international discourse as they sought to remake identifications for themselves whilst simultaneously trying to signify Orientalness for an Occidental readership. Transculturation moves both ways, and the terms available to Ottoman women were already by this period influenced by Western definitions of the Orient. The recognition of this continued to shock or surprise a West fond of imagining the Orient in general and the harem in particular as hermetically sealed.

This shifting set of identifications is important for an Orientalist discourse that sets such store by an authenticity whose guarantee rests on ethnic, Orientalist and gender allegiances. The concept of performativity is helpful for thinking through these varieties of racial and ethnic identity. In unpicking some of these complex positionings Vaka Brown, who was writing from the United States, emphasised her Oriental credentials by creating an affinity between herself and all that was best about Turkish Muslim female life. Thus, to her Occidental readership she might appear to be a reliable observer-participant (American enough to give judgements, Ottoman enough to gain privileged access). But to Ottoman Muslim readers she might appear more partisan. As was evident in Chapter Three, Halide Edib objected to Vaka Brown's version of harem life and to her romanticisation of polygamy. Edib wrote bitterly of the misery that polygamy brought to her childhood when her father took a second wife:

> Although this dramatic introduction of polygamy may seem to promise the sugared life of harems pictured in the 'Haremlik' of Mrs Kenneth [Vaka] Brown, it was not so in the least ... On my own childhood, polygamy and its results produced a very ugly and distressing impression ... (Edib 1926: 144–5)

Of all the writers I have read, Halide Edib had the least trouble establishing an ethnographic authority. As one whose identity meshed with all the variable terms that constitute the sign 'Oriental woman' – Ottoman, Turkish, Muslim, female – her claim to authenticity was powerful. She used her first-hand experience to dispute the 'sugared' vision of harem life for which Demetra Vaka Brown was nostalgic, and yet at the same time she stressed the relative autonomy of even segregated women. One consequence is that the question of contamination by the object of study (Melman 1992, Lewis 1996) is not as acute for Edib as it is for Vaka Brown. Against Edib, Vaka Brown's status as Oriental was quite differently inflected. As a self-designated 'child of the Orient', she presented herself as an explorer in a bewildering display of association with and disassociation from other Ottoman women. Returning to Turkey after six years in the United States, she wrote:

> I had returned to my native land with new ideas and a mind full of Occidental questioning, and I meant to find things out. Many of my childhood friends had been Turkish girls: them I now looked upon with new interest. Before, I had taken them and their way of living as a matter of course ... I had lived among them, looking upon their custom and habits as quite as natural as my own. But during my stay in America I heard Turks spoken of with hatred and scorn, the Turks reviled as despicable, their women as miserable creatures, living in practical slavery for the base desires of men. I had stood bewildered at this talk. Could it possibly be as the Americans said, and I never have known it? (Vaka 1909: 12–13)

Immediately the reader is told that she is like and not like the Oriental object of inquiry. What troubles her in this passage, is that the Turks are reviled by her new neighbours, the Americans. This resituating of her previously unproblematic partial identification with Turkish women continues to destabilise her narratorial position.

All the Ottoman women writers assume that ethnic difference exists and can be read from the body and behaviour. Sometimes they observe national characteristics in men or in children. Edib contrasts the brave endurance of Turkish soldiers to the 'childishness' of their Arab counterparts; she also detects obvious differences between Turkish, Kurdish and Armenian children. Vaka Brown, notably in her fiction, paints a world that is split by ethnic and national divides as much as it is by religion. Her 1911 novel *In The Shadow of Islam* is peopled by heroic but pleasure-loving Greeks, duplicitous Turks, betrayed Albanians and slimy, 'wretched' and irritating Armenians who, when not trying to fondle the heroine on the boat (he who so does is booted off the quay by her gorgeous, but strangely dangerous, Turkish suitor), are depicted as routinely cheating other foreigners in business transactions (Vaka 1911: 14, see also Chapter Three). But most often ethnic difference is registered through the representation of women and there are many references to a hierarchy of beauty which ran from Circassians down through Abyssinians (Ethiopans) to the least beautiful 'Negroes' (see Chapter Three).

The most conspicuous exponent of the construction of different female beauties is Demetra Vaka Brown, who institutes a gallery of female portraits that, even when they represent Turkish women as superior to American women, emphasise their difference. On her first visit to the polygamous harem of some old friends she enthuses:

> [they were both] sweet, commonplace women – not very different by nature from many commonplace American friends I have, whose lives are spent with dressmakers, manicures, masseuses, and in various frivolous pursuits … Except for the absence of men, I might almost have been visiting an American household. What difference existed was to the advantage of the Turkish girls. They were quite natural and spontaneous … They read a lot of French novels, without pretending that they did it for the sake of 'culture'. They took everything naturally and enjoyed it naturally. There was no unwholesome introspection – that horrible attribute of the average half-educated European and American woman. They never dreamed of setting the world aright. (Vaka 1909: 28)

Vaka Brown's descriptions become more and more Orientalised and eroticised. In the following scene she is trying to persuade her childhood friend Djimlah – to whose 'vigorous and original mind' she had been 'attracted' in her youth – that women do have a soul:

> She [Djimlah] laughed scornfully. 'You little petal of a flower, woman has no soul … she is all emotions and senses.'
> If an ugly girl had spoken as Djimlah spoke, it would have been very repulsive; but the radiant loveliness of the girl could not fail to modify the impression made by her words. While speaking, she would clasp her hands above her head, the sleeves falling away from her white arms; she would half close her eyes, in a way that made the light shining through them softer; and her lips forming her words were fresh and crimson, like a rose with the dew on it. The Greek in me, looking at her, forgave her words – one of the judges who liberated Phryne, because she was so beautiful, may have been an ancestor of mine … . (Vaka 1909: 60–1)

Vaka Brown offers a sexualised description of the Ottoman woman posing as an odalisque. She draws on the inventory of physical characteristics – arms, white skin, eyes – whose synecdochical function (in which a part stands in for the whole, here physiognomic detail standing in for Ottoman character, read as the cultural whole) had, as Melman (1992) demonstrates, been well established in women's travel writing from the mid-nineteenth century. As well as physiognomy, details of costume also functioned synecdochically to stand for the entireties of caste, class or race and these, as Suleri argues in the case of writings about India, were sometimes easier to itemise than physiognomy; which 'elicits the nervous terror of a possessor unable to record with any stability an understanding of what he may possess' (Suleri 1992a: 109). In women's travel writing, as Melman, and later Roberts (2002), have argued, detailed description of physical type and costume often served to code otherwise unrepresentable subjects, such as female sexuality or the author's own sexual desires (see also Chapter Five).

Indeed, as Roberts demonstrates, Oriental female beauty had a particular function for Western women travellers: in contrast to the male fantasy assumption of limitless harem beauties, women argued that most harem women were not beautiful – abrogating to themselves the quest to find the elusive beauty in the harem. The obsessive detailing of Oriental female physiognomy and dress that this quest involved was, as Roberts suggests, a mechanism by which Western women were able to access a moderated version of the stereotypically masculinist scopic pleasure involved in the objectification of Ottoman women. This, whilst based on the ethnographic authority of women's actual presence in the harem, was regularly transformed into a fantasy experience by their depiction of the harem in an evocative register derived from the popular tales of the *Arabian Nights*. In this guise, a space was permitted for a sexualised Western female gaze that rested on the appreciation of Orientalised female beauty. Vaka Brown engages in a comparable exercise half a century later, but she – herself part of the Orient – needs different mechanisms of observation and participation. And in this instance with Djimlah she aligns herself with a specifically male sexualised gaze by adopting the position of Phryne's judges who forgave her crimes when her naked beauty was revealed to them (a motif also popular with Orientalist artists such as Gérôme). The fancy flourishes of 'little petal' and so on, which already by page sixty pepper the text to underwrite the reality of Vaka Brown's Ottoman experiences, are simultaneously invoked as one of the pleasures of the Oriental *mise en scène* (honeyed language and excessive and exotic complement being expected tropes along with lovely ladies) and criticised in an invocation of stereotypical Oriental wiliness and duplicity. The reference to Phryne ends with the words:

> And she [Djilmah] prefaced all her blighting remarks with such endearments as 'little crest of the wave,' 'little mountain brook,' or 'flower of the almond tree'. It was as if I were being taken to a slaughter-house through a rose-conservatory. (Vaka 1909: 61)

Vaka Brown, who five lines earlier aligned herself with Phyrne's judges, now fancies herself the prisoner. But she does not only switch from judge to prisoner; later she becomes the agent who will enact the judgement or punishment when another Turkish woman, Aïshé Hanım, irritates her. Aïshé Hanım is the third wife of Djimlah's husband, given to the paşa by the sultan, in whose household she had arrived as a slave. Having the status thus of *seraigli* (one who has lived in the imperial harem) the woman was freed on marriage, as was the custom. But her husband – who did not approve of the gift wife system – maintained their marriage in form only. Denied access to a real marriage, Aïshé Hanım had taken great pleasure in her painting and had received instruction in Istanbul for some years. Yet she refuses to take seriously Vaka Brown's suggestion that she pursue her painting studies in Paris. Her response to every suggestion or explanation of why she should leave home and seek fame abroad is a quiet 'What for?', which frustrates and angers Vaka Brown. Though Vaka Brown admits to being 'somewhat afraid of' the elevated *seraigli* (aware of the respect due to the station), at this point even the author's intrinsic Greek appreciation of female beauty cannot save the Turkish woman from her punitive fantasy:

> She was very beautiful; not of the Turkish type, but of the pure Circassian, with exquisite lines and a very lovely, musical voice, and of things on this earth I am most susceptible to physical beauty. At that particular moment, however, I should have derived great pleasure if I could have smacked her pretty mouth. (Vaka 1909: 102)

So Vaka Brown is positioned first as magnanimous judge/connoisseur of female beauty, second as sacrificial lamb and third as both judge and executioner. But the reader is not the only one who finds this confusing. After she leaves Aïshé Hanım, Vaka Brown goes to her room feeling

> ... rather bewildered. Orientalism was like a labyrinth: the more I advanced in it, the more entangled I became. One woman after another was confronting me with a new problem, a new phase of life; and I felt stupid and incapable of understanding them. It hurt my vanity, too, to find how small I was in comparison with them. I should have liked really to sell myself to them for a year, merely to be able to live with them continuously, to try to understand a little more of their lives. They interested and charmed me: there was so much worth understanding. There was so much of the sublime in them, which is lacking in our European civilization. I felt petty and trivial every time I found myself facing one of those conditions which they understood so well. (Vaka 1909: 127)

Vaka Brown's attempts at an investigative social science protocol are thus regularly disrupted both by her desired closeness to her subjects and their bewildering ability to put her in her place. As Kalogeras (1997) argues, when put in the context of Vaka Brown's vague advocacy of Paris – '"Because," I answered lamely, "when a person has talent she generally goes to Paris or to some other great artistic centre,"' – Aïshé Hanım's repeated 'What for?' can be seen to represent a challenge to the presumed cultural supremacy of the West (Vaka 1909: 101). Indeed, as she points out, Vaka Brown becomes so frustrated at her inability to construct a reasoned explanation that she has to abandon the French in which they had been conducting the conversation and, resorting to her childish Turkish, ends up on the older woman's lap being comforted 'as if I were a little bit of thing, and was to be coaxed out of my foolishness' (Vaka 1909: 103).

Vaka Brown's oscillating relationship to the Ottoman women she describes reveals the tensions of her position. Like any Westerner she can be 'bewildered' by the illogical maze to which the Orient was often likened, yet she is also drawn to Ottoman women and wants to identify with them. This potential loss of (Westernised) self is not simply the projective fantasy common to Western Orientalism since, for Vaka Brown, the Orient is already experienced as part of self. The contradictions of this situation are there in her interactions. In representing herself as enslaved by Turkish women's sublime beauty Vaka Brown attests to the hold that the Orient has over her but, despite her alleged preference for the luxurious calm of Oriental life, she is not in Turkey to stay, and longs for the 'bustle' of the United States (Vaka 1909: 221). The passages' high-blown language and emotive imagery of total surrender suggest an investment that is strongly libidinal, an element that comes through even more strongly later in the book.

THE STRANGE LOVELINESS OF
THE PRE-RAPHAELITE WOMAN

The generic painterly references used for the odalisque-like Djimlah become more overt. This is Vaka Brown describing her first encounter with she whom she calls the 'Rossetti lady', at a bath-house party thrown in Vaka Brown's honour.

> I was especially attracted by a certain woman, whose type I had never met in flesh and blood before. To say that she looked like a Rossetti painting would be doing her scant justice, yet it was of the Blessed Damosel I thought when I saw her. (Vaka 1909: 234)

The woman begs Vaka Brown to visit her and of their next meeting Vaka Brown writes:

> There was a pathos in her voice that I had not detected at our previous interview. Rossetti's poem came back to me, and I said aloud, gazing at her beauty: –
>
>> 'Her body bore her neck as the tree's stem
>> Bears the top branches; and as the branch sustains
>> The flower of the year's pride, her high neck bore
>> That face made wonderful with night and day'
>
> 'Why do you say those lines?' my hostess asked.
> 'Because you make me think of them.'
> 'Do you mean that I look like Rossetti's paintings?'
> 'I rather think you look like his poems: you are the embodiment of them.'
> 'And am I this to you?'
> 'Yes, you are this to me. Ever since I first saw you I have been drawn to you.
> By rights I ought to be somewhere else tonight [Vaka Brown is meant to be travelling to Russia], but I am with you. It was of you I was thinking when you

came into my room. Do you know, I do not even know your name. That does not matter, though, for to me you are my Rossetti lady.'

The Turkish woman sat on a divan, near me, her fingers playing with my loose hair.

'You are a sweet-scented little bride,' she said irrelevantly. 'Where is the bride-groom, little one?'

'Your slave just gave me a heliotrope bath,' I explained: 'and as for the bride-groom, I am afraid his grandsire died heirless.'

'*Yavroum*, you are a very dear person, and I hope some day you will know the joy of being a wife.' She was silent for a long time, and then asked, suddenly: 'Shall I tell you why I insisted so strongly at the bath-party that you should come to see me?'

'Then it wasn't because you liked me?'

'Yes, indeed, little flower of the pomegranate tree. The minute my eyes met yours I knew that I liked you, and I knew that you belonged to us Oriental women. That is why I asked you to come. I wanted to ask you to do something for me, something which I can only trust to you … (Vaka 1909: 251–3)

How does one deal with the same-sex eroticism that seems so evident to early twenty-first-century readers and still establish what it might have meant to its original audience? Vaka Brown frequently depicts herself being touched and fondled by the Turkish women she spends time with (they hold her hand, sit close to her on divans, play with her hair) which, whilst it clearly activates the lesbian sub-texts that were a common feature of Western harem narratives, and which, though less so, were nonetheless present in women's accounts (Roberts 2002),[1] also disassociates the narrator and hence by implication Vaka Brown from any actual queerness. This is possible because, in the terms of this text, the homoerotic elements serve to emphasise the being-there-ness of Vaka Brown as narrator without tainting her as too sapphically Oriental. Whilst the text's performance of the familiar lesbian codings associated with the Oriental woman is part of Vaka Brown's presentation of herself as Oriental within the classification system recognisable to the West, she works to desexualise these most overtly masculinist stereotypes and to turn them to her own advantage. In her fiction and travel accounts, physical closeness is presented as typical of Oriental female manners: on a similar register of local authenticating detail to frankness in discussion and charming hospitality. Her ability to recognise all of these features as typical is one of the things that establishes the accuracy of her accounts. But, in seeking to authenticate herself as someone familiar enough with Oriental living and trusted enough by Oriental women to have valuable insider knowledge (in the context of a physical intimacy redolent of such titillating images as Ingres' *Turkish Bath* 1862), Vaka Brown risks becoming part of the Oriental spectacle. And if she does become part of the spectacle, what happens to the distance necessary for the establishment of the ethnographic authority which, at other moments in the book, she clearly desires?

What type of position is Vaka Brown taking up in relation to this 'Rossetti' woman? What other regime of representation does the Pre-Raphaelite reference introduce? The tragic vision of female beauty by which Vaka Brown is spell-bound reconfigures the Orientalist trope of the unhappy odalisque within an Occidental Pre-Raphaelite mode of imagery noted for its exotic/Italianate vision of mysterious, if not doomed, passionate female beauty. What is intriguing here, is that the stanza Vaka Brown quotes comes not from 'The Blessed Damozel', a tale of a dead maiden who pines in heaven for her male beloved left alive on earth below, but from another long poem by Dante Gabriel Rossetti, 'A Last Confession' (originally written in 1849, later revised and published in Rossetti's volume of verse, *Poems*, in 1870). Although Rossetti painted two versions of *The Blessed Damozel*, there is no painting to accompany 'A Last Confession', so the confusion between visual and literary analogies applies to more than Vaka Brown's reported conversation.

One of Rossetti's best-known poems, 'The Blessed Damozel' was first published in the short-lived Pre-Raphaelite journal *The Germ* in 1850. It appeared again in 1855 when William Morris and Edward Burne-Jones published a new version in their *Oxford and Cambridge Magazine*. This republication of Rossetti's poetry set the seal on his position as leader of the second group of Pre-Raphaelites. 'The Blessed Damozel' reached its widest audience when the final version appeared in Rossetti's *Poems* in 1870. Despite repeated requests from patrons (Riede 1992) Rossetti did not paint *The Blessed Damozel* until 1871 (Bennet 1988). This first version, for William Graham, was not completed until 1877 at which point Graham asked for a predella to be added featuring the earth-bound lover whose obsession with his dead mate brings him to a state of death-like trance (Bock 1981). The second section was finished in early 1878 and *The Blessed Damozel* was first exhibited at the Royal Academy in 1883 (see illustration 1, p. 152). The painting was bought by the American collector Grenville L. Winthrop and donated on his death to the Fogg Museum, Harvard University, in 1943.[2]

That Vaka Brown was able to characterise the woman as 'like a Rossetti painting' is not surprising: Dante Gabriel Rossetti and the other Pre-Raphaelite artists and writers were, by the last decades of the nineteenth century, known for a particular vision of a full-lipped, enigmatic but fleshly female type, whose monumental forms stared out from numerous paintings. Although Rossetti's earlier works featured ascetic, thin and pale women, his late work, of which *The Blessed Damozel* is one, inevitably included the strong-jawed, long-necked female forms that were distinctive enough to be caricatured by contemporary observers. Henry James visited William Morris and his wife Jane (née Burden) and he describes the scene in a letter to his sister Alice in 1869:

> Oh, ma chère, such a wife! *Je n'en reviens pas* – she haunts me still. A figure cut out of a missal – out of one of Rossetti's or Hunt's pictures – to say this gives but a faint idea of her, because when such an image puts on flesh and blood, it is an apparition of fearful and wonderful intensity. It's hard to say whether she's a grand synthesis of all the pre-Raphaelite pictures ever made – or they are a 'keen analysis' of her – whether she's an original or a copy. In

1. Dante Gabriel Rossetti, *The Blessed Damozel*, 1871–8, oil on canvas, 174 x 94 cm, with predella. Courtesy of the Fogg Art Museum, Harvard University Art Museums, Bequest of Grenville L. Winthrop

either case she is a wonder. Imagine a tall lean woman in a long dress of some dead purple stuff, guiltless of hoops (or anything else I should say) with a mass of crisp black hair heaped into great wavy projections on each of her temples, a thin pale face, a pair of strange sad deep, dark, Swinburnian eyes, with great thick black oblique brows, joined in the middle and tucking themselves away under her hair, a mouth like the 'Oriana' in our illustrated Tennyson, a long neck, without any collar, and in lieu thereof some dozen strings of outlandish beads – in fine complete. On the wall was a nearly full-length portrait of her by Rossetti, so strange and unreal that if you hadn't seen her you'd pronounce it a distempered vision, but in fact an extremely good likeness. (James, in Stanford 1970)

The cumulative cultural references (Swinburnian eyes, a Tennysonian mouth) reveal the cultural currency of not just Rossetti but of a more generic Pre-Raphaelite 'look'. Jane Morris was the great love of Rossetti's later life and it is her face, or a version of it, that stares out of so many of his later works, just as did that of Elizabeth Siddall from his earlier *oeuvre*. Challenging a romanticised response to this obsession with fascinating and unusual women, feminist critics Deborah Cherry and Griselda Pollock (1984) have pointed out that the Pre-Raphaelite investment in the figure of the woman as muse and in a vision of femininity that was mysterious and unavailable said more about their own pre-occupations than the actual women they so mythologised. What became the Pre-Raphaelite 'look', often associated with specific women in the Pre-Raphaelite circle such as Elizabeth Siddall, Jane Morris or Fanny Cornforth, was notori-ously recognisable by the last decades of the nineteenth century and remained so into the early twentieth century (Marsh 1987). As Barbara Munsen Goff demon-strates, this was widely discussed in the cultural media. The ability to identify this look did not apply only to the cognoscenti of the avant-garde; as a style it would have had a broader circulation and take-up. Initially remarkable as a valor-isation of individual women's idiosyncratic appearance, the Pre-Raphaelite style produced a visage that was in no way compatible with classical definitions of beauty. Goff refers us to Mary Howitt in *Household Words*:

> Only dress in the Pre-Raphaelite style and you will find that so far from being an 'ugly duck', you are a full fledged swan. [The Pre-Raphaelites] have made certain types of face and figure once literally hated, actually the fashion. Red hair – once, to say a woman had red hair was social assassination – is the rage. A pallid face with a protruding upper lip is highly esteemed. Green eyes, a squint, square eye-brows, whitey-brown complexions are not left out in the cold. In fact, the pink-cheeked dolls are nowhere; they are said to have 'no character' – and pretty little hands occasionally voted characterless too. Now is the time for plain women.[3]

It is not surprising to find such words of opprobrium in Dickens' journal *House-hold Words*, for his opposition to the Pre-Raphaelites was legendary and vociferous. Although today the Pre-Raphaelites are commonly seen as typical of Victorian painting, in their day they were regarded as counter-cultural, challenging protocols in both technique and subject matter. Their early insistence on truth to nature, rather than the ideal, was a displacement of the Raphaelite insistence on classical beauty as the externalisation of inner purity that enraged many. Dickens, for one, was horrified by John Everett Millais' painting *Christ in the House of His Parents* (1850) where the Holy Family, the highest in spiritual purity, were represented by figures whose physiology was read as ugly, common and deformed. The different ways in which the Pre-Raphaelite turn in art and literature was variously associated with a range of social ills from papism to degeneracy as they transgressed conventional links between beauty, morality and taste has been well-documented (See Riede 1992, Bullen 1998, Pearce 1991, Nead 1988). Yet, by the late nineteenth century the peculiar beauty of the Pre-Raphaelite 'stunner' – as Swinburne and others termed them – had become a type. It is this type that Vaka Brown invokes with the classification of the unnamed Turkish woman as a 'Rossetti' lady, further demonstrating her adroitness with Pre-Raphaelite language when she describes Aïshé Hanım's little slave girl as one who will grow up to 'make a stunner', with 'eyes that were that almond shape, the color, as Rossetti expresses it, like the sea and the sky mixed together' (Vaka 1909: 124). Notably, neither the earlier nor the later Rossetti imagery was a vision of normative and reproductive femininity.

When 'The Blessed Damozel' and 'A Last Confession' were published in *Poems* in 1870, the tenor of the criticism of his work changed. Rossetti, who for many years had not exhibited his paintings in public and whose verse was previously known mainly only by the inner circle, had prepared the ground for the publication of his poetry carefully. Apart from trying to secure favourably inclined reviewers he also specifically toned down some of the Catholic imagery in the earlier versions of his poems to avoid the criticisms of papism activated by the earlier religious paintings (Riede 1992). However, this time the attack came from another front, with Robert Buchanan's infamous assault on Rossetti as emblematic of the indecent and 'fleshly school' of art (published initially in 1871 in the *Contemporary Review*, and subsequently in pamphlet form in 1872). Unlike previous attacks that had criticised the ugliness of the ascetic and wan bodies in early Pre-Raphaelite paintings, Buchanan accused Rossetti of depicting bodies that were too beautiful and fleshly, seeing in this an indecent emphasis on the physicality of desire and the voluptuous fleshliness of the body. In 'The Blessed Damozel' even heaven is filled with reunited lovers, whilst the utterly corporeal and non-ethereal body of the Damozel is so warm that 'her bosom must have made / the bar she leaned upon warm'. Buchanan's diatribe against an immoral vision of flesh as flesh and not as an expression of the divine beauty of the soul, rekindled the debate started by Swinburne's *Poems and Ballads* in 1866 and anticipated the art for art's sake rationale of the final decades of the century. Rossetti, who always maintained that he was concerned with the soul and that he was as interested in content as in form (Ried 1992), was devastated by the assault.[4] By the end of the century, after Rossetti's death in 1882, the volatile status of his reputation had been somewhat codified by the influence that his life and work exerted over following generations of the avant-garde, notably the Aesthetes and the Symbolists (although they were also accused of degeneracy and decadence by their opponents). As the nineteenth century drew to a close, the dominant motif associated with Rossetti was the monumental siren of his later works, such as *Lady Lilith* (1864–) and *Astarte Syriaca* (1877), whose now typical Rossettian looks were coded as variously otherwordly, be it ancient, medieval, allegorical or Eastern. So Vaka Brown's allusion to Rossetti is the self-conscious invocation of what was by the early twentieth century a highly recognisable nineteenth-century image of femininity; one that was redolent of grandeur, transgressive passion, undying love and, often, tragedy.

By the time of Vaka Brown's schooling in Paris and her sojourn in the United States, Rossetti's reputation was riding high and he was the subject of several romanticised biographies (see Casteras 1990). Spurred partly by the dramatic disinterrment of the early poems from Elizabeth Siddall's coffin, and the self-revealing confessional read into the resultant volume of published verse, the myth of Rossetti as the romantic artist/hero, already developed in his lifetime, held sway for several years after his death in 1882. Vaka Brown assumes that her readers in America, Europe and the Ottoman Empire would be familiar with the name Rossetti and that the description of a character as Rossettian would make sense. As well as exhibitions in Britain, there were two large Pre-Raphaelite exhibitions in America prior to the publication of Vaka Brown's book in 1909. The first Pre-Raphaelite show in the USA was in New York in 1857. Then in 1892 in Philadelphia , Samuel Bancroft, the other great American collector of the Pre-Raphaelites, loaned many of his works to a public exhibition, including Rossetti's *Lady Lilith* and *Found* (Dickason 1953, Elzea 1997). But, although Bancroft owned *The Blessed Damozel*, the painting was not on display in either exhibition, even though the poem and the painting were seen as an important part of Rossetti's *oeuvre*, featuring prominently (including a full-page engraving) in Theodore Child's review of Bancroft's collection in *Harpers Monthly* in 1890.[5] Write-ups like this and the publicity for the American shows would have brought the Pre-Raphaelites to the attention of a public far wider than those who actually saw the exhibitions.

Both 'The Blessed Damozel' (poem or painting) and 'A Last Confession' are alluded to in Vaka Brown's text. The Rossetti woman's assumption that the reference to Rossetti's paintings is generic, 'Do you mean that I look like Rossetti's paintings?', indicates a familiarity with the Pre-Raphaelite female portrait as an easily recognisable type. At this point in the narrative, Vaka Brown does not know that the woman has spent time in Europe, but she does not seem at all surprised that an inmate of a Turkish harem should be so familiar with the concept of a Rossetti type. Nor does it seem at all remarkable that this woman is able to identify the author from the single, and misattributed, stanza that Vaka Brown recited to her. In this way the term Rossetti serves both as shorthand for a particularly allusive physical description, and as another example of the familiarity of Ottoman women with Western culture. The 'Blessed Damozel' that Vaka Brown invokes ('she looked like a Rossetti painting … the Blessed Damosel') is, in fact, twice displaced: once by not being quoted, even though she refers to it by name (something she never does for 'A Last Confession'), and again, by being side-lined when Vaka Brown redirects the woman away from the painting towards the poem, 'I rather think you look like his poems: you are the embodiment of them'. What does this movement from one artistic form to another and from one story to another signify, especially in relation to the power of the gaze in the visualisation of the Oriental woman?[6] To answer this, I need to discuss 'A Last Confession' in some more detail before I come back to the damozel that lurks uncannily in the background.

The stanza from which Vaka Brown quotes comes from the most intensely and overtly eroticised section of 'A Last Confession'. The poem, set in the recent past of Austrian-occupied Italy in 1848, tells the story of an Italian freedom-fighter that makes his final confession to a priest. In garbled flashback he tells his story. He had, eleven years earlier, adopted an abandoned girl child, whom he raised and loved. The young soldier who had left his family to join the freedom-fighters and the child whose parents abandoned her because of famine became a family in the face of adversity. The quoted stanza comes just at the point in his narrative when the speaker tells of the moment when he realised that the girl he had rescued and raised had turned into a desirable woman. His paternal love – 'the father's, brother's love' – turns into a man's love, as he notices for the first time that her body had matured and her beauty no longer reminded him of child angels but of lovely women. The stanza before Vaka Brown's quotation con-cludes with his recognition of her growing maturity and a revelation of her developing breasts:

> And when, remembering all and counting back
> The time, I made out fourteen years for her
> And told her so, she gazed at me with eyes
> As of the sky and sea on a grey day,
> And drew her long hand through her hair, and asked me
> If she was not a woman; and then laughed:
> And as she stooped in laughing, I could see
> Beneath the growing throat the breasts half-globed
> Like folded lilies deepset in the stream.

The next stanza continues

> Yes, let me think of her as then; for so
> Her image, Father, is not like the sights
> Which come when you are gone. She had a mouth
> Made to bring death to life, – the underlip
> Sucked in, as if it strove to kiss itself.
> Her face was pearly pale, as when one stoops
> Over wan water; and the dark crisped hair
> And the hair's shadow make it paler still:–
> Where the moon's gaze is set in eddying gloom.

Her body bore her neck as the tree's stem
Bears the top branches; and as the branch sustains
The flower of the year's pride, her high neck bore
That face made wonderful with night and day.
Her voice was swift, yet ever the last words
Fell lingeringly; and rounded finger-tips
She had, that clung a little where they touched
And then were gone o' the instant ...[7]

I put Vaka Brown's quoted passage in context because the erotic charge of the material she has selected cannot be ignored – even if it is taken out of its context in one poem and attributed to another. It is after this section that the narrator murders his beloved, having subsequently heard her laugh in such a way that reminded him of the laughter of a prostitute he heard in the village square whilst he was hiding from the Austrian soldiers. From this coarse and womanly laugh – contrasted to her earlier naive and childish laughter – he 'deduces' that she is no longer an innocent and that she has given herself to the enemy soldiers. When she mockingly refuses the jewelled dagger he has bought her as a token of his love, he hears betrayal in her laugh and murders her with the gift weapon. Although I have previously characterised the typical Pre-Raphaelite heroine as unlike a normative regime of representation – which ran between the chaste and asexual bourgeois wife and mother, the angel in the house, and the cautionary tale of her counterpart, the fallen woman – 'A Last Confession' is clearly a poem concerned with a woman assumed to have fallen. It is also conventional in its outcome since here the fall does lead inexorably to death. This is in contrast to other Pre-Raphaelite versions of the fallen, or, as J. B. Bullen prefers to put it, 'sexualised' woman, such as Rossetti's *Found* (*c.* 1855), *Bocca Baciata* (1859) or William Holman Hunt's *Awakening Conscience* (1853), which are not straightforwardly condemnatory of women that a dominant discourse would have seen as sexually deviant (Bullen 1998, Faxon 1989, Pearce 1991, Flint 1989). Bullen argues that paintings such as these acknowledge the possibility of a 'whole category of women in whom the expression of sexual desire or the possession of sexual attractiveness might be perceived as both powerful and enhancing' (Bullen 1998: 50). Pre-Raphaelite openness about the results of the fall central to so many moralised Victorian narratives puts in the foreground the potential erotic investment in the *event* of the fall. This explains the incitement of male desire, which structures these sexualised images of women. Yet it still says little about the active desire and agency of their female protagonists. The absence of any investigation of the woman's sexuality (aside from the narrator's projections) in 'A Last Confession' is, then, akin to the young male narrator in Rossetti's poem 'Jenny' (1857) who, revealing more about his masculinity than about her sexuality, cannot avoid eroticising the young prostitute even as he bewails the cruelty of her fate and yet still never wakes her to ask her opinion (Riede 1992, Bullen 1998).

But the female interest in Rossetti and the Pre-Raphaelites shows that for both men and women there were potentially counter-cultural meanings in some of Rossetti's self-absorbed phallic sirens. At this point analysis must consider narcissism, the phallic woman and revenge. Bullen (1998) likens the 'curious anonymity' of the narcissistic woman in 'A Last Confession' to the similarly anonymous female characters in some of Rossetti's paintings in the 1860s, such as *Woman Combing her Hair* (1864), *Lady Lilith* (1864–) and *Fazio's Mistress* (1863). These images of sexually alluring women narcissistically absorbed in the contemplation of their own beauty, he suggests, leave the male viewer spellbound but frozen out. Rossetti's late works are regularly discussed as narcissistic or phallic sirens and were seen even at the time as the result of a fascination with the 'female principle'.[8] Just as the woman in 'A Last Confession' takes pleasure in her own beauty and in the narrator's growing appreciation of it (note the auto-eroticism of the 'underlip / sucked in, as if it strove to kiss itself'), the female images in these paintings represent a phallic female body that is complete in itself, functioning for a male viewer as a fetish which both denies loss and constantly reinvokes it. Created by men as an absolute in female beauty, the Pre-Raphaelite siren does not provide the gratification her designers seek; instead her self-absorption and phallic potency destabilise masculinity, reactivating the uncertainties that the images were constructed to ameliorate. In 'A Last Confession', the woman's mocking laughter as she refuses the narrator's token of love, the obviously phallic dagger he then buries in her heart, is a sexual rejection of a magnitude that Bullen even calls a 'castration'. The sexual rejection also signifies a national betrayal – signalled by her earlier desertion of the previously beloved old Italian Madonna in the church in favour of a recent German import. By associating with the interlopers she uses her beauty against the narrator and against her country, and thus deserves to die. Whilst it is possible to read the narrative in this way, I think the poem leaves things more open. I am not convinced that her perfidy is confirmed. The poem presents it as possibly a misapprehension on the narrator's part. She may indeed spurn his love, but there is no evidence beyond his fevered imagination that she has been impure. The moment of the stabbing is tied to her refusal of the gift of the dagger and to his own lapse in self-control. This suggests that it is his social death, his loss of a sense of self that leads to her physical demise, not a judicious weighing up of guilt.

> 'Take it,' I said to her the second time,
> 'Take it and keep it.' And then came a fire
> That burnt my hand; and then the fire was blood,
> And sea and sky were blood and fire, and all
> The day was one red blindness; till it seemed,
> Within the whirling brain's eclipse, that she
> Or I or all things bled or burned to death.
> And then I found her laid against my feet
> And knew that I had stabbed her, and saw still
> Her look in falling. For she took the knife

> Deep in her heart, even as I bade her then,
> And fell; and her stiff bodice scooped the sand
> Into her bosom.

As he stabs her in the 'brain's eclipse' the boundaries between him and her and the physical world, 'she or I or all things bled', are dissolved in an experience of blood and burning, the 'red blindness' of total self-obliterating rage. The narrator's trauma is not just at his unlicensed killing, nor at the loss of his beloved, but at the loss of his own narcissistic sense of righteousness – essential to a soldier who sees himself as a freedom-fighter – and the threat of divine judgement. 'Tell me' Father, he pleads

> ... tell me at once what hope
> Can reach me still. For now she draws it out
> Slowly, and only smiles as yet: look, Father,
> She scarcely smiles: but I shall hear her laugh
> Soon, when she shows the crimson steel to God.

The laugh that he had interpreted as a sign of her fall may now signal his own fall from grace, as she shows the bloody evidence to God and her laugh becomes one of revenge. Adding the element of the revenge or vindication of the (possibly not) fallen woman to the general idea of a Rossettian beauty, opens up the multiple functions of the Rossetti woman in Vaka Brown's writing. But to what extent is this phallic, narcissistic image of femininity, 'significantly, if damagingly, empowered' (Bullen 1998: 147), pleasurable for the woman viewer/reader? Since the sexualisation of women in these images has so often been understood as inciting male sexual desire rather than signifying an active female desire, I want to consider why Vaka Brown chooses to invoke two poems which both deal with the (doomed) beauty of a dead woman. Elizabeth Bronfen locates the Pre-Raphaelites within a wider European cultural obsession with what was seen as the heightened beauty of the sick woman (Bronfen 1992). But, whilst it is evident that some women cultivated, indeed enacted, the cult of the sick and even dying woman as muse to a male artist (some would cite the consumptive and perpetually ill Elizabeth Siddall as a case in point), Bronfen says little about the female consumer of such 'deanimated' images. To what extent was the Pre-Raphaelite obsession with doomed or even dead female beauties available to women? Although the Pre-Raphaelites rarely ventured into overtly Orientalist subjects, the trope of the enigmatic and fated woman could be combined with the morbidity stereotypically attributed to Oriental woman, as could the idea of a death-inducing passion. Certainly, as Derek Stanford argues, Pre-Raphaelite poetry and, under its influence, Aestheticism, can be attributed a particularisation of beauty that led to a new definition of the beautiful. The ensuing cult of 'intensity' produced 'poetry which was often passionate [and] melancholy', whose potential for an Oriental setting is clear (Stanford 1973). So Vaka Brown's mixture of the Orient and the Pre-Raphaelite could meld two cultural currents together. But, her Rossetti woman is not doomed; so to what is she alluding with the introduction of Rossetti into her Oriental scene?

In response to feminist critiques that Rossetti's phallic sirens lack any sign of female agency, Bullen emphasises the potentially destructive power of the phallic woman. He argues that, because the fatal wounding of the narrator in 'A Last Confession' is tied to his murder of the woman, she displays 'an independence which brings death, not only to herself, but also to [him]' (Bullen 1998: 147). Raised by a man and made in an image of his own desire, the phallic woman problematises his masculinity rather than desiring it. Similarly, Lynn Pearce, in a discussion of *Beata Beatrix*, argues that the image of the beautiful dying woman suggests a masculinity that, unable to resolve the virgin/whore contradiction, can only love the Beatrix who dies whilst still a virgin and therefore incontrovertibly pure. She wonders if this avoidance of an active female sexuality might leave a space for a female viewer's pleasure that is other than masochistic (the result of a cross-gender identification with the male character's sadism); possibly in the compensatory knowledge that male power has its limitations and is in the end frustrated, even if at the cost of the woman's life (Pearce 1991: 54–5). I agree with Pearce and Bullen that *Beata Beatrix* and 'A Last Confession' reveal the unsustainability of male fantasies and the instability of masculinity, but where Bullen sees the double death at the end of 'A Last Confession' as testament to the phallicised woman's deadly power, I see the possibility that he has killed her wrongly, as it were, that she has not betrayed him with the Austrians. Rejection, yes, but betrayal, no: to conflate the two is to see the narrator as more reliable than he is. The hallucinatory quality of parts of his narrative, the instant association of her laugh when she spurns the dagger with that of the prostitute in the market place, do not make for reliable witnesses. This poem tells of a woman accused, possibly wrongly, who is not given the chance to defend herself or to be forgiven.

But the woman who prompts Vaka Brown to declaim Rossetti's lines, *is* guilty of perfidious adultery, yet she is forgiven. The Rossetti woman, relatively happy in her marriage and with three children, was wooed by Edgar, an English nobleman, whilst her husband was away, and ran away with him. They had a daughter, but after two years the woman repented and wrote to her Turkish husband begging forgiveness. He travelled to Scotland to reclaim her and although Edgar visited her in Istanbul pleading with her to return, she refused; at which point the Englishman committed suicide. Her husband then took the new daughter into his care as part of his family. The problem she now faces is that Edgar's mother, the duchess, wants her granddaughter to return to England (or Scotland). The Rossetti woman wants Vaka Brown to write to the duchess explaining that the girl will be raised in Turkey as an 'Osmanli noblewoman', and may return to England as an adult if she wishes. Vaka Brown offers crucial deviations from both the conventional narrative of the fall and from Rossetti's poems. Unlike 'The Blessed Damozel', the dead lover in this instance is the man, not the damozel, and unlike the woman in 'A Last Confession', this Rossetti woman is presented as having made a happy romantic alliance on her own terms, despite the potentially destructive implications of her illicit passion. Perhaps Vaka Brown switches to a generic Pre-Raphaelite position of sympathy for – yet eroticisation of – the fallen woman, rather than sticking to the details of either named painting or poem? Certainly, she responds only positively to the forgiveness offered to her Rossetti woman by the wronged husband.

Many women experienced the Pre-Raphaelite vision of femininity as enabling. Stanford concludes that the essence of its appeal 'lay in the nourishment it offered to the forces of feminism', noting that Max Beerbohm identified the Pre-Raphaelite fan base in 1880 as one in which 'the keenest students of the exquisite were women'.[9] As Henry James and Mary Howitt make clear, the Pre-Raphaelite vision of female beauty offered an alternative mode of taste and female behaviour that many women, trying to be unconventional in whatever way, found attractive and attempted to emulate (see also Shefer 1985). Goff insists that it is wrong to see the working-class women who were taken up by the Pre-Raphaelites as simply victims, patronised and remade in the image that their artist lover/husband desired (see also Marsh 1987, Marsh and Gerrish Nunn 1997, Faxon 1989). Making these women with their non-classical looks emblems of a new beauty, the Pre-Raphaelites valorised a mode of female appearance that was not the middle- and upper-class norm. Since the early criticism of Pre-Raphaelite works focused precisely on the ugliness of such unclassical bodies, this new look had come a long way to be accepted as a new (liberating and more inclusive) standard of attractiveness.

It was not just that a new definition of female beauty was emerging and being given cultural space: the 'cult' of this particular type of female beauty endowed her looks with more than a mere physical significance. The Pre-Raphaelite icon, as Rossetti's fans discovered (according to Stanford), had both a 'strong but refined sexual attraction' and 'the sense of woman as a vehicle of the divine; a creature affording man the means of identification with the cosmos' (Stanford 1970: 29). This 'splendid advertisement for woman' (Stanford 1970: 29) was, he argues, psychologically intriguing to men as well as to women. I like Stanford's point that women were attracted to the Pre-Raphaelite 'cult' of women because its championing of non-standard, enigmatic beauty enhanced their marriagability – the Pre-Raphaelite painters were held to be 'the plain girl's best friend' by Eliza Haweis in 1878.[10] But I want also to consider the pleasures possible for women in the consumption of these images and in the enactment of an identification with them. As Macleod (1995, 1997) has demonstrated, women were active in the patronage of the Pre-Raphaelites; either collecting in their own right (such as the rare example of Ellen Heaton) or, more often, collaborating with their husbands (such as Julia and George Rae) in a joint process of commissioning, acquisition and display. The materiality of this Pre-Raphaelite consumption came to constitute 'an integral aspect of their lives together' (Macleod 1997: 109). The installation of Pre-Raphaelite work in their homes was an integral part of its pleasure and women were often able to add to the purpose-made Pre-Raphaelite environment through the arrangement of interior furnishing and their own sympathetic self-display in Pre-Raphaelite mode. The Pre-Raphaelite literature and art that Vaka Brown adopted at the turn of the century had for some time offered women an opportunity for a profoundly aesthetic experience.

Stanford charts the change from earlier images that were 'sensual *and* refined' to the 'darkling Venus' of the later works by Rossetti and the later generation of Pre-Raphaelite or Aesthetic painters, Edward Burne-Jones, Simeon Solomon and Aubrey Beardsley. The sirens in Rossetti's later works are no longer docile as in *Ecce Ancille Domine* (1850) or transcendent as in *Beata Beatrix* (1863) but are devouring, as seen in *Astarte Syriaca* (1877) or sultrily narcissistic as in *The Bower Meadow* (1883) (Stanford 1970: 30). Stanford points the reader towards Arthur Symons' writings on Rossetti in the 1920s where Symons ponders this transition with some perplexity:

> ... as his dreams overpower him, as he becomes the slave and no longer the master of his dreams, his pictures become no longer symbolic. They become idols. Venus, growing more and more Asiatic as the moon's crescent begins to glitter above her head, and her name changes from Aphrodite into Astarte, loses all the freshness of the waves from which she was born, and her own sorcery hardens into a wooden image painted to be the object of savage worship. Dreams are not longer content to be turned into waking realities, taking the color of the daylight, that they may be visible to our eyes, but they remain lunar, spectral, a dark and unintelligible menace. (Symons 1923: 130–1)

What to Symons was unintelligible is now clear as a precursor of the vamp and the femme fatale; images of dangerously active female sexuality that were to dominate the *fin de siècle* and the early twentieth century. In the case of Vaka Brown both the quoted poem and the two paintings of *The Blessed Damozel* locate her interest in the later works. So what is enabled by the invocation of the fleshly Rossettis? One obvious answer would be to concentrate on the reconsideration of female beauty allowed by this new aesthetic. This would be attractive to a writer who wanted to endorse the beauty of non-European, Oriental female bodies. This might not apply to Vaka Brown herself, who as Greek can also claim a European – indeed classical – genealogy, but for the women she admires in the harems the Rossetti motif can stand as an absolute marker of individuated beauty. In contrast to her many other detailed female portraits, the Rossetti lady is never described: the allusiveness of the Rossetti label is enough. 'Rossettian' presumes a particularised beauty that, although it had become a stereotype by the later nineteenth century, still signalled a 'stunner' who was not in the common run of things. It is this exclusivity and specialness that Vaka Brown attaches to the woman about whom she is most admiring.

This new fleshliness is distinctly racialised. Symons' reference to the primitive and savage signalled by the movement to a pre-classical Syrian Venus, the *Astarte Syriaca*, echoes the language of Rossetti's brother William, the chronicler of the Pre-Raphaelite Brotherhood. Writing of the paintings done by Dante Gabriel after the publication of *Poems* in 1870, William acknowledged the validity of some criticisms of this later work, which took 'against the outre point of [his] style in painting – especially the peculiar and almost *mulatto* forms of his mouths, and the tumid elongation of his throats, almost (so W[atts] holds) goitred in form' (William Rossetti, quoted in Riede 1992: 152, my emphasis).

Similarly, Sidney Colvin in the *Magazine of Art* in 1883 (when the Liverpool *Damozel* was shown at the Burlington Fine Arts Club), lamented '… what a decay of the colour-sense is shown in the unwholesome pink stars and haloes, the *dusky hotness* and livid colours of the "Blessed Damozel"!' (Colvin, quoted in Bennet 1988: 179, my emphasis). The readiness to use a racial lexicon to describe these unusual female forms illustrates the unspoken whiteness inherent in normative, or even less obviously excessive, figures of female beauty. It also links the primitive or miscegenated with deformity and disease, not only returning to the medical discourse of disease and deformity utilised in early criticism of the Pre-Raphaelites, but also linking the racially indeterminate to the psycho-sexual discourse of deviancy and degeneracy that Bullen identifies as the dominant mode of critical response to the late Pre-Raphaelites and Aesthetics.

I do not know if Vaka Brown was aware of the *Astarte Syriaca*, but, as she was someone familiar with Rossetti's work, it is highly likely that news of a pre-classical Middle Eastern Venus would have caught her attention. Although interest by an artist she clearly admired in a non-European model of female desirability must have been attractive, it is unlikely that the negative associations of the primitive in Rossetti's later work would have been entirely welcome. She was, after all, partly associated with the non-European herself. Unlike Pierre Loti's Turkish female protagonists in *Les Désenchantées* who repeatedly explain that they are all 'little savages' at heart, Vaka Brown does not impute this to herself or very much to the Turkish women she represents herself living among. Whilst the primitive or atavistic connotations of these sirens were evident to some critics, the fact that self-presentation *à la Rossetti* remained popular with many women indicates that these associations were by no means dominant. The reaction to these 'whitey-brown' sirens could go either way and the evidence that some viewers did not see racial indeterminacy as a disadvantage suggests the potential that a Rossettian regime of representation could offer a writer like Vaka Brown. Jan Marsh, who wonders if 'Rossettian' had become a code for an attractive woman, notes that it could mean either a visual look or a feeling.[11] If this were the case, and Vaka Brown clearly assumes that her readers get the gist of the Rossetti reference, then the passions and transgressions of Rossetti's love life that were so well-rehearsed in the romanticised biographies popular at the turn of the century (that would doubtless have appealed to so romantic a writer as Vaka Brown) also come into play as her purple-tinged prose builds up the erotics of her fascination with the Rossetti lady. Does the non-standardised particularity of the Pre-Raphaelite mode of beauty provide any other way in to thinking about the pleasure available to the female consumer of an image whose male projective fantasies of the phallic woman seem often to override the idea of an active female sexuality?

PERFORMATIVITY: SEXUALISATION, RACIALISATION
AND TRANSCULTURATION

It is very significant that at the culmination of the highly charged exchange between Vaka Brown and the Rossetti lady, the Turkish woman identifies and claims Demetra Vaka Brown as 'belong[ing] to us Oriental women'. The problem that plagues Vaka Brown throughout her book is whether her ethnic and racialised identity is stable and is recognisable – to herself, to the characters in the book, and to the book's readers. Whilst is it precisely her ability to perform both Occidental and Oriental identifications that made her book a marketable product, it is also quite obviously troubling to the narrator to be so insecure and unstable. The authorial identity constructed within the text requires both a closeness to and a distance from the Orient and Orientalised femininity: the proximity is simultaneously one which the narrator desires, not least on behalf of her readers, and something to be avoided, or else she will be one of *them* and will risk being denigrated along with the Turks.

It is for this reason that Vaka Brown tries repeatedly both to invoke the stereotypes that make the Ottoman woman recognisable and to challenge and invalidate their negative aspects. Her distressed bewilderment in the passage I quoted earlier – could it have been like this all along 'and I never have known it' – is reminiscent of the impact of shame discussed by Eve Kosofsky Sedgwick (1993). She draws on Silvan Tomkins to argue that shame is an affect central to the formation of identities. Although what is considered shaming will vary across cultures, the result, she suggests, is the same: if shame 'is a bad feeling attached to what one is: one therefore *is something* in experiencing shame' (Sedgwick 1993: 12, original emphasis). Most importantly for my analysis, the effect of shame is not only prompted by shame at one's own behaviour but may also be activated by witnessing the shaming of another. In this light, the shame Vaka Brown feels at the belittlement of the Turks sets up the problematic of her book. Is she an Oriental or Ottoman woman or not? Can she risk this identification, when the shaming instance of having Turks re-presented to her through American eyes (as well as her own ambivalence about identifying with the Orient) has actually tarnished a previously acceptable identification? Her ambivalence about being identified with the Turkish women is not just another example of the problems of contamination faced by Occidental women travel writers as they attempted to claim the objectivity of an ethnographic authority. Rather, it signals the distress of a subject in the making that is under threat of being forced to give up an already only partial identification with a desired (and, in the context of her teenage emigration to the United States, nostalgic) Orientalised self. The customs of the Turks were only looked upon as 'quite as natural as my own', they never actually *were* her own.

But this partial ownership was a source of pleasure and pride. Her decision to write this, her first, and subsequent books speaks to a strong desire to retain the Ottoman self that has been partially diluted by her emigration to the United

States; yet Vaka Brown must also perform as an American and enact her new diasporic identifications in terms that her host country could tolerate. The threat of contamination by the East is indeed present in Vaka Brown's account. But here contamination works two ways: she also risked having her Ottoman-ness contaminated by too much American-ness. It is in this light that the eroticised conquest of her by the Rossetti woman needs to be seen: it is not just that Vaka Brown wants her to *like* her, but that she wants her to *claim* her, and, to claim her in such a way that her Oriental and Occidental qualities are recognised. It is important to note that the Rossetti woman has sought her out to help in a custody case over her daughter – something that she feels only a liberated part-Occidental woman could manage. Thus, for the twice-displaced Vaka Brown, already somewhat 'other' as a Greek in Turkey, and then again as an Ottoman in America, comes proof that her performance of a complex racialised identification has been properly recognised. The display of Ottoman femininities offered in the book serves to mark out for an audience assumed to be less than expert the reiterative elements essential to the racialised and ethnic performative identifications in relation to which Vaka Brown wants to be situated.

The ambivalence of her identification as Greek and Christian, which was tolerable in Istanbul because there was a context for the comprehension of those identifications (see Chapter Two), is rendered troublesome once she is relocated to America. There she is interpellated as Oriental within an Orientalist discourse that cannot recognise her differentiated Ottoman subjectivity. Shamed by the prejudice against Turks, which also threatens to envelope her if Americans persist in failing to recognise her performance of a nuanced Greek-Ottoman identification, Vaka Brown proffers a defence of Turkish women that is successful enough partially to redeem her Oriental roots, without capitulating entirely to the lure of the harem and too much contamination. In the context of emergent anti-immigrant prejudice directed at the Greek American community (Kalogeras 1989) Vaka Brown began to build her own version of an American identity, consolidated after her 1901 visit to Turkey by her marriage to Kenneth Brown in 1904.

Paradoxically, this American identity was unsettled in 1917 by shame at the actions of the Greek government, when she was distraught at King Constantine's abandonment of Greece's ally Serbia in the face of Bulgarian aggression. Writing in *In the Heart of German Intrigue* Vaka Brown reveals how her desired internationalism was under threat from an upsurge of bewildering race feeling:

> At that moment all my previous conceptions of my real state of mind fell away from me, and I stood revealed to myself as Greek and nothing but a Greek. A sense of shame overpowered me, as if I were personally responsible for this act of the race whose blood flowed in my veins. (Vaka 1918: 4)

Her Greek heritage now shamed her and interfered with her desired American-ness; an immigrant identity based on being not too much associated with the Greeks in America. Like all Greeks she maintained a diasporic loyalty to the

Hellenic dream of a unified Greece, but she also distanced herself from the Greek immigrant community, writing in English and living largely in American society: 'I gradually became an American in thought and in spirit … I did not care to go with people of my own race' (Vaka 1918: 1). The misadventures of Greece under Constantine jolted her back into a 'race' identity that linked her more than she liked with the American Greek community (itself vituperatively split between Constantine and Venizelos, see Saloutos 1964). The un-heroic role of Greece on the world stage also interrupted her 'pro-Hellenic' affiliation to the classical Greece of the Phryne legend that, in the tradition of Western Orientalism, also preferred to erase the troublesome modernity of contemporary Athens in favour of the classical past.[12] This could only be resolved by another journey of 'return', this time to Greece, after which, relieved to see Greece under safe leadership, she could once again associate herself with the valued elements of the Hellenic or the Byzantine that, along with her Ottomanism, coloured her chosen American identification.

In this context, aware of how shame could threaten the balance of her Greek and Ottoman affiliations, writing up her subsequent visits to the region caused further problems for her multiple identifications. When she returned to report on the Young Turk reforms in 1921, Vaka Brown rarely welcomed the sight of Turkish women working unveiled in the streets, offices and shops. Though this may seem contradictory, given her commitment to forging an independent life beyond the domestic, it makes sense since it was through an alignment with the old lifestyle of the elite harems that she could best demonstrate the particular Orientalised identification that she craved. Her displeasure with the unveiled Istanbul shop-girls in her account of 1923 takes a tone of such personal affront precisely because of the psychic loss she feels at the demise of a system of segregated life that was never hers in the first place, but in which she clearly had an over-determined investment (see Chapter Three).

Butler argues that performative actions only stand any chance of success if they have accumulated '*the force of authority through the repetition or citation of a prior, authoritative set of practices*' (Butler 1993: 19, original emphasis). Following Derrida, she insists that the performative statement relies for its success on conformity to an 'iterable model'; in other words, the norms through whose reiteration performativity works must have a history and be recognisable. The sources I have been discussing raise the question of whether performativity can work across cultures and languages and in terms of racial and ethnic identifications. This is not to say that a different culture will not have the regulatory and discursive modes of power that spur reiterative performative actions, but that, in trying to enact new identities, subjects risk remaining unrecognisable if their codings do not translate across cultures. Apart from the Western Rossetti reference, the history of the identificatory terms reiterated by Demetra Vaka Brown and the other Ottoman writers were largely unavailable to their Occidental audience. This rendered them either meaningless or inaccurate. Vaka Brown was trying to give voice to a different form of Ottoman femininity than that standardised by dominant Orientalist discourse. Yet the terms of intra-Ottoman differentiation, which were so important to her vision of her particular racialised space, had no comparable iterative history and hence no meaning in the Occident. Whilst some designations, like Circassian, might be familiar in the West (see Chapter Three), their particular histories would have carried different resonances in the Orient. There, their power as a distinguishing term among regional identifications was not overlaid with the same force of Orientalism, which attaches to each and every Oriental identification a similarly charged racialisation. In trying to use these terms Ottoman writers found themselves stuck between explaining the nuances of the classifications as they saw them and simultaneously challenging the blanket deformations of Orientalist structures of comprehension. In this light, Vaka Brown's oscillation between being of or separate from the Orient reveals both the lure of performative identificatory processes and the limits of the performative once it attempts to transculturate.

This is where the problem of authenticity returns. If authenticity is considered as performative, it becomes clear that the set of previously sanctioned codings whose reiteration signals authenticity will be differently constituted for different audiences. Halide Edib's condemnation of Vaka Brown typifies this dilemma. Edib is simultaneously trying to present herself to an Occidental readership as an authentic 'Oriental' woman (which requires that she reiterate and reconfirm signs of Orientalness that the West can recognise) and at the same time trying to discredit Vaka Brown's performance of Orientalness, by arguing that Vaka Brown's signs of belonging would not be recognised by an Ottoman audience. Edib is not only struggling because she is trying to codify herself within two overlapping but separate discourses: to be an authentic Ottoman in both regional/Oriental and Occidental terms. The problem is generic. Like the deadening effect of repeating a stereotype (in which one can only ever approximate but never quite fit a previously set classification), the invocation of authenticity will each time slightly miss the mark. Since the iterative elements of a performative action have to be familiar to the viewer before they can make sense, the 'authentic' Ottoman woman who wants her performance to be recognisable to the West must relate herself to a series of already available stereotypes operating within a previously existing Western classification system. Since every performative repetition is a dynamic intersubjective event, it will succeed or fail depending on who is involved and which histories and individual qualities they bring to their participation in the event. Furthermore, such stereotypes, as Emily Apter highlights (1996), are the Achilles heel of performativity. Using Homi Bhabha's emphasis on the stereotype's role in processes of subjectification, Apter argues that each new attempt to repeat the stereotype will, *qua* Bhabha, be a 'deadening' mismatch. The experience of not quite matching will alienate the subject from the image rather than tie them securely to it. Regarding authenticity as performative opens up the idea of the reiterative as not only referring back to but as also always misfitting, not quite matching, a prior or imagined 'original'. The difficulty of trying to be authentic is that one can never actually make a match, one can only ever approximate. And it is this dilemma that is so clearly manifested by these writers. Vaka Brown and Edib underscore the impossibility of totally reproducing a prior model – since, when this is combined with a transcultural scenario, the inbuilt problem becomes even more complex.

It is not just that cross-cultural iterations (like all iterative elements) need an interpretive community that can recognise and understand them. The gap between the Ottoman performer and the Occidental viewer/reader emphasises the always intersubjective quality of the processes by which a performative action is decoded. Where the different agents do not share a set of codings, the performance breaks down. The ways in which the stereotype misfits will not only be different each time, but the gaps and frayings from the original will themselves be differently recognisable to differently formed subjects. Hence, Edib's rejection of Vaka Brown's claim to fit the mould of the authentic harem respondent is couched both in terms of the mismatch of Vaka Brown's perform-ance to Edib's own experience (coded as truly Ottoman) and in relation to Edib's own attempt to remake the mould of the real Ottoman or Turkish woman to which she aspires. This quest to create alternative iterable qualities for a new type/image of Oriental women is also addressed to a 'home' audience of Otto-man/Turkish readers who will be able to read her self-representation within a different classification system. But, can the Western-educated and European-dressed Edib alter the terms of an Orientalist frame sufficiently for her primary Occidental audience to recognise the performative qualities she reiterates, with-out herself being deadened by the powerful stereotypes she must invoke in order to replace them?

SAPPHISM, DIFFERENCE AND DESIRE

It is in this light that the erotics of Vaka Brown's interaction with the Rossetti woman can be rethought. Like Edib, Vaka Brown has to operate within already existing codes and sometimes risks being overpowered by the stereotypes she invokes (in this case the lesbian overtones of the homoerotic Rossetti scenario). Activating the lesbian theme familiar to Orientalist representation may in part serve to mark her authenticity because she reiterates a code easily recognised in the West. But, because the lesbian codings come through most clearly in relation to the Rossetti woman, this section intermingles the two overlapping but differ-ently inflected discourses of beauty and of looking that operate simultaneously in Vaka Brown's book.

The first is a (necessarily feminised) version of a conventional Orientalist gaze, operating as a classificatory surveillance of Ottoman populations: in this Vaka Brown, like most Western sources, presents a gallery of racialised images of Ottoman women which identifies them as objects of a desirous but largely superior gaze. The earlier sections of *Haremlik* are closely aligned with a typical Orientalist range of imagery that generically presumes a male point of view but that, particularly when operating through an experiential description of female beauty, was also available to Occidental women observers. However, Western women were still faced with problems in adapting for themselves this masculine coded position – seen most often in the ways that their gender interrupted the establishment of the distance necessary for the maintenance of Orientalism's 'positional superiority' (Said 1978: 7). For Vaka Brown, whose portraits of women such as Djimlah and Aïshé Hanım seek to present them as exoticised beauties within well-established Orientalist conventions, it is ethnicity as well as gender which connects her so closely to the object of enquiry as to leave her 'bewildered'. This bewilderment is a symptom of the attempt to graft herself onto a Western and largely masculinist Orientalist viewing position signalled by the use of generic Orientalist tropes (remember the odalisque pose adopted by the hapless Djimlah?).

The second discourse of beauty owes its allegiance to another Western regime of representation that was already acknowledged as pleasurable and empowering for women. This utilises Pre-Raphaelite imagery to validate an alternative mode of female beauty. Just like her nineteenth-century Western predecessors who used the *Arabian Nights* to signal the fantastic, Vaka Brown by invoking Rossetti – especially through so loose and evocative a chain of association – enters into a realm of fantasy that was already highly sexualised and gratifying for female consumers. This connection to Rossetti in the context of her presence in the harem recasts the experiential as fantasy in a way that allows her access to a gender and ethnic specific sexualisation. Unlike some of the Ottoman terms that cannot translate for the West (*Perote*, harem) the Occidental Pre-Raphaelite terminology is presented as translating unproblematically to the Orient. This not only emphasises the Westernised knowledge of the harem women, but also points to the wish-fulfilment projective qualities that the Rossetti woman has for Vaka Brown: she shares Vaka Brown's cultural framework and can also read her mind to make an instant link between poem, painting and mood. Whilst I have previously used the term stereotype to describe the cumulative image of the Pre-Raphaelite woman, it does not operate in the same way as a stereotype relating to a social category such as race.

Apart from the obvious potential of a very particularised (not to mention dusky or sultry) vision of feminine loveliness for a non-European setting, the Pre-Raphaelite woman was frequently associated with a non-normative set of female behaviours and appearances. This potential to break with Western gender conventions gives Vaka Brown a space in which to assume an active viewing position that can avoid some of the masculinist sadism of the previous mode of viewing ('I could have smacked her pretty mouth') and allow for a female pleasure in looking that can play across the divide between voyeurism and narcissism. But the sapphic Orient is a dangerous trope to perform as it risks coding Vaka Brown as a sexualised object within the depicted scene. The text is partly successful in securing Vaka Brown as the observer and not the observed, which is one of its aims. But this separation from the Oriental object is put at risk once the

Rossetti woman fulfils her other purpose by identifying and claiming Vaka Brown as an Oriental woman. The dangers of being located as part of the (in this instance sapphic) Orient are clear. Although Vaka Brown wants her performance of Orientalness to be recognised, she wants it to be nuanced and remade in her own terms; not just to exist as an endlessly alienating mismatch of existing Orientalist stereotypes. The adoption of an objectifying gaze that classifies and evaluates the beauty of the Ottoman women she surveys is one way that Vaka Brown can claim authenticity on both (feminine) experiential and (masculine) objective grounds. This lets her occupy a more validated knowledge position through which to authenticate herself, while at the same time she is recognised as the owner of a body of knowledge that is self-experience. The Rossetti woman fully understands the nature of Vaka Brown's Ottoman identity. It is the intense desire of the text that this be recognised – at the very moment when Vaka Brown's appropriation of an eroticising gaze is at its most pronounced and most interactive – that produces the libidinal charge of the narrative. In an earlier version of this section I have argued that this eroticising gaze was masculine-coded and that it was this that produced the queerness so evident to modern eyes (Lewis 1999a). Although I still think that the assumption of an active gaze in a book bound by gender-specific authenticating conventions that can never overlook Vaka Brown's femininity will produce a masculinisation of sorts (since to do otherwise would sit at odds with the organising principle of the book's production and circulation), I now no longer see this binary as so absolute. The position of active desire that Vaka Brown takes up in relation to the Rossetti woman is able to traverse the continuum that runs between masculine and feminine, voyeuristic and narcissistic. This is because it is structured by the acknowledgement of differences other than sexual difference which, played out through her repeated stress on the differences between women, complicates any assumption of a narcissistic mirroring or matching.

Jackie Stacey (1988), on the visual pleasure of women film viewers, writes about the importance of such differences. Discussing how viewers are often fascinated by women characters in a film she notes that their fascination is not just one of identification (wanting to be like the female characters) but extends to a deep interest in the interactions between women in the movie. Arguing that such filmic relations between female characters often emphasise the differences between women on screen, Stacey demonstrates that viewers' 'fascinations … are precisely about difference – forms of otherness between women characters which are not merely reducible to sexual difference, so often seen as the sole producer of desire itself' (Stacey 1988: 122). Stacey suggests that what is often understood as simply a desire to be like the women in the film can be repositioned as a more complex desire to make an identification in the context of their differentiating interaction in the movie. Moreover, she suggests, the structure of films often disrupts identificatory fantasies even as they occur: in the film *Desperately Seeking Susan* (dir. Susan Seidelman 1984), for example, Roberta's (Rosanna Arquette) desire to become like Susan (Madonna), the object of her fascinated female gaze, is offered only a 'temporary narrative fulfillment' because 'the pleasures of this female desire cannot be collapsed into simple iden- tification, since difference and otherness are continually played upon, even when Roberta "becomes" her idealised object' (Stacey 1988: 129). Just as the film repeatedly contrasts the dissimilarities of the two female protagonists, so too does Vaka Brown's book construct endless points of differentiation between her- self and the Ottoman women who so fascinate her. With the Rossetti woman, to whom she is most drawn, the differences are emphasised even as the physical closeness between them develops. That these differences are 'not reducible to sexual difference' (Stacey 1988: 122) is axiomatic to the project: it is precisely the differences between racialised modes of femininity that are important here.

For all that Rossetti's paintings and poems reveal and revel in the full fleshli- ness of the female form, psychologically they were, as Stanford declares, 'enigmas; ideally intriguing, not the least to their own sex' (Stanford 1970: 29). Vaka Brown's Rossetti lady is precisely such an enigma: she draws Vaka Brown to her despite her previously made plans to leave Istanbul, and whilst she eventu- ally reveals the mystery of her past she remains a cipher to the reader since, as with the characters in 'A Last Confession', her name is never revealed – nor is she described in any detail. The repeated reference to her as 'my' Rossetti lady is too emphatic to ignore and suggests a level of erotic investment that is only just held in check by the chapter's heterosexual alibi. Her husband is met by Vaka Brown and described as suitably handsome and charming. The Rossetti lady con- stantly avows her love for him, her desire to repent her sins and her intention to fulfil the role of loving and obedient wife and mother. But Vaka Brown's desir- ous gaze at the Rossetti woman cannot be reduced to either an only masculinist objectifying gaze (built on an emphasis on difference) or a narcissistic gaze (built on the collapse of difference). She does both and it is the interaction between these two modes which creates the particular identificatory space she seeks. In this passage, Vaka Brown is invited to join the husband in admiring his wife's beautiful hair, again staging an identification with the man as owner of the desir- ous gaze rather than as woman as its object:

> As we sat on the divan, my Rossetti lady had her hair loose on her shoulders, except for a ribbon holding it back from her face. Ahmet Pasha [the husband] gathered a strand of it in his fingers, and turned to me.
>
> 'Did you ever see anything more exquisite in your life?' he asked.
>
> I had to admit that had I never had never seen anything equal to it.
>
> 'Nor is there a woman more charming,' he said, his Turkish politeness not permitting him to declare in the presence of another that she was the *most* charming of all.
>
> My Rossetti lady took his hand and kissed it in silence; and I thought I saw, together with love, the gratitude of a woman who has sinned and been forgiven. (Vaka 1909: 271, original emphasis)

Vaka Brown shares in Ahmet Paşa's appreciation of his wife's beauty and neatly deflects his compliment to her, by identifying with his unspoken assessment that the Rossetti lady is the most charming woman present. Yet earlier in the visit she had exclaimed when the Rossetti lady depreciated her beauty as now faded by age: 'Mashallah! Are you not [beautiful] now? ... I would give my soul to look like you' (Vaka 1909: 254). I am inclined to read this not only as an expression of envious identification but also as an insistence on the woman's beauty as the object of Vaka Brown's reverent gaze that highlights the difference between them, the other woman being older and more beautiful. In the extract above, Vaka Brown again resists a narcissistic identification with the Rossetti woman in favour of a partial identification with the husband as legitimate owner of the objectifying gaze. Her apparently selfless deflection of his well-intentioned compliment, along with the ownership implied by the oft-repeated nomenclature 'my Rossetti lady', serves to create a distance from rather than only an identification with the Oriental woman whose looks are so admired. This distance is necessary to puncture an overly close narcissistic dynamic, for it is just as important to Vaka Brown that the Rossetti woman can look at her and recognise her distinct forms of identification as it is that she is able to delight in the Ottoman woman's beauty. Like the movies discussed by Stacey, this is a moment depicting a female fascination with another woman where the attraction is partly identificatory, but where difference is also repeatedly demonstrated. The gallant attempt of the husband to position Vaka Brown also as an object of the admiring male gaze is rejected. This emphasises the differences between his wife and Vaka Brown, whilst not interfering with Vaka Brown's fascinated perusal of the woman whom they both know is really the '*most* charming', The Rossetti woman's triumphant claiming of a kinship with Vaka Brown, much as it is desired, is always only partial.

The narcissistic element in Vaka Brown's chapter is not simply a desire for the same, but a desire to be seen for what one is, or feels oneself to be, or wishes one were, or were recognised as (which in this instance is a gendered ethnic identity structured by differentiations that are not always easily decodable), by someone who reminds one of the experience of an earlier and unconditional love (Freud 1914). This earlier love, typified as the maternal–child dyad, is located in the pre-Oedipal prior to the recognition of sexual difference, hence the often troubling labelling of homosexual relations as pre-Oedipal and immature. But this does not have to have a negative gloss nor, as Stacey emphasises, do narcissism and voyeurism have to be conceptualised as polar divides (see also Evans and Gamman 1995, Lewis and Rolley 1996). Vaka Brown sets up a dynamic between the two women that is simultaneously narcissistic and differentiating because it can allow for a recognition of different types of femininity and of different ethnicities.

Macleod's argument that '[w]ays of seeing, like eating or speaking habits, are learned mannerisms' conditioned by location, gender and class helps to dissolve the idea of a singular gaze. Instead, 'individuals acquire a variety of spectatorship practices [in which] women in particular, because of the diversity of roles they are called upon to play in their lives, shift between a multiplicity of gazes from the dutiful and maternal to the pleasurable and transgressive' (Macleod

1997: 110). It is in the context of observing dress and female beauty that the female Orientalist gaze is most often reversed as Western women find themselves, their bodies and their clothes to be the object of Oriental women's curious gaze (Melman 1992, Roberts 2002, Ghose 1998). These moments of Western objectification occur most often in the harem or, notably, given where Vaka Brown is first solicited by the Rossetti lady, in the bath-house. Examined in this way Western women become spectacle for Oriental women and for their readers. Their accounts present them looking and being looked at within a play of gazes in which the Western women 'look [at Oriental women] vicariously from a male point of view, but they also derive their own pleasure from the sight – a pleasure that may well be inflected by homoerotic desire and that is, above all, attributable to the erotics of difference' (Ghose 1998: 60). But, whilst these Western accounts demonstrate the experience of Oriental scrutiny, their Western authors are able (often by using textual registers of fantasy) to reassert a Western superiority when needed. For the Orientalised female subject, speaking for herself rather then being spoken for, the range of viewing positions has to work differently. Vaka Brown's Rossetti interlude relies on a combination of (sometimes clashing) culturally and historically contingent habits of viewing whose mixture is essential to the author's identificatory practices. It is not enough simply for Vaka Brown and the Rossetti woman to have a touching moment of Pre-Raphaelite recognition. This must also be joined by the husband's invitation to Vaka Brown to join in an Oriental appreciation of Oriental female beauty that underlines that she is involved in an *Ottoman* consumption of the Pre-Raphaelite woman. This in turn permits to Vaka Brown an activation of the same-sex erotics long associated with the homosocial and homosexual function of Pre-Raphaelite images that were more often understood to operate on a male rather than female axis of desire (Morgan 1996, Dellamora 1990, Cruise 1995). The Oriental setting facilitates Vaka Brown's involvement in a reciprocal display of Oriental, Western and Pre-Raphaelite modes of viewing. Seeing and being seen in these ways allows her to demonstrate and integrate the diversity of differences on which are built her multiplicity of roles. Understanding difference in this, its widest sense, lets the Rossetti trope read as something that allows Vaka Brown a satisfying resolution to the questions of racial or ethnic difference that possess her writing.

This is where the reference to 'The Blessed Damozel' comes into its own once more. The damozel is described and painted as a woman looking down from heaven at her lover dreaming about her on earth below. In the painting, the monumental and typically Rossettian female figure (here modelled on Alexa Wilding) gazes out of the picture plane at, but not meeting the gaze of, the lover in the predella panel beneath. Separated from him in the poem by the 'gold bar of Heaven' she is divided from him in the painting by the frame that holds the two separate panels in place. Many times smaller than her and pictured lying prone on the ground, the male lover is almost of a size that could fit in her loosely clasped arms, like a child or a baby. So perhaps this is what Vaka Brown was thinking of when she confused the two works by Rossetti? The immense and

UNIVERSITY OF WINCHESTER
LIBRARY

otherworldly damozel is indeed phallicly replete and does offer a narcissistically pleasurable identification (to be that lovely and to be loved that much) but the picture and the poem are as much about the woman looking as they are about her being looked at or thought of. In this way, Vaka Brown's pleasure in the Rossetti woman is that the latter can really 'see' her for what she is, can recognise her as an Oriental woman, not as one who is the same as she is – whom the husband and Vaka Brown adore as the height of feminine desirability – but as one who is Oriental enough to communicate with her and Occidental enough to help her. The narcissistic allure of identification with the Rossetti woman, 'I knew that you belonged to us Oriental women', is one that can contain difference as well as similarity. This narcissism is also a desire to experience being looked at/adored as is the Rossetti lady – in the full recognition of her shortcomings – by both Vaka Brown and her husband. Vaka Brown does not want to be the object of a (Oriental) masculine gaze alone, but she can contemplate being, as the Rossetti woman is, the recipient of a combined male and female appreciation. The wish to be the object of such a pair of desirous gazes thus meshes gendered, sexualised and racialised positionings and allows for Vaka Brown the fantasy of a complete and resolved subjectivity, endorsed by a sympathetic recognition from others. The Rossetti woman is so important because she sees the ways in which Vaka Brown is at one with 'Oriental' women, without ignoring the things that make her different. Unlike the Turkish feminists (see Chapter Three) who value Vaka Brown's Occidentalness in all the wrong ways and for all the wrong reasons, thereby irritating her, the Rossetti woman instinctively responds to the best of both; loving her for the combined self Vaka Brown once was (or imagines/ remembers she was), that is now experienced as under threat from both the newly strange Orient and the never-quite home of the United States.

The Rossetti woman is invoked as both *The Blessed Damozel* and the nameless heroine of 'A Last Confession', this latter being the narrative of a sexualised woman who is not forgiven for her (possibly imagined) fall. Perhaps this is where the narcissism of the nameless woman in 'A Last Confession' re-enters as a pleasurable point of identification for women consumers? The forgiveness accorded to Vaka Brown's Rossetti lady corrects the unfair treatment meted out by Rossetti to his original creation. It is possible that part of women's pleasure in making narcissistic identifications with women represented as phallic is revenge against those who judge women wrongly; since male pleasure in the phallic woman is inevitably tinged with the pain of the castration (loss of power) it is intended to disavow. The ultimately phallic and Orientalised of Rossetti's images is the *Astarte Syriaca*, modelled on the unobtainable Jane Morris, whose type Bullen sees in the description of the woman in 'A Last Confession' and whose features David Riede detects in *The Blessed Damozel*, where the model Alexa Wilding is made to look as much like Morris as possible (Bullen 1998, Riede 1992: 158).[13] Just as the married Jane Morris is always a (partially) thwarted object for Rossetti, so too are the women of the Oriental harem for Occidental men. Yet to Vaka Brown, with her complex gender and ethnic identifications, the harem and its women are available as points of both identificatory/narcissistic and differentiating/voyeuristic desire.

The difficult to translate iterative elements of Orientalist stereotypes were open to a series of interventions that reveal glimpses of the different status that these performative tropes might have had in different discursive situations. In this light, claims to authenticity destabilise not only the stereotypes of the West – even as writers who invoke them risk being incorporated into them – but also hint, as I go on to discuss in Chapter Five, at the different histories and cultural meanings that could be attached to those performances. The possibilities offered by a homoerotic or homosocial engagement between Orientalised subjects in an Oriental setting can only be guessed at when represented in a source such as that published by Demetra Vaka Brown. Her mainly Occidental readership would have been ill-equipped to read her interaction with the Rossetti woman beyond the Western associations of the iterative terms she deploys. This is why Vaka Brown conspicuously plays up the fantastical nature of the Rossetti interlude (thus heightening its sexualisation) whilst simultaneously emphasising her own distinctly non-'Asiatic' racialised positioning. Meeting the Rossetti woman at the end of her trip (and the end of her book) the fascinated Vaka Brown is literally breathless with anticipation to hear her story, framing it as the fulfilment of her Orientalist fantasies:

> Every word she spoke seemed to add to the romance of the situation. I was to learn the story of my Rossetti poem, and I felt sure it could be nothing less than a wonderful love story. Bits of all the Oriental tales I knew came thronging to my mind. I was afraid to utter a word, lest I should break the spell and she should withhold her confidence from me. In my sojourn among the Turkish women I had always been expecting to come across some wonderful, out-of-the-common romance; but their lives, when seen near at hand, were generally as uneventful as the most conventional Western life. Now, at length, I felt that I was to learn of one that would come up to my expectations. (Vaka 1909: 254)

Yet though the story is as good a romance as Vaka Brown (and her readers) could desire; a glorious narrative of international aristocratic love, death and intrigue such as one could lose oneself in, and, despite the Rossetti woman's satisfying recognition of Vaka Brown's Oriental credentials, the text still underlines the gulf of difference between the two women. The sticking point for Vaka Brown is her doubts about the Rossetti woman's daughter remaining in Turkey. She feels compelled to challenge her Rossetti lady:

> 'She is English through her father, and she is the only child that grandmother has.'
>
> My Rossetti lady's face was again nearly as horror-stricken as before.
>
> 'Give the child to be brought up among that godless set of people. No! no! I could not do it!'

Vaka Brown writes that she 'protested, rather feebly',

> I was not happy in the situation. I had had my fill of romance, to be sure; but I had been dragged into playing a part in it that I did not particularly approve of,

although I knew the futility of trying to play any other part than that assigned to me. I looked out of my latticed window upon the Bosphorous, and as I looked the mystery of the East again stole over my senses. I turned my eyes to the woman, slim and graceful, and of a beauty that I could well believe had inspired the love it had in two men of alien races, and my Western prejudices fell from me.

The fantasy offered by the scopic pleasures of Oriental female beauty are able to see off the unwelcome realist intrusion of Vaka Brown's sense of Western (and Christian) responsibility. All resistance fades as she gazes at the Rossetti lady, now lying across a divan with her hands held up in prayer to Allah.

> … It seemed all in keeping with the night and the woman, looking more than ever like the embodiment of a poem, a greater poem now than Rossetti ever wrote. She was the East itself: the mysterious East, with its strange ideas of love, and death, and of religion. (Vaka 1909: 266–8)

Despite Vaka Brown's attempt to remind the child, Hope, of her English heritage the little girl prefers to be addressed by her new Turkish name and shows no desire to leave her mother. In the end Vaka Brown agrees to carry a photograph and a letter concerning the child's well-being to be posted from America. Of course, on the boat home she meets an Englishman who turns out to be Edgar's cousin, sent by the broken-hearted duchess to find her granddaughter. On the last leg of her journey and the last page of her book, Vaka Brown thinks of her complicity in the struggle over the child's social and racialised place in the world and writes, on hearing of the Englishman's failed mission, 'I thought of the addressed envelope down in my trunk, and of the miniature and the photographs of an English child. But this was not mine to tell, nor would it have helped him if I had' (Vaka 1909: 275). As the book closes, hybridity is put in its place. The Englishman assumes Vaka Brown to be Occidental and speaks to her in English about the problems he has encountered with the Turks, and the little girl, who a few pages earlier had a mixed heritage, is now identified as solely 'English': a child sacrificed to the 'true faith' that dominates the Orient and represents the unbreachable chasm between West and East. Up on deck Vaka Brown (the only other first-class passenger) passes as not Turkish and possibly not even Ottoman whilst, down below, the sealed envelope stays in the trunk; its safely hidden secret standing in for her camouflaged shifts in subjectivity, just as its eventual journey will seal her hybridity as envoy between Orient and Occident. Although this final passage seems to close down the opportunities for the recognition of multiple racial and gender identifications so fruitfully exploited in the Rossetti passages, this is not quite the case. Instead, the Englishman's inability to see beyond Vaka Brown's Westernised appearance, just as he had failed to discern that the Rossetti woman was Turkish when he met her previously in Europe,[14] underlines that the fluidity of racialised and sexualised identifications can only be seen by the perspicacious eye of a subject whose own identifications are/have been forged through similarly transculturated performances.[15] The rigidity of his identification as English renders him unable to detect the nuanced racialised identifications enacted by both Vaka Brown and the Rossetti woman.

NOTES

1 On male homoerotics in Loti see Barthes (1971), and on visual Orientalism see Boone (1995). On the place of the harem in Western erotica and the role of 'Oriental' homosexuality (male and female) see Schick (1999). See also Manton (1986) on lesbian harems in Orientalist pornography.

2 The second version, a replica of the first with some small modifications, was eventually bought in 1881 by F. R. Leyland, Rossetti's other main patron in the later period. This version now resides in the Walker Art Gallery, Liverpool. The second painting was begun at about the same time as the Fogg version, though not finished until after 1879 (Surtees 1971: 144).

3 Cited in Diana Holman Hunt, *My Father, His Wives and Lovers*, London, Hamish Hamilton, 1969, p. 137, in Goff (1982: 61).

4 Though, according to Ernest Vizetelly (1915), Buchanan later regretted the tone of his criticism.

5 Theodore Child, 'A Pre-Raphaelite Mansion', *Harpers Monthly Magazine*, 82, December 1890, in Casteras (1990).

6 On the optics of the Pre-Raphaelite movement between verse and painting see Smith (1995).

7 D. G. Rossetti, 'A Last Confession' (1842–70), in W. G. Rossetti, *The Works of Dante Gabriel Rossetti*, 1911, London, Ellis, p. 48.

8 Rossetti described *Lady Lilith* as an example of the perilous female principle; an image of 'self-absorption by whose strange fascination such natures draw others within their own circle', Rossetti, *Letters*, vol. 2, p. 850, quoted in Riede (1992: 103).

9 Max Beerbohm, '1880', in Stanford (1970: 28).

10 Eliza Haweis, *The Art of Beauty*, 1878, London, p. 273. I thank Kim Wahl for showing me this quotation.

11 I thank Jan Marsh for discussing these points.

12 Nina Athanassoglou-Kallmyer, 'Classicism and Resistance in Late Nineteenth-Century European Art: Victorians in Modern Greece', conference paper, 'Modern Art and the Mediterranean: Spaces, Bodies and Identities', The Art Gallery of Toronto, 2002.

13 Marsh, however, comments that by the 1870s Rossetti's paintings were 'so similar in composition and execution that there is little to distinguish one sitter from another', Marsh (1987: 56).

14 It is not only Vaka Brown whose Orientalness can be invisible; the Rossetti woman kept her Turkishness secret, known only to Edgar and his mother, whilst being squired around European society. The cousin, who had met her in Europe, and found her to be 'the kind of woman a man would go mad over', only learned of her ethnicity after Edgar's death.

15 On Vaka Brown's troping of ethnic history as romance rather than tragedy and her narratorial performance of gender, racial and ethnic transvestism in *Child of the Orient* (1914), see Kalogeras (1991).

CHAPTER FIVE

ᔓ CONTESTED BEHAVIOURS, ᔕ GENDERED SPACES

SPATIAL RELATIONS AND THE PLACE OF THE BODY

In Chapter Three I discussed how the harem system as an institution of seclusion was central to Ottoman and Occidental debates about female emancipation. Here, I return to the harem; this time discussing it as a space, an inhabited area whose institutions and relations affect and produce the subjectivities of those who dwell within it. By focusing on the harem's spatial relations and their gendering and racialising effects on the women who experienced and represented them, the racialised bodies discussed in Chapter Four can be seen as more specifically located organisms. In Western women's travel writing these bodies feature most prominently as dressed bodies, materialised through detailed description of dress, especially the 'veil'. Ottoman women's outdoor dress and the veil (see also Chapter Three) were the sartorial means by which the harem's architectural mechanisms of seclusion were extended beyond the harem walls. For Ottomans as well as Westerners women's dress (whether Ottoman or European) took on a particularly heightened significance in the run-up to the establishment of the Turkish Republic when women's outdoor and indoor dress, as I discuss in Chapter Six, were hotly contested in the battle over modernisation, Westernisation and emancipation. Female fashion was a subject which preoccupied commentators on all sides of the political spectrum. Books by Halide Edib, Grace Ellison, Zeyneb Hanım and Demetra Vaka Brown are animated by a concern with bodies and the spaces they occupy, as they compare women's lives in Istanbul, Europe and America.

Following the work of, most notably, Henri Lefebvre (1991) and Doreen Massey (1994), space can be considered as dynamic and productive rather than as simply a transparent and pre-existent zone in which events 'just happen'. Space is not neutral and static: a space, such as the harem, is experienced as a series of active spatial relations that are always socially situated and formative of social dynamics. It is not so much, as Massey puts it, that social relations occur 'in' space, as that 'both social phenomena and space [are] constituted out of social relations' which are also signifying practices (Massey 1994: 2). Thinking in this way about the 'spatiality of power' (Massey 1994: 2), it follows that the interpretation and representation of space will be constructed and understood in multiple ways by the individuals encountering it. Space positions the observer in particular ways, 'partly constitut[ing] the observer and the observer it' (Massey 1994:

3). So when, for example, Zeyneb Hanım visits Europe and writes about the Ladies' Club she stays at in London (see Chapter Six), it is not just her Turkish social framework which determines her experience and understanding of the unfamiliar London space. She is positioned in specific ways (as Turkish, woman and 'lady') through her interaction with the particular spatial relations which inhere in the club. Both these dynamics frame her experience and representation of the club and her place in it. Zeyneb Hanım's take on the club is quite different from that of its English members, demonstrating how shifting spatial identifications are calibrated by factors such as race, sexuality, gender and class. These delineations operate not just in local but also in *international* terms. This is not simply because of individual experience of travel, but because spatial relations are themselves inevitably located, experienced and understood in relation to their 'beyond' (Massey 1994).

As opposed to spaces in general, places often seem to be distinct from each other, invested with a (nostalgic) sense of fixity and authenticity. But places are also connected to places beyond themselves (Massey 1994: 120) so that individual subjects never only belong to one (spatial) community but experience and are positioned by multiple and fluid spatial frameworks. Just as Zeyneb Hanım in London is positioned as Turkish, female and classed, so too is Grace Ellison's experience of Turkish harems positioned not only by her Turkophile sympathies but also by her feminist oppositional interpretation of what she constructs as the 'beyond' of the harem: the spatialised gender relations of Britain. Similarly, Zeyneb Hanım's horror at the public humiliation she detects in the British feminist street meeting (see Chapter Three) is indicative of her desire to protect the class privilege, ensured by the otherwise much-hated restrictions of the harem system, which she is unable to recognise in the public behaviour of European 'ladies'. In neither case do the two women share an identical experience of space's gendering effects. The differences between women mean that there is no such thing as 'women as a group having a consistent relationship to spatial frameworks' (Mills 1996: 131).

The harem is a space with an overburdened signification in several clashing discourses, often in implicit or explicit contestation with each other. Like other spaces, harem spaces can be experienced as differently socialising by the various bodies that encounter them – or that are positioned by them. The European men who never actually entered a harem were nonetheless positioned as outsiders by its segregating spatial system, thereby encountering the gendering and racialising effects of the harem's spatial rules. The harem and related sartorial methods of seclusion produce a series of spatial relations which map the bodies moving through and around them with a force both socialising and symbolic. Focusing on the symbolic importance of spatial relations as signifying practices reveals their inherent link to representation and thus to narrative. In this light, the sources in this book can be understood as narratives of space which are also narratives of identity.

Emphasis on the politics of location – the history of power relations that marks each viewing/speaking subject position (Rich 1984) and hence determines the differences between members of what can appear as an apparently homogeneous group (e.g. women) – allows an elaboration of the locatedness of knowledge. The range of interpretations given to the spaces discussed in this chapter by their differently located authorial subjects is determined by a variety of elements. Some of these are consciously known to their authors, others are not. One factor that would have been known to women writers was the gender-specific market for female accounts of the harem (see Chapter One). As Indira Ghose illustrates, women writing on India knew that their unique selling point often rested on their ability – real or imagined – to access the segregated space of the harem or zenana (Ghose 1998). Whilst other elements of Orientalist scholarly enquiry or the wilder points of travel narrative might be male preserves, English women writers of all political persuasions were aware that as women there was 'one domain in which they [were] endowed with exclusive rights' (Ghose 1998: 30, see also Mills 1996).

Like the books in my study, most representations of the harem's spatial relations were intended for a primarily alien – that is non-harem dwelling – readership. My analysis of these representations of 'other' cultures (even when those making the representations were in some cases 'from' the culture positioned as alien to their target readership) connects me to critical work in anthropology and ethnography. This has in recent years taken a structuralist turn, emphasising the textuality of social and spatial relations. Clifford Geertz (1984), among others, has argued that spatial and social relations can be analysed as a text whose meaning is not innate but is produced through the decoding activity of participating social agents. Like a written text made up of words on a page, space is not meaningful in itself: in both cases meaning is generated in the interaction between reader and page, or between social agent and space, and is thus open to a multitude of possible meanings (see also Moore 1986). A social text, like a written text, is polysemic: no one reader will ever capture 'all' of its meanings since different readers/agents will produce different interpretations/experiences. The project of analysis therefore cannot be to find the one 'true' meaning but, as Henrietta Moore drawing on Pierre Bourdieu explains, must be instead to analyse the implicit as well as explicit knowledges employed in the reading/occupation of space (Moore 1986: 72). Space emerges as a densely marked terrain which is acted in and understood through the utilisation of a series of located knowledges, each with its own multiple and interconnecting histories. The observation and interpretation of space is never a neutral or 'obvious' act since the knowledges used (whether consciously or unconsciously) to understand and analyse it are all complicit in relations of power.

How are Ottoman and Western women's sources connected to these spatialised and historicised relations of power? The very specificity of their female and/or Ottoman point of origin tags them as situated knowledges, disallowing a vision of knowledge as objective and unbiased. Sara Mills (1996) has criticised the fantasy of transparent space and neutral knowledge as something that only makes sense from the point of view of the putatively objective Western sovereign subject. This universalising of a normative Western experience relies on the construction of a derogated other that implicitly codes local/non-Western knowledges as specific and generally inferior. Travel writing, ostensibly about somewhere foreign, relies, as Mills demonstrates, on the implicit norms of home to provide a counterfoil against which the exotica of the foreign can be given meaning. As Alison Blunt and Gillian Rose explain, the image of the Western controlling observer of space relied on the denial of this relationality. At the heart of imperial subjectivity was a being fixed in securely bounded space. Yet, just as self is constituted in opposition to an 'other', the imperial centre relies on its margins to prove the very essence of its existence (Blunt and Rose 1994). Although transparent space tends to homogenise (constructing undifferentiated group entities, be it Britons, women or Africans) it is both threatened by and reliant on the marginal spaces and figures whose exclusion gives the centre definition and meaning:

> [h]ence the paradox that the 'others' of the master subject are marginalised and ignored in its gaze at space, but are also given their own places: the slum, the ghetto, the harem, the closet, the inner city, the Third World, the private. These places haunt the imagination of the master subject, and are both feared and desired for their difference. (Blunt and Rose 1994: 16)

The books under consideration here are bound up in an interplay of imperial power relations but yet are by authors variously marginal to the imagined imperial centre. Ottoman writers (even if from the ailing Ottoman Empire) could never be positioned in books addressed to an English language readership as part of the imperial centre. European women representing the harem relied on their embodied identity as women to gain them special access, making impossible the Western position of disembodied invisible surveyor of transparent space. This is not to say that Western and Ottoman women, who were undeniably placed in a series of fluctuating and marginal relationships to dominant discourse, had no access to dominant discursive codes. As Mills explains in relation to British women travellers, the spatial dimension of power meant that the patriarchal gender relations of Britain were thrown into a different dynamic by their contact with racialising power relations in the colonies. British women's location in India gained them access to discourses of white superiority which, though gendered and often different to the colonial positions adopted by men, allowed them to enjoy the benefits of the imperial project and to adopt an imperial gaze in their writing (see also Nair 1990). As Mills and Peter Hulme (1986) discuss, there were always a number of colonial and Orientalist discourses in operation and authors to (variable) extents were able to choose which discursive strategy to employ from among the range available. Thus some male writers undercut the paradigmatic male imperial privilege whilst some women adopted a version of the masculinist 'master of all I survey' stance. A similar level of agency must be allowed on the part of Orientalised women. Despite the constraints of writing within a Western literary discourse, Ottoman authors made choices about how to represent themselves.

HAREMISED SPACE: STATUS AND GENDER

The space on which all these women focus is the Oriental female space of the harem, against which are contrasted the public and private spaces of Europe and the United States and the newly desegregating spaces of the modernising Otto-man Empire.[1] As I suggested in Chapter Three, the harem can be seen as both an actual space, the segregated space of women and children in elite Muslim house-holds, and an imaginary space – the isolated, sexualised realm of Orientalist fantasy. Both the architectural and sartorial mechanisms of seclusion (the divi-sion of household space into men's and women's quarters, and the use of the veil) were generally a privilege of the wealthy and often the urban. Indeed, harem, meaning sacred or forbidden, operated as a seclusionary activity to pro-tect status, not simply gender.[2] As Leslie Peirce has discussed, the sultan as ruler and caliph was secluded from all but the smallest number of strangers by the spa-tial organisation of the imperial palace and, when he ventured abroad, by the symbolic cordon provided by a large retinue (Peirce 1993). The harem was a form of spatial division experienced mainly by a small elite; these authors came from this stratum. Despite its rarity, the symbolic importance of this division of space came to define all Oriental domestic relations for the West and therefore had an impact on nearly all Ottomans who encountered Western attitudes. The overamplified status of the harem is similar to that of polygamy. As seen in Chapter Three, polygamy was also always a much rarer and restricted practice than its centrality to Western discourse – in which the harem was inevitably understood as polygamous – suggests. Duben and Behar (1991: 148–50) find that under 3 per cent of men in Istanbul were involved in polygamous marriages between 1885 and 1907 (though polygamy also had an inflated importance in Ottoman accounts). But the experience of space as segregated did not only apply to those women rich enough to live in the large mansions or *konaks* associated with the grandest harems. Most women were bound by imperial regulations about female dress in public. Respectable women were reluctant to be seen, even veiled, in many public spaces. Upper-class women often lived in houses arranged around the concept of seclusion, even if they were not in a polygamous family. But, for the West, the image of the harem remained a delightfully shocking one of polygamy and sequestration.

In the imaginary of what might be called dominant Orientalist discourse, the harem figures as a polygamous space animated by different forms of tyranny (from despot to women, from eunuchs to women, from mistress to slave, from favourite to rival); of excess (the multitude of women, the opulence of the inte-rior, the passions of the despot); and of perversion (the barbarity of polygamy, the violence of castration, the sapphism of the women locked up without 'real' men and the illicit affairs carried out behind the despot's back). All these things are found deplorable and enticing by turn. In this well-known and endlessly rehearsed knowledge about the Oriental harem, the stereotype of the actual impe- rial seraglio (the biggest, most hierarchical and richest of Ottoman harems) came to stand in as a signifier for all harems: dominant Orientalist discourse could talk of 'the' harem with a clear sense of what it meant and of the spatial relations it enacted. To this extent, the generic harem of Orientalist fantasy operated as what Mills calls an 'ideal/stereotypical level of space' (Mills 1996: 136). This refers both to the ideal social arrangements implicit in the architectural division of space (each type of house is premised on a culturally specific model of the ideal family who will inhabit it) and to the role of ideal/imagined relations in stereo- type. Writing on the division of space in colonial India, Mills explains how the intended division of towns into British cantonments and 'native' towns could only ever operate on an ideal level since these apparently impermeable spaces were always interconnected, from the Indian servants who populated the British homes to the British women working as prostitutes for both British and Indian men (Mills 1996, see also Çelik 1996 on the rebuilding of Algiers). Mills notes that the *zenana* – a mode of seclusion which only affected an elite minority of women in a small number of regions – came to operate at 'the ideal level of stereotype' as a paradigmatic descriptor of all Indian women's lives in British colonial discourse. The *zenana*, like the Ottoman harem, worked potently as an ideal space. It assumed centrality in several divergent and contradictory dis- courses, appearing as a symbol for female Indian experience in feminist, imperialist and anti-imperialist discourse (Mills 1996, see also Grewal 1996). Similarly, the harem in an Ottoman context had a significance far beyond its actual frequency as an experienced spatial relation. Representations of any indi- vidual harem always had to position themselves in relation to the imagined spatial frameworks attributed to the ideal harem of the generic stereotype.

That the harem's spatial relations were inevitably understood in specifically sexualised terms is highlighted by Grace Ellison, who set out to challenge the Orientalist reification of the harem (Ellison 1915). Notably, as seen in Chapter Three, she quoted Halide Edib asking English feminists to

> delete for ever that misunderstood word 'harem', and speak of us in our Turk- ish 'homes'. Ask them to try and dispel the nasty atmosphere which a wrong meaning of that word has cast over our lives. Tell them what our existence really is. (Ellison 1915: 17)

Both Ottoman and the English feminist understood the runaway signification of the term harem. Edib demonstrates an awareness of the gap between harem as a local denotation of a social and spatial organisation and its international connota- tions within Orientalist codes of knowledge. Her attempt to rebrand the space as a home rather than a harem was not an assertion that the two were interchangea- ble: the insertion of the qualifier 'Turkish' indicates that homes are not the same the world over and will produce specific spatial relations, an oscillation between being like and not like the Occident common to all these sources. Calling her book *An Englishwoman in a Turkish Harem* was an act of bravado for Ellison, who was quite aware that – although sales would be prompted by the assumed authenticity of her gendered access to the forbidden realm of the Ottoman harem – to associate herself with a space that was relentlessly sexualised in the minds of some of her readers (see also Schick 1999) was not without its risks (see also Chapter Three). Melman (1992, see Chapter One) has pointed out that European women writers developed a number of strategies for avoiding the contamination threatened by their imagined insertion into the harem's stereotypical spatial relations. Ellison followed the Victorian tradition of domesticating the harem. Using detail to establish the differences between individual harems and the generic Orientalist fantasy harem, she emphasised that:

> [t]he Turkish home in which I am staying at present has little in common with the harem described by most Western writers, and no doubt those readers accustomed to the *usual* notions of harem life will consider my surroundings disappointingly Western. (Ellison 1915: 19, original emphasis)

By refuting the 'usual' accounts of harem life, Ellison made clear her awareness of the range of discursive strategies available for representing Ottoman segregated space. Like much travel writing, these accounts have connections to the 'manners and customs' model of ethnography typified in the mid-nineteenth century by E. W. Lane and augmented by his sister Sophia Poole.[3] Women's writing needs to be positioned in relation to the protocols by which the developing human sciences of ethnography and anthropology sought to establish authority and authenticity for their knowledges. Any female signature on an account of the harem invested it with the authority of eye-witness privilege, since Western men could not observe these forbidden spaces. But this far too situated knowledge did not give women unimpeded access to the nominally transparent position of detached ethnographic knowledge and authority. The very codes of authenticity which guaranteed women's reports on the harem and the world behind the veil also located them as gendered *participants* in the sexualised space of the segregated harem. For Western women travellers and writers, this emphatic presence effectively disallowed a scientific mode of detached objectivity and risked contaminating them by too great a proximity to their object of study.

As Melman has argued, European women were not given easy access to the status of objective, scientific observer on which the disciplines of anthropology and ethnography came to rest. It was even more difficult for Orientalised women, who were always positioned as implicitly the object rather than the subject of such knowledge systems, to achieve an authoritative speaking position. Melman observes how European women's knowledge was coded as subjective rather than objective, as empathetic rather than detached and as descriptive rather than analytic. In some cases this was presented as an advantage by women, who made a feature out of the specificity of their knowledge and ways of inscribing it.

The authority to comment on harem life was predicated variously on authenti-cating codes of gender, class, ethnicity and religion, as seen in the titles of Zeyneb Hanım's and Ellison's books, both of which call attention to the gender and national specificities of their viewing position. But even in relation to the relentlessly gendered realm of the harem, women's authority was questioned – often by setting them against other women's accounts (see also Lewis 1996). Sometimes women writers signalled an awareness of the fragility of their claim to truth through a discussion of the ineligibility of others. Ellison begins her book by challenging the accounts of other female narrators depicted as ethnically unre-liable, talking of 'falsehoods that are put into circulation by expelled governesses and Perote ladies' (Ellison 1915: 15). This criticism of non-native observers leaves her own position somewhat insecure: hence the 'invitation' by a named Ottoman source (Halide Edib) to tell the 'real' story.

Like Edib, Ellison wants to disassociate herself from the stereotypical space of the ideal or generic harem. Emphasising the unremarkable aspects of the harem she lives in, she directly contrasts it to the imperial harem which she also visits. Picturing it as a an opulent place of ritual and state function rather than a regular domestic home, Ellison encounters the imperial harem during a highly formal court audience and admits that this:

> … remains the harem in the real sense of the word, the harem about which Western readers expect to hear … This is the first time since I have been back in Turkey that I have felt myself really within a harem. Even when I wear a veil, even when I forget I am not in England and try to push back the fixed lat-tice windows [even when I sit down to dinner] where not even the master of the house may be present, I do not realise the atmosphere of the harem. But within the palace, amidst its curious assembly of slaves and eunuchs, and in spite of its wide corridors and immense salons, there is a most uncomfortable feeling of bondage which would turn me into a raving lunatic at the end of a week. (Elli-son 1915: 36–7)

The distinction she sets up between the imperial harem and the elite harems in which she has been living offers an eye-witness and womanly challenge to the generalisations of Orientalist knowledge. But more than this, it also marks out as different and as healthier the domestic spaces which she depicts herself inhabit-ing. By emphasising the particularity of the imperial seraglio she is able to restrict the most negative and potentially morally contaminating elements of the harem myth (which she knows inform her readers' minds) to a space other than those in which she dwells in relative happiness. This splitting allows her to linger on the luxuries and hospitality of the elite Turkish home which, whilst evidently a source of great pleasure to her personally, will also provide some of the expected pleasures of Orientalism for her readers.

> In no other land have I met with such lavish hospitality – hospitality even that makes one feel a little uncomfortable, especially when one realises how little one has done to deserve it. The courtesy, also, is almost overwhelming. Every time I go in or out of the room the assembled company, men and women, stand,

and every time coffee, cigarettes, and sweets are brought by the slaves for the guests, my hostess rises to serve me herself. Always, too, I sit in the place of honour, as far away from the door as possible, and sometimes right in the draught of the window.

It is the custom, too, for the master of the house to pay all the visitor's bills. That I should have proposed to stamp my own letters hurt my friend. The result is that, nowadays, I write no letters and buy practically nothing. I feel almost guilty when I accept what I do and give nothing in return, and always I have before me the haunting fear of the terrible disappointment my friend will have when she visits my country, for our hospitality cannot be compared to this. (Ellison 1915: 22)

Whereas previous women writers frequently digressed from received wisdom about Oriental luxury and excess by describing humbler Ottoman interiors, for Ellison the luxury of Ottoman homes emerges as a fundamental characteristic and as key to her potential pleasure in the experience of segregated Ottoman space. The accounts of middle-income homes presented in the nineteenth century (see Chapter One) did shift representation away from the material and sexual excesses associated with the stereotype of the grand seraglio. But the cycle of disenchantment and re-enchantment described by Ruth Bernard Yeazell (2000) was still in evidence in women's sources. Rather than evince disappointment at a lack of sexual excess (a recurrent theme in men's accounts), nineteenth-century women expressed disappointment at the lack of the excessive luxury that they had learned to expect from the Oriental interior. This investment in luxury continued in Ellison's writing at the turn of the century. But, unlike her disappointed predecessors, she found impressive evidence of material ease in the elite Ottoman home even though – as she noted in an interview in *Votes for Women* in 1914 – that, with the Turkish economy in crisis, 'I do not suppose there is in Turkey now one man whom we should consider wealthy – the days of extravagance and luxury, the days of vast expenditure on the harem are gone …'[4] Despite her hosts' straitened circumstances Turkish hospitality was still able to provide delightful sensory pleasures.

Ellison enjoyed an elevated position as a result of her incorporation into Ottoman spatial relations where the privilege of her national identity and status as foreign guest allowed her to accede to a social status far above that to which she was accustomed. In her friend's house this included being allocated her own slave, a woman she renamed 'Miss Chocolate' and persistently referred to as a servant rather than a slave (see Chapter Six). Ellison's anxiety about Fatima's reception should she visit England was not just a reflection on the different customs of hospitality in England and Turkey. It also reveals the extent to which specific spaces modify a subject's gendered, classed and racialised position within social relations. For Ellison, to be contaminated by her presence in the Oriental female space was as often pleasurable as it was bewildering or frustrating.

Apter's (1996) work on French colonial literature is useful here; she describes a haremisation effect: a product of the harem experience which challenges the normative phallocentric ordering of Western colonial desire. Apter argues that, for Western writers, both male and female, the relentless intrusion of a sapphic subtext into harem narratives reveals as only ever partial the presumed power and sexual omnipotence of the sultan. This produces an 'other' eroticism which transcends the limitations of the harem regime and hints at forms of pleasure (*jouissance* in Apter's Lacanian scenario) outside of a Western libidinal economy. Apter discusses how in a story by Guy de Teramond (*Schmam'ha*, 1901) set in North Africa, a French woman is engaged in adulterous sex when she notices that her Kabylian maid is still in the room waiting to be dismissed. At this moment, the Oriental gaze that spectates on the French woman in her performance of abandon becomes a 'voyeurism [that] "haremizes" European eroticism by rendering it self-conscious, strange to itself' (Apter 1996: 213). This combination of sequestered female spaces, cultural voyeurism and fantasies of visual control can, then, 'make strange' both the stereotype of the fantasy harem and the experience of Western subjectivities.

But this haremisation effect, I contend, does not only apply to Europeans. Vaka Brown, too, found herself being newly overtaken by the haremising experience of Ottoman female spaces – even though she was keen to identify herself as an Ottoman woman after living in the United States for six years. Her ambivalence about the pleasures and dangers of contamination comes through most clearly at the end of the book:

> After six years of hurrying, of striving as if life counted only the amount of work done, of knowledge acquired, I was back again in the calm leisure of Turkey, where eternity reigned, and no one hurried. Not to stay, for I fear that he who tastes of American bustle can never again live for long without it. Yet as I stood at my window I was happy – happy to have nothing to do – happy merely to live for the pleasure of living … Among the Orientals I am always overwhelmed by a curious feeling of resigned happiness, such as the West can hardly conceive of. (Vaka 1909: 221)

Although she did not signal her geographical identification in her titles in the same way as Zeyneb Hanım, Vaka Brown relied on the value-added currency of being not only a female reporter on the harem but also a nearly-native informant (Ottoman but not Muslim) to establish her authority throughout her books. Despite the authenticating value of these insider knowledges (which were always situated in relation to her émigrée United States identification) she also found herself undercutting her very claim to power and knowledge:

> Orientalism was like a labyrinth: the more I advanced in it, the more entangled I became. One woman after another was confronting me with a new problem … and I felt stupid and incapable of understanding them. It hurt my vanity, too, to find how small I was in comparison with them. (Vaka 1909: 127)

The depiction of life *à la turque* was made more difficult for Vaka Brown because she had to present herself as sufficiently American to be a reliable witness for her readers but remain sufficiently Oriental to be a credible insider informant. Her work oscillates between being like and not like the Muslim Ottoman women she studies. This produces a hybrid identification whose authority is sometimes directly contested. Edib, as seen in Chapter Three, explicitly challenged the right of the Greek Christian Vaka Brown to represent Muslim life accurately (Edib 1926: 144). In turn, Vaka Brown anticipated such criticism by regularly including quotes from Muslim Turks attesting that she was one of the few who could really understand them and represent them fairly for the West (Vaka 1923: 60–5, see also Chapter Three). Travel reconfigured the spatialised elements of Vaka Brown's identifications in a number of ways. In her first volume in 1909 Vaka Brown, having become acculturated to American social life, was primarily concerned with the re-presentation of Ottoman segregated space. The Orient figures as something familiar made newly strange by her now partially Americanised eyes. In *Child of the Orient*, from 1915, she wrote about the journey to America, where America itself is presented as initially bewildering and strange. But in her first volume, Vaka Brown's complex ethnic identification was mapped out through the revisiting of Ottoman female spaces, held up in direct and indirect contrast to what had become a more normative United States lifestyle. It was only later, once she had established sales and an authorial reputation and, more importantly, firmed up a suitably acculturated (i.e. not too immigrant) Ottoman-American identification (Kalogeras 1989, see also Chapter Four), that she could write about the dislocating experience of travel to America. In 1909 the terms of her hybrid and authorial identity were still dangerously unstable. Consequently she was at pains not to be merged with the harem and its women.

For Grace Ellison, whose identification as an 'Englishwoman' in a Turkish harem was so emphatically signalled, the contradictions about closeness to the object of study were less acute. For her, the haremisation effect was clearly produced by the Ottoman organisation of domestic space. It was this and the interpersonal relations it fostered which impeded her ability to operate in her normal mode as a modern professional European woman.

> [T]he greatest obstacle to one's writing, setting aside the atmosphere, is the lack of solitude … as we understand it in the West, i.e. one's own self within one's own room, and the door locked … Several times I have escaped to my room to write. But my maid … follows me … and runs to fetch my hostess. She too, fails to understand why I go to my bedroom to write in solitude when I could write at a big desk in the salon with the other ladies to keep me company. (Ellison 1915: 9–10)

She will not find privacy in the Ottoman house since privacy, as Lefebvre points out, is a historically contingent (Occidental) concept, the spatial conditions for the emergence of which did not develop in Europe until the rising bourgeoisie adapted and changed the previously prevalent aristocratic form of residential space (Lefebvre 1991: 314–15). The concept and behaviours of privacy so central to early twentieth-century European feminists (witness Virginia Woolf's *A Room of One's Own*) were not a characteristic of Islamic cultures of the Middle East. Here, even in the most elite harems, the central reception hall was a multi-use space, operating as an area for eating, socialising, working, washing and sleeping that was quite unlike the strict division of the middle-class European home where food functions were separated from sleeping space, children's areas from adults and so on (Melman 1992, Küçükerman 1985). Typically, in traditional Middle Eastern harems that had room divides, individuals rarely experienced a sense of ownership about 'their' room: spaces were freely utilised by different household members for various purposes. Not surprisingly, in the face of this strange regimen, European women travellers regularly complained about the lack of privacy especially, as Melman discusses, since they saw privacy as a prerequisite for their treasured habit of journal-keeping: a 'private and highly individual activity of the self [that was] a statement of Western, middle-class identity' (Melman 1992: 154). Ellison, having internalised other forms of spatial compliance, experienced obedience to the spatial relations demanded by Ottoman architecture as acutely alienating:

> I cannot master Turkish architecture – at least, this funny place [Zeyneb Hanım's riverside house or *yali*, on the Bosphorous] has entirely upset my calculations … A hateful idea it is, to have rooms with more than one door; it's like having people with eyes in the back of their heads, and I wonder whether there isn't also a door under my bed and one in the ceiling. It's rather uncanny too, for in a country where doors have not locks and would not lock if they had, everyone flits unheard into one another's room. (Ellison 1915: 188)

But if she wanted more privacy at Zeyneb Hanım's riverside house, her visit to another such dwelling produced feelings of abandonment and loneliness that entirely threatened her sense of self. In a house where the husband was absent, Ellison's hostess instructed her to arrive without luggage and dressed her guest in a variety of clothing as they let down their bouffant coiffures in favour of 'flapper plaits' and wandered *déshabillées* through the drafty corridors. Separated from her clothes and her possessions, Ellison becomes delirious and, as Ternar discusses, needed her Turkish friends to reflect back to herself a clearer sense of her identity:

> But oh! The silence and loneliness of my bedroom. It frightens me. I wish one of my friends had offered to share it with me. I wonder how long the sturdy candle will last! What a distressing shadow the coiffeuse makes on the wall! There are little draughts coming from everywhere. The door, bereft of its handle, is attached by a string to a substantial nail and the window will neither open nor will it quite shut.
>
> … If only the trees would shiver as I am shivering! If only a dog would bark! If only I could sleep! But paradox of paradoxes, it is the silence that is keeping me awake. 'Yet I am not afraid,' I say to myself. 'I will sing to contradict this awful silence.' I try, but not one note will come, for terror has frozen my voice to my throat. Summoning up the little will-power that the soul-

crushing harem life has left me, I stagger to the mirror to see how I look – but the horror of it! Can that hideous, un-earthly face be mine? Where am I? And where am I going? My whole being is numbed, my ears are singing – I can remember no more. (Ellison 1915: 174–5)

The eruption of a gothic strain into the narrative suggests the threat to self that is rendered by the now unwelcome solitude of this alien place. Where Fatima's house is too potentially Western – 'Sometimes in the morning when I wake I still wonder where I really am. Am I in Europe or am I in Asia?' (Ellison 1915: 27) – the absolute difference of this place makes her mirrored image unrecognisable. Insufficient solitude threatens her ability to write, but too much threatens her sanity. Interrupted endlessly at Fatima's, in this scary *yali* she craves a room-mate and one is miraculously provided: '[e]xactly how I and my bed were transplanted to my friend's room I cannot tell. Did I faint? It is not a pleasant memory, nor one on which I care to dwell' (Ellison 1915: 175). The potential loss of dignity witnessed by her kindly responsive host is too much to bear. Ellison's ambivalence about the effects of Ottoman spatial relations surfaces time and again as she weaves a series of uneven and shifting identifications with Ottoman women. Whilst for Vaka Brown the American way wins in the end, Ellison is sorely tempted to prefer the Oriental, despite its deleterious effect on her literary ambitions.

The diary of my existence as a Turkish woman, which in England I imagined could be written in a very short while, lies day after day in the form of a pencil and exercise book, untouched on the little mother-of-pearl table in the most comfortable corner of my large bedroom. 'To-morrow', I say, like a true Turkish woman … (Ellison 1915: 3–4)

Both women were overtaken by this 'curious resigned happiness', a passivity in the face of destiny that was frequently identified as characteristic of Oriental attitudes, especially women's. Clara Erskine Clement specifically recommended it, urging the Western visitor to Istanbul not to resist 'the Oriental lethargy [that will] pervade your being, and convince you that nothing matters; that the thing not done is quite as good as the thing well done', for it was only by throwing 'off your Western unrest and your weighty sense of responsibility [that] you will be prepared to enjoy Constantinople' (Clement 1895: 171–2). For Ellison, Turkey was experienced as a refuge of calm and quiet after the noise and the rush of 'what we in the West call pleasures of society' (Ellison 1915: 2), making her ambivalent about her Orientalised loss of motivation: 'if we in the West possess what is known as the "joy of liberty" have not so many of us been denied the blessing of protection?' (Ellison 1915: 196).

CLAIMING SPACE:
TERRITORY, POWER AND INSURRECTION

Whatever the delights of the elite harem system, Ellison also celebrated the increasing ability of upper-class Ottoman women to inhabit spaces beyond the harem walls:

> Five years ago we never walked a step; now we not only saunter through the bazaar, but go to a big dressmaker's in Pera, whilst formerly all our goods had to be purchased from Greek merchants and Paris dressmakers who came with their goods to the harem. (Ellison 1915: 31–2)

Women's changing interaction with public spaces was often linked to developments in dress habits. To go shopping outside the harem and to venture into Pera, to be in proximity with the local minority populations and visiting foreigners, was a major event for a well brought-up Muslim Ottoman woman and was, just a few years before Ellison's excursion with Fatima, still being depicted as exciting and contentious in the women's press of the 1890s (Frierson 2000a). It was no coincidence that Ellison and her friend went shopping for clothes: dress was important not just in terms of women's increasingly visible consumer activities outside the home but more specifically in relation to the sartorial nature of socio-spatial frameworks themselves (see also Micklewright 2000). Individuals in what might be termed public space in the late Ottoman period were emphatically registered as dressed subjects, and the role of dress cannot be separated from discourses of female and social emancipation, modernity and, increasingly, nationalism.

In Ottoman society of the late pre-republican and early republican period women's clothes, in particular the veil, were seen as a crucial index of political and social change by politicians of all persuasions, and inevitably discussed as such by local and foreign commentators (Graham-Brown 1988, see also Chapter Six). Both women's and men's apparel had long been the subject of sumptuary legislation (Şeni 1995), with the state encoding dress rules that differentiated status according to religion and rank. Though the interaction with European fabrics and dress styles had been producing alterations in Ottoman dress since the sixteenth century (Scarce 1987), the most dramatic shift came in 1829 when Sultan Mahmut II required all officials (except the clergy) to wear a fez (generally accompanied by a frock-coat and trousers). Introduced as a modernising European style, the fez was intended to mould a uniform appearance for male state functionaries and was, ideally, to be extended to the rest of the male population – though many outside the state service rejected the fez in favour of the distinctive headwear that denoted class or trade affiliations (Quataert 2000). The engagement with Western styles continued to be pronounced during and after the Tanzimat reforms of the mid-nineteenth century (1839–76). Tanzimat ideology and the shift towards a market economy prompted the beginnings of what can be recognised as a modern industrial fashion cycle, in which changes in women's dress in particular assumed a key role in debates about the direction of state and society (Şeni 1995). On a macro-political level, apart from the epochal fez, this was often a very gradual change – the porte continued to legislate about male and female dress – and one that was inevitably contradictory and shifting. Court women acted as fashion leaders in the by now increasingly common partial or wholesale adoption or adaptation of European fashions among the elite.

Fatma Aliye Hanım, whose Ottoman publications against polygamy I introduced in Chapter Three, also wrote a book for translation, *Les musulmanes contemporaines*, to be published in France in 1894.[5] One-third of the book was devoted to women's dress and the veil (the other two-thirds were taken up with a discourse on polygamy and slavery). She described how the previously traditional indoor ensemble of *salvar* (wide, baggy trousers) and *gömlek* (large blouse) had given way to the use of an *entari*, a loose shift-like garment of Ottoman dress (increasingly waisted in this period) that had now been adapted to accommodate a corset (Şeni 1995). This produced a fitted silhouette radically different to the unstructured body so beloved of the Orientalists. The *entari*, Aliye Hanım claimed, now only looked good on a corseted body – a change in bodily relations so huge that Şeni is moved to call the *entari* the 'Trojan horse' that 'revolutionised' Ottoman women's wear. The alterations made by corseting to the self-perception of Ottoman women were immense. It is not only that the corseted figure fitted in with the different spatial behaviours required by fashionable pieces of Western furniture that shifted life from floor level upwards. Corsets also made women's interaction with Ottoman low-level living increasingly uncomfortable. By the 1870s in Istanbul and other main cities of the empire, elite women were increasingly wearing elements of European dress in conjunction with Ottoman clothes. Whilst urban and indoor clothing had changed, 'discrete outdoor dress' was still required; ensuring that women in public spaces conformed to expectations of modesty and seclusion (Scarce 1987: 79–80). Western visitors might encounter royal women wearing entire ensembles of imported French couture when indoors, though they were not necessarily equipped to recognise the Western-influenced changes to Turkish dress, nor could they (or male observers) detect Western dress underneath Ottoman outerwear (Micklewright 2000, Graham-Brown 1988: 118–43).

By the period leading up to the Young Turk Revolution of 1908, affluent Ottomans in Istanbul would expect to be au fait with Western clothing and manners, whose usage they chose selectively. After the revolution, people began to take more liberties with dress and adventurous urban women began to be seen outside without a male escort (Berkes 1964). Sometimes wearing Western clothes was part of a clear political statement. But at the very least throughout the periods on either side of the revolution, dress – like the consumption of other Western goods – signalled a vague sense of generally Westernised modernity, though the advantages of Western ways and the extent to which they should be embraced were hotly debated (Duben and Behar 1991, Göçek 1996, Berkes 1964). Even those women who passionately embraced all that was Western as a sign of modernity and progress found that their personal allegiances to traditional ways could not easily be overcome. When Halide Edib started writing for the radical press in 1908 she still felt unable to attend the newspaper office or to meet men unknown to the family, even at home (Edib 1926: 265).

For both Ellison and Vaka Brown, in her second book about Istanbul (*The Unveiled Ladies of Stamboul*, 1923), women's occupation of public spaces was the most conspicuous sign of change in Ottoman society during the second constitutional period (1908–18) and leading up to the republic in 1923. Dress, Ottoman and European, functioned within spatial relations as an element of gender and ethnic performance that registered differently to those who wore it and read about it in both Orient and Occident.

Ellison wrote in considerable detail about clothes, especially about the familiarity of elite Ottoman women with European clothes and furniture and the codes of conduct which accompanied these. Just as, despite her progressive feminist politics, she romanticised the Ottoman harem system (Melman 1992), so too did she aestheticise the veil, seeing it not as a mechanism of seclusion but as a fetching head-dress which she herself delighted in wearing. Her movements both veiled and unveiled in Ottoman spaces outside the home allowed her the opportunity to imagine that she had sampled the different ways in which these spaces could be experienced (as a European woman or a Turkish lady).

Fatima and Ellison's trips to the bazaar are indicative of a reconfiguration of public and previously masculinised spaces that was seen by many as a turbulent and challenging experience (Duben and Behar 1991). The use of Western goods and the behaviours associated with them invariably had political overtones (Göçek 1996) and were unevenly adopted by different sections of the population, where they were used in conjunction with conventional products in a number of ways. Even those few households which considered themselves extensively Westernised would still have been operating a mix of traditional and newly formulated habits in their homes. Melek Hanım, writing in the *Strand Magazine* in 1926 about how she came to be a Paris dressmaker, made very clear the spatialised nature of the Ottoman interaction with Western dress. The two sisters, who were veiled at the age of ten, were dressed, like many women of their class, in Paris fashions purchased from European dressmakers who visited them in their father's harem. The young Melek Hanım had already taught herself to sew but was keen to take proper training, even though this necessitated leaving the house. Her departure from the protected space of elite Ottoman femininity was far in advance of the (limited) vocational training for women that was to come during the second constitutional period (see Chapter Two) and so had to be undertaken in conditions of utmost secrecy. For Melek Hanım access to this education was gained by bribing a Greek merchant who provided a house for her to change in: she would depart her own home dressed in a 'shabby coat and veil of one of the slaves' and change into the 'coat and skirt and hat' in which she made her secret visit to a dressmaker's establishment for her daily instruction. Given the climate of fear that pertained to palace officials and their families during the Hamidian regime, she remarks that, not 'many dressmakers have had to risk their lives as I did to have my training' (Melek Hanım 1926: 131). The wearing and even the making of European clothes operated alongside traditional codes of behaviour and propriety in a dynamic series of checks and balances that created opportunities for change in the lives of Ottoman women and that perpetuated their restriction. Similarly, Ellison notes that Fatima's home, furnished in the best European empire style, was still policed by 'fanatical' old women whose adherence to conventional gendered uses of space curtailed Fatima's activities in the house and constrained her husband's desire to allow her more liberty of movement outside of it.

In encounters with spaces beyond the harem female dress was of paramount significance to both Ottoman and Occidental participants and observers. Although Ottoman female dress underwent many minor and major changes in this period, it was the veil which operated as signifier sine qua non for Western observers. The veil had for a long time been emblematic as the publicly visible signifier of Ottoman women's 'freedom', modernity or seclusion, whilst the many Western garments worn in domestic spaces which were equally significant to Ottoman women, had not such a currency to Westerners since they were not on display (Göçek 1996). Ellison describes Fatima's fearless incursion into the previously forbidden space of her hotel:

> She came at one to see me at an hotel. A Turkish woman visiting me at an hotel! Was it possible? Five years ago what would not have been her punishment for such reckless *license*? The customs of the country do not yet, however, allow women to visit hotels, and in taking every step forward she has to run the risk of offending the ignorant and fanatical mob.
>
> Fatima did not come in by the front entrance. Quite recently a restaurant for 'ladies only' has been opened by the same management as the hotel where I stayed and is, to some extent, a rendezvous for Turkish women. It is their first step towards a 'fashionable' club, and to me, the newcomer, another big step towards freedom. Let those Western critics [who take a stand against the new government] take into consideration such details … It is part of a great scheme of reform, and everything is going on in proportion. In 1908 more than two men sitting at a café together were 'suspect' and reported at headquarters; in 1913 Turkish *women* meet in a restaurant and discuss political subjects – certainly this is not the Turkey I expected to see. (Ellison 1915: 5, original emphasis)

Access to different spaces had captured the imagination of the elite secluded Turkish woman. Fatima had long been fascinated by the forbidden space of the hotel and was thrilled at her own audacity, arriving 'thickly veiled' and smuggling herself in unseen by a side door, when 'five years ago the zenith of [her] longing was to be taken up in a hotel lift' (Ellison 1915: 6). The liberties promised by the hotel and its exciting Western technologies were not only important for women: Ellison is careful to put Fatima's visit in the context of the general change in politicised spatial relations. The constitutional period made freedom of movement and of association more available to the whole population, although women's access to these new civil liberties always operated on a restrictive gendered axis. The occupation of newly gender-liberated spaces was not homogeneous or neutral: not all women were equally able to assume spatial rights though they might at times assert both traditional and unconventional spatial behaviours as political statements.

When Vaka Brown returned to Istanbul in 1921 her title – *The Unveiled Ladies of Stamboul* – illustrated the importance of dress (the veil) and place (Stamboul being the old Turkish quarter of the city) as composite signifiers of the changes she discerned after twenty years. Unable during the Allied invasion to find any of the old friends who had peopled *Haremlik* (presumed to be dead or hiding in proud poverty), she consciously sought new contacts, mapping the changed city through her determined interactions with older and younger generations of Turkish women. Their new occupation of public space functions as a visible marker of dramatic social and political change. Travelling through a city still occupied by foreign troops, Vaka Brown had frequently to position herself vis-à-vis the much-resented American and European imperialism being played out in the streets of the city. Although she identified herself in the dedication at the start of her book as a loyal Ottoman subject (see Chapter Two), her Western dress led passers-by to assume she was Occidental:

> The tram gave a jerk, a throb, and stopped [then] started again on its course toward old, sunlit Stamboul. The passenger who had caused the stop was a solitary Turkish woman. Carefully balancing herself on her excessively high heels, she came in by the front end, and scanned the 'harem' end of the car for a vacant seat. There was none.
>
> For a second she stood poised, taking in the fact that all the seats in the women's compartment were occupied. Through the opening in the curtains she could equally discern that beyond them were empty seats in the men's end. Her black lustrous eyes – so piquantly opposed to the gold of her hair – turned back from the men's compartment, and scanned the faces of such Christian women as were seated in the women's end. Then she advanced to where I sat, and with a motion of her small, white-gloved hand said in French:
>
> 'There is room for *you* in there.'
>
> She was within her rights. I yielded my place to her, and changed to one beyond the curtains. Yet the tone in which she had ordered me to give her my seat disturbed me. It was something new to me in Turkish women. Losing no sight of the fact that she had a perfect right to ask a European woman to go into the other end of the car when there were places available there, I yet wondered at her doing so. That right I had never seen them exercise before. And the tone she had used had nothing to do with rights. It smacked of hatred. It was as if she said: 'This opportunity I take to enforce in our capital that which belongs to us Turks.' (Vaka 1923: 122–3)

Vaka Brown found herself more and more positioned as either Euro-American or Greek (in the context of Turkey's war with Greece). By asserting her right to the gender-segregated space at the front of the bus the Turkish woman

reactivated the nationalising and racialising dynamic inherent in the bus's gendered spatial relations and the city through which it travelled. Vaka Brown's
surprise at encountering a so uncharacteristically haughty Turkish woman indicates some of the new ways of being that emerged with the different spatialities
of the changing city. Thinking about spatiality, the active agency of space
(McDowell and Sharpe 1997), demonstrates how the multiple subject positions
made possible for individuals by different socio-spatial relations can be experienced, and at times consciously enacted, in overlapping and contradictory ways.
Whilst Edib represented as frustrating her inability to brave the newspaper office,
this woman is depicted as manipulating codes of seclusion to make a political
point: the inference being that her aversion was not so much to sitting in the
mixed section of the bus as it was to the visible presence of foreigners in the bus
qua the city. The political and personal slippage between local minority populations (Christians) and foreign interlopers is suggested later in Vaka Brown's
account when she watched the same Turkish woman board another tram where
'several vacant seats in the women's end robbed her of the pleasure of ordering a
Christian woman out.' The switch between Occidentals/Europeans and Christians is indicative of how the European occupation reformulated previous social
and spatial relations of gender and ethnicity: not only the space of the bus and the
relative control of that domain by the Muslim woman[6] vis-à-vis non-Muslims but
also the relative control over domains of the city by the occupying foreign powers. Edib tells of similar turf wars on public transport during the occupation,
emphasising the class dimension of local responses. Whilst the 'fashionable
ladies',

> those in Pera mostly – were trying to express the national indignation and the
> unfitness of the Allied actions in their own fashionable way ... [by] giving tea
> parties to English and French officers and dancing with them, as well as telling
> them about the state of things, [elsewhere in the city] the entry of the Allied
> armies [increased] the insolence of the Greeks and the Armenians [whose]
> treatment of the peaceful Turkish citizens in the streets became scandalous.
> (Edib 1928: 4)

Though Edib kept herself out of fraternising parties 'with religious care', her
journeys around the city could not avoid involving her in incidents where the
'lower classes were expressing themselves in their dumb but very forcible way'.
Her tram story describes an Armenian Christian conductor unfairly 'taking [in]
the Christian women and pushing the Turkish women out' (Edib 1928: 9–19),
whilst on the Bosphorous ferry a 'violent-looking rabble (mostly servant class)'
of Christian women pushed their way into the first-class cabin with only second-
class tickets, threatening the mainly Turkish attendants with the Allied forces.
The working-class minority population women's presumed affinity with the foreign forces – '"I am Greek, and I am protected by the English and the French"' –
allowed them to transgress divides of class as well as those of ethnicity within
the gender demarcated ferry (Edib 1928: 7–9). For Muslim women, as in many
national liberation struggles, the assertive enactment of 'traditional' religious

spatial rights was re-animated as a sign of anti-imperialist allegiances. For progressives like Edib, who argued against the veil and other mechanisms of seclusion in the name of national progress and modernity, the segregated space was an unavoidable part of female life and a marker of the radically altered spatial behaviours necessitated in the occupied city.

Vaka Brown's encounter on the tram led to another vignette of women's resistance to the occupation, played out in spatial and sexual terms that reactivated to deadly purpose a simulacrum of the old-style Ottoman femininity for which she was so nostalgic. Obtaining an introduction to Azzizé Hanım, the woman who had demanded her seat, Vaka Brown learned that she was driven by a fierce hatred of the occupying European forces whom she held responsible for the death of her brother and her mother. Refusing at first to talk with Vaka Brown, Azzizé Hanım, having subsequently read (the French edition of) *Haremlik*, agreed to tell her story. In the context of the annexation of the city's space by the armies of occupation Vaka Brown's respondent had met her husband when he was sent to requisition her house for billets. After the resulting death of her brother she had married the infatuated Frenchman, intending to make his life misery and extract a fully feminine revenge. In a situation where Vaka Brown was saddened to find that the younger generation were no longer trained to be gracious otherworldly hanıms she was confronted with a self-conscious enactment of the old-style odalisque, here performed as a method of nationalist resistance.

> 'You have written of sweet women, of resigned women, of women who loved their husbands, of women who loved their lovers and died for them. I shall tell you a tale different from any in your former book. We have minds that can plan, we Turkish women; we have courage that can carry out our plans to the bitter end; and we have teeth that can bite, if need be.'
>
> Of a sudden she became rigid. She listened intently. Then quickly her extended hand unfastened the bejeweled net that held her hair. A torrent of gold covered her slim shoulders.
>
> 'Mashallah!' I cried, 'but you are beautiful!'
>
> Her eyes narrowed. Her lips quivered. Like an odalisk bringing out the full voluptuousness of her body, she sank back at full length on the settee. Leaning over to the vase on the table, she took from it a spray of hyacinth and brought it to her lips. Then nonchalantly she called out:
>
> '*Entrez*!'
>
> Unaware of any approaching footsteps, and having heard no rap at the door, I was quite amazed to have the door open and the same young French officer enter who had been so moved by the sight of her at the theater the day before. Azzizé introduced him by his name and made no use of the word 'husband.'
>
> 'I came very quietly and had no time to knock before you called out. Did you hear me coming?'
>
> 'My heart told me that you were near.'
>
> She brought the flower closer to her lips and inhaled its scent. Every motion, every act enhanced her enchantingness. The loose white silk garment, the

cascade of gold on her head, the pale pink of the flower with which the two small white hands were toying, were all a complement to the play of her eyes.

The Frenchman was overwhelmed, and the passion that surged through him was no more attractive to behold than an earthquake, and equally devastating. I gave a glance at him, and then wished I were not in the room. I wanted to look at anything else except at him, yet my eyes, mesmerized, kept on travelling from the man to the woman and back to the man again.

His voice was unsteady when he spoke. 'Will you make room for me here at your feet?' He indicated the settee on which she was reclining.

'No!' she answered, so softly that her refusal was a caress. 'Your – er – nearness is so disturbing, Armand, *mon ami*.'

Her mouth and chin were hidden behind the flower. Her eyes were veiled, somber and exciting. The Frenchman grew whiter.

'Am I *de trop*?' he asked.

'N-n-never that. No – only I wish to talk to madame – of you! Of you – and of – our union.'

Then, contradictorily, she gathered herself together like a kitten, and made room for him close to her.

He dropped on the seat like a man who was drunk. She passed one of her perfumed hands through his hair, brought her cheek close to his lips, but not so close that he could kiss her, while the hand that held the flower almost touched his face.

He made as if to take her in his arms, but she eluded him and was on her feet with a movement that from its perfect grace seemed slow, but which must have been swift.

'Now you must go – please, Armand.'

Passing her arm through his she led him to the door. Opening it she pushed him caressingly out, blowing him a kiss with her finger-tips. After closing the door, she stood listening to his soft retreating footsteps, then ever so quietly drew the bolt.

Slowly she returned to me. Every feature that nature had fashioned so lovingly was clouded by an inward tempest of unholy tumult. Her hands tore to fragments the flower she held and with loathing threw it into the waste-basket. With heaving breast, eyes dilated, nostrils quivering, she sank back on the settee. Of me she was oblivious. She laughed her low mirthless laugh, threw back her head and gazed up at the ceiling as if communing with some unseen power.

… Irresistibly compelled, I rose and went to her, and taking one of her hands patted it.

'I – torture – him,' She said brokenly. 'I am – driving – him mad, little – by little. But it is – killing me – too. Still – vengeance – is sweet. The price – is worth it.'

She let her head fall forward on my lap and lie there for me to pat and soothe. The insolent lady of the tram had no relation to the spent young woman whose head on my lap was inundated in its golden wealth.

… I bent over her. 'It isn't worth it,' I pleaded, 'because it is marring your very soul.'

… 'My soul! What do I care for my soul? And what do you know, you who have never suffered? … It was heroism in Belgium to defy the Germans. It was a crime in Turkey to resist the Allies … Because of me one Frenchman, at least, is suffering in purgatory. My husband! … He has never received from me more than I gave him in your presence. But I fan his passion – and then feed it with straws. My brother died from fever. My mother died from a broken heart. And he who killed them both shall be made to die from the fever of his all-consuming passion, by me – me, the avenger of her family and race.' (Vaka 1923: 136–42)

But this enactment of the odalisque was not merely a return to treasured, old-fashioned social mores. Rather, as Kalogeras (1997) discusses,[7] Azzizé Hanım knowingly creates a performance of the Orientalist fantasy odalisque, construct-ing the vision that will most compel and torment her victim – despite the cost to herself of inhabiting the artificiality of the role and the denial of her own true desires. For Vaka Brown, the self-acknowledged 'troubadour' of the old harem system, to be confronted by a Turkish woman who could perform a variety of resistant public and private identities was shocking. The unexpected haughtiness of Azzizé Hanım on the tram is revealed as merely one of her behavioural strate-gies, alongside her knowing self-Orientalisation. The image of the hanım that so plagued the nationalists in their domestic and foreign self-presentation (see Chapter One), was also available for a politicised recuperation within the gender segregated domain of public transport and the – now often internationally con-tested – territory of the supposedly private home.

DRESSING TO GO OUT: VEILS AND VISIBILITY

The changing ways in which veiled women populated public spaces continued also to fascinate Ellison. Her contradictory attitudes to Turkish female emancipa-tion and her investment in the exotica of Turkish dress and spatial relations are seen most acutely in 1928 when she returned to review the new Turkish Repub-lic. Although she was thrilled with its modernising reforms and the advances in women's social position, the veil remained a garment so tantalising to behold and to wear that when Mustafa Kemal, propounding his project of national and gen-der liberation, argued resoundingly that, 'All that nonsense is going to cease. Harems, veils, lattice windows … must go', Ellison was moved to intervene:

> I could not resist the feminine protest, –
> 'But veils are picturesque. No more becoming a head-dress has ever been invented for women.'
> 'We cannot remain in the Dark Ages to supply foreign writers with copy,' was the answer. (Ellison 1928: 23)

It was no coincidence that Mustafa Kemal prioritised getting rid of the veil; not only was he opposed ideologically to the Islamic gender division of society but he was also by then determined to limit the power of the conservative *ulema* (clergy) who had supported the sultan in his opposition to the nationalists

(Y. Arat 1994, Kandiyoti 1991a, Shaw and Shaw 1978, Norton 1997). Although often credited with banning the veil, Kemal never actually legislated against it. The veil was discouraged and frowned upon, but it was only male clothing that was the subject of new laws. In 1925 the turban and the fez were prohibited in public and hats were made the official male headwear. Kemal's inability to legislate against the veil reveals the extreme significance of changes in women's public presence where, unlike the draconian intervention in male apparel, to interfere too strongly with concepts of women's public modesty would have been politically dangerous. Musbah Haidar described how the legal alterations to men's attire exerted a keenly felt social pressure on women:

> women, who still wore the veil, found it to be ludicrous in contrast to the new headgear of their menfolk. Very soon there was hardly a veiled woman to be seen, and these few were looked at askance and even suspected of being doubtful characters. (Haidar 1944: 235)

But what was so delightful about the spectatorial pleasure offered by the figure of the veiled Turkish woman that it threatened the British feminist's political commitment to female emancipation? A liberation that Ellison clearly understood in 1914 was, for Turkish feminists, focused on the removal of the veil: 'The veil must go, of that they are assured, or no progress can be made', she told *Votes for Women* (10 April 1914, p. 442). Her partial embrace of the impact of haremisation is seen most notably in relation to the pleasures it offered in terms of cross-cultural dressing, luxury and wealth. Lovingly described in her 1913 volume, cross-cultural dressing not only gave Ellison the thrill of wearing such fetching items as the yaşmak. It also permitted her access to spaces forbidden to Europeans, since the spatialising dynamics of dress operated simultaneously as religious and ethnic as well as gender identifications. With her hostess Fatima's connivance, Ellison dressed in a veil to visit the mosque and holy tomb of Eyüp where, five years earlier, she had 'had the humiliating experience of being refused admission to the tomb because I was wearing a hat; now I am wearing a veil who can tell whether I am Muslim or Christian?' (Ellison 1915: 162).

> It was Friday afternoon. The Faithful were at prayer when we arrived. I wanted to see the mosque; but how could I, even as a veiled women, take my place amongst the women? Much as I admire the wonderful solemnity of the Eastern prayers – much as I, a Christian, would have loved to worship Allah with my Muslim sisters – I was just a little frightened; my action might be mistaken for irreverence. We went, however, into the gallery reserved for the Sultan, and through the lattice-work windows we had a good view of the mosque below. (Ellison 1915: 164)

The dual deception of her cross-dressed activity is signalled by two different representational registers. Her solemn tone above presents her as respectful worshipper. There is no room for the vengeful pique she felt at the earlier refusal. Her mischievous satisfaction in her indecipherable new (veiled) identification is aimed not at the custodians of the holy site but is redirected (jokingly, as if to defuse its power) at other Europeans she encountered as they trod their very limited Christian way through the religiously demarcated space. Fatima and Ellison had started to leave when:

> Just before we reached our carriage I saw a dear friend with her accustomed unselfishness escorting some English visitors round as much as they, Christians, could see of the holy city of Eyoub. She recognised my voice, and I was introduced as a Turkish lady to my compatriots.
>
> I felt just a little guilty at their delight in meeting a real Turkish woman, but it was too dangerous to undeceive them in those fanatical surroundings. 'And how well you speak English too!' they said. 'English was the first language I spoke,' I answered truthfully. I wonder whether Miss A. ever told them who I really was. (Ellison 1915: 169)

Ellison is all laughter at having fooled some Europeans – though this too is presented as unintentional. But though she romanticised it, Ellison was not unaware of the veil's negative qualities. Again, she reported a discussion with Edib:

> Is it [the veil] protection or is it not? Halide-Hanoum considers that it creates between the sexes a barrier which is impossible when both sexes should be working for the common cause of humanity. It makes the woman at once the 'forbidden fruit', and surrounds her with an atmosphere of mystery which, although fascinating, is neither desirable nor healthy. The thicker the veil the harder the male stares. The more the woman covers her face the more he longs to see the features which, were he to see but once, would interest him no more.
>
> Personally I find the veil no protection. In my hat I thread my way in and out of the cosmopolitan throng at Pera. No one speaks to me, no one notices me, and yet my mirror shows I am no more ugly than the majority of my sex. But when I have walked in the park [recently arranged by Abdülhamit on European lines], a veiled woman, what a different experience. Even the cold Englishman has summoned up courage and enough Turkish to pay compliments to our 'silhouettes'. (Ellison 1915: 69)

Ellison's delight in receiving the attentions directed (in Turkish) at a supposed Turkish woman indicates her investment in the thrill of passing as 'other'. It is not just that she adores the veil as an item of clothing, but that she also mistakes it for a sleight of hand way of temporarily inhabiting another identity. This in part explains her inability to realise the different significance of wearing the veil for Ottoman and English women. Notably she wrote mainly of her scrutiny by European men. The reference to Pera, the foreign quarter of Istanbul, and the new European-style park indicate that the role of veiling was being altered by the hybrid spaces of the modernising city. It was hardly surprising that the cross-culturally dressed Ellison should achieve a heightened visibility in Pera because, despite their increased public visibility, veiled women would still have been a rarity in this cosmopolitan section of the city and so would be of obvious curiosity to the many tourists and foreigners who resided there. To walk in the park, however, attracted attention from a different audience. Public parks were new spaces, designed to allow Turks a mixed gender public life, whose social etiquettes were not yet mapped out and where Turkish men also engaged in new and potentially perplexing behaviours.

This is not to say that men and women had never before met in public. Although ostensibly a segregated society, pleasure trips on boats and to the banks of the Sweet Waters of the Bosphorus had long been used by women as a cover for illicit meetings with men (Loti records secret assignations at the Sweet Waters with Melek Hanım and Zeyneb Hanım in *Les Désenchantées*) and were recommended as locations in which foreigners could catch a much-desired glimpse of Ottoman Muslim women. Clara Erskine Clement counted the Sweet Waters as unmissable, though already by 1895 she was nostalgically regretting the modern intrusion of carriages over the traditional *caiques*. To her experienced eye, much 'of the picturesqueness and air of romance that once pervaded Constantinople is lost; and the afternoon at the Sweet Waters that once seemed like a gala day in Mohammed's Paradise, now resembles a collection of picnic parties in the Prater of Vienna or the Bois de Boulogne' (Clement 1895: 249). But if Clement was determined to show her familiarity with the authentic Istanbul scene, the riverside display continued to be a feature of tourist spectacle and essential route to sightings of the elusive hanıms. Demetrius Coufopoulos in *Black's Guide Book* of 1910 advised visitors to attend the Sweet Waters of Europe (on the Golden Horn) on a Friday afternoon, noting that ladies of the upper classes were to be found at the more exclusive Sweet Waters of Asia (on the Bosphorous).[8] The shift in the location of public promenades from the Sweet Waters (used by minority populations but dominated by Muslims) to the parks in Pera also marked a transition in which elite minority population women came to replace women of the Muslim elite as fashion leaders (Quataert 2000).

Though the flirtations associated with the Sweet Waters point to the existence of mixed gender public interactions, they were always without sanction and hence qualitatively different from the respectable mixed social intercourse which the new parks were intended to facilitate.[9] But the unsegregated park was a novel space that, like other experiences of Turkish women's increasing licit presence in public, presented behavioural challenges for both men and women:

> Five years ago we never walked a step; now we not only saunter through the bazaar, but go to a big dressmaker's in Pera … But not only in the bazaar do we walk; we have walked in the magnificent newly laid-out park, where women are allowed for the first time to walk in a park where there are men. The men I must say, have not yet grown accustomed to the new and extraordinary state of things, and vie with the Levantine 'mashers' in their desire to see the features under the veil. It is not a very comfortable experience for the Turkish woman, but it is the darkness before the dawn. (Ellison 1915: 31–2)

Ellison presents the male response as an aping of a Levantine/Christian mode of masculinity, but it also makes sense within a traditional Muslim conceptualisation of space as sexualised and segregated. Fatima Mernissi reads the seclusion of women as part of a Muslim binarism that divides space into the public, men's space of the *umma* – the community of believers in which women only exceptionally had a justifiable place – and the women's space of the home, in which men were not encouraged to linger (Mernissi 1985). In this schema, restricting contact between the sexes serves to maintain the purity of the *umma* and to prevent *fitna* – the chaos and disorder threatened by illicit sexual thoughts and/or relations – which could be sparked by the seductive presence or visibility of women. The veil as a portable means of seclusion, Mernissi argues, allows women to pass through public spaces, symbolically unseen.

But the new space of the public park would not accord with these spatial relations and so the Ottoman woman, even when veiled, found herself positioned by Muslim as well as Christian men as a sexualised public spectacle. The indeterminate nature of the park space emphasised that, even when veiled, Muslim women should not be in public/men's space unless they had good reason (visiting a shrine etc) and, since frivolous public dalliance in the park would not count as good reason, women's respectability was bound to be called into question. However, Clement, listing the affluent woman's itinerary – Sweet Waters on a Friday, the cemetery at Scutari on a Tuesday, shops in Pera and in Stamboul, prayers at mosques and tombs – concluded, with echoes of Montagu, that 'Turkish ladies go about with a freedom that ought to be sufficient for those of any nation' (Clement 1895: 249–50). For all that Clement might idealise the movements available to the rich and for all that women's presence in public did increase dramatically after 1908, women's new spatial behaviours continued to cause concern. The potential frivolity of Ellison and Fatima's park visit combined with the acquired mode of 'foreign' male voyeurism, in which women's bodies were a legitimate object of surveillance, to activate in Muslim men a mode of behaviour which rendered women – veiled or otherwise – a spectacle in both Islamic and Western terms.

There is something odd about this account, since Levantine men (French- and Italian-speaking Roman Catholics of generally Venetian and Genoese extraction, whose residence in Pera dated back to the Italian colonies there) would have been quite used to moving among a veiled female Muslim population.[10] But despite this strict geographical definition, the term Levantine was often used with negative associations to refer to nefarious long-term residents of Istanbul and the Middle East:

> … [the] narrow, crooked streets [of Pera] are the playground and dwelling place of a nondescript people which, for the lack of a better name, people have agreed to call 'Levantines'.
>
> The Levantine is the parasite of the Near East. He has no country, no scruples, no morals, no honesty of any sort – in business or in private life. He is the descendant of foreign traders who have settled in the Near East at some period or another and have intermingled, not necessarily intermarried, with Greeks and Armenians or other non-Turkish elements of the country.[11]

In Ellison's instance, the attack on Turkish Muslim men becoming like a 'Levantine masher', or cad, is the male equivalent of the 'hat and ball' criticism aimed at *alafranga*[12] women by Edib in Chapter Three: both groups were guilty of a cultural hybridity that diluted and de-classed the manners expected of Ottomans. This pillorying of the Levantines, as Ternar points out in relation to Ellison's criticism of the Perote governesses whose untruths about the harem she intended to correct, served to separate Ellison from the less respected elements of Istanbul European society (Ternar 1994: 41–2). In both these cases the inference is that it is their hybridity that renders them unappealing. Pera also, as Kandiyoti (1989a) notes, signified an unhealthy cultural mingling in Turkish novels from the 1890s to the republic: acting as a lure for bored fashionable young men in contrast to the purity of the idealised Anatolian provinces; as a zone of corruption and collaboration between Turkish women and enemy troops during the Balkan and First World Wars; and as a general stand-in for the immodesty of the *alafranga* woman in contrast to the idealised purity of the chaste nationalist rural woman (see also Chapter Three).

For Ellison, this low-class mixing was not the appealing multicultural synthesis of upper-class Ottomanism. The English Turkophile's disassociation from Perotes (some of whom she feels obliged to mention she 'personally found … very charming') and Levantines fosters her alignment with the well-mannered Ottoman elite, providing her readers with further proof of her reliability as an informant. It was this elevated association specifically to which she attached herself socially and to which she aligned herself sartorially in her carefully selected cross-cultural dressing. Presenting herself photographically dressed *à la turque* could become therefore, as I discuss in the next chapter, one of the means by which her ethnographic authority was confirmed.

NOTES

1   For an overview of the public/private debate in feminist historiography and cultural geography see Helly and Reverby (1992).

2   On the use of veiling as a language of modesty and status in rural bedouin society see Abu-Lughod (1986).

3   See also Lewis and Micklewright (2004).

4   'The Turkish woman's awakening: interview with Miss Grace Ellison', E. I., *Votes for Women*, 10 April 1914, p. 442.

5   Aliye Hanım, *Les musulmanes contemporaines*, Paris, A. Lemerre, 1894, trans. Nazime Roukié, in Şeni (1995).

6   Non-Muslim women did generally sit in the 'harem' compartment in trams. Public transport was desegregated by the head of the Istanbul police on 24 October 1923, a few days ahead of the declaration of the republic on 29 October (Kandiyoti 1991b).

7   In a previous version of this section (Lewis 1999c) I had not dwelt enough on the significance of Azzizé Hanım's story. I am grateful to Yiorgos Kalogeras for causing me to reconsider.

8   See also Bohrer (2004).

9   I am indebted to Nancy Micklewright for her discussion of this point.

10 I am grateful to Claire Karaz for her information on the Levantine population in Istanbul.

11 Mufty-Zade, K. Zia Bey, 1922, *Speaking of the Turks*, New York, Duffield and Co., in Ternar (1994:168n).

12 *Alafranga* was a colloquialism meaning 'in the European or "Frankish" style/manner' and could refer to dress, behaviour, speech or other cultural elements. Its use was often, but not always, derogatory.

CHAPTER SIX

✺ Dress Acts: the Shifting ❧ Significance of Clothes

PHOTOGRAPHY, PLEASURE AND CROSS-CULTURAL DRESSING

Although, as I discussed in the last chapter, Ellison delighted in being mistaken for a Turk when touring Istanbul in a veil with her Ottoman friends, she also used the story of their encounter with unwanted male attention in the new park to remind her readers of her distance from her Ottoman objects of study. Male scrutiny was less burdensome to her than to them. This is hardly surprising, given the imperial privilege which cloaked her transactions in Istanbul. But it also emphasises her subject formation within different European spatial relations: just as her internalisation of European forms of spatial compliance made Ottoman architecture bewildering, so too did it produce different concepts of spatial resistance. Against the background of British suffragists' determinedly public demonstrations, it is easy to see how the usurpation of a previously segregated Ottoman civic space was likely to be a source of triumph and excitement to Ellison rather than the anxiety it caused to her Ottoman friends. Her intrinsic separation from Ottoman women is further emphasised when she tried to capture the 'features under the veil':

> There is a beautiful old woman in the household whom I long to 'Kodak.' Once I thought I 'had' her as she sat cross-legged on the carpet rolling her quarter-hourly cigarette, but she noticed me, alas! then cursed, screamed, and buried her head in her roomy pantaloons. I shall not try to repeat the experiment. (Ellison 1915: 183)

In this chapter I also look through the lens of the camera – using photographs to reconfigure the issues of dress and identity encountered in Chapter Five.

Throughout *An Englishwoman in a Turkish Harem* Ellison was torn between wanting to defend the Ottomans by presenting them as modern and modernising and her nostalgia for elegant Ottoman conventions. But the distinctive traditions which she described in such loving detail became exasperating when they thwarted her ethnographic and scopophilic desire to gather photographic evidence:

> Before I leave [Fatima's] house I hope to get some photos of the interesting persons it contains, but in undertaking to photograph a Turkish household I had forgotten first that the windows are dimmed by the inevitable lattice-work …

But there is another and greater difficulty, and this, photography is forbidden by the Moslem religion. My friend would certainly let me photograph the house if I asked her. The sacred law of hospitality is part of her religion ... But Fatima has to deal with a most fanatical entourage, the women much more than the men ... (Ellison 1915: 27–8)

It was not just superstitious old women who prevented her photographic aspirations, but the very materiality of Oriental architectural space. Yet even when Ellison managed to overcome Oriental scruples and shadows, and take some photographs, they were not always acceptable to her Western audience:

Had I been able, as I hoped, to send some photographs of the interior of my friend's house, those photographs would probably be considered 'fakes,' or perhaps even they might be returned (as they were returned to me when I last stayed in Turkey five years ago) with the comment 'This is not a Turkish harem.' (Ellison 1915: 19)

The presence of thirteen photographs proudly announced on the title page attests to the significance of photographic documentation and to Ellison's determination. Her photographs reveal the double bind of representing Ottoman domestic space: their production and circulation was hampered by an allegiance to the old and Oriental (religious interdiction) *and* the problematic signification of the new and Occidental (too much modern furniture). One of Ellison's rejected photographs, *A Corner of a Turkish Harem of Today* (Illustration 2, overleaf) was reproduced in Zeyneb Hanım's *A Turkish Woman's European Impressions*. Its caption read:

This photograph was taken expressly for a London paper. It was returned with this comment: 'The British public would not accept this as a picture of a Turkish Harem.' As a matter of fact, in the smartest Turkish houses European furniture is much in evidence. (Zeyneb Hanoum 1913: 192)

As an editor and a writer Ellison trod a delicate line between offering the expected pleasures of a recognisable Orient and challenging Orientalist stereotypes, wanting to show that Ottoman homes were not as Europe imagined but were in fact contemporary, respectable domiciles full of European furniture. But she also loved participating in old Ottoman customs and dressing up in 'traditional' clothes. Recognising this desire for an 'authentic' environment, Ellison's hostess Fatima started shopping for 'antiquated' Turkish goods in order to furnish a proper 'Turkish room' for her next visit, buying in the bazaar, 'those quaint and delightful souvenirs of the Turkey of the past, in much the same way as we English who can afford it indulge our tastes for the furniture and porcelain of a century that is gone' (Ellison 1915: 20).

Despite Ellison's experiences photography was increasingly available in the late Ottoman period (Çizgen 1987), although like all Western goods and technologies its consumption was uneven. The majority of professional Ottoman photographers were Greek or Armenian, with studios in the Rue de Pera (where Ellison and Fatima now shopped for clothes). Though their trade was largely aimed at foreign tourists, Ottoman Muslims also began from the late nineteenth century to visit the photographic studios and/or commission photographs to be taken at home. These professional images would have had a mainly private circulation, as would those of keen Muslim amateurs, such as Ali Sami, who were taking photographs of their families at the turn of the century. This can be seen in the framed photographs that decorate the room in Ellison's contemporary Turkish harem in Illustration 2 (see also Graham-Brown 1988: 81, Micklewright 1999). Outside the individual household the imperial dominions were documented photographically for Abdülhamit, whose commissioned photographs of new buildings and machinery as well as of his diverse population allowed him to access the sights of his empire that he did not visit in person. His vast photographic collection often presented the empire as a series of geographic spaces and ethnic groups in a way which shared much with the Euro-American use of

2. *A Corner of a Turkish Harem of Today* (Zeyneb Hanoum, *A Turkish Woman's European Impressions*, London, Seeley, Service and Co., 1913)

photography as a means of surveillance, classification and control in what John Tagg has identified as a regime of surveillance (Tagg 1988). Demonstrating an awareness of the power of photographic representation, the sultan also used photography to intervene in how his empire was displayed to the Occident, sending photographic albums to the Chicago Exposition in 1893 and presenting albums to the British and US governments (Çelik 1992). A photographic record of Ottoman costume had previously been made by Abdülaziz for the 1873 Universal Exposition in Vienna. As Micklewright and Çelik discuss in relation to Abdülhamit's commissions, the imperial desire for self-representation was instrumental to the development of Ottoman photography since many early photographers were trained during their time in the military. But by far the largest sector of photographs of the Ottoman Empire consisted of trade images for tourists and for export,[1] including the ever-popular souvenir photos of visitors to Istanbul dressed up in approximations of local costume.

The symbiotic relationship between the new technology of photography and the new investigative social sciences of ethnography and anthropology has been much discussed (Edwards 1990, 1992, Pinney 1990, 1992, Street 1992). Not only did the new technology and new disciplines develop coterminously, but photography had, by the late nineteenth century, come to be an established part of the fieldwork process. Photography did not simply document, it played a crucial role in the classification, conceptualisation and visualisation of 'other' peoples in the protocols of the emerging disciplines, though this was not without its problems and anxieties. As Christopher Pinney discusses, early concerns about the ethics of editing and 'touching up' photographs made in the field became more acute by the early twentieth century as the apparent denotative security of photography was increasingly undermined. In a context where anthropology looked to photography to shore up its classifications, the caption took on a heightened significance (Pinney 1990, 1992). For these and other reasons, such as the increase in amateur photography made possible by the development of easier to use and portable equipment such as Ellison's Kodak camera, Elizabeth Edwards identifies 1910–20 as a period in which photography was ceasing to be so central to the professional anthropological endeavour (Edwards 1992). This is also the period in which anthropology turned towards a more cultural relativist viewpoint, though the ideas of clearly visible racial superiority encouraged by nineteenth-century evolutionary thinking continued to be active in popular attitudes to racial and ethnic difference (Street 1992).

Redolent of the uneven application of this intellectual shift is the way that Ellison regarded photography as integral to her ability to present the Ottomans. She wished to show the Ottomans as they saw themselves and to challenge British assumptions about their barbarism but could not help presuming on the superiority of Western culture. Ellison's description of her 'Kodaking' experience shows the would-be amateur ethnographer's classic attempt to assume the invisible viewpoint implicit in early codifications of ethnographic objectivity, just at the point when the role of photography was being reformulated in the

3. *The Author in Turkish Costume* (Grace Ellison, *An Englishwoman in a Turkish Harem*, London, Methuen, 1915)

4. *A Contributor to the New Turkish Woman's Paper, Kadinlar Dunyassi (The Woman's World)* (Grace Ellison, *An Englishwoman in a Turkish Harem*, London, Methuen, 1915)

profession. The Ottoman woman is described in her 'natural' habitat, a local curiosity who is the subject of an 'experiment' to document a dying breed rendered antiquated by the contemporary modernisation of Ottoman social life. Kathleen Stewart Howe identifies the photographic moment as a contact zone, emphasising that the 'photograph is first an event before it becomes an object'.[2] Ellison's photographic experiences, with willing and unwilling sitters and involving herself as sitter, were processes of engagement which repositioned existing subject positions and produced new forms of racialised identification.

Whilst one particular old woman may have refused to be photographed, the looked-for pleasures of Oriental dress were more than adequately represented by photographs of Ellison's cross-cultural dressing. In the frontispiece to her book, entitled *The Author in Turkish Costume* (Illustration 3, above, p. 210), Ellison simultaneously enacted and frustrated the expectations that her book's title would have created in the minds of her Occidental readers. Having on several occasions identified the erroneous ideas of sex and violence that were aroused in the minds of Europeans at the mere mention of the word harem, she defiantly entitled her book *An Englishwoman in a Turkish Harem* and fronted it with a photograph of herself in 'native' dress. Captions, as Barthes (1977) has argued, are often crucial in tying down photography's bewildering polysemy and thus essential to the construction of realist reading conventions. In these books ethnographic and literary codes work in potent combination to locate the photograph within particular conventions of racialised meaning.

In Illustration 3 the caption identifies the pictured woman as the author, immediately keying into discourses of experiential realism and literary authority. It also differentiates this photo from other images of women in similar clothes by identifying this woman as English and not Turkish. How else to distinguish the racial identity of this figure from that of the unnamed female contributor to the women's magazine *Kadınlar Dünyası*, illustrated in Illustration 4 (p. 211)? Both are dark-haired, pale-skinned women in similar clothes and pose.[3] In the first plate the clothes are identified as 'costume', utilising the pseudo-scientific language of ethnographic description which renders 'native' clothing timeless and archaic collective costume, a world far away from the increasingly fast-moving and individualising fashion industry of the modern Western world. Since Ellison's book often discussed changes in Ottoman fashions, the use of terminology such as 'costume' may reflect the publisher's editorial choices rather than Ellison's own. This places the images, their captions and the rest of the written text in a dialectical relationship, all parts of the multifaceted narrative sold under Ellison's name but not necessarily all the result of her actual writing.[4] Adding to the ethnographic distanciation is the anonymity of the contributor to *Kadınlar Dünyası*. This is unusual for Ellison's book, where most of the pictured subjects are named; a form of individuation and recognition of social status that diverges from anthropological conventions of the unidentified, essentialised type. But, though unnamed, the Ottoman journalist is identified by her progressive occupation whilst the partially legible inscription, 'Grace Ellison ... affection', testifies to the personal provenance of the photograph, inscribing Ellison as participant in the photographic exchange rather than as invisible absent ethnographer.

Grace Ellison herself has a very peculiar and transitory status in the photographs. She appears as 'the author' at the head of the book, yet in *An Englishwoman Wearing a Yashmak* (Illustration 5, overleaf) the identity of the woman as well as her face appears to be veiled. In fact, both identity and face are only partially veiled; for this is clearly Ellison and her face is still visible, being only slightly obscured by the yaşmak. This form of veiling was temporarily replaced by the heavy black face veil or peçe (see Illustration 6, p. 215) insisted on by Abdülhamit at the turn of the century (see later this chapter) but the thinner and more revealing yaşmak was frequently described by Ellison as particularly attractive. When Fatima wore one on their court visit Ellison bewailed that 'now, alas!' it is obsolete, worn only at court, 'for to me it is one of the most becoming of head-dresses, showing the eyes to very great advantage' (Ellison 1915: 35). Having plastered her face all over the book, and not herself being bound by any Islamic scruples about photography, why was Ellison so coy about her identity in this image? The answer lies in the pleasures of cross-cultural dressing and Ellison's teasing of her readers.

Gail Low has written about the pleasures of cross-cultural dressing which, she argues, are often underpinned by a closely held sense of racialised differentiation. This might initially seem at odds with the profound delight taken by participants in dressing in local clothes and even passing as native. But for the Westerner, she suggests, the pleasure of wearing an exotic and splendid 'native' costume is enhanced by the knowledge of their white skin underneath the disguise (Low 1996). For Richard Burton or Kipling's Kim the ability to pass as a native is an important talent, both pleasurable (giving access to hidden native customs) and political (Kim, after all, spies for the Raj). Clothes, Low argues, are important to the fantasy of cross-dressing because they are 'superficial' and can always be removed when one needs to revert to type, to reassert one's racial or cultural superiority. In contrast, Apter maintains that cross-dressing undermines previous conventions of absolute difference, and instances Loti's delight in passing not only as a Turk, but also as a veiled Turkish woman, as an example of the fluidity of boundaries. I however agree with Low that it is the transitory nature of this boundary-breaking that is significant. For Loti, as for Ellison, the thrill of cross-cultural dressing is predicated on an implicit re-investment in the very boundaries they cross. Clothes operate as visible gatekeepers of those divisions and, even when worn against the grain, serve to re-emphasise the existence of the dividing line. Cross-dressing offers both the pleasures of consumption – the Orient as a space full of enticing goods to be bought, savoured and worn – and the deeper thrill of passing as native.

Both these pleasures are demonstrated in Ellison's interaction with Ottoman clothes. When Fatima puts her entire trousseau at Ellison's disposal, her guest admits that: 'I take out these precious gifts sometimes and examine them at leisure' (Ellison 1915: 23). This private reverie and the sensual satisfactions

5. *An Englishwoman Wearing a Yashmak* (Grace Ellison, *An Englishwoman in a Turkish Harem*, London, Methuen, 1915)

6. *Turkish Lady in Tcharchoff (outdoor costume)* (Zeyneb Hanoum, *A Turkish Woman's European Impressions*, London, Seeley, Service and Co., 1913)

obtained from her perusal of the fabulously bejewelled items illustrate the double desirability of Oriental artefacts. Spearheaded by Paul Poiret in 1911, these 'ancient' styles and motifs were becoming newly contemporary for Ellison's Western readers. Aiming to emancipate Western women from the corsets of the *belle époque* via the unfettered form of Oriental fashion, Poiret's plan relied, as Peter Wollen points out, not just on the use of Oriental colour and style but also on the sexualised stereotypes of the harem as a place of sadism and power (Wollen 1993). Coterminously, the Ballet Russes also embraced Oriental style, colour, vibrancy and texture in their dance and costumes, causing a sensation in Paris and London in 1910. Whether or not Ellison saw any of their performances she, and many of her readers, would have heard of Bakst's sensational costumes and may have visited the displays at London's Selfridges which tied in with this Orientalist craze (Wollen 1987, 1993, Nava 1998). By the time Ellison's reports from a Turkish harem were appearing in the *Daily Telegraph* in January 1914, their fashion coverage was dominated by the Poiret-esque elongated silhouette and adverts lured readers with reductions on Poiret cloaks in the winter sales. The style and feel of the Ottoman stuffs that Ellison was enjoying in Fatima's home would not have been entirely alien to her readers, they were part of the already codified covetable exotic. The freer movements of Dhiagilev's style also found their way into the popular arena through the dances of Isadora Duncan and of Maud Allen, whose explicitly Orientalist performances of Salome played to packed, largely middle-class, female audiences at London's Palace Theatre in 1918 (Walkowitz 2003, Bland 1998). In a number of ways a familiarity with – if not actual experience of – Oriental styles spread far beyond the avant-garde during the period in which Ellison was travelling and publishing. The fascination with the Orient and the body Orientalised through clothes and movement was becoming recognisable as one of the contours of women's cultural consumption, laying the ground for the outrageous success of Valentino's cross-culturally dressed role in *The Sheik* in 1921 (based on Edith Hull's steamy novel of the same name from in 1919), which prompted its own consumer crazes for Sheik-style dress and interiors.

As well as enjoying dressing in Turkish clothes with her women friends, Ellison delighted in going out and about in Istanbul in Turkish dress. As seen in Chapter Five she was thrilled when she hoodwinked people into thinking that she was Turkish. How does this link to the experience of hoodwinking her readers, who opened her book expecting one thing (disreputable 'smoking room' tales of polygamy) and got another? If the logic of the veil is that one cannot identify the wearer, why does the caption *Englishwoman Wearing a Yashmak* (Illustration 5, above, p. 214) identify the nationality or race of the subject, but not her name? By presenting herself as willingly acculturated to Ottoman Muslim life (though this cannot be deduced from the photograph alone, but only from the longer narrative) Ellison suggests the positive aspects of haremisation.

This links into another set of pleasures that Low associates with cross-cultural dressing, namely fantasies of power and surveillance. The undercover cross-culturally dressed agent embodies a mode of power based on a 'fantasy of invisibility' which imagines for an imperial gaze a state of omnipotence and omnipresence that is secret and voyeuristic rather than visible (Low 1996: 95). Like the fantasised invisibility of the ethnographic eye behind the camera (and the troublingly hidden gaze of the veiled woman), the undercover agent offers a possibility of looking without being seen to look. Ellison was well aware that her inquisitive gaze would be defeated if it became too apparent and worried about alienating the subjects of her interactive enquiry. Compensating for the impossibly masculinist position of objective scientific observer, the pleasure of cross-cultural dressing, knowing that one is white underneath the native garb, allowed a European woman like Ellison to demonstrate her impressive local knowledges and contacts.

By crossing both the gender and religious demarcations of 'harem', gaining access to spaces forbidden to non-believers, she could enjoy the pleasures of cultural transgression without having to give up the racial privilege that underpinned her authority to represent her version of Oriental reality. Ellison's reference to the danger at Eyüp of being discovered in the tomb's 'fanatical surroundings' (see Chapter Five) and her determination to go there because it was forbidden (she admits that other monuments were finer), align her with a site already made legendary by Loti's triumphant incursion in *Aziyadé* and evoke the dangers famously faced by that other English cross-cultural dresser Sir Richard Burton. He, among his many transgressive dress acts, disguised himself in 1853 as a Pathan pilgrim in order to enter the holy cities of Mecca and Medina, forbidden to infidels. Though Ellison was attempting to appropriate for herself the heroic transgressions of Burton's free-ranging excursions,[5] her temporary invisibility is presented as ultimately gendered and therefore limited: she can only access the already restricted spaces available to Muslim women. In contrast to her near contemporary Isabel Ebehart – who, at the turn of the century (after a history of cross-gender dressing in Europe), reinvented herself as an Arab boy in North Africa – Ellison retains a clearly gendered identity, looking instead for opportunities to imagine alternative femininities. Her access to the disembodied position of Western imperial invisibility is challenged (her photographs of the harem cannot be accepted as 'real'), but the thrill of cross-cultural dressing offers her the opportunity to temporarily align herself with the position from which authoritative discourse emanates. Ellison's access to this is partial both on the ground and in the text, where her ethnographic authority cannot but represent itself as having been challenged. The need to create an authenticating narratorial identity as a woman in the Turkish harem requires an emphasis on the pleasures of female finery which works in tension with the severe investigative rationale that apparently lies behind her public cross-cultural dressing endeavours. Male cross-cultural dressers also lovingly described the details of their exotic apparel (Garber 1992, Low 1996), but this potentially feminising vein of writing could be more effectively submerged in the heroic discourse of their exploits. In a colonial context where the burden of upholding cultural norms abroad fell on

Western women, Ellison's cross-cultural dressing, already potentially transgressing gender norms, reveals a series of contestations: her pleasure in racialised power sits in tension with a desire to challenge Orientalist knowledges; her attempt at ethnographic documentary invisibility is held in check by her awareness of the intimacy of the photographic process; and her would-be scientific objectivity runs alongside her inability to suppress her evident joy in the clothes. It is her feminine pleasure in these rich stuffs that anchors the gendered authority accruing to the woman's account of the harem.

The luxurious pleasures of the harem also centre on the allocation to Ellison of a slave, Cadhem Haïr Calfat, whom she renamed Miss Chocolate and with whom she posed in the photograph labelled simply *Miss "Chocolate"* (Illustration 7, opposite, Ellison 1915). Referring to her often as a maid rather than a slave – though she understood 'Calfat' to mean slave[6] – Ellison describes her as an 'elegant negress'. Whilst the Ottoman slave name denoted status and identity within the household, Ellison's jokey re-christening reduces her maid's status to a differentiation of skin colour. The new name sticks, permitting Ellison a sense of ownership in relation to Miss Chocolate – 'as *my* negress is now called by all my friends' (Ellison 1915: 11, my emphasis). Changing names and protecting true identities is a ploy that runs through all these sources (see Chapter One) but Miss Chocolate's name was not changed for reasons of personal protection. This renaming has more to do with the anthropologist's renaming of native informants (see also Ternar 1994) and the Victorian habit of renaming domestic servants for the greater convenience of their mistresses. Miss Chocolate is renamed twice, once by slavery and once by Ellison. Ellison's renaming attempts to assign to herself a relationship to the domestic labourer that simultaneously inscribes her ownership of and authority over that labour and that uses humour to side-step the brutal commodification of the original enslavement. So what is happening in the photograph of Ellison with Miss Chocolate?

Miss Chocolate looks 'off screen' with a slight smile on her face, but the viewer's eyes are directed back to her by Ellison's fond look within the frame. For the viewer outside the photograph, mimicking Ellison's ocularity, Miss Chocolate is the object to which the gaze is directed. With no presence in the title, it is not Ellison in her 'Turkish costume' who is constructed as the focus of curiosity,[7] but neither is she safely behind the lens. Who was handling the Kodak in this and the other shots when Ellison is in the picture? Few of the photographs in these books have clear provenance and, though Ellison here and in her later books evidently took many photographs herself, the others were not necessarily studio photographs. The photograph of Miss Chocolate is the most likely to have been made in a studio, with them posing against the ornate *mashrabbia* screen that, like the veil, regularly served in studio set-ups to signify the sequestration of the harem. But the women do not look directly at the camera, suggesting the absence of a professional photographer's direction. When Ellison appears in the frame the balance of power between observer and observed starts to shift as she becomes part of the Oriental spectacle. Yet, the narratorial voice in the written

7. *"Miss Chocolate"* (Grace Ellison, *An Englishwoman in a Turkish Harem*, London, Methuen, 1915)

text maintains a racialised difference which, however open to hybridity and however sympathetic to the Ottomans, is always that of an English woman with all the positional superiority it conventionally implies. It is this which allows Ellison to appear so easily hybridised since – having established her core identification as English – she, and by proxy her readers, can then enjoy the pleasure of cross-cultural consumption and costume. In this a discourse of luxury operated for women as a fantasy of Orientalist consumer excess, substituted for the more overt masculinist fantasies of the harem's sexual excess (Yeazell 2000). Ellison's emphatic delight in Turkish luxury and hospitality – particularly as experienced through dress and adornment – invests in a discourse of sensory pleasure coded in terms that were felt to be available to women tutored to recognise themselves as consumers. For a European readership already familiar with the fashion for things Oriental, Ellison's appearance in Turkish dress provided a vicarious version of the real thing and celebrated the Oriental experience in ways permissible for respectable women.

Whilst her book discusses and pictures elite Ottoman women's familiarity with Western fashions, Ellison herself only appears *à la turque*. Her presence in English dress would be too anti-exoticising, would too much trouble the transculturating drive of the book. If one of the declared intentions of the book was to show that Turkish homes were already partly Europeanised, then Ellison's visual presence reinforces the exotica that her written text so relentlessly undermines. This suggests why – like her readers who she knew would insist on holding onto outdated stereotypes about the harem – the feminist Ellison could not bear to relinquish Turkey's picturesquely exotic costumes. Despite her best intentions to challenge cultural stereotypes, Ellison is simultaneously interpellated within the larger structures of Orientalism. These power relations are often experienced consciously as an affront to her political sensibilities, yet they are also provide the source of much of her determined embrace of cultural difference.

This is where Miss Chocolate enters again, for it is the availability of slave labour that makes such hospitality possible. Ellison, like most writers on the subject (see also Chapter Three), elaborates on the differences between Atlantic/North American slavery and the Ottoman system; pointing out that, though officially freed by the 1908 constitution, most slaves chose to remain in the household and were well treated:

> Miss Chocolate ... is an excellent maid. She sews well, keeps my clothes well brushed and tidy, washes me well, and has an unending capacity for taking pains ... Miss Chocolate has never been beaten, she receives only kindness; she is invited, with all the other members of the 'domestic sisterhood,' to see us dance and hear the Western music when we dance and sing in the evenings, but we generally read and sew. And yet never does she or any other slave take advantage of her mistress's familiarity, standing always at the door, although bidden to come in. (Ellison 1915: 26–7)

The lavish hospitality so essential to Ellison's enchantment with Turkey (see Chapter Five) is only possible because Turkish homes are run by slaves and not servants:

> But the Eastern woman has not yet begun what we in the West know as 'the servant trouble.' With the abolition of slavery, however, this is on its way. When all the slaves in Fatima's household are married [and therefore freed in keeping with Muslim law] she must necessarily employ hired domestics; with education 'hired domestics' become *exigeants*. They will object to making coffee and emergency beds at all times and at all hours, then 'good-bye' to the charming unceremonious hospitality of the East … I asked a Turkish lady who had lived for some months in London what she most appreciated in our capital. 'What I know best,' she answered, 'is Mrs. —'s registry office for servants.' (Ellison 1915: 101, original emphasis)

Ellison's masquerade as Turkish is partly made possible by the unwilling masquerade of Cadhem Haïr Calfat as Miss Chocolate. As Ellison plays with disguising her own identity in the photographs, without losing the authority to provide commentary on Ottoman life, Cadhem Haïr Calfat's change of identity is enacted for her, rather than by her. Though the use of quotation marks in the photograph caption hints at the artificiality of Miss Chocolate's name, this is not problematised by the written text which, rendering it without quotation marks, naturalises the new nickname and Ellison's ownership. Ellison's slip in classifying Miss Chocolate as a servant rather than a slave is not just a way of avoiding complicity in an outlawed barbaric practice: in contrast to the privations inflicted on overworked domestic servants at home, Ottoman slaves had long been regarded by Western observers as having a preferable existence (Craven 1789, Pardoe 1837, Harvey 1871). In this Ellison aligns herself with the evaluative strategies of the Ottomans who, like other modernising or colonised cultures, often sought to resolve their ambivalent admiration for hegemonising foreign cultures by using alien cultural values to reveal the higher moral status of indigenous practices, especially those like slavery or polygamy that they themselves regarded as 'uncivilised' (van Os 1999).

When polygamy compared favourably to Christian marriage and slaves were better treated than servants (see Chapter Three), one must not assume that Ellison's sartorial adventures had no positive pleasures for the Ottoman hosts who assisted her. As an intimate interaction within the social relations of hospitality, dressing up at home provided an obvious chance for friendship and bonding. But, when transposed to public spaces, accompanying Ellison on her cross-dressed outings might vicariously offer a different but related set of transgressive thrills to her Ottoman accomplices. Collaborating in the joint misleading of Europeans could provide an opportunity to undermine and reposition racialised boundaries for subjects who must themselves have regularly been the recipients of a classificatory Orientalist gaze. Similarly, braving the uncharted social relations of the new park with a European woman 'masquerading' as veiled might put quite a different spin on the identificatory and sexualised assumptions projected onto her 'authentically' veiled companions by both European and Ottoman men. The reinvestment in racialised boundaries that underpins Ellison's cross-cultural dressing would have different connotations for her Turkish hosts than for Ellison herself and her British readers.

DE-VEILING: PERFORMING THE ORIENT IN EUROPE

The reverse side of Ellison's cross-culturally dressed charade is illustrated by Zeyneb Hanım and Melek Hanım. The power accruing to the European sartorial adventurer who can delight in the white skin underneath the native clothes is not available to two Ottoman women whose flight from the harem's constraints resulted in the differently restrictive spatialising gender relations of Europe. Having such an aversion to Oriental seclusion that they fled for a 'free' life in Europe, the sisters were unable to recognise the signs of Western freedom as truly valuable: they could not get over the pointlessness of sport or the crazy pace of a Paris Season. They looked with eyes that were both haremised and haremising, finding the harem in Europe. Zeyneb Hanım, writing to Ellison in Istanbul, reports on her stay in a 'Ladies' Club' in London and is not impressed with the experience:

> What a curious harem! and what a difference from the one in which you are living at present.
>
> The first time I dined there I ordered the vegetarian dinner, expecting to have one of those delicious meals which you are enjoying (you lucky woman!), which consists of everything that is good. But alas! the food in this harem has been a disappointment to me … In the reading room, where I spend my evening, I met … people, who spoke in whispers, wrote letters, and read the daily papers. The silence of the room was restful, there was an atmosphere almost of peace, but it is not the peace which follows strife, it is the peace of apathy. Is this, then, what the Turkish women dream of becoming one day? Is this their ideal of independence and liberty? … What I do feel, though, is that a Ladies' Club is not a big enough reward for having broken away from an Eastern harem and all the suffering that has been the consequence of that action. A club, as I said before, is after all another kind of harem, but it has none of the mystery and charm of the Harem of the East. (Zeyneb Hanoum 1913: 182–6)

Like the Kabylian servant in de Teramond's story (see Chapter Five), Zeyneb Hanım exerts a haremising gaze on the West that makes strange its familiar division of space and organisation of sexuality. At these points in her book, Zeyneb Hanım breaks off to address her respondent Grace Ellison directly – an exchange of opinions in which the presumed to be silent Orientalised woman speaks back with her observations on both Eastern and Western life. Zeyneb Hanım's haremisation effect is very particular. Though she makes no bones about how women are devalued in segregated society, she uses her experience of segregated life to counter the way the harem is sexualised in Western discourse and to domesticate it into a home (Melman 1992). Taking the positive evaluation of indigenous culture beyond a merely favourable comparison to the West, Zeyneb Hanım brings in the recurrent sexualised trope of Ottoman women's passivity in the face of fate and reattributes it to the London Ladies' Club. Having removed the excesses of sexualisation and privation from the Orient, she relocates them in the Occident, implicitly challenging the Orientalist sexualisation of Oriental female space and behaviours. Her sarcasm knows no bounds when she visits the Houses of Parliament.

> But, my dear, why have you never told me that the Ladies' Gallery is a harem? A harem with its latticed windows! The harem of the Government! No wonder the women cried through the windows of that harem that they wanted to be free! I felt inclined to shout too. 'Is it in Free England that you dare to have a harem? How inconsistent are you English! You send your women out unprotected all over the world, and here in the workshop where your laws are made, you cover them with a symbol of protection.' (Zeyneb Hanoum 1913: 194)

Positioning the Western and Eastern women's spaces in conjunction to each other, Zeyneb Hanım haremises in reverse. She specifically reassigns the sexualised projections of indolence and apathy back to their Western point of origin, the spectacular lack of luxury in the London 'harem' (with its grotesquely inedible food and unfriendly apathy) paradoxically serving to emphasise the domestification of the Istanbul harem. Her knowing gaze – 'my dear, why have you never told me?' – sees in the West what the West tries to project onto the East. But in Zeyneb Hanım's account neither the Oriental nor the Occidental spaces of female sequestration are highly sexualised. Rather than create an alternative erotic, Zeyneb Hanım's account emphasises the similarities between East and West whilst simultaneously criticising the limitations of both. Though the limitations of the Ottoman harem were not for her, the European alternatives are neither sufficiently better nor sufficiently *different*.

Zeyneb Hanım does not only find the harem in Europe, she also brings it with her through her staging of Ottoman clothes and interiors. Unlike Ellison, who appears solely photographed in Ottoman dress, there are only two 'cross-culturally' dressed photographs in Zeyneb Hanım's book showing the sisters in European clothes: *Melek on the Verandah at Fontainebleau* (Illustration 8, below, p. 224) and *The Balcony at the Back of Zeyneb's House [in Turkey]* (not shown). In all the other plates, the sisters wear some form of Ottoman dress even though in Turkey they would already have had access to Paris fashions.

Although Zeyneb Hanım's references to seeing the outside world without a veil make it clear that the sisters were not veiled in Europe, their written account says little about what they wore. But their wardrobe would have been European. At Fontainebleau Melek Hanım wears a fashionable Edwardian evening dress whose full bosom, covered in the deep lace characteristic of the turn of the century, accentuated the pushed out posterior typical of the desired 'S' bend shape, dating it between 1906 and 1908.[8] Appearing in a book published in 1913 this outfit would not have made Melek Hanım dowdy even if it were not quite the

8. *Melek on the Verandah at Fontainebleau* (Zeyneb Hanoum, *A Turkish Woman's European Impressions*, London, Seeley, Service and Co., 1913)

first rung of fashion (Gernsheim 1963). It is impossible to know whether the dress was purchased in Europe or Turkey but the two sisters, like many Ottoman consumers, would not have looked significantly out of date even if their clothes had been bought outside the European metropolis. Their knowledge of and ability to negotiate European sartorial norms are wryly illustrated when Zeyneb Hanım describes for Ellison the numerous gifts of hats which arrive almost daily. Sent by post from anonymous well-wishers, who, 'hearing of our escape, have had the thoughtfulness and the same original idea of providing us with hats', she cannot help noting the ridiculousness of the stereotypical but kindly intended response: 'it is curious, but charming all the same. Do they think we are too shy to order hats for ourselves, and are still wandering around Switzerland in our *tcharchafs*?' (Zeyneb Hanoum 1913: 66).

With these fashion skills at their fingertips, why do the photographs of them in their book about their travels in Europe mainly show them wearing Ottoman clothes? Many of the photographs not specifically in Europe are captioned with details about Ottoman dress, and are presented as an ethnographic or historical supplement on Ottoman female life rather than as a record of their time in Europe. The photographs of the sisters and other Ottoman women at home in Ottoman dress work generically to maintain the authors' Turkishness in the face of their potentially acculturating sojourn in Europe. But when Zeyneb Hanım and Melek Hanım are pictured in Europe, the significance of their Ottoman self-presentation goes into overdrive. It is, after all, the racialised specificity of their gendered gaze on Europe that supports the rationale of the whole book. Photographs like *Zeyneb in her Paris Drawing-room* (Illustration 9, below, p. 226) show a mixture of the two – a visibly Turkish woman in her Turkified room in the French capital. The same room is also seen in *Zeyneb in her Western Drawing-room* (Illustration 10, below, p. 227). If the frontispiece to Ellison's book of her in 'Turkish costume' is designed to testify to the actuality of her visit to Turkish harems, this photograph which opens Zeyneb Hanım's book shows her bringing the harem with her. Wearing a yaşmak, even in Paris, is important for the image of the book because the veil proves her authenticity as a Turkish woman in the way most easily recognisable to the West. Zeyneb Hanım cannot start her book with any hint of an unreliable narrator, unlike Ellison, who, as I discussed in Chapter Five, can leave it to captions to distinguish her racialised identity from that of similarly dressed Ottoman women. In contrast to the free play of Ellison's visual transgressions across racialised boundaries of identification, anchored in an easier to secure signification of Englishness, Zeyneb Hanım's 'Oriental' credentials are emphasised by the structure of the visual narrative in her book.

What is important here, and the quote about the hats is a clue, is that the 'Turkish' clothes worn in their books by both Ellison and the Ottoman sisters are outerwear: it is the contrast between veil and hat and all that this stands for that reads so significantly of the presumed differences in women's lives in East and West. The difference between hat and veil registered for women and their

9. *Zeyneb in her Paris Drawing-room* (Zeyneb Hanoum, *A Turkish Woman's European Impressions*, London, Seeley, Service and Co., 1913)

10. *Zeyneb in her Western Drawing-room* (Zeyneb Hanoum, *A Turkish Woman's European Impressions*, London, Seeley, Service and Co., 1913)

observers in both regions. The first hat was an oft-commented on acquisition for Ottoman women in the late nineteenth and early twentieth centuries (Duben and Behar 1991, Şeni 1995, Davis 1986), and Halide Edib referred to the negative associations of hats in her criticism of women's '"hat and ball" cravings' (Edib 1926: 229). Ellison equated the ability to manage one's hat with the potential – though not necessarily the desire – to integrate in European society: 'And those Turkish women who have come to Europe? How well they have adapted them-selves to our civilisation. When they were with us who could have supposed they were wearing hats for the first time ... And yet how glad they were to return to their home life!' (Ellison 1915: 198). The synecdochical function of the hat (male and female) as a stand-in for the whole of a civilisation was shared by Western observers and Ottomans, hence Mustafa Kemal's determination in the 1920s to remove the fez and encourage the hat over the veil (see Chapter Five). In the earlier period that Zeyneb Hanım writes about, it was the outerwear hat rather than the indoor Western dresses that had the heightened significance of being visibly *alafranga*.

Now I come to a procedural dilemma. Previously (Lewis 1999b) I had written that, although *A Turkish Woman's European Impressions* is the story of two women who resisted the restrictions of the harem system, the book did not permit the reader to 'see' their unveiled faces for almost sixty pages. The frontispiece shows Zeyneb Hanım in a yaşmak and at that point I thought that the second image in the book was *Turkish Lady in Tcharchoff (Outdoor Costume)* (Illustra-tion 6, above, p. 215), which made the unidentified woman even more remote from the viewer's gaze. Although this retreat is reversed on page 60, this is not another photograph but a sketch by Auguste Rodin of *Les Désenchantées* (Illus-tration 11, below, p. 229). This flimsy drawing sends Melek Hanım and Zeyneb Hanım back to their fictional existence as Loti's heroines, by which they were best known in Europe. The celebrity status of the Loti connection definitely helped to market their book: 'we have not had one free evening. The *Grandes Dames* of France wanted to get a closer view of two Turkish women, and they have all been charming to us' (Zeyneb Hanoum 1913: 156). However, Rodin's drawing does not access the photographic codes of realism promised by the fron-tispiece. The drawing keys into another order of representation and heightens the fantasy elements associated with Loti's *roman à clef*.

Subsequently I realised that my copy of the book had the plates in the wrong order and that in other copies the second image was Rodin's drawing, with the photograph of Zeyneb Hanım in the çarşaf coming after that. I had written in error. But later I realised that the book's visual narrative was unchanged: there is still no *photograph* of their faces until page 172. After a series of photographs of the sisters in Turkey and of other unidentified Turkish women in Turkey, the thir-teenth illustration finally shows the unveiled sisters receiving a visitor in the harem. The arresting photograph, *Zeyneb with a Black Face-veil Thrown Back* (Illustration 12, below, p. 230) suggests the emancipatory result promised by the whole project – though the fashionable Edwardian blouse worn under the thrown

11. *"Les Désenchantées" (by M. Rodin)* (Zeyneb Hanoum, *A Turkish Woman's European Impressions*, London, Seeley, Service and Co., 1913)

12. *Zeyneb with a Black Face-veil Thrown Back* (Zeyneb Hanoum, *A Turkish Woman's European Impressions*, London, Seeley, Service and Co., 1913)

back veil reveals the already Westernised hybrid nature of late Ottoman femininity, not some pure and absolute alterity.

This mix of cultures occurs more obviously in the second photograph of *Zeyneb in her Paris Drawing-room* (Illustration 9, above, p. 226), which enacts an
identification designed variously to signify Oriental (her Turkish dress and Turkish furnishings) and Westernised (being socially able and acculturated in Western
high society). But does an Ottoman woman wearing Western clothes count as
cross-cultural dressing? Whilst there is a long-established celebratory mode for
dealing with Western cross-cultural dressing as one of the pleasures of the imperial theatre, the practice of Orientals adopting European dress and behaviours not
only denies the Western gaze the exotica it expects and demands, but threatens
the viability of the West's pleasurable play at fashion *à la turque*. The West wants
to play at being exotic, but when the referent for that exotic reappears in their
midst, clad in Western clothes, the differentiating terms that secure the Western
masquerade begin to crumble: what is left for the West to dress in and
photograph?

As I argued in Chapter Four, Ottoman women's identifications can be understood as performative, as identifications that work through the reiteration of
socially and culturally recognisable signs of difference. Zeyneb Hanım's completely unnecessary wearing of the yaşmak in the frontispiece makes sense
because the veil (in all its versions) is the ultimate sign by which the West distin-
guishes the Oriental woman from the Occidental. The non-naturalness of this
coding is hinted at by the photographs in the room, some of which also show
veiled women. The presence of these mementos of the Orient in the Occidental
room, where Zeyneb Hanım does not need to be veiled, highlights the artificiality
of her performance. The dissonance between the montage of photographs and the
larger scene in which they figure makes Zeyneb Hanım's 'authentic' Ottoman
clothing look like drag. This is a woman who has specifically changed her life in
order to avoid the veil, alongside other elements of Ottoman seclusion, but who
dons it here in Europe in order to perform her Orientalised identification in terms
which the Western consumer can understand, aware that her authorial integrity
and book sales are both predicated on this.

With its mix of visuals and epistolary writing Zeyneb Hanım's book accords
with what James Clifford identifies as a strand within early twentieth-century
ethnography that allowed for polyvocality, and anticipated the postmodern shift
towards intersubjectivity in ethnographic writing (Clifford 1986). In this movement from a visual paradigm, based on a distant uninvolved observer who fixes
the world in a frozen moment of observation, to a discursive paradigm, 'it
becomes possible to think of a cultural poetics that is an interplay of voices, of
positioned utterances' (Clifford 1986: 12). Although in *An Englishwoman in a
Turkish Harem* Ellison retains the more traditional protocol of giving Ottoman
women's words as reported rather than direct speech, in her work as Zeyneb
Hanım's (and also Melek Hanım's) editor she implicitly recognises the intersubjective nature of her Ottoman experiences and elevates the Ottoman women to

the status of co-author rather than simply informant, named or anonymous. The sometimes contradictory relationship between the visual and literary elements of Zeyneb Hanım's narrative are not only evidence of the always-impossible attempt to fix photography's meaning (Berger and Mohr 1982). The visual evidence of Zeyneb Hanım's Turkishness makes visible in the text the contradictory nature of her activity as a located writing subject in a way that could not be done by the writing alone. In their inability to accede, for quite different reasons, to the putative authority of the (masculinist) Western ethnographer, both Ellison and Zeyneb Hanım in their various masquerades act as a limit case for the security of the identificatory terms on which their books are premised.

Zeyneb Hanım's staging of the Orient in the West produces an ersatz authenticity whose attempt to perform the two geographical categorisations signalled by the captions suggests the instability of both. But this does not mean that she is completely able to challenge the dominant Orientalist knowledges that she wishes to dispute: the very repetition that makes up the performance of identity can, as Dorinne Kondo uses Butler to argue, 'both consolidate [identity's] force and provide the occasion for its subversion' (Kondo 1997: 7). So, although thinking of identification as performative demonstrates the potential for dislodging the apparently essentialised identities of Orientalist discourse, it is difficult for the Orientalised subject to subvert hegemonic Orientalist knowledges without also being re-appropriated. When the Ottoman sisters present themselves as modern women, dressed in what are understood as Western clothes, the force of Orientalism means that they risk being reduced to the level of what Bhabha calls the mimic man – an uncanny imitation of the real thing, doomed to inauthenticity as never fully 'native' nor fully 'white' (Bhabha 1984). But in this indeterminacy lies the potential power of colonial mimesis: the weird uncanniness of 'the not quite, not white' haunts the coloniser and eats away at the naturalised sureties of colonial identity. Though such challenges are on a knife-edge of re-inscribing hegemonic knowledges and powers, they never simply replicate them. The shifting balance of power means that 'opposition may be both contestatory and complicit' (Kondo 1997), a contradictory dynamic that occurs in specific locations and is enacted and read by specific agents. This returns to attention the location of these photographs in Zeyneb Hanım's book, a commodity produced by her and Ellison in a particular set of circumstances for a particular audience.

That Zeyneb Hanım wears a yaşmak in Illustration 9 (above, p. 226) can only be for reasons of publication since she is no advocate of the veil. But this apparently transparent performance of the marker of racialised identity par excellence ends up destabilising the potential authenticity of the Turkish room. Like the Turkish textiles that do not quite cover the striped wallpaper and floral border of the Paris decoration in their attempt to Turkify the room, her cross-cultural musical behaviours suggest a diasporic hybridity (the caption to Illustration 10 reads 'Although Turkish women are now good pianists and fond of Western music, they generally play the oute, or Turkish guitar, at least once a day'). The personal and social relations of this transculturated identification are difficult for the book to contain since its sales are premised on her lived experience as a 'real' Turkish woman. Whilst Zeyneb Hanım's book is intended in part as an attack on the worst of Western stereotypes, the engraving on the front cover of a woman in a yaşmak and feraçe suggests the pervasive power of the exotic to which it must also appeal, revealing how the inevitably contradictory nature of her challenge to Orientalist knowledges impacts on the enunciation of the resistant voice.

If, by the turn of the century, objects signifying the 'authentic' Turkish past were already being recommodified as of quaint historic interest by the Turks (for both the domestic and souvenir market) what forms of Oriental spatial behaviour should Zeyneb Hanım be trying to enact in Paris? The gap between what is legible to her Occidental audience and personally meaningful to the expatriate Ottoman in a period of personal and social upheaval remains tantalisingly open in these visuals. Her hasty and clandestine departure gave little opportunity for arranging much luggage (Melek Hanoum 1926) and it is unlikely that the sisters had furniture shipped to France, so these photographs also testify to the circulation of Oriental (though not necessarily Ottoman) goods in Europe. The market for Oriental goods in Europe takes on a different meaning when these signs of the covetably exotic are used by a woman for whom they are mundane, if outdated, signs of a traditional set of domestic behaviours. The attempt by Zeyneb Hanım in Europe to dress to type reveals instead the inventedness of tradition. Like Fatima and her search for authentic artefacts of a now antiquated way of life (see Chapter Five), this dress becomes a form of historical re-enactment. The photograph shows Zeyneb Hanım dressing up as something which the West imagines she once was, but which was only ever part of the picture, as the rest of her book proceeds to demonstrate.

INTERCULTURAL EXCHANGE: COMPETING MODELS

The longer these photographs are looked at the more hybrid they become as the security of their apparent cultural distinctiveness disintegrates in the face of their obvious transculturation: that mingling of different cultures into a new form of social or cultural interaction that characterises what Mary Louise Pratt (1992) calls the contact zone. Within the dynamic productivity of cultural exchange (even in the most arduous of colonial experiences) the practices of both coloniser and colonised are altered by their experiences of each other. In the strange imperial context of Ottoman contacts with Europe the apparently closed court of the Ottoman sultans had been interacting with Western cultural codes, and social habits, for a very long time (Micklewright 1999, Germaner and Inankur 1989). Just as Ottoman court portraiture in the sixteenth to eighteenth centuries had engaged with European portrait conventions, so too did photography in the late Ottoman period reveal familiarity with European studio conventions. Ottoman sitters pose appropriately for the new medium, demonstrating photographic literacy as they 'naturally' stage themselves in the shapes and styles made commonplace by Occidental photography

As well as a familiarity with photographic coding, Zeyneb Hanım's photographs, like those in all these sources, testify to the incorporation of Western modes in Ottoman female dress and appearance. The yaşmaks worn by Melek Hanım and Zeyneb Hanım in Zeyneb Hanım's 1913 book and those featured in Ellison's 1915 publication are large enough to shroud loosely a typically bouffant Edwardian hairstyle without crushing its elaborately contrived fullness. The hatlike silhouette of Ellison in her yaşmak (Illustration 5, above, p. 214) hovers over a large hairstyle just as does Melek Hanım's in Illustration 13 (opposite). There is no discernible difference in the styling of the Ottoman and English women. Melek Hanım's fashionable Edwardian coiffure, dressed over the forehead, is best seen in her pose on the veranda (Illustration 8, above, p. 224). Compare these earlier photographs of Zeyneb Hanım and Melek Hanım with a plate from Ellison's 1928 volume (Illustration 14, below, p. 236) showing the delegates from the Union of Turkish Women meeting Kemal, and one can see underneath the hats and turbaned scarves a shift to a twenties-style bob, cut close to the head and dressed down the cheek. By the mid-1920s Kemal was encouraging Western dress and styling, so these changes are not surprising, but the contrast between two different versions of Western hair fashion in the earlier and later photographs indicates the incorporation of Western modes into late Ottoman style before the advent of government-sponsored dress reforms.

In *Turkey To-day* Ellison includes a pair of portraits (Illustration 15, below, p. 237), one of Melek Hanım (labelled as 'heroine of Pierre Loti's *Disenchanted*') and one of Suate Dervishe Hanım ('the Turkish writer, well-known in Germany'). Suate Dervishe Hanım is pictured in full movie-star glamour, with a low brimmed straw hat, a Mary Pickford dress and heavy make-up. In contrast, Melek Hanım wears a çarşaf. But her çarşaf follows almost exactly the same line over her face and hair as her compatriot's fashionable hat, skimming the brow like a cloche hat and revealing a flick of hair over the ear. Though Melek Hanım's photograph, which was also used to front her article in the *Strand Magazine* in 1926, was intended to signify something of the old Turkey as described by Loti, it is apparent that her enactment of this already anachronistic identification is laid over a modernised body whose flapper hair is now shorter than the Edwardian coiffure seen under yaşmaks and veils or revealed on the veranda in 1913. The easily adapted çarşaf could be worn draped loosely over a bouffant hairstyle, as in Illustration 3 (above, p. 210), or close to the face over a bob. The signification of Melek Hanım's çarşaf in Illustration 15 (below, p. 237) is complicated: on the one hand it signifies an authentic Oriental femininity premised on an apparently unchanging Muslim exotica (her 'traditional' head-wear is contrasted to Suate Dervishe Hanım's ultra-modernity), but on the other, the closer fitting çarşaf and lick of flapper hair indicate something of a European-style contemporaneity.

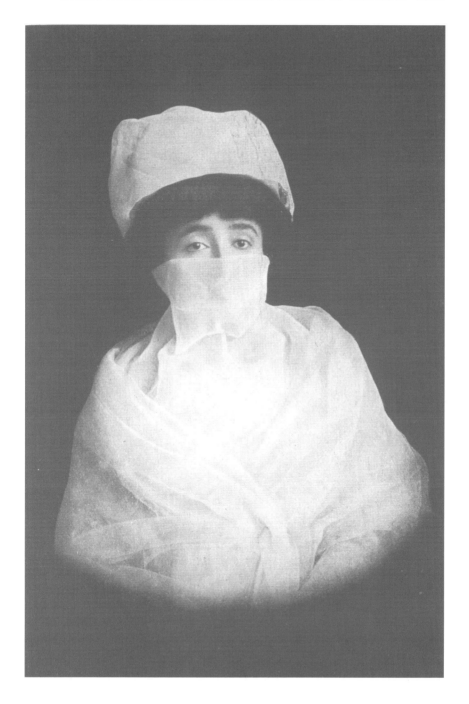

13. *Melek in Yashmak* (Zeyneb Hanoum, *A Turkish Woman's European Impressions*, London, Seeley, Service and Co., 1913)

14. *Mustapha Kemal Pasha with the Representatives of the "Union of Turkish Women"* (Grace Ellison, *Turkey To-day*, London, Hutchinson, 1928)

15. *"Melek Hanuom," Heroine of Pierre Loti's "Disenchanted" and Suate Der-vishe Hanoum, the Turkish Writer Well Known in Germany* (Grace Ellison, *Turkey To-day*, London, Hutchinson, 1928)

UNIVERSITY OF WINCHESTER
LIBRARY

This is hardly surprising since the çarşaf was itself a relatively recent phenomenon whose form had already gone through several permutations, as had the feraçe before it. The feraçe, worn with a yaşmak (as seen in Illustration 16, opposite), had been the object of much sumptuary legislation often, as in the eighteenth century, restricting ostentatious trimming and colour. An easing of codes concerning public female modesty during the Tanzimat era saw the emergence of the feraçe as a 'more frivolous' garment (Scarce 1987: 80). Generally held to be an elegant form of outerwear, coupled with the becoming yaşmak, the move towards the voluminous çarşaf may seem at first to have been retrograde, yet its varied usage illustrates the range of meaning that could be attached to women's public presentation. Sources vary regarding the introduction of the çarşaf but it is clear that it developed without the blessing of the palace (possibly brought from Syria, see Davis 1986). Initially a voluminous one-piece garment hanging cape-like from the head and gathered at the waist, the çarşaf was at first far more obscuring of the body's contours whilst also offering the benefit of being able to accommodate the wider sleeves of *belle époque* fashion not possible in the more narrowly cut feraçe.[9] Its popularity, Şeni claims, was due to the way that its baggy fit concealed the body and face (covered by the peçe, a dark veil attached at the hair line) so effectively as to permit women a greater freedom of movement without being identified. Abdülhamit, whose rulings on outerwear were contradictory, was at first opposed to the çarşaf, banning it in the Beşiktas district near to the palace for fear that men would enter the palace posing as women (Davis 1986, Şeni 1995). Not initially considering the çarşaf suitable for Muslim women, he subsequently banned the feraçe as offering women insufficient protection (Davis 1986) and insisted on the çarşaf and peçe instead. The çarşaf was therefore a garment whose origins did not lie with the palace but which came on other occasions to be associated with the conservatives. But whilst the effective modesty proved by the çarşaf might have endeared it to some traditionalists, the garment soon underwent changes that made it more revealing of the female form. Initially the cape was cut into two, creating an outerwear outfit of a loose skirt topped with a cape covering the chest to the waist. This was later amended to produce a much shorter cape (the arms now covered with long gloves) worn over a figure-skimming skirt or topcoat whose hems were, over time, on the rise. Like the feraçe, the çarşaf appeared in a variety of fabrics, the original dark cloth being replaced with European silks and light colours by fashionable women whilst conservatives retained dark colours for theirs. Both the loose-skirted and body-fitting forms of the çarşaf were owned by Halide Edib who, travelling to all parts of Istanbul on relief work in the war years, learned to dress her hair and her clothes to blend in with the local working-class population, for fear of assault (Edib 1926: 362–3).

Such choices were never regarded as neutral in the late Ottoman debates about modernisation and nationalism. Seen not just as a central index of morality, nor only in relation to the benefits or disadvantages of Westernising innovation, women's dress was also key to recurrent debates about the merits of formalising

16. *Yashmak and Mantle (Feradjé)* (Zeyneb Hanoum, *A Turkish Woman's European Impressions*, London, Seeley, Service and Co., 1913)

a national dress and harnessing women's consumption to nationalist trade protectionism. A national dress made from local cloth and manufactured by Muslim
tailors and seamstresses would act as a corrective to the patronage of Pera European seamstresses using imported textiles, such as those visited by Ellison and
Fatima. Much discussed but never finally designed, national dress was conceptualised as a frugal patriotic corrective to women's over-consumption of
Westernised fashion fripperies (van Os 1999). Those who wanted to wear Western fashion could be similarly patriotic: Fatma Aliye Hanım in the 1890s insisted
that Turkish textiles were of suitable quality for the production of European
styles (Şeni 1995: 28); and in 1914 Ellison noted that Fatima's court dress was
the last ensemble that would use imports, her friend having, 'like so many other
ladies here ... now awakened to the fact that the most costly embroideries of
Europe are but poor imitations of the work of her own land' (Ellison 1915: 35).
This longstanding politicisation of female consumption, dating back to protec-
tionist shopping strategies in the 1870s (Frierson 1995), operated across both
sides of the modernisation debate and was not only determined by whether
women wore Western fashions. By the 1890s the campaign to buy Ottoman was
becoming a campaign to buy Muslim and Turkish as the press and consumers
increasingly turned their backs on minority population traders (Frierson 2000a).
This trend was exacerbated by the Balkan Wars when minority populations were
believed to be colluding with enemies of the empire (van Os 1999) and continued
in women's determinedly Turkish fashion consumption in the republican 1930s
(Durakbaşa 1999).

The implementation of sumptuary laws was uneven and varied not only from
region to region but also from district to district within Istanbul. Davis cites
accounts of how, during the Young Turk era, when some women had started to
discard the skirt of the çarşaf and wear only the cape, the remonstrances of the
watchmen were simply ignored by fashionable ladies (Davis 1986: 200, also van
Os 1999). Kandiyoti (1991b) points to similar contradictions and resistances:
during the war years when women were recruited to the labour force an imperial
irade in 1915 authorised the removal of the veil during office hours, whilst police
posters in Istanbul in 1917 initially demanded a return to a thick çarşaf only to
repent of this in the face of massive opposition – the General Directorate blaming
it on 'old and retrograde women [who] were able to induce a subaltern
employee' into making the initial announcement in favour of the 'old fashions'.[10]
Allegiances to the feraçe or çarşaf signified class as well as modesty and also
often spoke to the characteristics of particular spatial communities. In the first
three decades of the republic, the desegregation of space and the involvement of
women in work did not lessen concern about *fitna* (see Chapter Five). Rather, as
Zehra Arat suggests, it increased anxiety about family honour, or *namus*, the protection of which now extended beyond male relatives to include employers and
state officials who all monitored women's dress and behaviour at work and in
school (Arat 1999b, 1999c, Durakbaşa 1999). The development and social connotations of different styles in outerwear were not straightforwardly

chronological: what was progressive and fashionable in one moment for one constituency could be subsequently replaced and then reclaimed. Garnett and Jenkins in 1911 noted that the çarşaf had, in recent years, come to replace the yaşmak and feraçe, yet by the end of the next decade the feraçe was again enjoying a period of fashionability. In Şişli, for example, a locale associated with modern apartment-living and the shift to nuclear families, women in the 1910s were already abandoning the previously fashionable çarşaf in favour of a feraçe with a yaşmak or even a hat with a veil, constructing a French-style appearance. Musbah Haidar (1944) similarly reported the decline of the çarşaf in the 1910s and 1920s, noting that the feraçe was augmented by the use of a manteau or cloak cut in a fashionable style. This look was associated with upper-class Ottomans, both Muslim and from the minority populations, whose congregation in the Şişli area north of Pera was conspicuous enough by 1924 to result in the sobriquet 'Şişli woman'.[11] In Fatih, on the other hand, within the walls of old Stamboul and therefore part of the traditionally Muslim quarter, women tended to be seen in a black loose-fitting çarşaf and a generally black face veil in keeping with the more conventional associations of the district. Those elite women who retained their çarşaf wore them in brightly coloured silks whose 'provocative and eye catching colour', as Scarce comments, 'effectively negat[ed] any concealing effect' (Scarce 1987: 85), whilst the peçe now thinner and lighter in colour 'came increasingly to resemble the yaşmak' (Davis 1986: 201).

The veil, national dress and all they stood for were covered regularly in the women's press and most often in *Kadınlar Dünyası*, whose parent organisation was committed to reform in women's outerwear as part of their mission to integrate women into the world of work and life outside the home (Demirdirek 1999). But the multifarious meanings possible for women's dress and the contested nature of changes in female fashion and consumption were often lost on Western observers. As Micklewright points out, the Western idea that there were a series of imagined absolute differences, boundaries which could be crossed, cannot adequately describe the late Ottoman attitude to Western goods and their use. This regarded Western commodities, including dress, as part of a continuum of goods whose partial or wholesale adoption was based on a sense of value concerned as much with rarity as with ideas of cultural difference (Micklewright 1999), seen in the Hamidian state's contestatory adaptation, rather than simply adoption, of Western capitalist production and consumption practice (Frierson 2000b).

The rejection by Ellison's editor of her photographs of a modern harem as unrealistic not only testifies to the desire to have the harem fit the expectations of Western Orientalist fantasy, but also reveals the assumption that the inclusion of Western furniture and associated behaviours would automatically invalidate the 'authentically' Turkish social relations presumed to inhere in the harem's space. These absolutes were inaccurate, as Göçek illustrates: on one hand the apartments of Sultan Selim III of 1789–1807 were painted with Western rococo motifs not hinted at by the traditional exterior architecture, whilst on the other,

Ottoman baroque architecture grafted Western exterior styles onto a traditional Muslim division of interior household spaces (Göçek 1996: 40). Domestic housing in Istanbul in the last decades of the nineteenth century followed similar patterns (Garnett 1891: 424–5) with a fusion of architectural styles in Istanbul stimulated by the Ottoman pavilions at the International Exhibitions from 1863 (Çelik 1992). Sections of the capital were rebuilt by Abdülaziz on the model of Hausman's grand boulevards in Paris after bad fire damage in 1865. The external spaces of Istanbul were, like its less visible interiors, already hybridised as a result of a longstanding and active engagement with Western architectural and cultural practices. This did not make them less Ottoman – the assumption behind the rejection of Ellison's photograph – rather, it was typical of Ottoman spatial, cultural and social relations. In the last century of the empire this mix was particularly pronounced in the lives of the Ottoman elite for whom the dynamic between Occidental and Ottoman habits of living was part of daily life. The Western furniture, which increasingly by the second half of the nineteenth century furnished the homes of the Ottoman bourgeoisie, existed in conjunction with older spatial habits of floor-level living and, in many homes, with the traditional Ottoman division of space and multipurpose room use. This accommodation of different spatial behaviours would have been the norm for elite Ottoman women, yet the depiction of the harem's gendered realm remained resolutely binary in the minds of the West. This presumption of categorial difference is what Ottoman writers set out to challenge but is also what they had to connect with if they were to find and keep an audience for their work.

The construction and reception of these photographs is therefore partly determined by the extent to which Ottoman (and Occidental) women writers consciously played with those clashing discourses. In their books and journalism Zeyneb Hanım and Melek Hanım knowingly presented themselves as the oppressed Turkish woman at the same time as they challenged this stereotype with evidence of the modernised contemporaneity of their lives and upbringing. The reader's resultant discomfiture is not just because they say contradictory things. It also derives from the difficulty faced by the Orientalised writing subject in trying to show the experience of living within overlapping and competing discourses in a period of accelerated social change and of trying to translate those local discursive structures for an alien readership. Like all discursive shifts the take-up of new ideas was uneven and the accommodations made with existing practice were varied and flexible. The fixity that is attributed to the 'Turkish' clothes seen in *A Turkish Woman's European Impressions* derives from the closing down of nuance that happens when the book presents the Ottoman sisters in clothes signalled as authentic in a way that cannot or does not wish to indicate the contemporaneous fashionability of these apparently antiquated garments. By showing outer garments whose adaptation to Western and local changes in fashion was indecipherable to her target readership and by not showing very much the Western fashion worn under the 'veil', Zeyneb Hanım freezes Ottoman dress and keeps present in the reader's mind the stereotype of the authentically exotic Oriental woman.

In contrast to this fossilisation, the *Kadınlar Dünyası* contributor in Illustration 4 (above, p. 211) adopts a pose quite in keeping the European society photograph. Her hands delicately placed in a muff, the slightly tilted head and the dreamy gaze contrast to the bombastic sprawl of Ellison in her guise as *The Author in Turkish Costume*. Where Ellison lounges expansively across the chaise, one arm messily exceeding the picture frame, her gaze caught by something out of shot, the journalist sits demurely and offers a clear and unanimated visage to the viewer. This studio photograph may have had many purposes but it is also reminiscent of the careful self-presentation of British feminists. Faced with critics and a hostile press that revelled in the stereotype of suffragists as ugly and masculinised spinsters, Edwardian British suffragists were determinedly respectable and feminine in their appearance. As Lisa Tickner elaborates, they utilised versions of contemporary female dress that were neither so excessively fashionable as to appear frivolous nor so outré as to seem dangerously avant-garde or deviant (Tickner 1987). Intended as an antidote to their insurrectionary political activities, this style strategy may also have been adopted by Ottoman women, such as Ellison's contact, who were daring enough to write for the press in pre-republican Turkey and to do so in a journal noteworthy as the first to print photographs of Muslim women (Demirdirek 1999). The Ottoman journalist who gave Ellison her photograph was already involved in transgressive representational practices, simply by having her photograph in the public domain. In contrast to Ellison's informality, her more compliant pose may be, like the British feminists, determined by a concern to present as respectable.

FASHIONING ALTERNATE SELVES: CROSS-CULTURAL DRESSING IN EAST AND WEST

How, then, to explain the oddity of the photographs of Zeyneb Hanım and Melek Hanım in Europe? It is evident that elite Ottoman women wore and adapted elements of European fashion. And it is evident that photography was increasingly available by the late nineteenth century in Istanbul, and that Ottomans were aware of Occidental photographic conventions. But whilst this gives an insight into dress and appearance in photographs taken in Istanbul, it is still not enough to really work out what mix of style and subjectification is going on in the photographs from Europe. Just what is it that they are wearing? The frontispiece identifies Zeyneb Hanım's garments as a 'yashmak and feradjé, or cloak' (the loose hooded manteau). But is hard to tell if the garment underneath is of Ottoman or European origin. The fringing is typically Poiret, although he was certainly not mainstream by 1913. It could be an Ottoman garment, though the loose caftan-like dress sported by Zeyneb Hanım in the sister shot with the *oute* could just as easily be a Western teagown. If Zeyneb Hanım were very fashionable, it may be that the Ottoman woman in Paris is wearing a Oriental-inspired dress of modern European manufacture. In the context of the emerging vogue for all things Oriental, Zeyneb Hanım may be staging her own version of fashionable Orientalness. Or it could be that the garment is an Ottoman version of French Orientalist chic.[12] The point is that it is impossible to tell: the division of East and West can never be fully secured. Indeed as Yeazell elaborates in her reading of J. F. Lewis' 1876 painting *The Siesta*, the scene of a woman reclining in a room furnished with Oriental drapes and lattice screens was inevitably read as one of his Orientalist paintings, even though it does not have the locational title typical of his other works. The imagined boundaries between East and West were blurred by the transnational exchange of commodities and cultural trends. Just as yaşmaks could miraculously accommodate roomy Edwardian coiffures, so too could a London lady purchase in London all that was needed to recline in Oriental splendour. Zeyneb Hanım's Paris drawing room is therefore an indeterminate space in which the boundaries between what is Eastern and Western are blurred, mixing nefariously Oriental furnishings with a Western piano (itself increasingly commonplace in Ottoman society) and presenting Ottoman outerwear in an interior clearly identified as European. But yet the way these Ottoman sisters photograph themselves encourages a view of Ottoman dress that antiquates a changing and modern phenomenon. In order to emphasise the unique selling point of their ethnicity they need *to be seen to be* Turkish women, the hybridised *mélange* of the drawing room needs to be tied down.

But when Zeyneb Hanım exhibits herself in Turkish clothes in her book, her native dress no longer looks natural. This is not just because she is in Europe but because the identity she enacts in Europe can only signify in relation to previously existing European classificatory terms. These, with their allegiances to stereotypes of the Oriental woman, are unable fully to encompass her performance of self as educated, cosmopolitan Ottoman. The racialised identifications performed by Zeyneb Hanım and Melek Hanım in these photographs are always also classed identifications and it was (as seen in Chapter Three) important to Zeyneb Hanım to be recognised as a lady. It was for this reason that she feared the degentrifying implications of the suffragists' occupation of public streets in meeting and demonstrations. She was not imagining the threat: the suffragists' own carefully respectable self-presentation was designed specifically to mitigate the radical transgression by women ('particularly upper-class women') of British gender and class spatial norms (Rolley and Ash 1992). For the Ottoman writer, the content of her book – working through the interaction of image and text – must underline not only the sisters' ethnicity but also their gentility. As well as producing them as authentic Ottoman women, or rather *ladies*, the photographs and letters also testify to their familiarity with the social mores of elite European culture. If Zeyneb Hanım, who would 'rather groan in bondage' than suffer the indignity of demonstrating on the public street (Zeyneb Hanoum 1913: 89–91), is to be a hybrid subject it must be in genteel terms. For Melek Hanım, whose aristocratic husband was ruined by the Russian Revolution, her ability to support her family through dressmaking is a matter of honour. She portrays her phlegmatic 'fatalism' in accepting this reversal of fortune as a particularly Ottoman virtue, drawing on the Ottoman's innately democratic social manners to retain her composure when rich women who had once been her guests now patronised her dressmaking establishment, whispering condescendingly about her 'better days' (Melek Hanoum 1926).[13]

Zeyneb Hanım's self-presentation in Turkish dress knowingly exploits the Orientalist paradigm for her own ends. Without downplaying the frustration of being positioned by and trying to intervene in a Western discourse that cannot recognise the nuanced specificity of her Ottoman identification, it is evident that the émigrée Ottoman is consciously trying to manoeuvre cultural codes to her advantage: hence the inclusion of photographs of herself veiled alongside the jibe at Europeans who imagine her to be wandering around Switzerland still wearing a çarşaf. Both the literary and visual elements of her volume invoke the already circulated image of the maltreated yet beautiful and cultured Oriental woman, sometimes to endorse elements of this iconography, at others to challenge the divisions on which it rests. The masquerade as oppressed veiled Turkish woman helps Zeyneb Hanım's sales just as Ellison's cross-cultural dressing, the epitome of the exoticised Turkish stereotype Ellison claims to challenge, helps hers.

Wearing Ottoman dress had offered a range of potential advantages to Occidental women for some time. Macleod argues that from the late eighteenth century to the 1920s unconventional and progressive elite English women paraded in the bifurcated dress of Ottoman women as a way of invoking for themselves the greater civic freedoms associated with Ottoman society (Macleod 1998, Melman 1992, see also Chapter One). Though bifurcated dress was an item of female Ottoman apparel, in England Turkish trousers were read as masculine attire, offering avant-garde Aesthetic and Bloomsbury women an 'appropriately feminised male costume' through which to stage alternative gender identities. They inverted for their own ends, Macleod argues, 'the Western male sexual stereotype of the Turkish harem woman' (Macleod 1998: 64). Associating bifurcated dress with the image of Turkish women as cultured, elegant and, most importantly, docile, was also important for British women in the 1850s keen to wear modest but unrestrictive garments without the negative associations of the infamous Mrs Bloomer's aggressive and masculinising American feminism. That a suitably desexualised Oriental femininity might be able to compensate for the potentially unsexing effects of bifurcated dress explains in part the constant fascination with Turkish dress.

But, it was never possible to desexualise entirely the Orientalist stereotype. As Grace Ellison's own account reveals, sexualised stereotypes about Ottoman women continued to hold sway into the first two decades of the twentieth century despite all evidence to the contrary. Her dressing in Turkish style would not have been able to avoid the sexualised associations of appearing as an odalisque. Or rather, it would have mattered to her if her self-presentation was tainted by the unrespectable hint of sex. For the aristocratic women in Macleod's sample such niceties were far less of a problem: class, as she points out, was a contributory factor in their ability to disregard convention and also helped obviate the sexualised connotations of their harem outfits. In contrast, Grace Ellison was not aristocratic and was not sashaying round Bloomsbury or a country retreat. She was presenting herself in photographs for a wider readership and was at some pains to avoid the most unflattering aspects of such a resolutely sexualised Orientalist stereotype. She appears in items of Ottoman outerwear that in the West would only have been coded as female. Macleod's approach suggests another way to conceptualise the pleasures available to Occidental women in their engagement with Ottoman dress. Significantly, Ellison in her first two books on Turkey was writing before the end of the 1920s – the moment according to Macleod when Ottoman textiles and dress, which had 'once been a locus of transgression among an elite group of cross-cultural cross-dressers who longed to stretch social boundaries by assimilating Ottoman values', were 'appropriated by consumer culture'. Now available via Liberty's in London, Ottoman styling became 'the standard fare in the polite parlours of middle-class housewives' (Macleod 1998: 77). Even though, as I discussed earlier, Poiret's innovations had changed the look of mainstream fashion by the time of Ellison's first book in 1915, actual Poiret-style trousers would have still been the prerogative of his elite patrons. Women might be wearing longer, leaner skirts (some with front splits and draperies that echoed the divide of 'harem trousers') but most women's wardrobes still centred on skirts and dresses. The use of trousers in women's war work (which did so much to legitimise trousers for women) would not yet have had a great impact on everyday wear. Bifurcated dress remained beyond the bounds of most women's sense of acceptable clothing.

If cross-cultural dressing, especially in masculine-coded trousers, facilitated forms of reinvention for elite English women, was a similar dynamic being activated by Grace Ellison? For someone who was ostensibly concerned with female emancipation in England and abroad, her performance as Ottoman was inflected to the exotica of the stereotypes that she critiqued rather than to the possibility of sexual transgression. Her pleasure lay more in the fantasy of passing, and the English women dressing up *à la turque* at home were in no way attempting to pass. Ellison's contact with bifurcated dress would not have come from the progressive women she befriended: the rare reference to trousers relates to older and fanatical women of their households, such as the woman in the 'roomy pantaloons' whom she unsuccessfully tried to 'Kodak'. To depict herself as a trouser-wearing Turkish woman, therefore, would tie her too closely to the forces of conservatism within Ottoman society, whilst to present herself in yaşmak and çarşaf was to associate herself with the outerwear worn by her forward-looking friends. Though she could easily have dressed in a trousers ensemble for a studio photograph, the plates in her book link to a written narrative concerned with experiencing outside life as a veiled Turkish woman and the thrill of passing that cross-cultural dressing in indoor clothes would not have facilitated. Given the

shift away from a late nineteenth-century sexual libertarianism towards a consciously respectable mode of dress and public presentation in the appearance of
Edwardian suffragists (Tickner 1987), it is not surprising that the scope for 'subversive sexualities' evoked by bifurcated dress, that were so valued by Macleod's
aristocratic avant-gardes, were not the first point of reference for Ellison. Her
nostalgia for elements of old Ottoman society and her fondness for the veil did
not extend to a wish to associate with the pantaloons of the superstitious old
guard. Though Ellison invoked the sexual stereotypes about Oriental women that
she wished to disavow, she was discriminating in her interaction with the overtly
sexual elements of Orientalist discourse, restricting herself to references to sala-
cious presumptions about polygamy and to the flirtatious connotations of the
veil. Birfucated dress was not attractive to her because her presentation in Turkish dress was concerned with adventure, authenticity and passing, without it
undermining her moral authority as feminist and as English (based not on an elite
class origin). In this light it is notable that a Turkophile like Ellison, who had
already been to Turkey, showed no sign of having previously taken advantage of
the opportunity to acquire Ottoman clothing. If she had wanted to drape herself
in a Turkish ensemble at home or abroad, she could have done so. Instead she
enjoyed moments of cross-cultural dressing in a specific setting. Her veiled masquerade let her imagine that she experienced *selected* elements of Ottoman
women's lives. But, unlike Loti – whose description of his cross-cultural dressing, Barthes argues, is driven by a desire to become part of his Oriental tableau
(to 'transform oneself into a describable object', 1971: 115) – Ellison could not
risk being incorporated into a louche Orientalist spectacle: hence outerwear but
not pantaloons. In her delightful promenades with her progressive friends her
risk of being misread as the classically sexualised and inferiorised odalisque was
only the same as theirs – since the outside viewer could not distinguish the reality
of the Ottoman women's emancipated subjectivity – but she was certainly not
about to present herself squatting with stubbornly old-fashioned old women.

Ellison repeatedly reminds the reader that she was found to be attractive and
that her celibacy was a matter of choice and not necessity. Ternar reads this
emphasis on the importance of male regard as an indicator that in the harem
'Grace could give vent to a feminine self which could only exist as a fantasy in
England, in view of her ideological beliefs, social position, and career ambitions'
(Ternar 1994: 158). Whilst the ostensible object of revelation was the harem and
its inmates, Ellison's writing also reveals her own conflicted desires. Her willingness to identify with the gracious charm of elite Ottoman femininity suggests
how the harem's apparently isolationist spatial relations actually gave her access
to men in a fruitfully different way. She could move from the all-women zone of
the harem into encounters with men who supported her political cause without
relinquishing the pleasures of dressing-up and toilette designed to gain affirma-
tive male attention. The effort to desexualise the harem was crucial to her
political project: representing the reality of Ottoman women's lives rendered the
harem a suitably respectable space for her to be seen to be living in. But her

disavowal of the harem's sexualisation relied on a process of repeated titillation and denial that kept (her own highly selective and restricted version of) the sexual at the forefront of the reader's mind. Though she did not want herself or her Ottoman friends to be associated with the worst Orientalist sexual stereotypes, she did want to claim for herself a fantasised relationship to the chivalric 'blessing of protection' (Ellison 1913: 196) that in her mind substantially ameliorated the evils of Ottoman women's seclusion.

The availability of male support for female emancipation stunned Ellison and Vaka Brown (see Chapter Three), who were used to the adversarial gender politics of Europe and North America. Progressive Ottoman society provided a glimpse of a sexualised femininity that was often felt to be unavailable by Western feminists, anxious to avoid being accused of using potentially belittling feminine wiles, among other things. The struggle of positioning oneself as a professional woman journalist, writing on international affairs as well as 'women's issues', required a vigilance about appearances that could rarely encompass the elegant, respectable mode of female desirability that seemed to be available to Ottoman women. The 'suppressed' femininity of which Ternar speaks is not the subversive and outrageous female sexuality of the English avant-garde but is, rather, a moderate reformist femininity that wishes safely to enjoy male attention without fearing that the recognition of one's desirability would devalue one's politics. If it seems surprising that Ellison, the avowed feminist, should interpret Ottoman segregation in this way,[14] remember how she later came to criticise severely the British feminists whose insistence on total equality deprived women of men's 'protector instinct' (Ellison 1923: 10–11, see Chapter One). As Bordieu points out, it is not the field of possible interpretations that is important so much as why it is that 'particular actors interpret space as they do' (Bordieu, in Moore 1986: 84). As I discussed in Chapter Three, the ability of Ellison's predecessors to avail themselves of Orientalism in order to mount a proto-feminist argument illustrates how colonial fantasy was differently accessible to different social subjects (Mills 1996, Garber 1992). Here, Ellison's choice of interpretation is suggestive of the tensions inherent in all gender performativity and a demonstration of how one can be compliant and subversive to spatial relations at the same time (McDowell and Sharpe 1997). Part of Ellison's pleasure in wearing a veil was the imagined affinity it allowed her with the observed and fantasised luminosity of Ottoman female sexuality – an opportunity to perform a different femininity without relinquishing the right to critique the backwardness of the harem system even as she despaired of the hardships of Occidental gender relations.

For Ottoman women European clothes might have signified fashionability and modernity, but they were not worn with the self-conscious theatricality of the English avant-garde discussed by Macleod. This was partly because the adoption of elements of Western fashion was, by the early twentieth century, quite commonplace, but also because de-veiling as a *public* gesture involved the exposure of the face not the whole body. When Halide Edib caused a commotion in 1910 at the American College (see Chapter Three), it was the face veil that she appeared without, her head remained covered. Similarly a decade later in Egypt, Huda Sha'rawi's much-hyped de-veiling in 1923 was again the removal of the face veil only, retaining the *hijab* just as Edib retained a head scarf of some sort throughout most of her life.[15] For elite Ottoman women, already accustomed to European dress, it was the absence of the veil as a mechanism of seclusion that registered the most significantly. Western fashion could signify the imagined pleasures of Western-style non-segregated life but, since these clothes were already worn in the harem, it was the different spatial relations with which Western apparel could be associated that had the most potential for hopes of female re-invention. For Melek Hanım, recollecting her arrival in France, the ability to venture out without a veil was directly linked to the sequestration previously associated with interior female spaces:

> We were just overjoyed to see the sun streaming into our rooms at Nice, to look at the landscape all around without a veil. This was the first time we had seen life out of doors except through a veil, and indoors through latticed windows ... (Melek Hanoum 1926: 135)

Here, it is not the wearing of French fashions that thrilled – they did that already – but the absence of the veil and the *mashrabbia* at their windows. Cross-cultural dressing offered different pleasures to Occidental and Ottoman women and signified within different discourses.[16] For women in Istanbul wearing European clothes may have keyed into a fantasy of experiencing life without the seclusion of the harem system, but the clothes themselves were already indigenised into the spatialised protocols of Ottoman dress.

The ways in which dress acts and their representation can be understood depend not only on discourses local to the dress itself but also on the location of the reader/viewer and the racialised point of origin constructed for the cross-dresser or author (see also Mohanty 1995). The activity and depiction of cross-cultural dressing was not equally available to all individuals, neither can contemporary theories of cross-cultural dressing be equally applied to all cross-dressing subjects.[17] The different cross-dressing experiences of Zeyneb Hanım and Ellison demonstrate how it can be either or both a re-investment in the boundaries of difference and/or a performative action creating new hybrid subjects whose clothes cannot veil the impossible sureties of authenticity imagined by their readers.

However oppositional Ellison's gender identity was as a feminist in England, her cross-cultural dressing worked to endorse the racialised boundaries she transgressed: when she appears in a veil her readers know who she 'really' is underneath. In contrast, Zeyneb Hanım's cross-cultural dressing does undermine Western differentiating categories. She becomes an indeterminate subject in a way that Ellison does not because for her, practised in Ottoman habits of consumption, the boundaries are not there to cross in the same way. As Gen Doy has demonstrated, some Orientalist representations did 'fail as stereotypes'; such as the 1856 photograph of an Ouled-Nail woman whose pose suggests that she has 'not yet internalized or externalized compliance' with the requirements of the Western Orientalist gaze (Doy 1996: 31). But where this visual resistance to stereotype derived from a colonial moment in which elements of the Algerian population were still relatively unfamiliar with French Orientalist cultural codes, Zeyneb Hanım is more than adept at negotiating Orientalist conventions. Her manipulation of the stereotypes that accrued to the Orientalised 'harem' woman indicates a level of agency in her interaction with the Orientalist paradigm that is not usually imagined to be possible for the unequal partner. But to imagine this was ever an easy process would be to underestimate the complexity for each woman of her own subjective investments in cross-cultural codes of dress, narrative and identification. The ability of Ottoman and Western women to negotiate this whilst producing accounts of Ottoman femininity suitably commodified for the market in harem literature forms the basis of my final chapter.

NOTES

1   On potentially counter-hegemonic representations within the export trade see Woodward (2003).
2   Kathleen Stewart Howe, 'Contact Printing the Ottoman Other: The Case of Mr. Benecke', conference paper, Middle East Studies Association, November 2000.
3   On the difficulty of deciphering ethnicity and nationality in photographs of cross-cultural dressing see Micklewright (1999). On the ethnographic conventions of ethnic 'contrast' and the interpretive role of captions see Malmsheimer (1987).
4   On Ellison's editorial interjections in Zeyneb Hanım's book see Ternar (1994: 138).
5   I am indebted also to Indira Ghose for points on Burton.
6   Kalfa is now more commonly rendered as stewardess or supervisor of female servants. Ternar (1994), translates the rest of the name to mean 'eternal blessing'.
7   See also Lutz and Collins (1994).
8   I am grateful here and elsewhere in this chapter to Katrina Rolley for discussions about clothes and photographs.
9   My understanding of this and of other developments in Ottoman dress is indebted to discussions with Nicole van Os.
10 J. Melia, *Mustafa Kemal ou la Rénovation de la Turquie*, Paris, 1929, quoted in Kandiyoti (1991b: 31).
11 The magazine *Resimli Ay* classified the women of the city by district, the contemporary (Westernised modernity) Şişli woman, the middling Kadıköy woman and the vulgar Beyazıd woman (Duben and Behar 1991: 102).
12 I am grateful to Sarah Graham-Brown for her discussion of this point.
13 At this stage Melek Hanım is writing about her work in Paris though Ellison (1928: 119) also cites her as working at Redfern, a British-based couture company with shops in many international locations including Paris. I am grateful to Susan North for information on Redfern.
14 As Melman (1992) points out, it was more common for conservative anti-feminist women who oppose legislative reform in England to valorise the liberties afforded by

segregation: women with specific emancipatory projects could rarely recognise the potential gains of seclusion. Ellison is therefore quite unusual among liberal and feminist writers in valuing and, indeed, romanticising the harem system.

15 Sha'rawi's de-veiling marked the public validation of a practice already reasonably widespread among Egyptian women in progressive circles by the early 1920s (El Guindi 1999). On British campaigns to 'liberate' Egyptian women from the veil see Badran (1996), Heffernan (forthcoming). On the class implications of veiling in the region see Chatty (1997). On the strategic use of de-veiling and re-veiling by Algerian women in the anti-colonial struggle see Fanon (1959); on women and the postcolonial Algerian state see Woodhull (1991).

16 Ottoman women did have themselves photographed at home and in studios masquerading in 'Eastern' clothing across divides of period, class and ethnicity; styled as odalisques, peasants, or in the traditional garb of another local ethnic community (Graham-Brown 1988). In Zeyneb Hanım's book two plates, listed as 'A Turkish Dancer' and 'A Turkish Lady Dressed up as a Greek Dancer' (not shown), are accompanied by the note that 'Turkish women spend much of their time dressing up'. Such dressing up came in handy on one of Ellison's linguistically challenged harem visits where, 'since we cannot speak, we try on all kinds of costumes and drink coffee' (Ellison 1915: 190).

17 As well as Garber (1992) see also McClintock (1995). For a critique of Garber see Elizabeth Wilson, 'Crossed Wires in the Gender Debate', *Guardian*, 2 May 1982.

ഇ Conclusion: ര
Commodification, Time and Nostalgia: the Search for Authenticity

All travel writing starts from a real or putative location of home, whose spatial norms are internalised and naturalised. Conventionally harem literature relied on the fertile contrast between the known space of the Western home and the exotica of the Eastern harem. But for Ottoman writers it was segregated society that was the (variously) familiar starting point. The distances covered by Zeyneb Hanım, Melek Hanım, Demetra Vaka Brown, Halide Edib and, in different ways, Grace Ellison, brought them up against the interpretive dynamism of spatiality in the context of the commercial forces of Orientalist publishing practice. For Ottoman authors this meant they certainly had something to sell, but the costs could be high. In preceding chapters I have traced how they faced competing definitions of Oriental or Ottoman authenticity and fought to express a sense of self that their readers could understand, without being overwhelmed by the brutalising force of Orientalist discourse. The ways in which they, and Ellison, negotiated the construction of ethnographic authority and the commodification of authenticity is explored in this final chapter in relation to the twin terms of modernity and nostalgia that also framed the creation and reception of their books.

Lefebvre cautions against seeing space as primarily a legible text (see Chapter Five). For him its principal purpose is to produce subjects obedient to spatial rules, 'command[ing] bodies, prescribing or proscribing gestures, routes and distances to be covered' (Lefebvre 1991: 143). Reading remains secondary, 'a rather superfluous reward to the individual for blind, spontaneous and *lived* obedience' (Lefebvre 1991: 143, original emphasis). This obedience is an important factor in the experience of 'foreign' spatial relations where, for Occidental travellers like Ellison, the segregations of the harem system produced a conformation to Ottoman spatial relations even as she was able to move within an alternative spatiality permitted to *gaiours*. This would be true for Occidental men as well as women. But these spatial relations were rarely internalised in a normative way. It is this disjuncture of conflicting spatial expectations and rules that makes alien spaces so particularly available for interpretation. For Ellison, the bewildering experience of being made compliant to a space whose social regulations were unfamiliar produced a discontinuity that enabled her to read it and represent it textually. This reading was not straightforward and logical, however much she might try to make it so. The assault on her sense of self is sometimes terrifying (her panic at the riverside house), sometimes delightful (an excuse to slow down her work rate and enjoy luxurious leisure), and sometimes provides an imagined alternative self replete with power and exoticism (her masquerades as a hanım).

In all of these experiences her presence as a dressed body in gendered spaces is paramount. Ellison's emphasis on clothes is not surprising since Western women, as Rose (1993) suggests, were inclined to represent space as bodily in contrast to the male tendency (ability) to present space from the position of an abstracted disembodied visual gaze (see also Clifford 1986). The stress on dress and the veil makes something special and saleable from the particular access women had to certain spaces (the harem) in the context of their presumed limitation in access to the paradigmatic position of distant, uninvolved, sovereign observer of all spaces. Paradoxically, it was the veil that allowed Ellison most clearly to mimic the masculinist viewing position of the disembodied observer – the ultimate ethnographer who is sees but is not seen. The peculiar productivity of the veil is also seen in the way that Zeyneb Hanım and Melek Hanım used it to masquerade as Orientalised tragediennes when they wanted to gain Loti's attention for their campaign to highlight the plight of educated Ottoman women. The spaces and habits of Ottoman female life that restricted Ellison's opportunities to write and, more importantly, altered her desire to do so were differently understood by Ottoman women whose compliance with the harem system was internalised but was also resisted. Their experience of Ottoman spatial relations was already in part mediated by their knowledge of Western spatiality, acquired not least through their interaction with Western goods in a context of intercultural penetration. Inhabiting an elite harem furnished with a mixture of Western and Ottoman furniture meant living within a changing space, accommodating clashing bodily gestures and learning to see Ottoman life through the lens of Occidental norms.

It was this mixture of Islamic spatialisation and late Ottoman Westernisation that Zeyneb Hanım took to Europe. Her different experience of subordination to European spatial rules is presented textually as a form of hybridity that disarticulates them at the same time as it reveals the internalised Orientalist gaze. Zeyneb Hanım's voice emerges from the frozen timeless space previously accorded to the Orientalised other, to tell a story of experiences that cannot but be the result of habitual exchange between East and West and that are narrated in ways fully cognisant of her Western readership and its preoccupations. But it is hard for her to find a way of recounting her story that can include her experiences of modern life in Turkey when her Occidental readership is deeply caught up in an alternatively fantasised knowledge about Oriental women that is intrinsically nostalgic in its emphasis on the unchanging nature of Oriental female life. With the veiled harem woman figured as key trope, the East appears to the West petrified in a pre-modern 'primitive' time, operating as a location for pleasurable fantasies of sexuality and excess perceived as increasingly unavailable in the spaces of Western modernity. Whilst this is what creates a market for Melek Hanım's, Vaka Brown's and Edib's 'authentic' insider accounts, it also operates in tension with their (very different) attempts to re-animate some of the classic signifiers of 'Ori-entalness' for their own recuperative purposes.

That time is so crucial to the potential success of Ottoman women's books is not surprising: as Johannes Fabian has powerfully elaborated, space (for exam-ple, the harem, *qua* the East) must be understood as always linked to time. His history of how anthropology created its object of study shows how the societies to be studied were located 'in terms of distance, spatial and temporal' that kept them in a different time to that of the Western observer (Fabian 1983: xi). Although the fieldwork process so essential to the discipline is based on an apparent proximity to the object of study, the transformation of this ethnographic experience of closeness into an authoritative anthropological discourse is achieved through a process of writing and teaching that turns 'the Other's empir-ical presence ... into his theoretical absence'. Emphasis on tribal, or traditional practices presented as unchanged and unchanging denies 'coevalness' (the state of inhabiting the same time) and produces the anthropological other in a space outside time, stuck in primitive behaviours that modern Western societies have left behind. At its most extreme, the Western observer could feel that to visit native cultures (or read accounts of others' visits) was to step backwards in evo-lutionary time.

Within the racialised hierarchy of colonial and imperial discourse, the Otto-mans were not as primitive as Africans and those other societies which formed the archetypal fieldwork study. But Ottomans could nonetheless be considered to exist in a separate temporal zone – in the Middle Eastern pavilions at the Inter-national Exhibitions, Muslim 'inhabitants' were displayed in clothes that could be read as authentic (certainly not in Paris fashions), engaged in similarly authentic (i.e. traditional, pre-modern) tasks (Çelik 1992). The harem in particu-lar occupied a temporal otherness, signified most easily by the sense of static space and inactivity encasing the stereotypically listless odalisque. Part of the attraction of visiting or reading about the harem was that it permitted Westerners to imagine they had access to this separate temporal realm, a space that was for them infused with nostalgia. This nostalgia is initially presented as a desire to experience and even save a way of life that they knew to be under threat from the rapid modernisation (Westernisation) of Ottoman society. But, as Renato Ros-aldo (1993) points out, their 'imperial nostalgia' was in fact driven by a Western agenda about the pace of modernity in the West itself and the sense of loss that characterised responses to such changes.

Bhabha (1994) has shown that keeping the colonies out of modernity, render-ing their spatial distance as a temporal distance, was essential to the construction of Enlightenment modernity and the universal category of rational 'Man' on which it depends. The temporality at the heart of this schema is revealed by the non-Western subject who, like Frantz Fanon, experiences the 'time lag' of com-ing 'belatedly' to the possibility of sovereign subjectivity. Fanon's consciousness of himself as negro, as not part of the unmarked universal category of 'Man', comes from outside as 'Look, a Negro!' is forced upon him. This different experience of becoming creates conditions of enunciation in which his discourse can disrupt the fantasised transparency of modernity's transcendent 'now'. His experience reveals the hidden importance of the marked non-Western subject whose exclusion boundaries the universalised subject of Western modernity. In contrast, colonial space appears as a 'non-place' whose 'history has to be begun' (Bhabha 1994).

The Orient's presumed temporal distance was problematic for Grace Ellison. Setting out to demonstrate the educated modernity of Ottoman women, she wanted to challenge the view that the Ottomans inhabited a separate time even as she re-inscribed it. She mourns the intrusion of elements of the very modernity that she feels compelled to emphasise – Ottoman harems are full of modern furniture but could Fatima please make her a comfortingly old-fashioned room. The link between dress, space and temporality is highlighted in her account of the reception at the palace, that harem of ultimate alterity that I discussed in Chapter Five. After a long description of Fatima's Paris gown and Miss Chocolate's finery, Ellison relays the garishly colourful – '[they] made one's eye's ache' – ensemble of the palace slaves: arrayed in outfits that could only 'behind the footlights, perhaps ... pass muster', their dresses 'defied both time and fashion' (Ellison 1915: 40). She imagines '[h]ow strange we [the fashionably dressed ladies] must have looked to the uncorseted women, who made no attempt at fashionable coiffure ... and whose dresses could have been made into 3 or 4 of our present day creations' (Ellison 1915: 40). Lucy Garnett, who similarly wanted to stress the power of Ottoman women relative to their Western counterparts, also could not avoid a nostalgic regret at the arrival of Western furniture and clothes. Like Ellison she found Oriental taste vulgar, but for her it was not the authentic aesthetic which was the problem but the unwholesome mix of East and West.

> Native costume and native furniture however rich and varied in colour and material, never offended a cultured Western eye when used in accordance with Oriental custom ... but the Oriental mind generally seems to get confused in endeavouring to assimilate its own notions of magnificence and luxury to those suggested by Western upholstery and French fashions; and this bewilderment finds expression in combinations of material and colour which would harrow the soul of the least aesthetic Englishwoman. (Garnett 1891: 425)

For both women the register for the nostalgic was the visual and the aesthetic. With the uncorseted body signifying the enormity of the temporal gulf, Ellison lays out verbally the gratifying ethnographic display of the 'contrast' photograph such as were produced, as Lorna Malmsheimer (1987) discusses, from the United States 'native schools' of the 1880s. Here, students were photographed before and after the education programme: the pair of portraits demonstrating the progress from 'wild' to 'civilised', a testament to the benefits of the government's assimilationist programme. The imperial harem produces a living contrast of pre-modern and modernising Turkey, the different time zones of cultural distance visible in one deliriously strange space – this is, after all, the place that threatened to drive Ellison mad 'at the end of a week'. Her writing betrays the lure of the other time of the Ottomans and the struggle to distance herself from it. Throughout her books, Ellison's intensely personal tone is at odds with the would-be anthropological distance of the investigative reporter writing in a genre of literature that relies on her feminine presence. The feminist subject struggles to align the 'freedoms' of the West with the 'protections' of the East that provided access to an imagined femininity now lost to the modernised West. The superior social status she enjoys as visitor to Turkey makes for a nostalgic investment in the imagined niceties of the almost obsolete (i.e. becoming past before her very eyes) world of the elite harem. Her self-mockingly rendered cry of despair to Mustafa Kemal at his plans to discontinue the veil (see Chapter Six) shows Ellison experiencing the 'transformation of other cultures as if they were personal losses' (Rosaldo 1993: 70). Agreeing that a (Westernising) model of progress is ultimately right and inevitable, Ellison's 'innocent yearning' is typical of imperialist nostalgia, working to absolve her of responsibility like the 'agents of colonialism [who] long for the very forms of life that they have intentionally altered or destroyed' (Rosaldo 1993: 69). Arrogating to herself the trauma of Ottoman cultural change Ellison mourned the loss of a fantasised association with an elegant and sensual femininity. But the codes of chivalry for which she was so nostalgic had not vanished: rather, as Durakbaşa elaborates, they had been transmogrified into the nationalist modernising project in which state-sponsored female emancipation was accompanied by the continuation of traditional attitudes to gender difference. Although the veil was to disappear, the persistence of codes of female modesty meant that anxieties about the masculinisation of women, which plagued the West, were not a major issue. When Ellison reached Ankara in the 1920s, the loss of harem femininity was compensated by the heroic but still sexual femininity now made available by the nationalist ideology of gender difference and the chivalric behaviours of the male elite. The respectability of nationalist elite women, coded in overtly 'feminine' terms, allowed Ellison access to a mode of female desirability that, unlike the restrictions of the harem or the 'sex wars' of Britain, augmented rather than undermined her professional identity.

But if this is what was available to the Western writer and reader, what about the nostalgia of Ottoman writers? How could a transnational subject's nostalgia be indexed when the Orient was a location that was, for the West, forever fixed in the past? All of the Ottoman sources I have discussed use their writing to construct an image of their Oriental past for their Occidental readership, each attempting to mark out an authenticating Oriental identity. Their desire to do this whilst also inscribing for themselves a meaningful transnational writing subjectivity produces a play of competing nostalgias. But registering any nostalgia is made more difficult if it is impossible for the West to recognise the temporality of the Ottoman present.[1] This is not to say that nostalgia – which has been the subject of so much debate in relation to postmodernity[2] – is essentially progressive when deployed by the non-Western subject. Spivak (1999) and others correctly criticise nostalgic narratives of origin in third world politics, among which can be instanced the imagined originative past employed in the Turkist conceptualisation of the new nation (see Chapter Two). But, as Kondo (1997) discusses, it can be empowering for minorities to represent their own nostalgia rather than be sold their past exclusively in the exoticised terms of Western nostalgia. The use of nostalgia in Ottoman sources shows the difficulty faced by writers in fashioning a modern self that does not have to break absolutely with the Ottoman past in the context of the existing commodification of Ottoman female life within an Occidental discourse. For subjects whose own recent past was rapidly being displaced (by emigration and by the social changes leading up to the second constitutional period and then the new republic) a nostalgic narrative redolent of exilic longing, also punctured by a gendered critique of sequestration, runs in tension with the invocation of Western stereotype necessary for engagement with Occidental attitudes. Unwilling to condemn totally the Ottoman ways, even as they argue for progressive social change, each woman attempts to construct herself as a reliable insider informant whose own version of her past, which always stands for a collective female experience, is authentic and incontrovertible. But they encounter contradictory versions of Ottoman female life not only from the West, but also from each other.

Vaka Brown, like Ellison, prevailed upon her Muslim hosts to enact for and with her scenes of Orientalist nostalgia: where Ellison begged a 'Turkish' room, Vaka Brown insisted on old fashioned 'Turkish' carriages. But Vaka Brown had always to choose American modernity, achieved, however, through a textual strategy (and successful writing career) that allowed her endlessly to return to the sybaritic qualities of her internationally connected childhood. It is this originary experience of Ottoman femininity that makes Vaka Brown's nostalgia qualitatively different from Ellison's: where Ellison laments an imagined loss of something that was never hers, Vaka Brown is torn by an affiliation to the modernity that is presented as her ethnic and immigrant destiny and the comfort of a treasured childhood experience that offered her protection from the rigours of that destiny. It was brought home to her that her present in 1901 was so materially challenging when she was reunited with her childhood friend Djimlah (see also Chapter Three), who was now the fourth wife of 'one of the most powerful pashas in the sultan's entourage ... in our girlhood we had been on the same social footing; but with the turning of the wheel of fortune I had gone under and had become a breadwinner – she had been carried up to the top' (Vaka 1909: 59–64). As a young child, the home of Djimlah's grandfather had been a refuge from Vaka Brown's strict school regime and, after the death of her father, a haven from the straitened circumstances of her mother's home. Now, for the young adult Vaka Brown, struggling to earn a living in New York, her friend's much-elevated marital social status highlights the material differences in their destinies, and the privations that were the cost of Vaka Brown's hard-won independence.

Vaka Brown's construction of her own authentic Oriental identity requires Ottoman Muslim women to remain somewhat otherworldly so that they can provide flattering contrast to her mediated American modernity and act as a

reminder of previous pleasures. It is imperative that this modern identity is calibrated by Vaka Brown's distinct ethnic identification. This allows her to be
unlike the other girls (those overeducated American women whose pretensions
she pillories, see Chapter Three) but also not quite like the Ottoman women who
must operate as a contrast to her adaptive modernity. Although in her writings
she must avoid being sucked back into the pre-modern time of the Orient, her
performance of an immigrant modernity that is nonetheless marked as Ottoman
is threatened by the potential modernisation of Ottoman women. On her visit in
1921 the ungraciousness of the woman on the tram (see Chapter Five) disallows
her previously pleasurable interactions with charming Ottoman women, and her
1923 account is marked by a nostalgic regret for this fast disappearing social
mode. The delightful affinities of the old order, which positioned her as relatively
modern but not entirely American, may start to unravel if Turkish women enact
too emphatically their own versions of modernity. Her horror at the brazen
modernity that transforms women into street sweepers suggests how modern
Turkey will defeat her by disallowing her desired nostalgic identification. Vaka
Brown's ability to recognise that these once great women have been brought low
in an ill-advised attempt at modernity mirrors Fabian's comments (1983: 10) on
the power accruing to those who have knowledge of time, in which the 'posited
authenticity of a past (savage, tribal, peasant) serves to denounce an inauthentic
present (the uprooted, évolués, acculturated)'. Though this formula usually
applies to the Western observer of a non-Western society, in the case of Vaka
Brown her position as non-Muslim observer of Muslim society allows her to
judge the degradation of the previously authentic Ottoman past in order to accrue
to herself the power to classify the Ottoman present as inauthentic.

Notably, she does not, in her accounts of her visits in either 1901 or 1921,
present the Greeks of Istanbul as part of her ethnographic exploration – though
the Ottoman minority populations were a regular feature of nineteenth- and early
twentieth-century Western travel writing.[3] The version of the Ottoman past in
which is anchored her complex identification as Ottoman (not quite like the
Turks) can then be pictured as authentic, if becoming obsolete. In this her alignment with a Western position is reminiscent of the way that colonial elites
aligned themselves with modern European time by relegating the peasantry to a
pre-modern time of superstition rather than reason. As Codell (1998c) describes
in relation to the Raj, the native informant can depict himself as a modern Westernised subject existing in a pre-modern society, separated by the colonial time
lag from the rest of the population for whom he can operate as a mediator with
modernity. Vaka Brown's temporalised distance from Muslim Ottoman women
in terms of religion, ethnicity and geographical location is understood by her and
them to be flexible: it is this mix of intimacy and difference that makes her such
an acute observer in their eyes. Vaka Brown's Greek Ottoman nostalgia recuper-
ates for Turkish women benefits of the old regime that the Young Turk
Revolution had dismantled and discredited. *Haremlik* is praised by the older
Ottoman lady Dilara Hanım for reminding Ottoman women of 'the attractive part

of the [old] system'; themselves, they could see only 'the things that stabbed' (Vaka 1923: 65).

For Vaka Brown, the journey back to Turkey is experienced as a journey through time as well as space: the old order which she cherishes and needs to find again is an imagined past on which is built her present writing self. The new Turkey emerging from these last days of the Ottoman Empire threatens to defeat her by disallowing the nostalgia essential to her desired identification. Yet it is Dilara Hanım who demonstrates the possibility of an oppositional reading practice, '[y]ou wrote for us – for Turkish women, not for the Westerners' (Vaka 1923: 65), and of living with the contradiction of opposing the harem system's restrictions on women whilst cherishing its forms of femininity now devalued by the Young Turks. It is at this point that Vaka Brown can allow herself literally to enter the picture. Whilst there are no photographs in *Haremlik*, she appears in a strangely ersatz Greek costume at the start of *Child of the Orient* (Illustration 17, below p. 260, see also Chapter One) and in action shots in *In the Heart of German Intrigue* in 1918: her presence behind the Greek lines during the First World War testify to her journalistic investigations. But the photographic presentation of Vaka Brown's body as part of her exercise in nostalgia really comes into its own in the pages of *Unveiled* where she appears with çarşaf and parasol as *The Author in Turkish Costume of Bygone Days*, paired tellingly and incongruously with that icon of Turkish modernity, *Girl Serving in the Turkish Shop* (both Illustration 18, below, p. 261). What sort of cultural ownership can Vaka Brown claim of these items of antiquated apparel? And why is it only once they have become antiquated that she can appear *à la turque*? The positional distance that needs to be preserved during the physical and emotional intimacies of *Haremlik* can – by the time she visits twenty years later as an established American author – now be reconfigured as an embodied photographic presence once it can be safely troped as nostalgia. The consumption of Ottoman costume (and class, these being the robes of the hanım, after all) has by 1921 become an important marker of her claim to an Ottoman identity. Wearing modern Western clothes is not cross-cultural dressing for the minority population and Americanised Vaka Brown, but neither does her apparel speak to the reality of her identity as she sees it. Returning in 1921, she is distressed that the dog on her old street, aptly named *gaiour*, does not at once recognise her. Having finally won him over, her moment of doggy validation is ruined by the horror of being taken for a stranger by an Englishman:

> 'I beg your pardon,' he said shyly, lifting his hat, 'but you are a stranger here, and those [dogs] are dangerous. Besides they are unhealthy.'
> This was the last straw: he took me for a foreigner.
> 'Thank you,' I replied, 'but I am not afraid. The fact is, we are of the same kennel, Gaiour and I.' (Vaka 1914: 286–7)

Vaka Brown must do all she can to be accepted as the loyal Ottoman that she signs herself as in the book's dedication to the Ottomanist Prince Sabaheddine

17. *Demetra Vaka* (Demetra Vaka, *Child of the Orient*, London, John Lane, 1914)

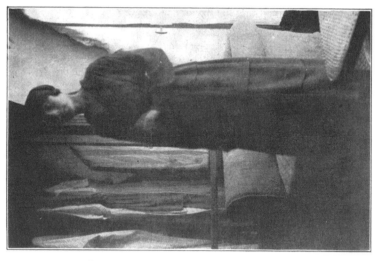

18. *The Author in Turkish Costume of Bygone Days,* and *Girl Serving in the Turkish Shop* (Demetra Vaka, *The Unveiled Ladies of Stamboul,* Boston and New York, Houghton Mifflin, 1923)

(see Chapter Two). Indeed, it is more than once left to Turkish Ottomans to demonstrate that they recognise the affinity between Greeks and Turks *as* Ottomans, whilst the British occupiers presume she will encounter animosity. In contrast to the foreigners who understand nothing of the East, her allegiance to a multi-ethnic and supra-national Ottoman identification is presented as a benefit for herself and for the Turks, who must otherwise resort to an ethnic isolationism that denies them a link to their own past. Her Ottoman Greek identification allows her to offer back to Muslim Turkish women her semi-outsider's nostalgia and Dilara Hanım's valediction returns to Vaka Brown a link with the old world in which her identification is anchored. This allows the paradoxes of Vaka Brown's nostalgia to co-exist with her ultimate belief in the advancement of Turkish women. The problem of framing that nostalgia to make sense for herself and for her Western readers without being subsumed under the West's overarching nostalgia is what makes her particular project so difficult.

Zeyneb Hanım faces similar problems but uses the West's nostalgia in a quite deliberate way. Her whole story is framed by her and Melek Hanım's self-conscious staging of themselves to Loti in the terms of not just any old generic Western Orientalist nostalgia but in the terms of what was by then a well-established vein of specifically Lotiesque nostalgia. Zeyneb Hanım's difficult process of presenting herself as authentic can be considered in relation to what Yeğenoğlu (forthcoming), in the context of contemporary tourism, calls the process of 'becoming native'. This refers to how the local population in Turkish holiday resorts earns a living by exhibiting itself engaged in 'authentic' artisanship in which the 'native' performing the task in front of the tourists is part of the spectacle that is purchased and consumed. This process of subjectification produces 'natives' just as colonial discourse allows the Westerner to 'become Western'.[4] Although the individual must adopt a touristic perspective in order to perform what is held to be an authentic identity (one that is already commodified by the tourist industry) this alteration to their sense of their space is not simply alienating. The informed, more cynical, stance that this practice can produce provides a chance to manipulate a discourse that threatens to colonise the terms and features of local identity. It is this tense process of enacting authenticity within a discourse that has already commodified (as nostalgic) Ottoman female experience whilst also trying to intervene in that discourse for her own ends that is seen in Zeyneb Hanım's book. Predicated from the first on the fruitful contrast of the educated woman trapped in the Orientalist harem that she and her sister use to hook Loti into their scheme, it continues to be haunted by the irresolvable conflict of selling an authenticity that would inevitably locate her in the past whilst also trying to insist on her modernity and acculturation. This is the tension that holds the photographs and the text in such uneasy alliance. This conflict, inherent in the presentation of Ottoman women as in any way modernised, is also faced by Ellison. But it runs deeper in a product sold as 'Oriental' in origin, where neither photographs of the harem in Turkey nor of Ottoman women in Europe can be easily secured as authentic.

In a book that is held to emerge from the East, 'a realm of tradition, and of the past' (Morley 1996: 328), the presence of Western furniture and clothes in photographs of the harem (Illustration 4, above, p. 211) marks an intrusion of recognisable signs of Western modernity into a space fantasised as the repository of unchanging tradition. But the Western goods that the Western reader (and at times Ellison) read as inauthentic are in fact given a new sense and meaning in their new location. Recognising that the ingestion of foreign elements is an intrinsic part of cultures, not an alien imposition into some previously 'pure' bounded native society, David Morley advocates an emphasis on 'local consequences not local origins' (Morley 1996: 330): consider, for example, how Western gloves came to be incorporated into the Ottoman çarşaf ensemble that ensured Islamic modesty for women in public.

The local consequences of the global movement of goods can also help make sense of the transfer of Ottoman objects to Europe seen in the photographs of Zeyneb Hanım's Western drawing room (Illustrations 9 and 10, above, pp. 226 and 227). Here the transnational subject uses generic 'Oriental' artefacts (probably acquired, and possibly manufactured, in Europe) alongside articles of Ottoman clothing (brought from home) to perform in Europe for her Western readers an identity as Turkish. And all this in a book that seeks to challenge the notion of the harem as an uncontaminated space existing outside modernity. At home in Istanbul her yaşmak was a quite natural piece of outerwear that – worn over her fashionable Paris gowns – would have been experienced as part of a modern identity. But taken out of the local situation, wearing a yaşmak is no longer unremarkable; it becomes instead a highly self-conscious act in the forging of a hybrid identity. The yaşmak, as discussed in Chapter Six, ran in and out of fashion in turn of the century Istanbul and for the stylish Ottoman women who wore it part of its appeal may indeed have been what would now be called 'retro'. But it would have been seen as very much of the moment. The West's nostalgic inability to recognise Ottoman modernity keeps this garment resolutely in the past, secured as the signifier of a imagined lost moment. But despite the urge to deny coevality, the very temporality of turn of the century Western Orientalist nostalgia makes Zeyneb Hanım's Western drawing-room look disconcertingly *à la mode*. With its Arts and Crafts lilies and elegant draperies, its simulation of the Oriental interior reminiscent of Lord Leighton's famous Arab hall in London's Holland Park, the room begins to look like the already commodified nostalgia of fashionable early twentieth-century interior design.

It would be wrong to look for a pure authenticity in the Ottoman women's self-presentation.[5] Their depiction of self must always be relational and cannot avoid the terms of dominant Orientalist discourse, but within this they demonstrate a knowingness that allows them to manipulate cultural codes to their benefit. Despite the obvious political regressiveness of much nostalgia maybe, when one considers the implications of recuperating signs of Ottoman-ness from Orientalism's appropriation, a form of oppositional nostalgia can be seen to be strategic for the putatively de-historicised non-Western subject. Writing of the

nostalgic packaging of old-style Kyoto in a contemporary urban Japanese fashion magazine, Kondo discusses how the pleasures of regaining an authentic
Japaneseness (signified by Kyoto) rely not just on experiencing the 'unchanged'
city but on the opportunity when there to purchase a combination of selected 'traditional' Japanese goods and the latest Western fashions. Mourning for the lost
past is combined with 'a kind of ironic reappropriation of a Western gaze' that
valorises Japaneseness as consumption, using a model of identity through consumption to reduce signifiers of both Japan and the West to commodities (Kondo
1997: 84). When in Chapter Six I labelled Zeyneb Hanım's self-display in a
yaşmak in Paris as a form of historical re-enactment, I was referring to the re-
enactment of a dress mode from her own recent past in Istanbul. But the clashing
temporality staged in these photographs also invokes the sense in which Zeyneb
Hanım would have been seen to be emerging from the other non-modern time of
the Orient. As such her costume from her own past in Paris enacts a crossing of
temporal boundaries akin to the temporalised cultural boundaries traversed by
cross-cultural dressing. In both these senses, the particular historical and spatial
positioning of the Ottoman female subject makes her dress acts shimmer on the
porous skin of the imagined boundaries that differently positioned subjects can
conceive of as impermeable. The bodily experience of the dressed Ottoman
woman creates opportunities for the performance of non-binary identifications –
if only the West can manage to read them.

For Zeyneb Hanım, dress is central to her staging of identity and it behoves
one to imagine the possible pleasures of presenting herself in Western and Ottoman clothing as well as the forms of political agency her complicated dress acts
express. In this light can be analysed Zeyneb Hanım's packaging of Ottoman
female experience as nostalgia whilst she Orientalises herself for Loti. The terms
of this creative self-fashioning are not solely determined by the outside, they also
point to the power of the choices made by the Ottoman émigré. For Halide Edib
the conditions of emergence necessary for the textual representation of the
agency of the Orientalised subject hang specifically on her participation in
national politics. Where Zeyneb Hanım and Melek Hanım relied on the presumed power of Loti's fiction, Edib experienced the power of her own fiction
made possible by the revolution of 1908.

Writing her memoirs some years later in England, Edib, in keeping with the
determined modernity of nationalist ideology, was resolute in her rejection of any
nostalgia for the ways of the old regime. For the nationalist soldier and heroine,
the elegant femininity of the hanım held little attraction, though her first volume
presents the many benefits as well as the disadvantages of growing up in an elite
segregated home. Edib is different to the other Ottoman authors covered here in
that she was the only one with sufficient public profile to sell a book without
recourse to the usual Orientalist codifications in her title. Marketing her first volume as *Memoirs of Halidé Edib* demonstrates a different form of self-
commodification. The decision to write in English was about her desire to make
a strategic intervention into local Turkish historiography (see Chapter Two), not

19. *Halide Hanoum, the Best Known of Turkish Women Writers and a Leader of the Woman's Movement* (Grace Ellison, *An Englishwoman in a Turkish Harem*, London, Methuen, 1915)

just about correcting Western presumptions. The public staging of so much of her life (from her prominence as the child of an eminent father to her own war-time escapades) traversed the limits of sequestration. The Ottoman lady becomes a version of a former self happily relinquished in the drive to national self-determination (see Chapter Three). Although Edib's account puts the agency of Ottoman women centre-stage, as an antidote to Kemalist visions of Atatürk single-handedly 'giving' women their liberation, she shares with the Kemalists the distaste for the image of the hanım – now coded as decadent – that so worry-ingly determined Western attitudes to the whole nation. In this way, Edib's private history is always packaged with a concern for local and foreign opinion. Noticeably, for a woman famous at home and abroad, she does not picture herself in the first volume of her memoirs at all, though her photographic image was already in international circulation. She had previously appeared in Ellison's 1915 book, as a young woman in an interior studio shot, elegantly dressed in Edwardian fashion (hailed as 'the best known of Turkish women writers and a leader of the woman's movement', Illustration 19, previous page), and sub-sequently was widely imaged addressing the crowds in her çarşaf during the Istanbul rallies of 1918.[6] Edib did later picture herself in the *Turkish Ordeal* of 1928, where she figures in a commercial photograph as the Halide of Sultanah-ment and in snapshots as Corporal Halide – astride her horse or standing with other nationalist leaders in the 'uniform' she had created for herself (Illustration 20, opposite). Edib's description of the delicate business of concocting an outfit suitable for travel and rough terrain but sufficiently modest to permit her move-ments among the troops, tells of a differently motivated sartorial agency. As well as needing to equate herself stylistically with her comrades, the outfit in Illustra-tion 20 arose from a desire to retain for herself a sense of femininity, albeit modified. After not seeing her reflection for some time in Ankara, Edib was shocked by the 'stranger' in the mirror and set about recasting the 'woman in black with high boots' into something less alienating:

> I put on a gray suit consisting of an ample skirt which buttoned both front and back (all my skirts were made in that way for riding), a Russian blouse with a leather belt, and a long gray veil which covered my hair and fell in folds, leav-ing my face exposed. I then felt like an ordinary civilized woman in spite of my high boots. (Edib 1928: 240)

Breaking with the clothes and customs of the elite Ottoman female past for per-sonal and national reasons, any nostalgia that is allowed to enter Edib's text is focused on the stoic loyalty of the Turkish peasantry (a standard trope in Turkist romanticisations of national identity) rather than on the mannered life of the elite lady. Though her detailed account delights in relaying the old customs of her childhood, they are presented as historically contingent elements of a changing society, not as adornments of a rarefied pre-modern realm. Reviews of her work demonstrate that the value of her insider political knowledge went some way toward compensating for the disappointing lack of the usual harem exotica, even

20. *Major Tewfik, Corporal Halide, Major Tahsin, and Galib Bey* (Halide Edib, *The Turkish Ordeal: Being the Further Memoirs of Halidé Edib*, London, John Murray, 1928)

though her hybrid cultural product (spanning the divide between harem literature and political autobiography) was still associated in the West with the scarcity value of the harem tale.

In today's postcolonial times the commodification of the view from behind the veil has not gone away. The immediacy of the hanım stereotype may have faded, but the Western fascination with the exotic continues and the desire to see the unveiled face is re-activated by new veiling practices in the context of global postmodern politics. One of the reasons why I have been at such pains in this book to draw out the nuance of specific historical experiences and representations of veiling, de-veiling and segregation is to provide a corrective to the continued tendency to talk about 'the' veil and women from Islamic societies as a single group. Although I started this book by identifying the early twentieth century as the last gasp of harem literature, the concerns that drove that market have transmogrified into a postcolonial obsession with the veil that, though it might manifest itself through different cultural and discursive forms, remains in alarming ways loyal to earlier Orientalist models.

But, as I have shown, the obsession with the veiled woman and with the local and international significance of visible Islamic practice is not confined to the West: the veil has reappeared (if it ever went away) both as a choice, newly energised by a generation of young women who reject the secular modernity of many postcolonial states in the Muslim world, or worn as a badge of pride by women in diasporic communities, or adopted strategically to facilitate otherwise transgressive gender behaviours;[7] and as an imposition, remodelled by Islamic revivalist forces reliant on their own nostalgic investment in narratives of an imagined prior golden moment of organic Islamic religiosity.

For all these reasons, the analysis of the history of segregated life remains contentious both as part of postcolonial revisions of the past and in relation to reprises of the veil. Fought over by politicians and activists of all political persuasions, fetishised by news reports, reclaimed within the creative arts, and prioritised in postcolonial studies, the body and the voice of the veiled and unveiled woman continues to transfix observers from inside and outside veiling communities.[8] This book has been an attempt to bring into play a set of historical voices not only as a process of information retrieval (Spivak 1999) but in order to attend to the way that as cultural artefacts they problematise the very issues of authenticity that ensured their initial value. That these sources remain fascinating is not just because of the spellbinding stories they tell but because of the problems they raise for contemporary conceptions of identity, power, authority and resistance.

NOTES

1 For examples of incidents in the nineteenth century when the image of Oriental time-lessness could not be sustained see Doy (1996).

2 Much of this is prompted by Fredric Jameson (1991), who detects the emergence of nostalgia as the dominant form of Western postmodernity. Arguing that the present has become colonised by 'the nostalgia mode', he notes the increased production in the West of nostalgia films set in the 1930s to the 1950s. Their careful rendition of an imagined past – with all clues to contemporary life relentlessly excised from the screen – produces a generalised sense of era, 'some eternal thirties, beyond real historical time', rooted in a desire for an imagined lost origin. Responses to Jameson have underlined the Euro-American specificity of his apparently universal model of postmodernity (for an overview see Morley 1996). Not only do all subjects not experience postmodernity in an equal way or even at the same time, but, as Spivak (1999) points out, the West's nostalgic repackaging of the past does not in itself apply equally to all pasts or all territories. Unlike the elaborate effects needed to produce a convincing staging of the European past, films such as *Out of Africa* are able to shoot in contemporary rural Africa whose 'un-retouched' spaces can stand in for colonial Africa on the assumption that time has not moved on in the same way as it has in the West. In the moment of modernity that frames my sources it can be said that the harem, to paraphrase Jameson, operates as the lost object of desire for Western nostalgia, functioning as a vague, timeless but highly evocative zone signalled by 'stylistic connotation[s]' producing an 'eternal [Orient], beyond real historical time' (Jameson 1991: 19–21).

3 Though she does not include the Greek populations as Oriental spectacle in *Haremlik* or *Unveiled*, Vaka Brown does present some of her mother's religious convictions as amusing superstitions in *Child of the Orient* (1914) and in the posthumous biography in *Athene* (1947–52). On mid-twentieth-century ethnographers from the Greek American community see Kalogeras 1988.

4 See also Dean MacCannell (1994) on the performance of authenticity by 'ex-primitives'.

5 See also Lewis (2004) on how harem accounts of uncertain provenance function as a limit case for discussions of attributable authenticity.

6 Though the Turkish press generally showed her wearing her çarşaf (though no face veil), American accounts from the period, especially missionary biographies, took especial delight in including photographs of her completely unveiled. I thank Hulya Adak for drawing this contrast to my attention.

7 See Abu Odeh (1993), Ghoussoub (1987, 1988), Hammami and Rieker (1989).

8 In addition to sources previously cited see also: *Interventions*, 1:4, 1999, special topic 'The Veil: Postcolonialism and the Politics of Dress', Copjec (1994), Bailey and Tawadros (2003), Moors (2000), Lowe (1996).

❧ BIBLIOGRAPHY ❧

PERIODICALS AND NEWSPAPERS CONSULTED

(place of publication is London, unless otherwise stated)

Daily Telegraph
The Times
The Times Literary Supplement
Votes for Women
The Englishwoman
Kadınlar Dünyası (Istanbul)
Levant Herald (Istanbul)
The Oriental Advertiser/Le moniteur oriental (Istanbul)

MANUSCRIPT SOURCES

Houghton Library, Harvard University
Houghton Mifflin manuscripts
Correspondence, Houghton Mifflin – Demetra Vaka Brown: BMS/Am 1925 (267)
Correspondence, Amy Lowell – Demetra Vaka Brown: BMS/Lowell 19 (152), BMS/
    Lowell 19.1 (165)

WORKS CITED

Abadan-Unat, Nermin (1981a) (ed), *Women in Turkish Society* (Leiden, E. J. Brill).
—— (1981b), 'Social Change and Turkish Women' in Abadan-Unat (1981a).
—— (1991), 'The Impact of Legal and Educational Reforms on Turkish Women', in
    Keddie and Baron (1991).
Abu-Lughod, Ibrahim (1963), *Arab Rediscovery of Europe: A Study in Cultural
    Encounters* (New Jersey, Princeton University Press).
Abu-Lughod, Lila (1986), *Veiled Sentiments: Honor and Poetry in a Bedouin Society*
    (Berkeley, University of California).
—— (1998) (ed), *Remaking Women: Feminism and Modernity in the Middle East*
    (Princeton, Princeton University Press).
Abu Odeh, L. (1993), 'Post-Colonial Feminism and the Veil: Thinking the Differ-
    ence', *Feminist Review*, 43, pp. 26–37.
Adak, Hulya (2003), 'National Myths and Self-Na(rra)tions: Mustafa Kemal's *Nutuk*
    and Halide Edib's *Memoirs* and *The Turkish Ordeal*', *South Atlantic Quarterly*,
    102: 2–3, pp. 511–29.

Akatali, Fusun (1981), 'The Image of Woman in Turkish Literature', in Abadan-Unat (1981a).

Al-'Azm, Sadiq Jamal (1984), 'Orientalism in Reverse', in Jon Rothschild (ed), *Forbidden Agendas: Intolerance and Defiance in the Middle East, Khamsin: An Anthropology* (London, Al Saqi Books).

Anderson, Benedict (1983), *Imagined Communities: Reflections on the Origin and Spread of Nationalism* (London, Verso).

Apter, E. (1992), 'Female Trouble in the Colonial Harem', *Differences*, 4, pp. 205–24.

—— (1996), 'Acting Out Orientalism: Sapphic Theatricality in Turn-of-the-Century Paris', in Elin Diamond (ed), *Performance and Cultural Politics* (London, Routledge).

Arat, Yeşim (1994), 'Women's Movement of the 1980s in Turkey: Radical Outcome of Liberal Kemalism', in Göçek and Balaghi (1994).

Arat, Zehra F. (1994), 'Turkish Women and the Republican Reconstruction of Tradition', in Göçek and Balaghi (1994).

—— (1999a) (ed), *Deconstructing Images of 'The Turkish Woman'* (New York, Palgrave).

—— (1999b), 'Educating the Daughters of the Republic', in Arat (1999a).

—— (1999c), 'Introduction: Politics of Representation and Identity', in Arat (1999a).

Ashcroft, Bill, Griffiths, Gareth, and Tiffin, Helen (1995) (eds), *The Post-Colonial Studies Reader* (London, Routledge).

Badran, Margot, and Cooke, Miriam (1990) (eds), *Opening the Gates. A Century of Arab Feminist Writing* (London, Virago).

Badran, Margot (1991), 'Competing Agenda: Feminists, Islam and the State in 19th and 20th Century Egypt', in Kandiyoti (1991).

—— (1996), *Feminists, Islam, and Nation* (Cairo, American University in Cairo Press).

Bailey, David A., and Tawadros, Gilane (2003) (eds), *Veil: Veiling, Representation and Contemporary Art* (London, Institute of International Visual Arts).

Bammer, Angelika (1994) (ed), *Displacements: Cultural Identities in Question* (Bloomington and Indianapolis, Indiana University Press).

Baron, Beth (1994), *The Women's Awakening in Egypt: Culture, Society and the Press* (New Haven, Yale University Press).

Barthes, Roland (1971), 'Pierre Loti: Aziyade', in Roland Barthes (1990), *New Critical Essays*, trans. Richard Howard (Berkeley, California University Press).

—— (1977), *Image, Music, Text*, trans. Stephen Heath (London, Fontana).

Başci, K. Pelin (1999), 'Shadows in the Missionary Garden of Rose: Women of Turkey in American Missionary Texts', in Arat (1999a).

Beaulieu, Jill, and Roberts, Mary (2002) (eds), *Orientalism's Interlocutors: Rewriting the Colonial Encounter* (Durham, NC, Duke University Press).

Benjamin, Roger (1997) (ed), *Orientalism: Delacroix to Klee* (Sydney, Art Gallery of New South Wales).

Bennet, Mary (1988), *Artists of the Pre-Raphaelite Circle, the First Generation. Catalogue of Works in the Walker Art Gallery, Lady Lever Art Gallery and Sudely Art Gallery* (London, National Museums and Galleries on Merseyside).

Berger, John, and Mohr, Jean (1982), *Another Way of Telling* (London, Writers and Readers).

Berkes, Niyazi (1964), *The Development of Secularism in Turkey* (Montreal, McGill University Press).

Bhabha, Homi K. (1984), 'Of Mimicry and Men', *October*, 28, pp. 125–33.

—— (1994), *The Location of Culture* (London, Routledge).

Bhavnani, Kum-Kum (2001), *Feminism and Race* (Oxford, Oxford University Press).

Birkett, Dea (1989), *Spinsters Abroad: Victorian Lady Explorers* (Oxford, Blackwell).

Bland, Lucy (1995), *Banishing the Beast: English Feminism and Sexual Morality 1885–1914* (Harmondsworth, Penguin).

—— (1998), 'Trial by Sexology? Maud Allan, Salome and the "Cult of the Clitoris" Case', in Lucy Bland and Laura Doan (eds), *Sexology in Culture: Labelling Bodies and Desires* (Cambridge, Polity Press).

Blunt, Alison (1994), 'Introduction: Women's Colonial and Postcolonial Geographies', in Blunt and Rose (1994).

—— and Rose, Gillian (1994) (eds), *Writing Women and Space: Colonial and Postcolonial Geographies* (London, The Guilford Press).

Blunt, Lady Anne (1881), *A Pilgrimage to Nejd: The Cradle of the Arab Race. A Visit to the Court of the Arab Emir, and 'Our Persian Campaign'*, 2 vols (London, John Murray).

Bock, Carol A. (1981), 'Rossetti's *Found* and *The Blessed Damozel* as Exploration in Victorian Psychosexuality', *The Journal of Pre-Raphaelite Studies*, 1: 2, May, pp. 83–90.

Bohrer, Frederick (2004), 'The Sweet Waters of Asia: Representing Difference/Differencing Representation in the Nineteenth Century', in Hackforth-Jones and Roberts (2004).

Boone, Joseph A. (1995), 'Vacation Cruises; or, the Homoerotics of Orientalism', *PMLA*, 110: 1, January, pp. 89–107.

Bouhdiba, Abdelwahab (1975), *Sexuality in Islam*, trans. Alan Sheridan (London, Routledge).

Brah, Avtar (1996), *Cartographies of Diaspora: Contesting Identities* (London, Routledge).

Bristow, Joseph (1991), *Empire Boys: Adventures in a Man's World* (London, Harper Collins).

Bronfen, Elisabeth (1992), *Over Her Dead Body: Death, Femininity and the Aesthetic* (Manchester, Manchester University Press).

Brontë, Charlotte (1847), *Jane Eyre* (London, Penguin, 1966).

Bullen, J. B. (1998), *The Pre-Raphaelite Body: Fear and Desire in Painting, Poetry, and Criticism* (Oxford, Clarendon Press).

Burke, W. J., and Howe, Will D. (1963), *American Authors and Books 1640 to the Present Day,* 2nd edition, augmented and revised by Irving R. Weiss (London, Vane).

Burton, Antoinette (1992), 'The White Woman's Burden: British Feminists and "the Indian Woman" 1865–1915', in Chaudhuri and Strobel (1992).

Butler, Judith (1990), *Gender Trouble. Feminism and the Subversion of Identity* (London, Routledge).

—— (1993), 'Critically Queer', *GLQ*, 1: 1, pp. 17–32.

Carrier, James G. (1992), 'Occidentalism: the World Turned Upside-Down', *American Ethnologist*, 19: 2, pp. 195–212.

Casteras, Susan P. (1990), *English Pre-Raphaelitism and Its Reception in America in the Nineteenth Century* (London and Toronto, Associated University Presses).

Çelik, Zeyneb (1986), *The Remaking of Istanbul: Portrait of an Ottoman City in the Nineteenth Century* (Seattle, University of Washington Press).

—— (1992), *Displaying the Orient: Architecture of Islam at Nineteenth-Century World's Fairs* (Berkeley, University of California Press).

—— (1996), 'Colonialism, Orientalism and the Canon', *Art Bulletin*, 78: 2, pp. 202–5.

Chatty, Dawn (1997), 'The Burqa Face Cover: An Aspect of Dress in Southeastern Arabia', in Lindisfarne-Tapper and Ingham (1997).

Chaudhuri, Nupur, and Strobel, Margaret (1992) (eds), *Western Women and Imperialism: Complicity and Resistance* (Bloomington, Indiana University Press).

Cherry, Deborah, and Pollock, Griselda (1984), 'Woman as Sign in Pre-Raphaelite Literature: A Study of the Representation of Elizabeth Siddall', *Art History,* June, pp. 206–27.

—— (2000), *Beyond the Frame: Feminism and Visual Culture, Britain 1850–1900* (London, Routledge).

Childs, Elizabeth Catharine (1989), 'Honoré Daumier and the Exotic Vision: Studies in French Culture and Caricature, 1830–1870', unpublished PhD thesis, Columbia University, School of Arts and Sciences.

Chinn, Sarah E. (1997), 'Gender Performativity', in Andy Medhurst and Sally Munt (1997) (eds), *Lesbian and Gay Studies: A Critical Introduction* (London, Cassell).

Chow, Rey (1994), 'Where Have All the Natives Gone?', in Bammer (1994).

Çizgen, Engin (1987), *Photography in the Ottoman Empire 1839–1919* (Istanbul, Haset Kitalevi).

Clarke, J. J. (1997), *Oriental Enlightenment: The Encounter Between Asian and Western Thought* (London, Routledge).

Clement, Clara Erskine (1895), *Constantinople: The City of the Sultans* (Boston, Estes and Lauriet).

Clifford, James (1986), 'Introduction: Partial Truths', in James Clifford and George E. Marcus (1986) (eds), *Writing Culture: The Poetics and Politics of Ethnography* (Berkeley, University of California Press).

Codell, Julie F. (1995), 'The Artist Colonized: Holman Hunt's "bio-history", Masculinity, Nationalism and the English School', in Harding (1995).

—— and Macleod, Dianne Sachko (1998a) (eds), *Orientalism Transposed: The Impact of the Colonies on British Culture* (Aldershot, Ashgate).

—— —— (1998b), 'Introduction: the "Easternization" of Britain and Interventions to Colonial Discourse', in Codell and Macleod (1998a).

—— (1998c), 'Resistance and Performance: Native Informant Discourse in the Biographies of Maharaja Sayaji Rao III (1863–1939)', in Codell and Macleod (1998a).

Cole, Juan R. I., and Kandiyoti, Deniz (2002) (eds), 'Nationalism and the Colonial Legacy in the Middle East and Central Asia: Introduction', *International Journal of Middle East Studies*, Special Issue, 34: 2, pp. 189–203.

Contopoulos, Michael (1992), *The Greek Community of New York City: Early Years to 1910* (New York, Aristide D. Caratzas, Publisher).

Copjec, Joan (1994), *Read my Desire: Lacan Against the Historicists* (Cambridge, MA, MIT Press).

Coufopoulos, Demetrius (1910), *Constantinople,* 4th edition (London, Adam and Charles Black), first edition 1895.

Craven, Elizabeth (1789), *Journey Through the Crimea to Constantinople. In a Series of Letter to His Serene Highness the Margrave of Brandenbourg, Anspach and Bareith. Written in the Year MDCCLXXXVI* (London, G. G. J. and J. Robinson).

Cruise, Colin (1995), '"Lovely Devils": Simeon Solomon and Pre-Raphaelite Masculinity', in Harding (1995).

Davis, Fanny (1986), *The Ottoman Lady: A Social History from 1718–1918* (New York, Greenwood Press).

Dellamora, Richard (1990), *Masculine Desire: The Sexual Politics of Victorian Aestheticism* (Chapel Hill, University of North Caroline Press).

Demirdirek, Aynur (1999), 'In Pursuit of the Ottoman Women's Movement', trans. Zehra F. Arat, in Arat (1999a).

Deringil, Selim (1999), *The Well-Protected Domains: Ideology and the Legitimation of Power in the Ottoman Empire, 1876–1909* (London, I.B. Tauris).

DeRoo, Rebecca J. (1998), 'Colonial Collecting: Women and Algerian Cartes Postales', *Parallax*, 4: 2, pp. 145–57.

Dickason, David Howard (1953), *The Daring Young Men: The Story of the American Pre-Raphaelites* (Bloomington, Indiana University Press).

Didur, Jill, and Heffernan, Teresa (2003), **'Revisiting the Subaltern in the New Empire',** *Cultural Studies, Special Issue: Revisiting the Subaltern in the New Empire*, 17: 1, Fall, pp. 1–15.

Dodd, Anna Bowman (1904), *In the Palaces of the Sultans* (London, Heinemann).

Donnell, A. (1999), 'Editorial: Dressing with a Difference: Cultural Representation, Minority Rights and Ethnic Chic', *Interventions. Special Topic, The Veil: Postcolonialism and the Politics of Dress*, 1: 4, pp. 489–99.

Donzel, E. van, Lewis, B., and Pellat, C. (1978), *The Encyclopaedia of Islam,* vol. 4 (Leiden, E. J. Brill).

Doy, Gen (1996), 'Out of Africa: Orientalism, "Race" and the Female Body', *Body and Society*, 2: 4, December, pp. 17–44.

Duben, Alan, and Behar, Cem (1991), *Istanbul Households: Marriage, Family and Fertility, 1880–1940* (Cambridge, Cambridge University Press).

Durakbaşa, Ayşe (1993), 'Reappraisal of Halide Edib for a Critique of Turkish Modernization', unpublished PhD thesis, Department of Sociology, University of Essex.

—— (1999), 'Kemalism as Identity Politics In Turkey', in Arat (1999a).

Edib, Halide Adivar (1926), *Memoirs of Halidé Edib* (London, John Murray).

—— (1928), *The Turkish Ordeal: Being the Further Memoirs of Halidé Edib* (London, John Murray).

—— (1930), *Turkey Faces West: A Turkish View of Recent Changes and Their Origin* (New Haven, Yale University Press).

—— (1937), *Inside India* (London, George Allen and Unwin).

Edwards, Elizabeth (1990), 'Photographic "Types": The Pursuit of Method', *Visual Anthropology,* 3, pp. 235–58.

—— (1992) (ed), *Anthropology and Photography 1860–1920* (New Haven, Yale University Press).

Ekrem, Selma (1931), *Unveiled* (London, Goeffrey Bles).

—— (1947), *Turkey, Old and New* (New York, Charles Scribner's Sons).

El Guindi, F. (1999), 'Veiling Resistance', *Fashion Theory,* 3: 1, pp. 51–80.

Ellis, Ellen Deborah, and Palmer, Florence (1914), 'The Feminist Movement in Turkey', *The Contemporary Review,* June, pp. 857–64.

Ellison, Grace (1914), 'Life in the Harem', *Daily Telegraph*, Saturday 24 January, p. 8; Monday 26 January, p. 7; Tuesday 27 January, p. 6; Wednesday 28 January, p. 7; Thursday 29 January, p. 8; Friday 30 January, p. 6; Saturday 31 January, p. 7; Monday 2 February, p. 9; Tuesday 3 February, p. 7; Friday 6 February, p. 7; Monday 9 February, p. 11.

—— (1915), *An Englishwoman in a Turkish Harem* (London, Methuen).

—— (1922), *The Disadvantages of Being a Woman*, 'The Blue Booklet Series', 4 (London, A. M. Philpot Ltd).

—— (1923), *An Englishwoman in Angora* (London, Hutchinson).

—— (1928), *Turkey To-day* (London, Hutchinson).

—— (1934), *The Authorised Life Story of Princess Marina* (London, Heinemann).

Elzea, Rowland (1997), 'Samuel Bancroft: Pre-Raphaelite Collector', in Watson (1997a).

Evans, Caroline, and Gamman, Lorraine (1995), 'The Gaze Revisited, Or Reviewing Queer Viewing', in Paul Burston and Colin Richardson (1995) (eds), *A Queer Romance: Lesbians, Gay Men and Popular Culture* (London, Routledge).

Fabian, Johannes (1983), *Time and the Other: How Anthropology Makes its Objects* (New York, Columbia University Press).

Fanon, F. (1959), 'Algeria Unveiled', in Haakon Chevalier (1989) (trans.), *Studies in a Dying Colonialism* (London, Earthscan Publications).

Faxon, Alicia Craig (1989), *Dante Gabriel Rossetti* (London, Phaidon).

Fernea, Elizabeth Warnock, and Bezirgan, Basima Qattan (1977) (eds), *Middle Eastern Women Speak* (Austin, University of Texas Press).

Finn, Robert P. (1984), *The Early Turkish Novel 1872–1900* (Istanbul, Isis Press).

Fleischmann, Ellen L. (1999), 'The Other "Awakening": The Emergence of Women's Movements in the Modern Middle East, 1900–1940', in Meriwether and Tucker (1999).

Fleming, K. E. (1999), 'Women as Preservers of the Past: Ziya Gökalp and Women's Reform', in Arat (1999a).

Flint, Kate (1989), 'Reading *The Awakening Conscience Rightly*', in Pointon (1989).

—— (1993), *The Woman Reader 1937–1914* (Oxford, Oxford University Press).

Fortna, Benjamin (2002), *Imperial Classroom: Islam, the State and Education in the Late Ottoman Empire* (Oxford, Oxford University Press).

Freud, Sigmund (1914), 'On Narcissism: an Introduction', in J. Strachey (trans. and ed), *The Standard Edition of the Complete Psychological Works of Sigmund Freud*, vol. 14 (London, Hogarth Press).

Frierson, Elizabeth B. (1995), 'Unimagined Communities: Woman and Education in the Late-Ottoman Empire', *Critical Matrix*, 9: 2, pp. 55–90.

—— (2000a). 'Cheap and Easy: The Creation of Consumer Culture in Late Ottoman Society', in Quataert (2000).

—— (2000b), 'Mirrors Out, Mirrors In: Domestication and Rejection the Foreign in Late-Ottoman Women's Magazines', in Ruggles (2000).

Garber, Marjorie (1992), *Vested Interests: Cross-Dressing and Cultural Anxiety* (London, Routledge).

Garnett, Lucy M. (1890), *The Women of Turkey and their Folklore*, vol. 1 (London, D. Nutt).

—— (1891), *The Women of Turkey and their Folklore*, vol. 2 (London, D. Nutt).

—— (1911), *Turkey of the Ottomans* (London, Sir Isaac Pitman and Sons Ltd).

Geertz, Clifford (1984), *Local Knowledge: Further Essays in Interpretative Anthropology* (New York, Basic Books).

Germaner, Semra, and Inankur, Zeynep (1989), *Orientalism and Turkey*, trans. Nigâr Alemdar and Jeremy Salt (Istanbul, Turkish Cultural Service Foundation).

Gernsheim, Alison (1963), *Victorian and Edwardian Fashion: A Photographic Survey* (London, Dover Publications).

Ghose, Indira (1998), *Women Travellers in Colonial India: The Power of the Female Gaze* (New Delhi, Oxford University Press).

Ghoussoub, Mai (1987), 'Feminism – or the Eternal Masculine – in the Arab World', *New Left Review*, 161, pp. 3–18.

—— (1988), 'A Reply to Hammami and Rieker', *New Left Review*, 170, pp. 108–9.

Göçek, Fatma Müge, and Balaghi, Shiva (1994a) (eds), *Reconstructing Gender in the Middle East: Tradition, Identity, and Power* (New York, Columbia University Press).

—— —— (1994b), 'Introduction: Reconstructing Gender in the Middle East Through Voice and Experience', in Göçek and Balaghi (1994a).

—— (1996), *Rise of the Bourgeoisie, Demise of Empire: Ottoman Westernisation and Social Change* (New York, Oxford University Press).

—— (1999), 'To Veil or not to Veil: The Contested Location of Gender in Contemporary Turkey', *Interventions*, 1: 4, pp. 521–35.

Goff, Barbara Munsen (1982), 'The Politics of Pre-Raphaelitism', *The Journal of Pre-Raphaelite Studies*, 2: 2, May, pp. 57–70.

Goffman, Carolyn McCue (2002), '"More than the Conversion of Souls": Rhetoric and Ideology at the American College for Girls in Istanbul, 1871–1923', unpublished PhD thesis, Ball State University, Muncie, IN.

Graham-Brown, Sarah (1988), *Images of Women: The Portrayal of Women in Photography of the Middle East 1860–1950* (London, Quartet).

Grewal, Inderpal (1996), *Home and Harem: Nation, Gender Empire and the Cultures of Travel* (Leicester, Leicester University Press).

De Groot, Joanna (1996), 'Gender Discourse and Ideology in Iranian Studies: Towards a New Scholarship', in Kandiyoti (1996a).

—— (1998), 'Coexisting and Conflicting Identities: Women and Nationalisms in Twentieth-Century Iran', in Ruth Roach Pierson and Nupur Chaudhuri (1998) (eds), *Nation, Empire, Colony: Historicizing Gender and Race* (Bloomington, Indiana University Press).

Hackforth-Jones, Jos, and Roberts, Mary (2004) (eds), *Edges of Empire: Orientalism and Visual Culture* (Oxford, Blackwells).

Haidar, Musbah (1944), *Arabesque* (London, Hutchinson).

Halid, Halil (1903), *The Diary of a Turk* (London, Adam and Charles Black).

Hammami, Reza, and Rieker, Martina (1989), 'Feminist Orientalism and Orientalist Marxism', *New Left Review*, 170, pp. 93–106.

Harding, Ellen (1995) (ed), *Re-Framing the Pre-Raphaelites: Historical and Theoretical Essays (*Aldershot, Scolar Press).

Harvey, Annie Jane (1871), *Turkish Harems and Circassion Homes* (London, Hurst and Blackett).

Hatem, Mervat (1992), 'Through Each Others' Eyes: The Impact on the Colonial Encounter of the Images of Egyptians, Levantine-Egyptian, and European Women, 1862–1920' in Chauduri and Strobel (1992).

Heffernan, Teresa (forthcoming), *Across the East/West Divide: Orientalism, Feminism and Women's Travel Narratives.*

Helly, Dorothy O., and Reverby, Susan M. (1992), *Gendered Domains: Rethinking Public and Private in Women's History. Essays from the 7th Berkshire Conference on the History of Women* (Ithaca, Cornell University Press).

Hélys, Marc (Marie Léra) (1923), *L'Envers d'un roman: le secret des Désenchantées* (Paris, Perrin).

Holman-Hunt, Diana (1969), *My Grandfather, His Wives and Loves* (London, Columbus Books).

Horne, Peter, and Lewis, Reina (1996) (eds), *Outlooks: Lesbian and Gay Sexualities and Visual Cultures* (London, Routledge).

Hulme, Peter (1986), *Colonial Encounters: Europe and the Native Caribbean, 1492–1797* (London, Methuen).

Hume-Griffith, M. E. (1909), *Behind the Veil in Persia and Turkish Arabia. An Account of an Englishwoman's Eight Years' Residence Amongst the Women of the East*, 2nd edition (London, Seeley and Co.).

Inalcik, Halil, with Quataert, Donald (1994), *An Economic and Social History of the Ottoman Empire, 1300–1914* (Cambridge, Cambridge University Press).

Jameson, Fredric (1991), *Postmodernism; or, The Cultural Logic of Late Capitalism* (Durham, NC, Duke University Press).

Jayawardena, Kumari (1986), *Feminism and Nationalism in the Third World* (London, Zed Books).

Jenkins, Hester Donaldson (1911), *Behind Turkish Lattices, the Story of a Turkish Woman's Life* (London, Chatto and Windus).

Jones, Amelia, and Stephenson, Andrew (1999) (eds), *Performing the Body/Performing the Text* (London, Routledge).

Kalogeras, Yiorgos (1988), 'The "Other" Space of Greek America', *American Literary History*, 10, December, pp. 702–24.

—— (1989), 'A Child of the Orient as American Storyteller: Demetra Vaka Brown', in R. Parkin-Gounelas (1989) (ed), *Working Papers in Linguistics and Literature* (Thessaloniki: Aristotle University Press).

—— (1997), 'Nationalism Unveiled: A Greek American View of the Harem', in Ekaterini Georgoudaki and Domna Pastourmatzi (1997) (eds), *Women, Creators of Culture, American Studies in Greece: Series 3* (Thessaloniki, Hellenic Association of American Studies).

Kandiyoti, Deniz (1989a), 'Woman as Metaphor: The Turkish Novel from the Tanzimat to the Republic', in Kenneth Brown et al (1989) (eds), *Urban Crises and Social Movement in the Middle East* (Paris, L'Hartmattan).

—— (1989b), 'Women and the Turkish State: Political Actors or Symbolic Pawns?', in Nira Yuval-Davis and Floya Anthias (1989) (eds), *Woman – Nation – State* (Basingstoke, Macmillan).

—— (1991a) (ed), *Women, Islam and the State* (Basingstoke, Macmillan).

—— (1991b), 'End of Empire: Islam, Nationalism and Women in Turkey', in Kandiyoti (1991a).

—— (1991c), 'Islam and Patriarchy: A Comparative Perspective', in Keddie and Baron (1991).

—— (1996a) (ed), *Gendering the Middle East: Emerging Perspectives* (London, I. B. Tauris).

—— (1996b), 'Contemporary Feminist Scholarship and Middle East Studies', in Kandiyoti (1996a).

—— (1998), 'Some Awkward Questions on Women and Modernity in Turkey', in Abu-Lughod (1998).

—— (2002), 'Post-colonialism Compared: Potentials and Limitations in the Middle East and Central Asia', *International Journal of Middle East Studies, Special Issue: Nationalism and the Colonial Legacy in the Middle East and Central Asia*, 34: 2, pp. 279–97.

Keddie, Nikki R., and Baron, Beth (1991) (eds), *Women in Middle Eastern History: Shifting Boundaries in Sex and Gender* (New Haven, Yale University Press).

Keddie, Nikki R. (1991), 'Introduction: Deciphering Middle Eastern Women's History', in Keddie and Baron (1991).

—— (2002), 'Women in the Limelight: Some Recent Books on Middle Eastern Women's History', *International Journal of Middle East Studies*, 34: 3, pp. 553–73.

Kondo, Dorinne (1997), *About Face: Performing Race in Fashion and Theatre* (London, Routledge).

Kopan, Andrew T. (1987), 'The Greek Press', in Sally M. Miller (1987) (ed), *The Ethnic Press in The United States: A Historical Analysis and Handbook* (New York, Greenwood Press).

Küçükerman, Onder (1985), *Turkish House: In Search of Spatial Identity* (Istanbul, Turkish Touring and Automobile Association).

Kushner, David (1977), *The Rise of Turkish Nationalism 1876–1908* (London, Frank Cass).

Lefebvre, Henri (1991), *The Production of Space*, trans. Donald Nicholson-Smith (Oxford, Blackwell).

Lerner, Michael G. (1974), *Pierre Loti* (New York, Twayne Publications Inc.).

Lewis, Bernard (1968), *The Emergence of Modern Turkey*, 2nd edition (Oxford, Oxford University Press).

—— (1990), *Race and Slavery in the Middle East* (Oxford, Oxford University Press).

Lewis, Reina, and Rolley, Katrina (1996). 'Ad(dressing) the Dyke: Lesbian Looks and Lesbians Looking' in Horne and Lewis (eds).

Lewis, Reina (1996), *Gendering Orientalism: Race, Femininity and Representation* (London, Routledge).

—— (1999a), 'Cross-Cultural Reiterations: Demetra Vaka Brown and the Performance of Racialized Female Beauty', in Jones and Stephenson (1999).

—— (1999b), 'On Veiling, Vision and Voyage: Cross-Cultural Dressing and Narratives of Identity', *Interventions*, 1: 4, pp. 500–20.

——(1999c), 'Racialised Bodies, Gendered Spaces: Women Represent the Harem', in Louise During and Richard Wrigley (1999) (eds), *Gender and Architecture* (London, John Wiley).

—— and Mills, Sara (2003) (eds), *Feminist Postcolonial Theory: A Reader* (Edinburgh, Edinburgh University Press).

—— (2004), '"Oriental" Femininity as Cultural Commodity: Authorship, Authority and Authenticity', in Hackforth-Jones and Roberts (2004).

—— and Micklewright, Nancy (2004) (eds), *Gender, Modernity, Liberty: Middle Eastern and Western Women's Writings, a Critical Sourcebook* (London, I. B. Tauris).

Lindisfarne-Tapper, Nancy, and Ingham, Bruce (1997) (eds), *Language of Dress in the Middle East* (London, Curzon Press in association with the Centre for Near and Middle East Studies, SOAS).

Loti, Pierre (Louis Marie Julien Viaud) (1879), *Aziyadé* (1989) trans. Marjorie Laurie (London, Routledge).

—— (1906a), *Les Désenchantées. Roman des harems turcs contemporains* (Paris, Calmann-Levy).

—— (1906b), *Disenchanted (Désenchantées). A Romance of Harem Life*, trans. Clara Bell (London, Macmillan).

Lott, Emmeline (1866), *The English Governess in Egypt: Harem Life in Egypt and Constantinople*, 2 vols (London, Richard Bentley).

Low, Gail Ching-Liang (1996), *White Skins/Black Masks: Representation and Colonialism* (London, Routledge).

Lowe, Lisa (1991), *Critical Terrains*, (Ithaca, NY, Cornell University Press).

—— (1996), *Immigrant Acts: On Asian American Cultural Politics* (Durham, NC, Duke University Press).

Lutz, Catherine, and Collins, Jane (1994), 'The Photograph as an Intersection of Gazes: The Example of *National Geographic*', in Taylor (1994).

MacCannell, Dean (1994), 'Cannibal Tours', in Taylor (1994).

McClintock, Anne (1995), *Imperial Leather: Race, Gender and Sexuality in the Imperial Contest* (London, Routledge).

McDowell, Linda, and Sharpe, Joanne P. (1997), *Space, Gender, Knowledge: Feminist Readings* (London, Arnold).

MacKenzie, John M. (1995), *Orientalism: History, Theory and the Arts* (Manchester, Manchester University Press).

Macleod, Dianne Sachko (1995), 'The " Identity" of the Pre-Raphaelite Patrons', in Harding (1995).

—— (1997), 'Pre-Raphaelite Women Collectors and the Female Gaze', in Watson (1997).

—— (1998), 'Cross-Cultural Dressing: Class, Gender and Modernist Sexual Identity' in Codell and Macleod (1998a).

Malmsheimer, Lorna M. (1987), 'Photographic Analysis as Ethnohistory: Interpretive Strategies', *Visual Anthropology*, 1: 1, pp. 21–36.

Manton, Richard (1986) (ed), *The Victorians in the Harem* (New York, Grove Press).

Marsh, Jan (1987), *Pre-Raphaelite Women: Images of Femininity in Pre-Raphaelite Art* (London, Weidenfeld and Nicolson).

—— (1995), '"For the wolf or the babe he is seeking to devour?" The Hidden Impact of the American Civil War in British Art', in Harding (1995).

—— and Gerrish Nunn, Pamela (1997), *Pre-Raphaelite Women Artists* (Manchester, Manchester City Art Galleries).

Massey, Doreen (1994), *Space, Place and Gender* (Cambridge, Polity Press).

Melek Hanoum (1872), *Thirty Years in the Harem: or the Autobiography of Melek-Hanoum, Wife of H.H. Kibrizli-Mehemet-Pasha* (London, Chapman and Hall).

—— (1873), *Six Years in Europe: Sequel to Thirty Years in the Harem* (London, Chapman and Hall).

Melek Hanoum and Ellison, Grace (1913), *Abdul Hamid's Daughter: The Tragedy of an Ottoman Princess* (London, Methuen).

—— (1926), 'How I Escaped From the Harem and How I Became a Dressmaker', *The Strand Magazine*, February, pp. 129–38.

Melman, Billie (1992), *Women's Orients: English Women and the Middle East, 1718–1918. Sexuality, Religion and Work* (Basingstoke, Macmillan).

Meriwether, Margaret L., and Tucker, Judith E. (1999) (eds), *A Social History of Women and Gender in the Modern Middle East* (Boulder, CO, Westview Press).

Mernissi, Fatima (1985), *Beyond the Veil: Male-Female Dynamics in Muslim Society*, 2nd edition (London, al Saqi books).

Meyer, Susan L. (1989), 'Colonialism and the Figurative Strategy of *Jane Eyre*', *Victorian Studies*, 33: 2, pp. 247–68.

Micklewright, Nancy (1999), 'Photography and Consumption in the Ottoman Empire' in Donald Quataert (1999) (ed), *Consumption in the Ottoman Empire* (New York, State University of New York Press).

—— (2000), 'Public and Private for Ottoman Women of the Nineteenth Century' in Ruggles (2000).

Mills, Sara (1991), *Discourses of Difference: Women's Travel Writing and Colonialism* (London, Routledge).

—— (1994), 'Knowledge, Gender and Empire' in Blunt and Rose (1994).

—— (1996), 'Gender and Colonial Space', *Gender Place and Culture*, 3: 2, pp. 125–47.

Mohanty, Chandra (1988), 'Under Western Eyes: Feminist Scholarship and Colonial Discourses', *Feminist Review*, 30, Autumn, pp. 65–88.

——, Russo, Ann, and Torres, Lourdes (1991) (eds), *Third World Women and the Politics of Feminism* (Bloomington, Indiana University Press).

Mohanty, Satya P. (1995), 'Colonial Legacies, Multicultural Futures: Relativism, Objectivity, and the Challenge of Otherness', *PMLA*, 10: 1, pp. 108–18.

Montagu, Lady Mary Wortley (1763), *Embassy to Constantinople: The Travels of Lady Mary Wortley Montagu*, Christopher Pick (1988) (ed), intro. Dervla Murphy (London, Hutchinson).

Moore, Henrietta (1986), *Space, Text and Gender: An Anthropological Study of the Marakwet of Kenya* (Cambridge, Cambridge University Press).

Moors, Annelies (2000), 'Embodying the Nation: Maha Saca's Post-Intifida Postcards', *Ethnic and Racial Studies*, 23: 5, pp. 871–87.

Morley, David, and Robins, Kevin (1992), 'Techno-Orientalism: Futures, Foreigners and Phobias', *New Formations*, 16, Spring, pp. 136–56.

Morley, David (1996), 'EurAm, Modernity, Reason and Alterity: or, Postmodernism, the Highest Stage of Cultural Imperialism', in David Morley and Kuan-Hsing Chen (1996) (eds), *Stuart Hall: Critical Dialogues* (London, Routledge).

Morgan, Thais (1996), 'Perverse Male Bodies: Simeon Soloman and Algernon Charles Swinburne', in Horne and Lewis (1996).

Müller, Mrs Max (Georgina Adelaide Grenfell) (1897), *Letters from Constantinople* (London, Longmans, Green and Co.).

Nader, Laura (1989) 'Orientalism, Occidentalism and the Control of Women', *Cultural Dynamics*, 2: 3, pp. 323–55.

Nair, Janaki (1990), 'Uncovering the Zenana: Vision of Indian Womanhood in Englishwomen's Writing, 1913-1940', *Journal of Women's History*, 2: 1, Spring, pp. 8–34.

Najmadi, Asfaneh (1993), 'Veiled Discourse – Unveiled Bodies', *Feminist Studies*, 19: 3, Fall, pp. 487–518.

Nava, Mica (1998), 'The Cosmopolitanism of Commerce and the Allure of Difference: Selfridges, the Russian Ballet and the Tango', *International Journal of Cultural Studies*, 1: 2, pp. 163–96.

Nead, Lynda (1988), *Myths of Sexuality: Representations of Women in Victorian Britain* (Oxford, Blackwell).

Nelson, Cynthia (1996), *Doria Shafik, Egyptian Feminist: A Woman Apart* (Cairo, American University in Cairo Press).

Nochlin, Linda (1983), 'The Imaginary Orient', in Linda Nochlin (1991), *The Politics of Vision* (London, Thames and Hudson).

Norton, John (1997), 'Faith and Fashion in Turkey' in Lindisfarne-Tapper and Ingham (1997).

Ong, Aihwa (1995), 'State versus Islam: Malay Families, Women's Bodies and the Body Politic in Malaysia', in Aihwa Ong and Michael G. Peletz (1995) (eds), *Bewitching Women – Pious Men: Gender and Politics in South East Asia* (Berkeley, University of California Press).

van Os, Nicole A. N. M. (1999), 'Ottoman Women's Reaction to the Economic and Cultural Intrusion of the West: The Quest for a National Dress', in Katja Füllberg-Stolberg, Petra Heidrich and Ellinor Schöne (1999) (eds), *Dissociation and Appropriation: Responses to Globalization in Asia and Africa* (Berlin, Verlag Das Arabische Buch).

Ostle, Robin (1991) (ed), *Modern Literature in the Near and Middle East 1850–1970* (London, Routledge).

Overton, Grant (1928), *The Women Who Make Our Novels*, 2nd edition (Freeport, NY, Books for Libraries Press).

Paidar, Parvin (1996), 'Feminism and Islam in Iran', in Kandiyoti (1996a).

Paker, Saliha (1991a), 'Turkey', in Ostle (1991).

—— (1991b), 'Unmuffled Voices in the Shade and Beyond: Women's Writing in Turkish', in Helena Forsås-Scott (1991) (ed), *Textual Liberation: European Feminist Writings in the Twentieth Century* (London, Routledge).

Pardoe, Julia (1837), *City of the Sultan: and Domestic Manners of the Turks, in 1836*, 2 vols (London, Henry Colburn).

Parker, Andrew, Russo, Mary, Sommer, Doris, and Yaeger, Patricia (1992) (eds), *Nationalisms and Sexualities* (London, Routledge).

Pearce, Lynn (1991), *Woman/Image/Text: Readings in Pre-Raphaelite Art and Literature* (Hemel Hempstead, Harvester Wheatsheaf).

Peirce, Leslie (1993), *The Imperial Harem: Women and Sovereignty in the Ottoman Empire* (Oxford, Oxford University Press).

Penzer, N. M. (1936), *The Harem: An Account of the Institution as it Existed in the Palace of the Turkish Sultans With a History of the Grand Seraglio from its Foundations to Modern Time* (London, Spring Books).

Pinney, Christopher (1990), 'Classification and Fantasy in the Photographic Construction of Caste and Tribe', *Visual Anthropology*, 3, pp. 259–88.

—— (1992), 'The Parallel Histories of Anthropology and Photography', in Edwards (1990).

Pointon, Marcia (1989) (ed), *The Pre-Raphaelites Re-Viewed* (Manchester, Manchester University Press).

Poole, Sophia (1844), *The Englishwoman in Egypt: Letters from Cairo, Written During a Residence There in 1842, 3 and 4 with E.W. Lane Esq, Author of 'The Modern Egyptian', by his Sister*, 2 vols (London, Charles Knight and Co.).

Pratt, Mary Louise (1992), *Imperial Eyes: Travel Writing and Transculturation*, (London, Routledge).

Quataert, Donald (1991), 'Ottoman Women, Households, and Textile Manufacturing 1800–1914', in Keddie and Baron (1991).

—— (1994), 'Part 4: The Age of Reforms 1812–1914', in Inalcik and Quataert (1994).

—— (2000) (ed), *Consumption Studies and the History of the Ottoman Empire 1550–1922* (New York, State University of New York Press).

Rich, Adrienne (1984), 'Notes Toward a Politics of Location', in Rich (1987), *Blood, Bread and Poetry: Selected Prose 1979–1985* (London, Virago).

Richon, Olivier (1985), 'Representation, the Harem and the Despot', *Block*, 10, pp. 34–41.

Riede, David G. (1992), *Dante Gabriel Rossetti Revisited* (New York, Twayne Publishers).

Roberts, Mary (2002), 'Contested Terrains: Women Orientalists and the Colonial Harem', in Beaulieu and Roberts (2002).

Rofé, Husein (1969), 'Turkish Literature in the West', *Eastern Horizon*, 8: 1, pp. 56–62.

Rolley, Katrina, and Ash, Caroline (1992), *Fashion in Photographs 1900–1920* (London, B. T. Batsford Ltd).

Rosaldo, Renato (1993), *Culture and Truth: The Remaking of Social Analysis* (London, Routledge).

Rose, Gillian (1993), *Feminism and Geography: The Limits of Geographical Knowledge* (Cambridge, Polity).

Rossetti, William M. (1911), *The Works of Dante Gabriel Rossetti* (London, Ellis).

Ruggles, Dede Fairchild (2000) (ed), *Women, Patronage, and Self-Representation in Islamic Societies* (Albany, State University of New York Press).

Said, Edward W. (1978), *Orientalism* (London, Routledge).

—— (1993), *Culture and Imperialism* (New York, Knopf).

Said-Ruete, Emily (1888), *Memoirs of an Arabian Princess: Princess Salme bin Said ibn Sultan al-Bu Saidi of Oman and Zanzibar* (London, Ward and Downey).

Saloutos, Theodore (1964), *The Greeks in the United States* (Cambridge, MA, Harvard University Press).

Sandoval, Chela (1991), 'U.S. Third World Feminism: The Theory and Method of Oppositional Consciousness in the Postmodern World', *Genders*, 10, Spring, pp. 1–24.

Scarce, Jennifer (1987), *Women's Costume of the Near and Middle East* (London, Unwin Hyman).

Schick, Irvin Cemil (1999), *The Erotic Margin: Sexuality and Spatiality in Alteritist Discourse* (London, Verso).

Sedgewick, Eve Kosofsky (1993), 'Queer Performativity: Henry James's *The Art of the Novel*', *GLQ*, 1, pp. 1–16.

Şeni, Nora (1995), 'Fashion and Women's Clothing in the Satirical Press of Istanbul at the End of the 19th Century', in Sirin Tekeli (1995) (ed), *Women in Modern Turkish Society* (London, Zed Books).

Sharpe, Jenny (1993), *Allegories of Empire: The Figure of Woman in The Colonial Text* (Minneapolis, University of Minnesota Press).

Shaw, Stanford J., and Shaw, Ezel Kural (1978), *History of the Ottoman Empire and Modern Turkey. Volume II. Reform, Revolution, and Republic: The Rise of Modern Turkey 1808–1975*, 2nd edition (Cambridge, Cambridge University Press).

Shefer, Elaine (1985), 'Pre-Raphaelite Clothing and the New Woman', *The Journal of Pre-Raphaelite Studies*, 6: 1, November, pp. 55–67.

Smith, Lindsay (1995), *Victorian Photography, Painting and Poetry: The Enigma of Visibility in Ruskin, Morris and the Pre-Raphaelites* (Cambridge, Cambridge University Press).

Sönmez, Emel (1969), 'Turkish Women in Turkish Literature of the 19th Century', *Die Welt des Islams*, 12: 1–3, pp. 1–73.

Spivak, Gayatri Chakravorty (1985), 'Three Women's Texts and a Critique of Imperialism', *Critical Enquiry*, 12, Autumn, pp. 243–61.

—— (1988a), *In Other Worlds: Essays in Cultural Politics* (London, Routledge).

—— (1988b), 'Can the Subaltern Speak?', in C. Nelson and L. Grossberg (1998) (eds), *Marxism and the Interpretation of Culture* (Basingstoke, Macmillan).

—— (1999), *A Critique of Postcolonial Reason: Toward a History of the Vanishing Present* (Cambridge, MA, Harvard University Press).

—— (2000), 'The New Subaltern: a Silent Interview', in V. Chaturvedi (2000) (ed), *Mapping Subaltern Studies and the Postcolonial* (London, Verso).

Stacey, Jackie (1988), 'Desperately Seeking Difference', in Lorraine Gamman and Margaret Marshment (1988) (eds), *The Female Gaze: Women as Viewers of Popular Culture* (London, The Women's Press).

Stanford, Derek (1970), 'The Pre-Raphaelite Cult of Women: From Damozel to Demon', *Contemporary Review*, 217: 1254, July, pp. 26–33.

—— (1973), *Pre-Raphaelite Writing: An Anthology* (London, Dent).

Street, Brian (1992), 'British Popular Anthropology: Exhibiting and Photography the Other', in Edwards (1992).

Suleri, Sara (1992a), *The Rhetoric of English India* (Chicago, University of Chicago Press).

—— (1992b), 'Woman Skin Deep: Feminism and the Postcolonial Condition', *Critical Inquiry*, 18, Summer, pp. 756–69.

Surtees, Virginia (1971), *The Paintings and Drawings of Dante Gabriel Rossetti (1828–1882). A Catalogue Raisonnée* (Oxford, Clarendon Press).

Symons, Arthur (1923), *Dramatis Personae* (Indianapolis, Bobbs-Merril Co.)

Szyliowicz, Irene L. (1988), *Pierre Loti and the Oriental Woman* (Basingstoke, Macmillan).

Tagg, John (1988), *The Burden of Representation: Essays on Photographies and Histories* (Basingstoke, Macmillan).

Taşkiran, Tezer (1973), *Women in Turkey*, trans. Nida Tektas, ed Anna G. Edmonds (Istanbul, Redhouse Yayinevi).

Tawadros, Çeylan (1988), 'Foreign Bodies : Art History and the Discourse of Nineteenth-Cenetury Orientalist Art', *Third Text*, 3: 4, Spring/Summer, pp. 51–67.

Taylor, Lucian (1994) (ed), *Visualising Theory: Selected Essays from Visual Anthropology Review* (London, Routledge).

Tekeli, Sirin (1986), 'Emergence of the Feminist Movement in Turkey', in Drude Dahlerup (1986) (ed), *The New Women's Movement: Feminism and Political Power in Europe and the USA* (London, Sage).

Ternar, Yeshin (1994), *The Book and the Veil: Escape from an Istanbul Harem* (Montreal, Véhicule Press).

Tickner, Lisa (1987), *The Spectacle of Women: Imagery of the Suffrage Campaign 1907–1914* (London, Chatto and Windus).

Toledano, Ehud R. (1982), *The Ottoman Slave Trade and its Suppression: 1840–1890* (Princeton, Princeton University Press).

Tugay, Emine Foat (1963), *Three Centuries: Family Chronicles Of Turkey and Egypt* (Oxford, Oxford University Press).

Vaka, Demetra (Mrs Kenneth Brown) (1909), *Haremlik* (Boston and New York, Houghton Mifflin Co.).

—— (1911), *In The Shadow of Islam* (Boston and New York, Houghton Mifflin Co.).

—— (1914), *A Child of the Orient* (London, John Lane, the Bodley Head).

—— (1917), *The Heart of the Balkans* (Boston and New York, Houghton Mifflin Co.).

—— (1918), *In the Heart of German Intrigue* (Boston and New York, Houghton Mifflin Co.).

—— (1923), *The Unveiled Ladies of Stamboul* (Boston and New York, Houghton Mifflin Co.).

—— (1947–52), '"For a Heart for Any Fate": The Early of Years of Demetra Vaka (Mrs. Kenneth Brown), Told by Herself', *Athene* (1947) 8: 3, pp. 87–90; (1948) 8: 4, pp. 10–15; (1948) 9: 1, pp. 21–3, 35–6; (1949) 10: 3, pp. 28–30, 66, 68–9; (1950) 10: 4, pp. 16–19, 36–7; (1950) 11: 1, pp. 17–22; (1950) 11: 2, pp. 22–3, 36; (1950) 11: 3, pp. 33–5, 47; (1951) 11: 4, pp. 24–5, 50–4; (1951) 12: 1, pp. 24–7, 46, 54; (1951) 12: 2, pp. 22–5; (1951) 12: 3, pp. 22–4, 70–2; (1952) 12: 4, pp. 14–15, 41; (1952) 13: 1, pp. 26–7, 52–3; (1952) 13: 2, pp. 22–3, 47–51; (1952) 13: 3, pp. 15–17.

Vizetelly, Ernest Alfred (1915), *Loves of the Poets* (London, Holden and Hardingham).

Walkowitz, Judy (2003), 'The "Vision of Salome": Cosmopolitanism and Erotic Dancing in Central London, 1908–1918', *American Historical Review*, 108, pp. 337–76.

Ware, Vron (1992), *Beyond the Pale: White Women, Racism and History* (London, Verso).

Watson, Margaretta Frederick (1997a) (ed), *Collecting the Pre-Raphaelites: The Anglo-American Enchantment* (Aldershot, Ashgate).

—— (1997b), 'Introduction: "Crossing the Big Pond": The Anglo-American Appeal of Pre-Raphaelitism', in Watson (1997a).

Who Was Who 1929–1940 (1976), 2nd edition (London, Adam and Charles Black).

Williams, Patrick, and Chrisman, Laura (1993) (eds), *Colonial Discourse and Post-Colonial Theory: A Reader* (London, Harvester Wheatsheaf).

Wollen, Peter (1987), 'Fashion/Orientalism/The Body', *New Formations*, 1, Spring, pp. 5–33.

—— (1993), *Raiding the Icebox: Reflections on Twentieth-Century Culture* (London, Verso).

Woodhull, Winifred (1991), 'Unveiling Algeria', *Genders*, 10, Spring, pp. 112–31.

Woodsmall, Ruth Frances (1936), *Moslem Women Enter a New World* (London, George Allen and Unwin).

Woodward, Michelle (2003), 'Between Orientalist Clichés and Images of Modernization: Photographic Practice in the Late Ottoman Era', *History of Photography*, Winter.

Yapp, Malcom (1991), 'Modernisation and Literature in the North and Middle East, 1850–1914', in Ostle (1991).

Yeazell, Ruth Bernard (2000), *Harems of the Mind: Passages of Western Art and Literature* (New Haven, CT, Yale University Press).

Yeğenoğlu, Meyda (1998), *Colonial Fantasies: Towards a Feminist Reading of Orientalism* (Cambridge, Cambridge University Press).

—— (forthcoming), 'Inhabiting Other Spaces: Tourists and Migrants in the Postcolonial World', in Kamran Asdar Ali and Martina Reiker (eds), *TransActions: Tourism in the Southern Mediterranean* (Bloomington, Indiana University Press).

Young, R. (1990), *White Mythologies: Writing History and the West* (London, Routledge).

—— (2001), *Postcolonialism An Historical Introduction* (Oxford, Blackwell).

Zeyneb Hanoum (1913), *A Turkish Woman's European Impressions, edited and with an introduction by Grace Ellison* (London, Seeley, Service and Co. Ltd).

Zonana, Joyce (1993), 'The Sultan and the Slave: Feminist Orientalism and the Structure of *Jane Eyre*', *Signs*, 18: 3, Spring, pp. 592–617.

INDEX

Numbers in italics refer to illustrations.

UNIVERSITY OF WINCHESTER
LIBRARY